10Tac

Parliament & Congress

KENNETH BRADSHAW AND DAVID PRING

Parliament & Congress

UNIVERSITY OF TEXAS PRESS, AUSTIN

Printed in Great Britain

CONTENTS

CONTENTS

INTRODUCTION

IN the last years of the eighteenth century Thomas Jefferson
turned his polymath mind to the law and practice of Congress.
Elected Vice-President in 1796, he had to preside over the
Senate, and with characteristic diligence he set down on paper
his conclusions about the bases on which a legislature should
operate. His *Manual*, carefully annotated by later officers of
Congress, remains a standard work. It is bound up and published with successive editions of the Rules of the House of
Representatives and of the Senate.

Jefferson's *Manual*, in the notes now added to the version
printed by the House of Representatives, is described as being
the best statement of what had been at that time the law of the
British Parliament. Nothing could make plainer the shared
heritage of the two greatest legislatures of the free world. Yet
today the two are separated by a width of incomprehension, an
Atlantic of the mind, which prevents each from benefiting from
the acquired wisdom of the other.

How has this divergence come about? Largely as a result of
the absence from Congress of what now gives Parliament its
leadership; this is, the government or executive.

Over the last two centuries the government has strengthened
its leadership within Parliament. Today it relies upon, and almost
invariably receives, the support of a Commons majority which is
largely susceptible to party discipline; and with rare exceptions
it can have its way in the House of Lords, whose powers are now
declared by statute to be in important respects inferior to those of
the Commons. As a result since Jefferson's time the structure of
power in Parliament has become comparatively simplified.
Debate in Parliament, unlike debate in Congress, is a constant
exchange between the government and the governed through
their elected representatives. The government states its policy
and its needs, and individual members or groups of members
compel a full disclosure and explanation. In particular, debate is a

confrontation between the government who have power and the official opposition who do not. When the government introduces a bill, it is likely to pass. Moreover, such is the government's power to retain control over the content of the bill during its passage through both Houses, it is likely to pass substantially as introduced.

Congress does not have—has never had—this governmental motive force. Much legislation, it is true, emanates from the Executive. But power within Congress is far more widely distributed than in Parliament. In the first place, the Senate and the House have broadly equal powers and rights, and the assent of both is necessary for most congressional decisions. In each House the leaders of two great national political parties propose national policies, but their influence is much modified by the independence of the representatives of the Union's fifty states; and the national electoral process may well relegate the members of the President's party to the minority in each House of Congress. In this setting the British concept of an opposition—as well as a government—within the legislature can have no meaning.

Since Jefferson's day Congress has fragmented power still further. It has created many standing committees, with powerful chairmen chosen by the caprice of seniority, each with its own responsibility. As a result, for example, taxing decisions are taken independently of spending decisions, which are themselves taken by different bodies from those which reach policy decisions. Every legislative step forward in Congress has thus to be by agreement between a number of power-possessing bodies. No stance can be struck too soon, no commitment reached too early, because a great many compromises may have to be made before a bill can pass. The bill proceeds, with syncopated movement, to a final grand conciliation between the House and Senate; before perhaps they need to combine in a naked test of strength with the Executive.

The extent of these constitutional differences seems to have discouraged a comparative approach to the legislatures in this century. It is remarkable that, when each country has been concerned with the health of democratic institutions throughout the world, and when the legislation of each is often the subject of study in the other, no detailed, side by side comparison of how they work has been attempted. In the 1950s George Galloway, a senior specialist in American Government in the Library of Congress and the author of major works on Congress, took a step in this direction. His short book, *Congress and Parliament*, published only in the United States, has proved invaluable. Its purpose was however deliberately prescriptive; he was examining the working methods of Parliament to see how far they might provide solutions for the problems of Congress. It was he who suggested to one of us that the comparison between the two legislatures needed to be made in greater detail and without an overriding prescriptive purpose. George Galloway died in 1967. We warmly acknowledge the debt our work owes to him.

Our aim has been to describe the working methods of each legislature in as much detail as the practitioners and students of each may require. By placing them whenever necessary in their constitutional and historical setting, it is possible to show why they have taken their present form. We do not attempt to make judgements, or to show that one system, or within that system one set of practices, is better than another. We have tried to describe objectively the origin and nature of each system in enough detail for its advantages and disadvantages to emerge. The debate on merits can continue, but with its factual basis more secure.

This book is published at a time when, it seems, both legislatures are likely to take breath after at least a decade of procedural debate and change. In the United States the Legislative Reorganization Act of 1946—which among other things entirely reshaped the system of committees in both Houses of Congress—did not exhaust the appetite for change. Steady pressure inside and outside Congress to modernize its workings led to the appointment of the Joint Committee on the Organization of Congress of 1965–66. After much controversy and some abortive legislation, many of the Joint Committee's conclusions found a place in the Legislative Reorganization Act of 1970. In the United Kingdom there has been a like sequence of events. The changes that resulted from the comprehensive inquiry of 1945–1946 into the working methods of the House of Commons primarily benefited the government, since most of them helped it to get its business through Parliament more swiftly. This governmental thrust touched off a reaction. Pressure built up during the 1950s and 1960s to mitigate in some degree what was thought to be the excessive hold exerted by governments over Parliament. These efforts issued in the appointment of the Procedure Committee of 1958–59, itself the precursor of a series of similar committees appointed sessionally from 1962. The results of all this inquiry should not be exaggerated. But it is fair to say that by the end of the 1960s a new balance between government and Parliament, based on developed procedures by which the latter scrutinize the activities of the former, had been struck. In the session of 1970–1971 this new balance was seen to have wide support within both government and Parliament, and it is unlikely to be disturbed in essentials for some years. In the session 1970–71 a committee of the House of Lords has been looking closely at the workings of that House, and has made a series of ten reports. In Britain as in the United States, therefore, the early 1970s is an apt time to describe and compare the two legislatures. We have sought to take account of developments in both of them up to the end of 1970, though reference has been made to some later developments in 1971.

One special problem should be mentioned. Was it Bernard Shaw who remarked that the Americans and British are two peoples separated only by their use of a common language? His epigram has a special relevance for the student of Parliament and Congress. Many words in current use have different meanings in each legislature. An example is 'the legislative process'. In Parliament this phrase is generally understood to mean only the process by which a bill becomes a law. Yet George Galloway used the phrase as a title for his authoritative study of Congress,[1] and applied it to every facet of the work of a legislature. Many other words—budget, standing committee, adjournment, recess, division—carry not only different but sometimes the opposite meanings in the United States from those they bear in Britain. We have tried to draw attention to these potential sources of confusion as and when they come into view.

In any work of this kind the authors must lean heavily on advice of practitioners in the legislative business of both countries. We are conscious of our indebtedness to many people whose expert guidance gives to this book whatever authority it may be thought to possess. In the United States we mention first Dr Floyd Riddick, Parliamentarian of the Senate and author of

1. *The Legislative Process in Congress* (1955).

The U.S. Congress: Organization and Procedure (1949), still the standard work on its subject. Together with Mr Murray Zweben, an Assistant Parliamentarian, Dr Riddick read most of the book in manuscript and all of it in proof. We were indeed fortunate to be able to draw so freely on such experience and authority. In the House of Representatives our manuscript was to have been read by Dr Charles Zinn, lately Law Revision Counsel of the House's Committee on the Judiciary and President of the Association of Secretaries General of Parliaments. Charles Zinn, who achieved the remarkable feat of making his booklet *How our Laws are Made* into a best-seller, gave us unstinted encouragement and shed light for us on many dark corners of congressional habits and practice. His sad and untimely death early in 1970 robbed us of a close friend as well as a valued collaborator. As it transpired however, we were fortunate in being helped by Mr William Cochrane, the House's Assistant Parliamentarian who, with his colleague Mr William Brown, read several chapters in manuscript and helped us immeasurably with fundamental matters of fact and interpretation. One of the happiest by-products of this book was to have worked so closely and formed lasting friendships with our professional counterparts in both Houses of Congress.

Our debt is as heavy to colleagues and friends in the British Parliament. Mr Richard Barlas, Second Clerk Assistant and Clerk of Committees in the House of Commons, read Chapters I, II, V and VIII in manuscript and the entire work in proof. Mr Kenneth Mackenzie, Clerk of Public Bills, read the other four chapters, while Mr Peter Henderson, Reading Clerk of the House of Lords, looked over the whole of the text to ensure that the working methods and practice of that House were adequately and accurately presented. We gratefully acknowledge their invaluable contributions to the pages that follow.

We wish also to thank specifically a number of persons in Washington and London who read various parts of our manuscript and helped us with expert advice and guidance on the parts of it which touched on their own functions. In Washington Mr Elmer Staats, Comptroller General of the United States; Congressman John Monagan, a member of the House Foreign Affairs Committee and the Government Operations Committee; Mr Paul Wilson and Mr John Martin, staff directors of the House Appropriations Committee and Ways and Means Committee, and Mr Walter Pincus, consultant to the Senate's Foreign Relations Committee, helped us with the chapters on Finance or on Scrutiny and Control of the Executive or on both; while in London the same expert help was given by Sir Robert Speed, the Speaker's Counsel, Sir Edmund Compton, the first British Ombudsman, and Sir Bruce Fraser, the British Comptroller and Auditor General.

For our chapter on Leadership we were much indebted to an old friend, Mr Charles Clapp, the sage of Georgetown, author of *The Congressman* (1963) and currently an aide in the White House; to Mr Mike Reed, Assistant to the Speaker of the House of Representatives; to Mr Gary Hymel, Assistant to the Majority Leader; and to Mr William Pitts, Assistant to the Republican Whip in that House. Their closest equivalents at Westminster, Mr Freddie Warren, Secretary to the Government Chief Whip; Mr Frank Barlow and Mr Harry Mitchell of the Parliamentary Labour Party; and Miss Felicity Yonge of the Conservative Party did us the same kind service for the British Parliament.

For the chapters on Members and on Committees we wish to mention gratefully Mr Pat Jennings, Clerk of the House of Representatives and Mr Paul Wohl, his Legislative Counsel; Mr John Swanner, staff director of the House's Committee on Standards of Official Conduct; Mr Del Goldberg, a staff member of the House's Committee on Government Operations, and Mr Murphy, Counsel to the Joint Committee on Atomic Energy.

On specific points and on some of our conclusions we were fortunate to have been able to consult others with long experience of the Washington scene or with comparative knowledge of Parliament and Congress. They included Mr Douglass Cater, Mr Darrell St Claire, Mr Henry Fairlie, Mr Hugh Gallagher, Dean Ernest Griffith, Mr D. B. Hardeman, Mr Walter Kravitz, Mr Neil MacNeil, Mr Carl Marcy and Mr William M. Miller. In addition we were much helped by conversations with the then British Ambassador, Mr John Freeman, and with Mr William Drower, Counsellor at the British Embassy, who gave us many useful introductions on Capitol Hill.

It would be impossible in the space available to record in full the help we received from many people in and around Congress— members of both Houses, officials, scholars, librarians, journalists, diplomats and politicians—in whose company we were able to explore the topics we were interested in and to test out such tentative conclusions as we had reached. We can only ask them to accept this collective expression of thanks for the courtesy, time and thought invariably accorded to our requests.

At home our labours have been eased by the collaboration of many friends in the Clerk's department of each House of Parliament and in the Library of the House of Commons. We should like to express our thanks for their efforts to improve our work.

Finally, we must record our gratitude to the Ford Foundation, whose generosity did much to make our most recent visit to Washington so fruitful and agreeable.

Westminster, 1972

CHAPTER ONE

LEADERSHIP

AMONG legislatures in the world today Parliament and Congress stand out as models, each being a classic statement, within its own constitutional terms, of popular representation. The two systems, sometimes described as the parliamentary and the presidential systems, stem from a common root. Parliament since the Restoration and Congress since its beginning have an uninterrupted history of protecting the freedoms of the people and of giving expression to their will. Their continuity and strength have encouraged other countries across the world to build constitutional systems on the same lines. So a comparative study of how the two models work can be widely useful.

Of major importance in such a study is the way in which power is wielded. Leadership in each legislature is, then, the first subject to be considered. Once elected or constituted an assembly must have leaders to focus its energies and crystallize its will. The leaders in their turn must direct, or oversee the direction of, the governmental machinery which gives effect to that will. The line of responsibility from the electorate to that executive machinery has to be traced separately in each political system.

In Britain that line is clear and direct. It runs from the electorate to the House of Commons, through the majority party to the Prime Minister and the cabinet. This is the result of centuries of development in the powers of the monarchy. The Civil War (1642–49) and the Bill of Rights (1688) at last decided that those powers were to be exercised on behalf of the monarch by ministers responsible to Parliament rather than by the monarch himself acting outside and above it. The simplicity of the structure derives from the government's being placed in Parliament. The leader of that government, supported by the cabinet and specifically by the Leader of the House and the Chief Whip, provides policy and leadership in the House of Commons for as long as he is supported by the majority. He and his cabinet are individually and collectively accountable to the House of Commons. There they confront an opposition which opposes, criticizes and offers alternative policies: Her Majesty's Government faces Her Majesty's Opposition. The killing-ground, as it were, is the floor of the House. The work and expertise of government are carried on elsewhere under the direction of the Prime Minister and the cabinet and are subject to oversight by Parliament.

The description of the British system as 'parliamentary government' should not convey the implication that Parliament governs. Parliament does not and cannot. The phrase has meaning only if it conveys that the government governs through Parliament. 'Constitutional monarchy' is another phrase used to describe the British system. This again misleads, if it suggests that the monarch has power. But it is an accurate description if it is realized that the prerogative of power, once exercised by the monarch in person, is now exercised on her behalf by ministers. They too, by the strength of their party support in a single dominant chamber and without any formal constitutional limits placed on them, can largely control the content of the statute book. The combination of these powers, exercised for a maximum of five years at a time, enables a Prime Minister to lead Parliament and the country at the same time and gives to his leadership a different character from that exercised in the United States.

In the United States by contrast the line of responsibility running from the electorate is by no means so clear. The Constitution formally separates legislature and executive and expects them to operate independently, though with certain links between them. Within Congress itself power is fragmented. For a start Congress has two elected chambers of more or less equal powers. In each chamber the party leaders—the Speaker of the House, floor leaders and whips—have constantly to take account of the wishes and intentions of other members whose claims to leadership derive from the system of seniority, that is, the chairmen and senior (ranking) minority members of the committees of both Houses. For his part the President is elected by and is responsible to the people who elect him. He is not responsible to Congress. Nor is he hedged, as is the British Prime Minister, by the need to secure the agreement of his cabinet, since American ministers are neither elected nor are they members of Congress. Moreover while electing a President, the electorate may at the same time elect a Congress of different political colour and crucially alter the degree and area of possible co-operation between the arms of government.

Even without this complicating factor, the tension between legislature and executive is a characteristic feature. While the British have a monarchical executive tempered by parliamentary accountability, the American system is a sharing of power between institutions which are constitutionally separate. The executive, in carrying out the President's policy and programme (his 'platform'), makes an important contribution to the legislative business of each session. Congress, the legislature, through its power of oversight amounting in some areas to control, vitally influences the actions of the executive branch. From this system of checks and balances, from the constant process of criticizing, thwarting, interfering and controlling, each with the other, emerges what has been termed a 'government by consensus' in which final decisions draw strength from endorsement by a majority of both Houses of Congress and by the President, each with distinct and direct links with the electorate.

This difference in the basic constitutional arrangements— between the concentration of power in the British system and its diffusion in the American—will colour every comparison made in this book between Parliament and Congress. It is apparent, too, in the nature of the party systems to which both countries adhere and in the manner in which the parties organize themselves, both outside and inside the legislature.

THE PARTY SYSTEM

In both countries there are two major parties. The two-party system can be dated back at least to the Civil War (1642–49) and the 'glorious revolution' (1688) in Great Britain and, in part by derivation, to the first Congress in the United States (1789).

'Third' parties and other groupings have frequently emerged in both countries. In Britain a variety of groups—National Liberals, National Socialists, Co-operative Party, Independent Labour Party, Irish, Scottish and Welsh Nationalists, Communists—have achieved representation in Parliament, but only one, the Labour Party, has succeeded in displacing one of the two major parties (the Liberals) and relegating them to the status of 'third party'. In the United States, despite a colourful crop of parties and groupings—among them Barnburners, Locofocos, Bucktails, Abolitionists, Free-Soilers, Know-Nothings, Progressives, the non-Partisan League, the Prohibitionists, several kinds of Socialist and Labour parties and latterly the followers of Henry Wallace and Governor Wallace—the predominance of the two main parties has been steady for more than a hundred years. In both countries the two-party system has been reinforced by the method of election. Both elect their legislators in single member constituencies by simple majority vote, a system which makes it difficult for third or other parties to win as many seats as they would be entitled to according to a more purely arithmetical system. Nevertheless, though deeply rooted in the tradition of both countries, the two party systems serve a very different purpose in each.

In Britain the system focuses and clarifies the choice which the electorate has to make. In practice at a general election the electorate decides which party is to be in majority and which in minority. In other words it decides either to sustain or to dismiss the government in power. This is the electors' chief democratic right—their only one according to some political theorists. The tradition and character of each party will no doubt be widely known, but in any event the alternatives will be stated and canvassed before and during the election. An elector can choose one party either because he likes its leaders or programme or because he dislikes the leaders or programme of the other party. The leader of the party winning the majority of seats in the House of Commons becomes Prime Minister and forms a cabinet from members of either House, usually belonging to the same party. The government can be expected if not to implement every detail of the party programme, at least to act continuously in the spirit of it and so to translate into governmental terms the message conveyed by the electors.[1] In this way a strong and stable executive backed directly by the authority of the electorate can be combined with periodic and necessary verdicts on the government's performance.

1. More parties (than two) would make minority governments more probable and lead to coalitions of parties and compromises on matters of policy. Whatever their merits, these deals would mean a blurring and muting of the electorate's message. See Henry Fairlie, *The Life of Politics*, Chapter 3, for a persuasive development of this point set in its historical context.

In the United States the Constitution by separating executive from legislature rules out a party government as understood in Britain. Candidates have to be found for election to the Presidency, to each House of Congress and to the corresponding offices at state and local level. The voters can, and often do, vote one way for the President and another for a congressional candidate or a state governor. If an independent candidate offers himself for any of these offices the voters can vote a third way. In Britain a voter may vote for one party at national and another at local level. But at national level he has only one vote, addressed primarily to the choice of alternative governments. In the absence of this choice in the United States, and in the atmosphere of greater independence and more cross-voting, what purpose is served by the two-party system there?

Its working has first to be set against the size and population of the country. The area of the United States is broadly the same as that of the whole of Europe, including the Soviet Union about as far east as a line running north from the Caspian Sea. The population, 202 million in 1969, compares with 186 million in the six countries presently comprising the European Economic Community, and with 55 million in Great Britain (1969). The electorate in the United States is about 120 million (in 1968) compared with about 40 million in Britain (in 1970). These physical facts have two corollaries for political organization. First, except for an election to the Presidency, and despite the efforts of some senators to campaign on national issues, the prime political interest of the voters is in local and state rather than national issues. In the context of American politics this is not surprising. Londoners do not normally take a close interest in social conditions in Bucharest, yet it is only half as far away as is Los Angeles from New York. Secondly, the business of the parties is, first and foremost, a problem of organization; from the diverse interests, needs and aspirations of 50 states, the concept of a national party has somehow to be nurtured. The complexity and expense of this exercise weight the system heavily in favour of two parties, that is, the minimum number required for a political choice.

These two features of the American party system—local or state orientation and the preoccupation with organizational problems—have been given emphasis by the Constitution. Candidates for both Houses of Congress have to be 'inhabitants' (the word is in the Constitution) of the state that they are to represent, and the choice of a candidate is motivated primarily by his stance on local and regional issues. A further tug against the national orientation of party loyalties is to be found in the 'primaries'— elections in which the membership of each party at local or state level choose the candidates who are to carry the party standard in the elections for Congress. In some states 'membership' for purposes of primary elections is so loosely defined that members of one party can invade the primaries of the other.

The result has been well described by Dean Griffith:[1]

> ...the system of state and local party control, together with the direct primary, weights the scales in Congress heavily in the direction of a sprinkling of *both* parties on the side of any point of view on an issue strongly felt by a *particular region*. Public power and irrigation are widely and strongly supported in the West. The St Lawrence Seaway was supported in the states bordering the Great Lakes, while it was opposed in New England and the Lower Mississippi Valley because of fear that commerce would be deflected. Silver subsidy attracts the Rocky Mountain states, and parity of price for farm products unites agriculture in the Middle West. Strong support for collective bargaining and organized labor characterizes both parties in industrial areas. The Eastern seaboard states favor foreign trade. The West Coast is concerned that our policy in the Far East be strong. Agrarian radicalism is strong in North Dakota and Minnesota. The South opposes social and political equality for the Negro....

The successful parties have been able to weld together some of these interests into durable alliances. Their prime function has been to bring together a diversity of interests and sections behind their candidates. In the words of M. Duverger they are:

> founded on no ideological or social bases ... they include elements and doctrines that are completely heterogeneous ... fundamentally they are simply organizations for the conquest of political office.[2]

Each party has national aim and reach, and its purpose is fundamentally unifying. When an election has been won (or lost), the parties continue the search, in Congress and elsewhere, for

1. Dean Ernest Griffith, *The American System of Government* (1965 ed.), p. 137.
2. Maurice Duverger, *Political Parties* (1964 ed.), p. 210.

alliances and agreements as a basis for policy and action. This is the essential difference from British parties. Being a relatively compact political unit, and without the American preoccupation with local issues, Britain has thrown up the main parties of 'organized opinion' embodying separate and contrasting traditions of an economic, social, even ideological character. As in the United States each party system is national in scope. But whereas in the United States the purpose of party is unifying, in Britain it is divisive. Party in Britain is the means by which the views and programmes endorsed by supporters are given expression through majority government and minority opposition in the House of Commons. From this basic distinction flow the contrasts in party organization and party discipline in Congress and Parliament.

POLITICAL ORGANIZATION

In Parliament

Once Parliament has assembled, how are the two main parties organized to give effect to the will of the electorate? There are important differences between them in organization and structure, though the relationship between the leader and his supporters in both parties is broadly similar. The organization of each party varies according to whether it is in power or in opposition.

The Parliamentary Labour Party comprises all the Labour members of both Houses. When in opposition the party elects annually its Leader, Deputy Leader, Chairman and Chief Whip. Since World War II the sitting tenant in each of these posts has invariably been re-elected, though not on occasion without challenge; nor has there been any elevation from one post to another. These four leaders, together with eight others elected by the Parliamentary Labour Party and three peers, constitute the Parliamentary Committee or 'shadow cabinet', which directs the work of the Parliamentary Labour Party. The three peers are the Leader of the Labour members in the House of Lords, the Labour Chief Whip in that House and one other Labour peer (all elected by the body of Labour peers). The Leader in the Commons allocates duties, appointing each member of the shadow cabinet to mark one or more ministries or departments. Since 1955 the

Labour leader has named additional shadow ministers to give his shadow cabinet the range and balance that he thinks desirable.

When the party is in power, the Leader becomes Prime Minister. His choice of cabinet and other ministers is not inhibited by the last elections to the shadow cabinet, though he obviously takes into account the standing of individuals in the party as revealed in the elections and the experience that they have gained as shadow spokesmen. To provide and preserve contact between the government and its backbench supporters a liaison committee is set up. It consists of a chairman—usually a senior member of the party with ministerial experience—and three vice-chairmen, all elected by the Parliamentary Labour Party, a Labour peer (elected by the Labour peers), the Leader of the House of Commons and the Chief Whip. The committee, which is served by a secretary drawn from the party organization, meets weekly while Parliament is sitting, keeps the government informed of how opinion is moving on the backbenches and arranges for ministers to meet backbenchers concerned about particular aspects of policy. Between 1968 and 1970 these meetings were supplemented by a regular weekly talk between the Prime Minister and the chairman of the parliamentary party.[1]

The organization of the Conservative Parliamentary Party is formally different. All members of the party in the House of Commons belong to the Conservative Members' Committee, better known as the 1922 Committee since its formation in that year for the express purpose of keeping ministers informed of backbench views. In 1965, when the party was in opposition, the Leader (Mr Heath) was for the first time elected by 'a ballot of the party in the House of Commons'.[2] Before that date he had been chosen as Leader after soundings taken from members of the party in and out of Parliament, or, when the party was in power—as for example in 1957 (Mr Macmillan) and 1963 (Sir Alec Douglas-Home)—chosen as Leader following appointment by the Sovereign as Prime Minister after similar soundings. It is worth noting that neither party—Labour since its inception or

1. See *The Times*, 28 August 1969: article by the Chairman of the Parliamentary Labour Party on 'giving backbench MPs a role in decision making'.

2. *Procedure for the Selection of the Leader of the Conservative and Unionist Party*, issued by the Conservative Party in February 1965.

Conservative since 1965—has elected a Leader while the party was in power. What would happen if the leadership were then to fall vacant is uncertain. In most circumstances the electoral body in each party would probably meet at once to decide upon a new Leader and so help the Sovereign to make the choice of Prime Minister.

When in opposition the Conservative Leader picks his own 'shadow cabinet'. He is not, like the Labour Leader, inhibited in so doing by the election of other members alongside him. If the party is in the majority, the Leader becomes Prime Minister and, like a Labour Prime Minister, will choose cabinet and other ministers. The leadership of the party is distinct from the hierarchy of the 1922 Committee. The officers of that Committee are the chairman who is always a respected and senior member of the party, usually without ministerial experience; two vice-chairmen; a treasurer; and two secretaries. All these officers are elected from the membership. When the party is in power ministers attend meetings of the 1922 Committee by invitation only;[1] when in opposition leading members (or ex-ministers) take a regular part in its proceedings. The chairman of the 1922 Committee has direct access to the Leader of the party and in particular reports criticisms made in the Committee of policies advocated or pursued by the Leader or his colleagues.

Professor McKenzie has summed up the difference between the two parties as follows: whereas in opposition the Parliamentary Labour Party observes certain 'democratic' practices in its organization (such as the annual election of its Leader and the Parliamentary Committee) which distinguish it from the Conservative Party, in office it does not do so, believing those practices to be incompatible with cabinet government as it has developed in Britain. For its part the Conservative Party carries into opposition certain aspects of cabinet practices. Its leaders are not subject to annual elections, though broadly speaking, like the Labour Leader, they can move only in the direction that the bulk of their supporters are prepared to follow.[2]

1. Commons ministers do, however, have the right to take part in any election of a Leader. The 1922 Committee is thus distinguished from the 'party in the House of Commons' which chooses the Leader.

2. Robert T. McKenzie, *British Political Parties*, 2nd edition (1964), p. 412. Prof. McKenzie's analysis of the power structures of each party remains valid and is of great importance to students of British politics.

A similar contrast can be drawn between the powers of the leaders over the formation of party policy and over the party 'machines'. The powers of the Conservative Leader are the easier to state. He has traditionally been entrusted with exclusive duty to decide party policy. In so doing he may and does consult his cabinet (actual or shadow) and seeks the advice of any relevant committees or working parties within the party organization. He will also have regard to resolutions passed by the annual party conference—that is the conference of the National Union of Conservative and Unionist Associations. But he is not bound by any of this advice: final determination of policy remains his prerogative.

This power is reinforced by the Leader's absolute control of the Conservative Central Office and the Conservative Research Department. At the Central Office are based the chairman of the party, a deputy chairman, three vice-chairmen, the chairman of the Research Department and chairman and deputy chairman of the advisory committee on policy. The chief function of the Central Office is to see that the party's organization throughout the country is efficient and able to win elections. The Research Department is independent of the Central Office, and its director, besides directing the party's research, acts as secretary to the advisory committee on policy. The advisory committee comprises the chairman and deputy chairman of the party and fifteen others, seven from Parliament (five chosen by the '1922 Committee' in the Commons and two by the Conservative peers) and eight representing Conservative associations outside Parliament. All the officers of these bodies are appointed by the Leader and are responsible to him.

Taken with his responsibilities for making policy, these controls add up to an impressive sum of personal powers. Yet as Professor McKenzie has pointed out, the Leader holds and exercises them subject to the consent of his followers in and out of Parliament. Precedents for the withdrawal of that consent have not been lacking in modern times: Balfour (1910), Austen Chamberlain (1922) and Neville Chamberlain (1940) were in fact driven from office by their followers.[1]

1. Ibid., p. 66. On the question whether Mr Harold Macmillan should be included in this group differing views have been expressed. See McKenzie, op. cit., p. 594H and John P. Mackintosh, *The British Cabinet* (1968 ed.), pp. 432–3.

The formal arrangements in the Labour Party are more complex. On the face of it the responsibilities placed on the Conservative Leader for making policy and for controlling the party organization rest in the Labour Party with the National Executive Committee (NEC) and the Labour party conference. The NEC consists of twenty-eight members of whom the Leader and deputy Leader of the party are members ex officio. A third member, the treasurer, and five women members of the party are elected by the conference. The remaining twenty members are either nominated or elected by the various organized elements within the party such as the affiliated trade unions, affiliated co-operative organizations and the constituency parties. These are powerful and constitutionally entrenched elements. They apply to the Labour leadership an insistent and well organized pressure of a kind to which the Conservative leadership is not exposed.[1]

The NEC is the administrative authority responsible to the party conference for the operations of the party outside Parliament; so its field of activity is clearly differentiated from the Parliamentary Labour Party operating within Parliament. The NEC has the important duty of submitting statements of policy to the conference, and the conference is then empowered under the party's constitution to decide on specific proposals for inclusion in the party programme. No proposal can, however, be included unless carried by a two-thirds majority of the recorded votes, a rule which makes it difficult for minorities, however vociferous, to get their views accepted by the conference. But even when the conference has decided on specific proposals for inclusion in the programme, they are not automatically included. The final say in the content of the programme belongs jointly to the NEC and the Parliamentary Labour Party. As already shown the two leading figures on these bodies, namely the Party Leader and his deputy are common to both, and in practice members of the Parliamentary Labour Party are usually in a majority on the NEC. In addition the Chief Whip is invited to attend meetings of the NEC.[2] These arrangements have enabled the party

1. This point is discussed in detail by Ian Gilmour in *The Body Politic* (1969), pp. 106–13.
2. The general secretary, or top official of the Labour Party's head office, is invited to attend the liaison committee (when the party is in power) and the parliamentary committee (when the party is in opposition).

leader to exert a crucial influence over the formation of policy. In the most notable instance in recent years of a conference rejecting the advice of the leadership (on the issue of unilateral nuclear disarmament in 1960) the then Leader of the Labour Party was able in the following year to secure the reversal of the decision. Throughout he had retained the support of the Parliamentary Labour Party.

The other responsibility of the NEC is to direct the work of the Labour Party Head Office (Transport House). In contrast to the position of the Conservative Central Office, Transport House has never come structurally under the command of the Leader of the party. Here again, however, the close links between, and overlapping membership of, the PLP and the NEC in practice lessen this formal difference.

To sum up, when either major party is in power each respects the right of the Prime Minister to appoint his cabinet and determine policy. When in opposition, various constitutional safeguards against the power of the Leader figure more prominently in the Labour Party's arrangements. In practice, however, the power of both leaders, once chosen, derives less from a party than from a more purely constitutional context. Each is either the Prime Minister or the shadow, alternative Prime Minister. The position of shadow Prime Minister, as Leader of the Opposition, is officially recognized by the payment to him of an annual salary from public funds,[1] and he is by practice consulted directly by the Prime Minister on such matters of importance as national security. Both the Prime Minister and the Leader of the Opposition are, or are likely to be, in a position, by disposing of cabinet and other appointments, to affect decisively the political destinies of their colleagues. Argument about policy and programme is likely to be crucially influenced by this ultimate power.

In Congress

The contrasting division of powers and leadership in the United States between Congress and the President is reflected in the organization of the two chief parties. Elections every two years

1. In 1970 this salary was £4,500 a year which compared with £14,000 a year paid to the Prime Minister. For the salaries of members of Parliament see p. 118.

determine which party is to control proceedings in the House of Representatives and, depending on which senators are seeking re-election, the Senate. In every fourth year these elections coincide with the election of the President. But at every election a large number of other posts at state and local level are being filled, and indeed polls are being taken on a variety of local issues, on the same ballot paper as for membership of Congress. Whereas in Britain steps are taken to ensure that national and local elections do not coincide (the latter taking place at regular intervals and the former being within the discretion of the Prime Minister (see p. 81), in the United States elections are never held solely to choose members of Congress; and even in 'off' years, when the President is not being selected, the election of congressmen may not be considered by voters the most important decisions that they have to make.

Faced with this welter of electoral activity, the party organizations of Republicans and Democrats tend to divide into two branches. On the one hand the national committee of each party is concerned with the preparation of the national convention at which the presidential candidate is chosen and with related national and international issues. On the other hand the state and local committees are chiefly concerned with local and regional problems. The two halves interact, notably in state primary elections of presidential candidates. But the specific responsibility of these bodies for backing the campaigns of senators and congressmen is by no means always clear. According to one experienced Democratic congressman:

> I don't think there is any element of the party that is particularly interested in or concerned with the election of members of Congress. The national committee is preoccupied with the White House. The state committee has its eyes on the state house and the country committee is interested only in the court house. The Congressman is just a sort of a fifth wheel on the whole wagon.[1]

The extent of the help given to congressmen by the national committees of the two parties may depend upon the political colour of the occupant of the White House. If he is a Republican, for example, Democratic congressional candidates may expect more active support from the party's national committee as part

1. Cited in Charles L. Clapp, *The Congressman* (1964 ed.), p. 397.

of a broad attack across the whole country aimed at unseating him. Nevertheless the need to combine in face of this ever-threatening isolation explains a feature of the congressional party organization of both Republicans and Democrats that has no counterpart at Westminster. Since World War I both parties have set up campaign committees biennially, from election to election, in each House of Congress. In the House of Representatives the committee—named Congressional Campaign Committee—of each party consists of one member for each state represented in the House; where there is more than one member, he is chosen by the others. States with both Republican and Democratic congressmen are represented on both committees. The equivalent committees in the Senate are smaller, consisting of twelve to fourteen senators elected by each party. The two campaign committees of the same party in each House work closely together with a general aim of securing the election of congressmen of their own political persuasion. Party activity in primary elections is regarded as the province of the locality; but with the primaries completed, the campaign committee takes an active part in election notably by raising and distributing funds and by arranging to support each other on the hustings.

Once the elections are over, the basic party organization within Congress is similar to that at Westminster. Each party in each House has a group consisting of all members of the party in that House. The Democrats call their group a caucus, the Republicans a conference. For convenience here the term 'caucus' is used throughout, as the term 'conference' is also used officially in Congress to describe joint meetings of members of each House to discuss and resolve differences over the content of legislation.

In the days immediately before the opening of a Congress, each party caucus in each House holds its first meeting to elect its chairman and secretary and to choose its floor leader. At the same time the majority party in each House chooses its candidates for the posts of Speaker of the House and President pro tempore of the Senate, each to be elected by the House and by the Senate at their first meetings. Both these high positions are in the gift of the majority party.

In each House, too, the Democratic and Republican caucuses elect committees to frame policy on each bill and to recommend a course of action for it on the floor. The committees carry out these policy and steering functions in different ways in each House, the more elaborate organization being found in the Senate. These must now be described.

The importance of the policy-making function within Congress becomes evident against the background (described above) that the two major parties rely for their strength in the country on alliances of regions and areas rather than a coherent statement of nation-wide policy. A major recommendation of the Joint Committee on the Organization of Congress in 1945 was that each party should establish a policy committee, distinct from the steering committees which had hitherto discharged both the policy and steering function. The House of Representatives did not accept the proposal, largely because the leaders of both parties were content with the existing arrangements. But the Senate went ahead, both parties setting up policy committees with professional staff to advise them. Today the policy committee of each party in the Senate consists of the floor leader, whip and caucus chairman and secretary and from six to ten other senators. The steering committees, with an overlapping membership and with the floor leader, whip and caucus chairman as again the key figures, are larger bodies whose aim is to give effect to the conclusions of the policy committee by action through the standing committees and on the floor.

In the House of Representatives each party has only one committee for policy and steering. The Republican organization is the more active. In 1959, as part of an agreement under which the new Minority Leader was chosen, the Republicans changed the name of their steering committee to the policy committee, at the same time enlarging its membership and giving it a more positive function. In the 91st Congress (1969–70) it consisted of thirty-six members.[1] During the session it meets when the leadership considers that a bill or matter is of such consequence that there should be a party stance taken on it—in practice about a dozen times a session. The policy committee, working with leading Republicans on the legislative committees, then makes

1. Ten were ex officio, being the chairman and secretary of the caucus, the floor leader, the whip, the chairman of the Congressional Campaign Committee and the five Republican members of the Rules Committee (see below), and the remainder were elected regionally or otherwise, with an element of representation for the newest members.

recommendations which are circulated to all members of the caucus.

The Democrats have chosen to work differently. In the 91st Congress (1969–70) they had a steering committee of twenty-four members.[1] But it had no policy-making responsibilities, though it was used by the body of Democratic members as a channel for making their views on bills known to the leadership. The difference from the Republican organization is that the Democrats, having had a majority in both Houses of Congress for all except two Congresses[2] since World War II, have tended to rely upon the Speaker, Majority Leader and Whip on the one hand and the Democratic chairmen of the standing (legislative) committees on the other to furnish the necessary guidance on policy matters. By contrast in the Senate, where the same explanation might be thought to apply, the move towards separate policy and steering committees has stemmed from efforts of some Democratic senators to make Democratic policy more liberal.

Within each caucus, therefore, the location of leadership and the supporting committee structure is clear. But the leaders themselves, in making their dispositions, have to take account of other claimants for power.

There are first the senior members of the standing (legislative) committees—twenty-one in the House, seventeen in the Senate. These are the chairman of each committee, invariably the senior member of the majority party on the committee, and the senior or ranking member of the minority party. The results of the biennial congressional elections determine which of these two is to be chairman and which the ranking minority member. The advantages and disadvantages of the seniority system as a method of choosing chairmen are discussed in a later chapter on committees. Here its consequence for congressional leadership has to be noted. Because he has succeeded to one or other position by virtue of seniority, that is, by his own efforts and ability to survive rather than by his party's efforts on his behalf, a chairman's independence of party is strongly fortified. It is true that

1. There were six ex officio members: the Speaker, floor leader, the whip, the secretary and chairman of the caucus, and the chairman of the Congressional Campaign Committee; and eighteen elected regional representatives.

2. The 80th Congress (1947–48) and the 83rd Congress (1953–54).

each committee has its own rules, and it can amend those rules, or otherwise act, to restrain a chairman who constantly flouts its desires or intentions. Nevertheless, being in charge of committees which are largely autonomous in their allotted fields, the chairman and ranking minority member can influence decisively not only the content of the bills coming out of committee but also the dates by which they are reported. In particular they guide the leaders of their respective parties as to the choice of bills which should be accorded priority, though where there is a conflict of views the leaders have to decide what line to take.

Another important strand in the pattern of leadership is the Rules Committee of the House of Representatives (the Senate has no equivalent committee). This famous committee has for long stood at the centre of the controversy surrounding the reform of procedure in the House of Representatives. Its defenders see it as a 'traffic director on the legislative highway', its critics as 'an obstruction to orderly traffic'. As George Galloway has well said 'whether such a concentration of power in one committee is good or evil depends on whose ox is gored'.[1] That power is beyond doubt. A bill which has been favourably reported by another committee can be advanced by the Rules Committee if it recommends a special order or a 'rule' governing its further progress on the floor of the House.[2] Alternatively a rule can be withheld sometimes indefinitely.

The action taken by the Rules Committee is likely to reflect its composition, which is of crucial importance to the leadership of the two parties. Unlike most House committees which reflect the balance of parties in the House, the Rules Committee has ten majority and five minority members. This balance was struck by the House in 1961, the previous composition of eight to four having enabled two conservative Democrats (including the chairman), by voting with the four Republicans, to withhold rules from liberal measures. The effect of the new composition, which was tailored primarily to the requirements of President Kennedy's 'New Frontier' legislative programme, has been to reinforce the liberal element on the Committee. In this way the Committee's conservative approach, deriving from the working of the seniority

1. *The Legislative Process in Congress* (1955), p. 341.
2. An example of a rule is given on p. 283.

rule and the fact that most of its members are usually from safe seats, was offset in some degree. The way in which the Committee has worked since has made it unlikely that the House would tolerate a reversion to the practices which led to the change in the balance of majority to minority.

The powers of the chairmen of committees over the shape of bills, and in particular the proceedings of the Rules Committee, are considered in later chapters. Here what matters is the broad picture of the structure of leadership within Congress. In essence it may be summed up as follows. Within the House of Representatives there are two groups. On the one hand there are the policy or steering committee men, among whom the Speaker and Majority Leader of one party and the Minority Leader in the other stand out. This group concentrates generally on moving forward the party's legislative programme as proclaimed nationally by the party's leaders. On the other hand there are the twenty-one chairmen or ranking minority members of standing committees, among which the Rules Committee has a special importance. Those in this group tend to follow their several inclinations on legislative matters, thus making it difficult to present and follow through a coherent legislative programme. These two groups, whose membership in some degree overlaps, keep in touch with the movement of opinion in their parties. From a blend of compromise and leadership a programme emerges and is steered along a frequently unpredictable course in committee and on the floor. In the Senate the two groups within each caucus are reproduced, with differences of size and organization already noticed. This duplicated structure, in a second chamber of comparable power, means that the authority of leadership is still further diffused. In each House the majority decides the order of business, but it does so in consultation with the minority. The opportunities to obstruct the progress of business, more especially in the Senate, enforce this consultation.

Finally, there is the President's contribution to congressional leadership, in pursuance of the constitutional injunction that he is to recommend to Congress such measures as he judges necessary and expedient.[1] Much more than the parties—whose preoccupations at election times have been shown to be various— Presidents have often identified themselves as candidates with

1. Article II, 3.

political manifestoes of national scope and extent (for example, the New Deal, the New Frontier, the Great Society or Creative Federalism). Once in office they have sought either to translate them into detailed legislative programmes, or at least to press desirable legislation already before Congress. President Truman assigned two assistants to act as his informal liaison with Congress. President Eisenhower formalized this arrangement by setting up the legislative office within the White House. His interest in liaison was chiefly to ensure the flow of foreign aid. His three successors expanded and fully exploited the new office in support of their New Frontier, Great Society and Creative Federalism programmes of legislation.[1] When his own party has a majority in Congress, the President can work closely with the House and Senate majority leaders. Weekly conferences at the White House and day to day contact at various levels are the norm. But this favourable majority will not by itself assure the passage of his proposals. In Chapters VI and VII the way in which Congress deals with financial and other bills sent to it by the President, and the extent to which they are altered, are considered in some detail. The examples are taken from the 90th Congress (1967–68) when the President and the majority in each House were of the same political persuasion. When they are not, the President does not remit one iota of his constitutional right to recommend legislation. Nor are the ordinary congressional procedures for handling bills emanating from the executive altered in any respect. Nevertheless the legislative programme develops without any feeling on the part of the majority leadership that the President has to be unduly obliged, except naturally on bipartisan legislative policies. In the search made by that leadership for compromise and consensus on a legislative programme, this may be a crucial factor.

The contrast between this diffused leadership in Congress and the concentrated leadership in Parliament is striking. In Parliament power centred in the Prime Minister and his cabinet is deployed under the scrutiny and oversight of the opposition. As Professor Mackintosh has shown, an opposition cannot

1. For President Eisenhower's relations with Congress, see Arthur Larson, *Eisenhower* (1968), pp. 28–33. For President Kennedy's relations with Congress over the New Frontier, see T. C. Sorensen, *Kennedy* (1965), pp.339–65; Arthur M. Schlesinger, *A Thousand Days* (1965), pp. 612–17.

dislodge a Ministry with a working majority.[1] But it can by continually stating and recording alternative policies establish its claim to be the next government. It is this degree of confrontation which is missing from the congressional scene. In the years since World War II (1945–70) the majority in Congress has been of the same political colour as the President in fifteen out of twenty-five years, so that there has more often than not been a broad sympathy between the White House and the congressional leaders. But in the other ten years the congressional process has continued to operate, albeit less smoothly. The reason is that in Congress the leaders, while taking account of what the President is saying and doing, are working towards a consensus which as a rule runs across party lines. It is true that at the end of a congressional session each party publishes statements in the Congressional Record showing how far the party's programmes and policies have been translated into legislation. These records focus on what happened to measures recommended by the President. In the 91st Congress (1969–70), for example, the Republicans gave a favourable account of the President's achievement, while the Democrats emphasized the legislative contribution made by Congress itself and suggested that the whole sessional achievement compared unfavourably with that of the 90th Congress (1967–68).[2] But there are many other leaders in Congress operating within the majority and minority from various bases of power. Their interaction and the resulting decisions do not correspond in essentials to the British concept of an official opposition holding up to the electorate a clear alternative to the government in power. It is this contrast which accounts for the different style and purpose in Congress and in Parliament and for the different relationship between the leaders and the led.

FLOOR LEADERS, WHIPS AND DISCIPLINE

In Parliament

Party and power in Britain are united in the person of the Prime Minister and the other members of the cabinet appointed on his advice. This book is not concerned with the division of power

1. John P. Mackintosh, op. cit., p. 569.
2. Congressional Record, 5 January 1970 (Extensions of Remarks), E11171.

within the cabinet between the Prime Minister and other leading ministers and the extent to which the Prime Minister acts on the advice of an inner cabinet.[1] It is concerned with the way in which the Prime Minister, with the cabinet, secures the acceptance and support of his party for the policies and programmes laid before Parliament. Here his principal lieutenants are the Leader of the House and the Chief Whip.

Floor Leaders in Parliament

Until 1942 Prime Ministers in the twentieth century, with the single exception of Lloyd George, acted as Leader of the House of Commons. During World War II Churchill devolved the post, and this practice has been followed ever since. The Leader is not formally appointed by the Crown; the Prime Minister designates a member of the cabinet to lead the House on his behalf. Although some Leaders have been asked to carry at the same time important departmental responsibilities, it is no longer the practice so to do.

The Leader's most important function is the arrangement of government business in the House of Commons. He is chairman of the committees of the cabinet which draw a broad plan for legislation over the lifetime of a Parliament and choose the bills to be brought before Parliament in each session. The day to day details of the business for each session are worked out by the Chief Whip after consulting the Opposition Chief Whip (who together comprise what are referred to as 'the usual channels'). But the Leader of the House remains responsible for the general arrangements. It is he who in answer to a question asked by the Leader of the Opposition every Thursday states the business for the next week and the Monday following; and it is he who then deals with requests from members to find time for debates on matters currently interesting them.

The practice of questioning the Leader of the House on business matters is about as old as the devolution by the Prime

1. For contrasting views on how the power of the Prime Minister compares with that of the President of the United States, see R. H. S. Crossman, Introduction (1963) to W. Bagehot, *The English Constitution*, pp. 51–56; J. P. Mackintosh, *The British Cabinet* (1968 ed.), pp. 428–54; Ian Gilmour, op. cit., pp. 205–41; and P. Gordon Walker, *The Cabinet* (1970), pp. 80–96.

Minister of his duties as Leader. The length of the questioning is at the discretion of the Speaker: it usually lasts about twenty minutes. This close questioning of the Leader entertains the House and is both a test and an opportunity for him. It is also important for members. Nearly two-thirds of the time available in the House of Commons is devoted to government business and general debates, the remainder being for the official opposition or for private members. The colloquy with the Leader on Thursdays bears chiefly on the disposal of the time available on the initiative of the government. For example, a private member may seek to extract a pledge from the Leader for a debate on this or that topic that interests him. But some, indeed most, questions raised at this time have a more limited objective of calling public attention to a matter without serious expectation of obtaining time. The Leader often has to make a swift assessment of these different approaches and, consistent with maintaining the integrity of the government's programme, bow to strong parliamentary pressures, because it is his duty as Leader to ensure that the House has reasonable opportunity of debating matters which deeply concern it.

This is the wider aspect of his office: besides being the cabinet minister responsible to the Prime Minister for the government's programme in the House, he is the custodian of the rights of the different sections of the House—government, opposition, other parties and backbench members. He guides the House on questions of privilege and procedure, himself taking the chair of the important and long established Committee of Privileges. He also leads on matters of domestic concern, often being chairman of the House's Services Committee which inquires into such delicate questions as the accommodation and living conditions of members and the publication and broadcasting of House debates.

Two recent developments have added to the organized forces within the House with which he has to deal. The first is that since 1967 the chairmen of select committees have developed the practice of meeting informally at regular intervals as a liaison committee to co-ordinate their inquiries and where necessary to keep the Leader acquainted of the needs and wishes of select committees. Secondly, the chairmen's panel, from which chairmen of Standing Committees debating the committee stages of bills and other matters are chosen, has become more active. This panel, first appointed in 1883 and later empowered to report to the House their opinions on the procedure of standing committees, have recently made use of this power to bring to the notice of the Leader their disquiet on several procedural matters in which they are involved under the existing rules.

Whips in Parliament

The term 'whip' derives from the whippers-in of the hunting field who keep the hounds working as a pack and prevent them wandering. All parties in Parliament have some kind of whip to give their activities coherence and organization. Special and important duties fall to the Government Chief Whip in the House of Commons. His official style and title is Parliamentary Secretary to the Treasury or Patronage Secretary, though his ministerial ranking understates his real power and authority. For example, he regularly attends cabinet meetings, a practice begun during the tenure of Mr Buchan-Hepburn (now Lord Hailes) from 1951 to 1955. He is assisted by the Deputy Chief Whip and up to thirteen junior whips who are remunerated as ministers from public funds. Some hold junior posts in the government. Others have positions in the Royal Household; one of them sends to the Sovereign a daily account of proceedings in Parliament. A third category do not hold any post other than that of whip. All these whips are members of the Commons.

The other main party has a similar organization. The importance of the Opposition Chief Whip is recognized by the payment to him out of public funds, as to the Leader of the Opposition, of an annual salary.[1] Other members of the same party, not so remunerated, are appointed deputy to the Chief Whip and assistant whips.

The first duty of the Government Chief Whip is to help the Leader of the House prepare a sessional time-table of business. Within that frame he will work out the business of each sitting on a weekly basis. In this duty he is assisted by his private secretary, an influential and permanent civil servant whose tenure of this post is not disturbed by a change of government. This officer makes contact with government departments and

1. In 1970 this salary was £3,750.

various authorities within the House to ensure that the business is ready for the House to consider in accordance with the Chief Whip's plan. The plan has to take account of the time allotted by the standing orders to private members; of the customs according to which on certain occasions the subject of debate is chosen by the opposition; and a number of statutory provisions requiring certain kinds of business (notably the annual finance bill) to be completed by specified dates. Once an outline of the week's business is drawn, it is discussed in 'the usual channels', as meetings of the Government Chief Whip (or his private secretary) and the Opposition Chief Whip are generally known. Here the talk will turn on the topics to be debated, the amount of time to be given (or taken) on each, and the form that the debate will take. Other interested persons may also be consulted from time to time but it is the working of the usual channels which will decide whether the House's business is organized efficiently. One measure of that efficiency is the extent to which the House can be kept clear of argument about the order of proceedings and so enabled to spend its time and effort on the substance of the business before it. Good personal relations between the two Chief Whips lubricate the usual channels and contribute visibly to the smooth flow of the business of the House. Morrison has suggested that the need for them to be continuously on speaking terms and to avoid public and personal recrimination explains why traditionally they do not take part in debate.[1]

The other major duty of the Chief Whip is to inform all members of his party of the government's detailed proposals and intentions, and conversely to inform members of the government of the movement of opinion within the party on the policies and performances of ministers. This is an indispensable work of organization if on the one hand the party's support for the government is to be effectively directed and on the other if ministers are not to become the prisoners of their departments, and isolated from the party. The opposition whips provide the same link between the leaders of the other main party and the led. Both sides so spread their network of whips that the Chief Whip is kept in touch with all segments of opinion—whether regional (Scottish, Welsh, Northern Irish or the different quarters of England) or political (right, centre or left)—within the party.

1. Herbert Morrison, *Government and Parliament* (1954 ed.), p. 103.

Discipline in Parliament

Party policy and attitudes are discussed week by week within the parliamentary party organizations. The whips tie these discussions to the day to day business of the House by sending out a weekly circular, likewise known as a 'whip', to every member of the party. This written whip sets out the items of business for each day of the following week (as already announced to the House by the Leader) and requests the member's attendance in support. The relative urgency and importance of each item is indicated by the number of times the request for attendance is underlined—a one-, two- or three-line whip—and the degree of stress in the language of the request. A three-line whip indicates that an important vote is expected and that a member is expected to be present, unless illness or some other reason approved in advance by the whips keeps him away. Two-line or one-line whips indicate occasions of lesser importance when the government whip will be concerned with marshalling a large enough attendance to ensure a majority—often by informal 'pairing' between the two sides—and if necessary to carry a motion to closure a debate (see p. 152), thus assuring the passage of government business.

Why does a member of Parliament accept this kind of indication as to how he should vote? The practical answer is that this is a helpful and efficient method of informing members of the issues coming before the House and the importance attached to each of them by his party. So large and complex is the range of business coming before Parliament that it would be impossible for a single member to study each item in enough detail to decide his own line. The circular whip gives him convenient guidance, as do the personal whips standing at the doors of the division lobby, on how he may cast his vote in line with the party to which he belongs.

One constitutional answer is that a member is returned to the House of Commons primarily to support (or oppose) the party obtaining a majority at the general election and forming the government. If he declines so to act, the line of responsibility between the declared will of the electorate and the action of the government breaks down. To say absolutely that the prerogative of dismissing a government today rests with the electorate alone, and not with the House of Commons, would be an overstatement. But the realities come close to it. A member would have been pressed by his government far beyond the limits of what was acceptable before voting in a way that would have such a result. In reply to a critic of the government's incomes policy the Government Chief Whip stated his view of the position in December 1969 as follows:

> I would remind you . . . you were elected not because you were [an individual with a very good record] but simply because you were a Labour candidate. I cannot speak for your constituents but I am certain that they expect you, as mine expect me, to vote for the Labour government and to ensure its continuance in office.[1]

This is the spirit of the standing orders of the Labour Party which every Labour candidate has to sign. Its implications are set out in the code of conduct[2] of the Parliamentary Labour Party. The following paragraph from the code will allow a direct comparison to be struck with the freedom and obligation of a congressman (see p. 42):

> While the party recognizes the right of members to abstain from voting in the House on matters of deeply held personal conviction, this does not entitle members to vote contrary to a decision of a party meeting, or to abstain from voting on a vote of confidence in a Labour Government.

The demands made by the Parliamentary Labour Party of its members are more formally stated than those of the Conservative Party. A Conservative candidate is not called upon to make a pledge of loyalty, nor does the party use written codes or rules. As Professor Jackson has pointed out, this lack of formality is in tune with the power and authority accorded to the Leader: this hierarchical idea of authority is combined with a belief in individual freedom and initiative.[3] But the end product in both parties is similar. A member is expected to vote for his party except on questions touching matters of 'conscientious' conviction,

1. Letter quoted in *The Times*, 16 December 1969.
2. See the Report of the Annual Conference of the Labour Party (1968), p. 58.
3. R. J. Jackson, *Rebels and Whips* (1968), p. 30.

when he is expected to abstain rather than vote against his party. A 'free vote', that is, a vote on which the whips do not give prior guidance, is rare. It is a tolerance extended more often by an opposition than a government leadership. For a government the level of voting is regarded as a matter of prestige. Free votes would probably result in a lower figure of support than a whipped vote, and a lower majority would be regarded as a serious loss of face, depressing the morale of the party workers in the country and conveying to the electorate, accustomed to well measured differences between government and opposition, the belief that all was not well in high places. For this chief reason the whipped vote on party lines is the general rule both in the House and in Standing Committees considering government bills.

The obligations of membership are backed by sanctions. The Labour Party's code of conduct provides for a number of disciplinary actions of increasing severity. The first is a written reprimand from the Chief Whip. The second is a 'suspension', in effect a period of probation in which the member though excluded from party colloquies is expected to comply with the party whip. A more serious sanction is the withdrawal of the party whip which (like suspension) is decided upon by the Parliamentary Labour Party. The effect of a withdrawal is that a member no longer receives the weekly circular of guidance from the whips and is in effect no longer a member of the parliamentary party. By itself this weapon may prove a boomerang, in that the de-whipped member can then speak and vote as he pleases and may cause more trouble outside than inside the parliamentary party. A further step is to expel him from the national party and refuse him readoption as the party's candidate in his constituency. He may be readmitted after treaty with the leadership. But if not readmitted before the next election, he would be denied the organization and resources of the constituency party and would have to rely on his own efforts and reputation to secure re-election as an independent. The dangers of embarking on this course were dramatically illustrated at the general election of 1950. In the previous year four Labour members had been expelled from the party after differences over foreign policy. At the general election of 1950 they stood as independents, official party candidates being put up against them with the approval of the party's national executive. All four were defeated, and only one was subsequently reinstated as an official Labour candidate.

The initiative in a divorce between a Labour member and his party does not always come from the party. A member may himself decide that to resign the whip is the right course for him to take. As a rule he will seek to make peace with the party before the next general election. One who did not was Desmond Donnelly, Labour Member for Pembroke since 1950, who resigned the whip in June 1968 after disagreements over policy. He was expelled in March 1969 and in April launched a New Democratic Party. In the general election of 1970 the Labour Party's new candidate won 32·5 per cent of the vote at Pembroke as compared with Donnelly's 21·5, but the seat was lost to the Conservatives with 34·7 per cent.[1]

In the Conservative party the absence of written standing orders or code of conduct means that the sanctions underlying party discipline are less closely defined. The withdrawal of the whip is a matter for the Leader exclusively. In fact the Conservative whip was last withdrawn from a member in 1942, the usual practice being for a member who disagrees with party policy or is in serious contention with his constituency association to resign the whip. No member has been expelled from the Conservative party since World War II. The most recent study of party discipline has suggested that even in the Labour party, which last expelled members in 1950, the weapon of expulsion may be obsolete; in the Conservative party it is not used.[2]

A government Chief Whip's alternative title of Patronage Secretary is another indication of his power. According to Lord Morrison, most Prime Ministers consult the Chief Whip as well as senior colleagues in forming a government or replacing ministers. The scope for influence is considerable. In October 1969, of the 328 members in the majority, 81 held ministerial appointments. The principle of collective responsibility for the government's decisions binds the support of an important group to the leadership. Their unity, and the aspirations of other members to join them, are factors lending cohesion to any party in government. The prospect of government likewise helps to unite the

1. David Butler and Michael Pinto-Duschinsky, *The British General Election of 1970* (1971), pp. 112–13, 411–13.
2. R. J. Jackson, op. cit., pp. 216, 252.

party in opposition. On both sides, irrespective of the gift or prospect of office, the whips can be, and are, helpful to their members in a variety of matters of convenience within the House such as appointments to committees. They can be just as unhelpful to members not in favour.

The strength of the party leadership is mitigated in some measure by unseen but effective currents of communication between the two sides. There is no crossbench in the Commons, as there is in the Lords, providing a physical link between government and opposition, as well as a home for the unaligned. But contact is real enough. A large proportion of every government's legislative programme is common ground—as Churchill once said, four-fifths of one party agree with four-fifths of what the other side are trying to do.

This ready co-operation is nurtured by service on select committees, out of which cross-party policies frequently emerge, and by joint endeavours further afield at international parliamentary assemblies or on commonwealth delegations. It is also rooted in an awareness that 'pairing' between the two sides eases the burden of constant attendance at the House to fulfil the requirements of the whip. Moreover in every Parliament some members are less impressed by party requirements than others. Some are not interested in the pursuit of office; others have regained the relative freedom of the backbenches; still others are not seeking re-election. These and other motivations result in a varied reaction to the touch of the whip. But, potent as all these influences may be, they do not affect the final arbitrament, which is that, by and large, with occasional spectacular exceptions, the government gets its way. In later chapters on Legislation and Finance the enactment of a government's programme will be looked at in greater detail and the extent to which it can be altered, or disrupted, is considered. Here it need only be noted that the result of the effort by the government leaders and whips is that their programme is usually enacted after debate in the House in which they are tested and examined, notably by a rival leadership with governmental aspirations.

Leadership in the House of Lords

In the House of Lords the structure of leadership is the same as in the Commons: there is a Leader of the House and a Leader of the Opposition, each supported by a Chief Whip and other whips.[1] The presence of a Conservative majority in the House of Lords means that only when the Conservatives are in power are negotiations between the Leaders conducted in the same way as in the Commons. When the Labour party is in power, confronting, as it were, a hostile majority of the floor of the House, discussions depend more on the tact, restraint and wisdom of the Leaders. They negotiate in the knowledge that a defeat for the government on the floor may be overborne by the preponderant powers of the Commons. The powers of the two Houses are considered in Chapter IV. Here it need only be noted that special problems may be posed for the Lords leadership of a kind not found in the House of Commons as a result of the differing powers of the two Houses.

In Congress

In the two Houses of Congress the absence of members of the administration is the most striking feature to the British eye. In Washington the authority of leadership is exercised by the Speaker of the House of Representatives and by the majority floor leaders and whips in both Houses. To preserve the symmetry of comparison with their British opposite numbers the powers and functions of the presiding officers are considered in the next section of this chapter. But it has to be remembered that in the House of Representatives the Speaker (unlike his opposite number in the Senate) is the supreme commander of the majority's troops, while the majority leader is merely the general commanding in the field. The primacy of the Speaker is emphasized by the normal avenues of promotion to the apex of a parliamentary party, which is from Majority Leader to presiding officer. The post of presiding officer is in a sense the apex for both parties, in that it belongs by tradition to the majority party; when the minority becomes the majority, the former minority leader is likely to become Speaker. Due reservation being made of this special position of the Speaker in the House, the responsibilities of the floor leaders are substantially the same in both Houses of Congress, and may for easier comparison with the

1. The Leader of the Opposition and Chief Whip (Opposition), like their counterparts in the House of Commons, are paid official salaries.

House of Commons, be mainly described in terms of the House of Representatives.

Floor Leaders in Congress

The post of the floor leader seems to have been created in the early nineteenth century in response to the need for a leader to organize and direct the growing quantity of business coming before the House of Representatives. According to Dr Riddick, the earliest titular floor leaders were the chairmen of the Ways and Means Committee (then responsible for questions of expenditure as well as taxation). It was a practical arrangement because this committee reported most of the bills coming before the House, so that the chairman was the logical choice to arrange the House's programme of business. When in 1865 an Appropriations Committee was set up to take over questions of expenditure, supply and appropriation, the chairman of that Committee, which came to handle most of the legislation, frequently became the Leader.[1] The post of Majority Leader was not identified as such in the House of Representatives until 1899.

From 1899 to 1910 the Majority Leader of the House of Representatives was designated by the Speaker. Since that date he has been elected by the party caucus. Once elected he ceases to be a chairman or a member of a legislative committee. It is noteworthy that in an assembly so dedicated to the principle of seniority, no special weight is given to this qualification in choosing the floor leader. In the 90th Congress (1967–68), for example, no fewer than twenty-seven Democrats had more seniority (measured as at Westminster by consecutive membership) than Congressman Carl Albert, the Democrat's choice for Majority Leader.[2] Seniority and experience are not by themselves enough for election to the leadership.

The Majority Leader, like the Leader of the House of Commons, is primarily concerned with the legislative programme. Like him too, his first duty is to be his party's spokesman on that programme. The reliance placed by the Democrats on the Majority Leader (as part of the triumvirate of Speaker, Majority Leader and Whip) in policy-making has already been noted

1. F. Riddick, *Congress: Organization and Procedure* (1949), p. 86n.
2. He held the post from 1962 to 1970. In January 1971 he was elected Speaker.

(p. 23); and on the Republican side, the Leader is an ex officio member of the party's policy committee. Moreover, when the majority in Congress is the same political colour as the President, it is the Majority Leader's responsibility to ensure that as much as possible of the President's own legislative expectations are realized. In conjunction with the Speaker and the Whip he brings together the different strands of party opinion—from the President, the party organization and from members of Congress—and weaves them into a legislative programme as a rallying point for the majority party.

Like the British Leader he makes a weekly statement (usually on the last sitting day of the week) in reply to a question from the Minority Leader about the business for the following week. But there is an important difference. He cannot bring to his statement the certainty of his British opposite number who knows that in the House of Commons the time of the House, subject to predetermined exceptions, is controlled by the government. In the House of Representatives the weekly statement is less precise especially in regard to the last few days of the following week. The Majority Leader has to keep in day to day touch with the chairmen of committees over the progress of bills. He has to weigh the many imponderables in Congress—such as whether the report of a conference between the two Houses will be available or whether the member in charge of a bill scheduled for a particular day can be present—so that the discussion of future business is couched in flexible language.

The Minority Leader in the House is also elected by the party caucus, and he too gives up committee assignments, once elected. But his position has proved less secure than that of the Majority Leader. Since 1931 the Republicans have been the minority party in all except two Congresses (1948–49 and 1954–55). The frustration of continuing minority status—which applies to all committees as well as to the floor itself—may have accounted for the more frequent changes of Minority than of Majority Leaders.[1]

1. Randall Ripley has made the following analysis of Majority and Minority Leaders in this century: of the twelve Majority Leaders, six became Speaker; four gave up the position when their party became the minority, and two ran for the Senate; of the thirteen Minority Leaders, two died or were defeated at the polls, three were ousted by their party, three ran for the Senate and two retired from the House. See *Party Leaders in the House of Representatives* (1967), pp. 28–32.

There are differences of emphasis in the Senate. The two parties did not formally vote to elect floor leaders until after World War I, though individual senators carried out comparable duties before that time.[1] Today the duties of Majority and Minority Leaders are broadly the same as those of their opposite numbers in the House, though the Senate leaders continue to serve on standing committees. Senator Mansfield, Majority Leader through the 1960s, was a member of the Senate's Appropriations Committee and Foreign Relations Committee; Senator Scott, who became Minority Leader in 1969, was a member of the Committee on Commerce and on the Judiciary. But the Senate looks for the same kind of qualities as the House in choosing its leaders, that is, a blend of experience (in 1970 twelve Democratic senators had more seniority than Senator Mansfield), firmness of purpose, skill in negotiations and an ability to inspire the confidence of his fellow members in all quarters of the Senate. The same qualities are found in successful leaders at Westminster.

Whips in Congress

Each party in the House of Representatives is served by a member known as the Whip. The Democratic Whip—first officially so described in 1913—is designated by the floor leader (in consultation with the Speaker, if the Democrats are in the majority) and subsequently approved by the caucus. Nineteen assistant whips are named by the nineteen geographical groups or zones into which the members of the Democratic caucus are divided. The Republican Whip—first officially so described in 1899—was formerly chosen by the party's committee on committees (see p. 46); but since 1965 he has been elected by the full Republican caucus. Once elected, he chooses a deputy and nineteen other regional or area whips.

The majority and minority whips work closely with their respective leaders, and when they are absent act on their behalf. Though the last two Democratic Majority Leaders had been Democratic Whips, promotion from one post to the other is not automatic; no Republican Whip has ever become a Leader. Like the Leader the Whip is not chosen on grounds of seniority,

1. Floyd Riddick, *Majority and Minority Leaders of the Senate* (1969), pp. 3–5.

though he is likely to be an experienced member of the House. The majority Whip in 1970, Congressman Hale Boggs, had the same continuous service as his Leader and was a senior member of the Ways and Means Committee, the Joint Economic Committee and the Joint Committee on Internal Revenue Taxation.[1] Both majority and minority whips are assisted by small administrative staffs paid for out of public funds.

As at Westminster the whips carry out an essential two-way communication, conveying the views of the membership to the party Leaders, and informing the membership of the views of the leadership. Also as at Westminster, following the business statement by the Majority Leader, the Whip sends out to every member of the party in the House a letter stating the programme of business for the next week. This letter simply reflects what has been said in the House by the Majority Leader. It does not contain any of the special markings (one-, two- or three-line whips) that distinguish its British equivalent, but it provides a basis on which the Whip's organization can seek to unify party opinion in support of the measures to which the party attaches importance, and, when the time comes, to rally members for votes.

In the Senate with its smaller numbers communication within the membership of each party is easier than in the House. Four senators are appointed in each party on a regional basis to assist the Whip; but in practice the routine work is done by two officials, the secretary for the majority and the secretary for the minority. Indeed the Majority and Minority Whips are no longer officially described as such. Their present titles—Assistant Majority Leader and Assistant Minority Leader—indicate that they are more concerned with helping their Leaders and in particular with their party's policy and steering committees than with whipping. This concern, as well as the different style of proceeding in the Senate, may account for the contrast in tone of the whip notices circulated in the Senate and in the House of Representatives.

Discipline in Congress

How do the Leaders and their Whips succeed in mobilizing party opinion behind measures which the party regards as important?

1. He was elected Majority Leader in January 1971.

They operate against the unpromising background already noticed that members of Congress, though elected as Democrats or Republicans, tend to have secured election on, and therefore to have a prime concern for, local, state and regional rather than national issues. There is a built-in tension between their approach and the approach of the floor leaders who, though by no means impervious to the importance of local issues, have a professional concern with national party government and, where the Majority Leaders are in harness with a President of the same party, a responsibility for turning the President's own programme into legislation.

In these circumstances the Leaders on both sides have tended to press their requests for support only on a few, carefully selected occasions. No doubt they could secure more voting on party lines. But being congressmen themselves they have recognized that the first obligation of each member is to 'vote his district'; that is to say, when he comes to vote, the call of his district (constituency) or the demands of his state and his own need to secure re-election as its member are expected to take precedence over his status as a party man in the national representative body. This tolerant attitude towards party affiliation is echoed in the rules of the party caucuses. The following paragraph is taken from the rules of the Democratic caucus in the House of Representatives:

> In deciding upon action in the House involving party policy or principle, a two-thirds vote of those present and voting at a caucus meeting shall bind all members of the caucus: *Provided*, The said two-thirds vote is a majority of the full Democratic membership of the House; *And provided further*, That no Member shall be bound upon questions involving a construction of the Constitution of the United States or upon which he made contrary pledges to his constituents prior to his election or received contrary instructions by resolutions or platform [declaration of policy] from his nominating authority.

The contrast in tone and temper to the text cited on p. 33 from the British Labour Parliamentary Party's rules could hardly be more striking. The effect of the Democratic rule is that Democratic members are bound to back a party decision only if it has commanded a vote of two-thirds of the full party membership in the House. Even then important exceptions are allowed, if

contrary election pledges have been given or—vital for Southern
Democrats—the party decision involves an unacceptable interpretation of the Constitution. In all other cases, according to the
rule, a member can vote as he thinks best. In practice even
the two-thirds requirement has become a dead letter because the
Democratic caucus rarely takes a formal stand on an issue. Policy
direction, as already shown, has been left to the Speaker, the
Majority Leader, and the committee chairmen.

It is not surprising in these circumstances that votes on party
lines—all Republicans versus all Democrats—seldom take place.
Cross-voting is the norm. At least since World War II it has been
possible to identify five broad voting groups in both Houses of
Congress, namely, liberal and conservative Republicans, liberal
and conservative Democrats and Southern Democrats.[1] Legislation has often been a product of varying alliances between these
groups tempered always by the play of local and regional
interests.

An analysis of twelve key votes in 1968 selected by the *Congressional Quarterly*[2] shows how extensive this cross-voting is.
In 1968, the last year of President Johnson's administration, the
main issues were the open (multi-racial) housing bill, the tax
surcharge, various cuts in the President's budget, crime and gun
control, foreign aid and the (anti-) poverty programme. On not
one of these issues did the twelve key votes follow party lines. On
seven out of twelve in the House and five out of twelve in the
Senate a conservative coalition of Republicans and Southern
Democrats was found voting against Northern Democrats. One
vote may be set out in detail to show that even within these groups
there is not unanimity. In the House an amendment to reduce
the funds for the Office of Economic Opportunity (the anti-
poverty Agency) by 100m. dollars was rejected by 220 votes to
181. The votes broke down as follows:

1. Within these groups are several informal organizations of like-
minded members, which frame proposals or do research on behalf of
their membership. The Democratic Study Group; its Republican equivalent, the Wednesday Club; and the Southern Caucus are three examples.

2. The *Congressional Quarterly* is a privately owned, non-party, weekly
publication (with a consolidated almanac) giving a detailed and systematic
account of business transacted in both Houses of Congress and their Committees. It is an indispensable work of reference for students of Congress.
There is no equivalent coverage of proceedings in Parliament.

	For	Against
Northern Democrats	11	132
Southern Democrats	60	24
Republicans	110	64
	181	220

In the Senate a vote to restore 215m. dollars to the Agency's budget was carried by thirty-seven votes to twenty-six. Here the breakdown was as follows:

	For	Against
Northern Democrats	27	1
Southern Democrats	2	11
Republicans	8	14
	37	26

The flexibility of this voting—it is not untypical of the twelve key votes cited in the Congressional Quarterly—explains the minute attention given to a Congressman's voting record, by himself, his constituency, his state, and all other interested bodies and persons. High among those interests is his party, whose pressure on him through the leadership, though tactful, is constant. Whatever the precise nature of his mandate or the extent of the pledges he has given locally, he is still a Republican or a Democrat. There are solid advantages to be gained from party government, of however attenuated a kind, working through Congress. He knows it, and the leadership know it. This is the strongest weapon at the disposal of the leaders. A member may know what bill he wants, or is required by previous pledges, to bring forward. It will be unlikely to make swift progress if he habitually withholds co-operation from the leadership. Direct penalties are rare and are only imposed when the provocation is extreme. In January 1965 the Democratic caucus stripped Congressmen John Bell Williams (Mississippi) and Watson (South Carolina) of their committee seniority for giving public support to the Republican presidential candidate in the election of 1964. The same treatment was accorded to Congressman Adam Clayton Powell (New York) in January 1967 for alleged improprieties in his conduct as chairman of a committee and to Congressman Rarick (Louisiana) in January 1969 for giving public support to the candidature of Governor Wallace in the presidential election of 1968. The softer tactic is however the usual practice. The leadership can achieve much by a timely concession to a particular member or co-operation with a particular group. Asked[1] what steps he could take to secure the co-operation of members of the House Appropriations Committee in his own point of view, the chairman of the Committee replied: 'Sometimes the only way to keep your troops in line is to go right over there and join them'. The same spirit has animated many prudent congressmen in positions of leadership.

Besides extending a prudent measure of co-operation, a Leader has other weapons. There is patronage. In the House of Representatives a committee on patronage is composed of three members appointed by the Speaker from the majority party. The Committee distributes about 200 minor posts, such as doorkeepers and pages. Each majority party member—except committee chairmen who appoint the staff of their committees—is in order of seniority entitled to dispose of one of the minor posts. There is an equivalent committee of minority members, who dispose of about thirty posts, though the most important—such as the Clerk of the Minority, Minority Sergeant at Arms and Minority Doorkeeper—are elected by the minority caucus. In the Senate there is less organization, most patronage appointments being made after informal consultations, with the Leaders making proposals to the party caucus if important posts are in question. Political patronage, however, embraces not only posts within Congress but also a range of federal positions of greater or lesser importance located all over the country. It is the practice of the President to consult members of his party in both Houses when filling these posts. The knowledge that these consultations have taken place, and the appointments resulting from them, help to smooth the way of members of Congress and their staffs in carrying out their functions locally, regionally and nationally.

Then there are the rewards or preferments which the leadership can influence or directly control. For example, the Speaker of the House of Representatives chooses members to preside over the House in his stead. To be chosen is a cherished honour. In both Houses, too, the leadership can influence appointments to delegations for international meetings.

But most important for a congressman's satisfaction and indeed

1. By one of the authors.

for his future career in Congress is a desired assignment to a standing (legislative) committee. In each House members are nominated for membership of committees by a 'committee on committees' in each party. These nominations are approved as a matter of course by the House in question. In the House of Representatives the Republican committee on committees consists of one (usually the senior) member for each state having Republican representation in the House, selected by each state delegation. The committee includes the Republican floor leader who acts as chairman, though without a vote. The Democratic committee on committees, by contrast, consists of all the Democratic members of the Committee of Ways and Means who are elected by the party caucus. This Committee does not include the Democratic floor leader, because he does not take an active part in legislative committees. But his informal advice on committee assignments does not necessarily fall on deaf ears. One channel for that advice could be a senior member of the Ways and Means Committee, more especially when—as happened between 1962 and 1970—such a member is also the Democratic Whip. Charles Clapp has concluded that while formal leadership of the Republicans is the more prominent in exerting influence on committee assignments, both leaderships exert much influence, though it is done 'with discretion and with a light rather than a heavy hand.' Only in the choice of the membership of the Ways and Means Committee—of crucial importance because tax and tariff policies go to the heart of party programmes and because the Democratic members of it are to make committee assignments for their fellow Democrats—is the hand applied heavily and always decisively.[1]

In the Senate the method of appointment is different. The Republican committee on committees is appointed by the chairman of the party caucus subject to confirmation by the caucus itself. Usually the Republican Whip is a member of this committee. The Democratic committee on committees is in fact the Democratic Steering Committee (see above) whose membership is nominated by the Democratic floor leader subject to the caucus's approval. In both these groupings, therefore, the leadership has a clear avenue of influence over committee assignments.

1. Charles L. Clapp, *The Congressman* (1964 ed.), Chapter V, especially pp. 217–19.

Finally the leadership can—and does—positively help its party members. It is commonplace that a good voting record on legislation helps a congressman towards re-election. But what constitutes a 'good' record in state or local terms may need careful consideration. He may also need help from the leadership in avoiding or disguising necessary party votes with awkward regional implications. This act of reconciliation is supremely the business of the Leader. As Dr Riddick has observed,

> The work of the Leader in making party government function must not be underestimated: he is the great 'mitigator' of individual members' ills; to the party he is the cement that holds it together.[1]

Some of these powers at the Leader's disposal find a parallel in the kind of persuasion used by British leaders and whips. But the spirit and object of the whole exercise is different. Parties in the United States being agglomerations of sectional interest, legislation in Congress is always the search for a compromise or a bargain. In mapping out his programme of business the Leader in Congress has to collaborate with other key figures in the field— the chairmen and members of the relevant committee, the representatives of the affected areas, the liberal and conservative elements within the party, and always the other party with its own internal groupings and problems. The business of the leadership is so to strike the compromise or bargain that a majority can be found for the measures he wants. It calls for a high degree of political skill and sensitivity, a clear grasp of what needs to be done and what can be done. Not surprisingly, since the needs and the possibilities are matters of judgement, the leadership is often criticized—in a way seldom heard at Westminster—for not giving its followers a clear enough lead on policy or pressing them hard enough to support it with their vote.[2]

It is a curiosity that while the party asks less of its members in Congress than in Parliament, it is accorded a much higher degree of official recognition. Before a Congress convenes, each party in each House meets for 'organization'. These—and other— meetings are held in the Senate chamber or the House chamber. In Parliament it would be unthinkable to use either chamber for

1. F. Riddick, op. cit., p. 90.
2. Charles L. Clapp, op. cit., pp. 325–6, 329–30.

a party meeting (even if the seating arrangements—government confronting opposition—were not likely to encourage fissiparous tendencies within the parties). Another example is pairing, long established in Washington and Westminster as a method of allowing members to be absent without upsetting the balance of parties. In the House of Representatives and the Senate statements of pairing submitted by absent members are given to the clerk who reads out the list at the end of a vote and publishes it in the official record as part of the proceedings. At Westminster pairing is unknown to the official proceedings of the House of Commons. A third instance is the status of party organizations. In both Congress and Parliament the organizations serving the parliamentary parties are allowed offices in the parliamentary buildings. But in Congress some of the staff are borne on public funds. For example, about 50,000 dollars (£22,000) was included in the House's budget of 1969–70 for the staff of the House Democratic steering committee and the same amount for the House Republican caucus; the equivalent staff in the Senate are paid for in the same way. At Westminster all party officials working within the Palace are supported wholly from party funds. More striking still is the relative status of the notice of the following week's business circulated by the whips' organization. In the House of Commons this is a party document, circulated to party members and officials only, with the prime object of securing the attendance of members in the necessary numbers to back or oppose each item of government business. In the House of Representatives the equivalent documents are widely circulated for general information outside as well as within each party organization, and in some measure are a substitute for the order paper (agenda) put out officially in the House of Commons.

These, and other, contrasts make the point that in Congress parties, though less influential, work more openly; in Westminster where party discipline and influence alike are stronger, their operations are more covert. The basis of the contrast may be that in Congress, especially in the House of Representatives, the status of party is bound up with the status of the presiding officer, so that operations of the parties draw strength and respectability from the link with the official operations of the chair. At Westminster, where the Speaker severs himself from his party membership on election to the chair, there is no such link.

SPEAKERS AND PRESIDING OFFICERS

The final contrast in the leadership of Parliament and Congress is between their presiding officers and chief advisers in both Houses. The most instructive contrast here is between the Speaker of the House of Commons, an impartial umpire, and the Speaker of the House of Representatives who combines the leadership of a party with the duty to preside as impartially as possible. The presiding officers of both the House of Lords and the Senate also have extraneous duties which differentiate their status and influence as presiding officers. These four high officers can conveniently be treated in this order.

The Speaker of the House of Commons

The Speakership of the Commons draws strength from its antiquity: the line stretches unbroken from Sir Thomas Hungerford in 1377, the first Speaker to be so styled, to the present incumbent. The Speaker is at once the representative of the House of Commons and a condition of its existence: until he is elected, it cannot proceed with business.

The longstanding tradition and functional significance of the office is reflected in the high status and dignity accorded to its occupant.[1] He lives in the Speaker's House within the Palace of Westminster and receives a salary and expenses equivalent to that of a cabinet minister.[2] On state occasions he wears a gold-embroidered gown over court dress, and cuts a splendid figure in his large state coach drawn by two dray horses which Whitbread's Brewery traditionally provides. In the House he wears a black silk gown over court dress and a full-bottomed wig, entering the chamber in procession with the mace borne before him. The mace is set on the table of the House when the Speaker is in the chair. Its symbolism has been variously described: it is a sign that the House is properly constituted—the Speaker ruled in 1961 that no vote could be taken by the House unless it were on the table—and that the Speaker's authority, as derived from the House, is paramount.

1. He ranks sixth in the official order of precedence—after the Archbishop of Canterbury, the Lord Chancellor, the Archbishop of York, the Prime Minister and the Lord President of the Council.

2. In 1970 £9,750 a year, with no specific allowances for entertainment.

The procedure for electing the Speaker brings out a link with the monarchy. When the House assembles to elect a Speaker at the beginning of a Parliament (or after a Speaker's death or resignation), the Clerk of the House acts as presiding officer, and the mace, though brought into the House, is put on a bracket below the table (the same position as for a committee of the whole House, when the Speaker does not preside). When the Speaker is chosen, the mace is placed on the table, but he cannot yet be preceded by the mace on entering or leaving the chamber. The reason is that though Speaker-elect, he does not become Speaker until the Sovereign has signified approval to the election.

The royal approval was last withheld by Charles II in 1679. It is unlikely to be withheld today, just as the Royal Assent is unlikely to be withheld from a bill passed by the Lords and the Commons. But like so many formal observances, this one makes a point about the original status and function of the Speaker. While the title of his office indicates his duty 'to speak before the King', that is, to convey the Commons' desires and conclusions, the Speaker was just as much a royal servant. In Tudor times he was the Crown's business manager in the House. Sir Edward Coke, Speaker from 1593 to 1598, for example, is recorded by Philip Laundy as follows:

> having mastered the difficult art of serving two masters, [he] showed a remarkable dexterity in the manipulation of procedure and precedent in order to expedite business and comply with the wishes of the Queen.[1]

By the beginning of the eighteenth century, if the Speakership was freed from royal power, it remained within that of the party in power. Robert Harley was able to combine it with the office of Secretary of State in the last year of his tenure (1701–05). The advent of the Speaker as impartial servant of the House took much longer. The distinguished tenure of Onslow (1728–61) set a standard of impartiality not approached by his predecessors or by his successors for another three-quarters of a century. Shaw Lefevre (1839–57) is generally regarded as the first of the modern Speakers. Thus in close to 600 years of the unbroken succession of Speakers (1377–1970) only in 164 (including Onslow's 33 years) could modern standards of impartiality be said to have existed.

1. Philip Laundy, *The Office of Speaker* (1964), p. 182.

The need for an impartial Speaker rules out the candidature of a high temperature or strongly partisan member. The successful candidate is likely to be a senior member of the House with experience of presiding over committees of the House. Alternatively he may be drawn from those with ministerial experience. On being selected, he forswears political connections and ceases to be a member of his party. As Dr Horace King put it, on first being elected Speaker:

> I now sever myself completely from all party politics. This is no light matter. No man can easily break with the political faith which has given the whole of his life purpose and meaning, except for the even greater faith that he has in political freedom itself.[1]

He remains a member of the House and must stand at the next general election if he wishes to continue as Speaker. He stands for election as an independent candidate. Provided that he is returned, it has been the custom in this century to re-elect him as Speaker for as long as he wishes to continue. The severance of former political ties is confirmed by the conventions surrounding his behaviour. Outside the chamber he keeps to his own quarters, avoiding contact with other members in the social and working rooms of the Palace. Nor does he take part in debate (Speaker Denison was last to do so in 1871); he votes only to decide a tied vote, and then 'only in accordance with rules which preclude an expression of view upon the merits of a question'.[2] When he vacates the office, he invariably quits the House of Commons (Addington was the last Speaker to stay on as a member; he left the chair to become Prime Minister), usually accepting a Viscountcy or a life peerage.

The impartiality of the Speakership is shown chiefly in his concern for minorities—that is, not only for the official opposition and other opposition parties but the various strands of opinion within each organized group, as well as for unaligned members. His chief weapon for making this concern felt is his power to call upon individual members to speak in debate. He respects the traditions of the House in calling upon spokesmen for the government and opposition to open and wind up major debates and in

1. H. C. Deb. (1964–65), 718 c. 11.
2. Erskine May, *Parliamentary Practice*, 18th ed. (1971), p. 225. (See also p. 52.)

according a measure of priority to members of the Privy Council (usually ministers or ex-ministers). But he will ensure that all views can be expressed. Since power in the House is disposed of primarily by the government members, the Speaker, in extending his protection to minorities, has to take stances which are disagreeable to the government, while at the same time preserving the government's rights, under the orders and customs of the House, to transact its business. In discharging his duties as presiding officer he has constantly to preserve a fair balance between these contending elements.

Another facet of his impartiality is the convention applying to the way in which the Speaker casts his vote. In theory he is as free as any other member to vote as he thinks fit, and may give or withhold a reason for the way in which he votes. In practice he votes only when the numbers are equal, and then, in order to avoid any possible stain on his impartiality, casts his vote according to well understood principles: in general he will try to avoid a change that depends on his sole vote, and if possible will so cast his vote as to enable the matter to be discussed again by the House.

To help make its debates more effective the House has given the Speaker certain discretionary powers. The most important are the power to select amendments to a bill or a motion before the House, that is, in the interests of more efficient debate, to decide that one (or more) and not another (or others) is to be discussed and voted upon; the power to refuse a delaying or dilatory motion if he thinks it an abuse of the rules or to accept a motion to bring a debate to a close after it has, in his view, been debated enough; and the power to decide whether or not to allow a proposal to move the adjournment of the House to discuss 'a specific and important matter that should have urgent consideration'.[1] In all his exercises of these powers the Speaker has to balance the claims of several affected parties—government, opposition, private member—before giving his ruling. Wherever possible he will act in accordance with precedent, and the House accepts his rulings because they are habitually so grounded. But it is worth noting that in the exercise of one of the discretionary powers—to decide whether an 'urgency' debate should take place—the House has lately relieved the Speaker of the need to be bound by prece-

1. Standing Order No. 9.

dent. Decisions from the chair on applications for urgency debates had cumulatively resulted in the virtual extinction of this procedural opportunity, and in 1967 the Speaker was in effect encouraged to make a political judgement, in order to restore flexibility to this Rule.[1]

Besides these important powers the Speaker has the 'bread and butter' duties of most presiding officers of parliamentary assemblies, namely to keep order in debate, to put questions to the vote and declare the results, and to deal with points of order raised by members.

To keep order the House has given him a graduated series of powers while retaining for itself the ultimate authority. Thus the Speaker checks minor breaches of order as they arise. If a member persists in irrelevance or tedious repetition of argument, the Speaker may after due warning direct him to discontinue his speech. Similarly if a member is guilty of grossly disorderly conduct, he may be ordered to withdraw from the House for the remainder of the sitting. These steps a Speaker can take on his own authority. But if a member continues to disregard the authority of the chair or to obstruct the business of the House, the Speaker can 'name' him for so doing. In that event, a motion is at once moved, usually by the Leader of the House, to suspend him from the House's service; in other words the House itself, on the initiative of the Speaker, exercises the extreme disciplinary power of withdrawing a member's rights. Finally if grave disorder arises, in effect preventing further debate, the Speaker can adjourn the House on his own authority, or suspend the sitting for an interval. The occasions when passions run so high as to prevent further debate are fortunately rare: one such suspension occurred during the Suez crisis (1956); another on the motion to apply a restrictive motion (guillotine) to proceedings on the Industrial Relations Bill 1971.

The Speaker's decisions can only be debated, in the words of Erskine May, 'on a substantive motion which admits of a distinct vote of the House'. Such a motion is rarely put down, but when it is, it is the custom for the government to make time for it to be debated so that the matter can be disposed of as soon as possible. Only four motions have been debated in this century, and none pressed to a vote.

1. The urgency adjournment, as a means of criticizing government action, is described on pp. 372–3.

The duties of presiding over the House are shared with two other members, the Chairman of Ways and Means and the Deputy Chairman. Each takes the chair as Deputy Speaker when asked by the Speaker, though if the Speaker is unavoidably absent for a significant period the House has to be informed. The Chairman, assisted by his Deputy and by a panel of temporary chairmen appointed sessionally by the Speaker, also takes the chair in committee of the whole House. The Chairman of Ways and Means and his Deputy are appointed for the life of a Parliament on a motion moved by the government. By tradition they take no public part in the activities of their party during their tenure of office and do not speak or vote in the House. If a government of a different political colour takes power, however, it is not the practice to reappoint them. They may then return to party political activity. This power of re-entry differentiates them from the Speaker and may explain why their conduct in the Chair has not always been as free from criticism as his.

The Speaker of the House of Representatives

The Speakership in Washington is, like so many other elements in Congress, of British derivation. Yet his status as a recognized political leader, in addition to being presiding officer, of the House of Representatives contrasts strikingly with the non-party president of the House of Commons. The inspiration for this development in the United States is reasonably clear. Of the sixty-five members of the first House of Representatives in 1789, thirty-nine had served in a state or colonial legislature; so it was natural for them to assimilate to their new surroundings the practices of those legislatures. One of these was to choose a Speaker, a prominent political personage who could direct their business and proceedings besides acting as their spokesman in negotiation with external authorities. This was in some respects the status of the Speaker in the House of Commons of that time. American politicians were well aware of the nature and conduct of the British speakership, as Jefferson's manual makes clear.[1] But it was not then the independent or impartial office that it was later to become. The impartiality and authority of Onslow (1728–

1. See *House Rules and Manual* (1971), paras. 283, 312, 314–15.

61) was followed by the political ineffectiveness of Cust (1761–70) and Cornwall (1780–89) and the open and violent partisanship of Norton (1770–80). So far as the British speakership was an influence on the House of Representatives in 1789, it was to confirm the concept of an active politician with an avowed political allegiance in the chair.

The requirements of the American Constitution are minimal: 'The House of Representatives shall choose their Speaker and other officers'.[1] Nothing is said about whether the Speaker was to be a member of the House, though the corresponding provision for the Senate—that the presiding officer is to be the Vice-President of the United States—carries the clear implication that the presiding officer of *that* House is not a Senator. In practice the Speaker of the House has always been chosen from the membership, and no doubt it was unthinkable for members of former colonial assemblies to look elsewhere for their Speaker.

Once chosen from among the prominent figures in the House, the pre-eminence of the Speaker was assured by the more fundamental provision of the Constitution that the President and his ministers were not to be seated in Congress. In their absence it was natural for members of the majority to look for leadership to the man they had elected as Speaker. In some of the early Congresses and on occasion in modern times Speakers have been content to exercise their duties as presiding officers, allowing other figures such as the chairman of the Ways and Means Committee, the Majority Leader or the Whip to make the running on behalf of the majority party. But the potentialities of the speakership were present from the beginning, and they have been fully realized in the last hundred years.[2] With a strong Speaker the leadership and activity of the House is concentrated, its business focused, and its standing relative to the other elements in the legislative struggle—the President and the Senate—enhanced.

Today the office is recognized as being one of the two or three greatest offices in the American machinery of government. In

1. Article I, 2.
2. A recent analysis of twenty Speakers (1861 to 1967) concluded that fourteen made a positive contribution, either of a personal kind or jointly with other leaders in the same party, and six were figure-heads. See Randall B. Ripley, *Party Leaders in the House of Representatives* (1967), pp. 13–18.

protocol the Speaker ranks seventh in the order of precedence,[1] but in power and status he is probably exceeded only by the President and the Chief Justice. He follows the Vice-President in the line of succession, if anything should remove the President during his term of office (no Speaker has ever become President by this means). But whereas the Vice-President achieves office by election on the same 'ticket' as the President, the Speaker derives his authority from a personal election by the House of Representatives, without the subsequent endorsement of any outside authority. In practice he is first selected by the majority caucus, and his selection by the House is then a formality. But he carries the authority of the House itself. He is given an imposing office and quarters in the Capitol for his district's business; and he receives substantially higher pay and allowances[2] than other members. He remains Speaker for as long as his party keeps control of the House and wishes him to continue. If control is lost, the (former) Minority Leader is likely to be elected Speaker and the (former) Speaker, having been ousted, to become Minority Leader. If the President is of a different political colour, the Speaker can be the national leader of his party. In the six years that Rayburn was Speaker and Eisenhower was President (1954–59) Rayburn was for practical purposes the national leader of the Democratic Party.

The greatness of the American speakership springs from the combination of the functions of presiding officer and party leader. As presiding officer he has much in common with the British Speaker. The manner of their election is similar in each House: the Clerk presides over the House, receives the names of candidates and puts any necessary questions to decide the matter, after which the successful candidate takes the chair. The American, like the British, Speaker is expected to protect the rights of individual members and to be fair as between one member and another. In calling on members to speak—in Washington as at Westminster an important weapon in the Speaker's armoury—he has to respect the practice of the House. The chairman or other

1. After President, the Vice-President, the Chief Justice and former Chief Justices, former Presidents, Ambassadors and widows of former Presidents.

2. In 1970 62,500 dollars a year, with an allowance of 10,000 dollars a year (a total of about £30,000).

members of the committee which reported a bill, for example, have to be called first when it comes before the House. Consistent with such priorities the Speaker will respect the rights of all members of the House.

In both countries the Speakers have to act within the rules and practices of the House and the decisions made by their predecessors. In both countries, too, there have been spectacular exceptions. The action of Common Speaker Brand, in personally closuring a lengthy filibuster by the Irish nationalists in 1881, may be likened to Speaker Reed's action in the House of Representatives of 1890 in refusing to entertain a motion on the grounds that it was dilatory and by counting members who were present but not voting as part of the quorum. A British Speaker may be challenged by motion. He rarely is. Rulings and decisions by an American Speaker are subject to immediate appeal and vote, though appeals are not in order in several important instances, such as a ruling that a motion is dilatory or a decision to call a particular member to speak. In practice appeals are rare, and a reversal is rarer because the majority usually supports the Speaker. Since the Speakership of Nicholas Longworth (1926–31) no ruling has been reversed.

Like his British counterpart the American Speaker has the routine duties of a presiding officer—to keep order in debate, to put questions to the vote and declare results and to deal with points of order raised by members.

There is however a significant difference in the order-keeping powers of the two Speakers. The House of Representatives has conceded less power to its presiding officer. If a member transgresses a rule of the House, the Speaker or any other member calls him to order, and he must sit down. It is then the practice to take the House's opinion on a motion 'that the gentleman be allowed to proceed in order' or that he be permitted to explain. The House decides this question without debate. If the decision is favourable, the member may continue, but not otherwise. Again, if disorderly words are spoken in debate, a member can specify the words to which he takes exception and have them taken down at the Clerk's desk and read out to the House. At this point it is for the chair to decide if they are in order, and from that decision there is no appeal. The House then decides what action should be taken. The Speaker may name a member for the purpose of referring his actions to the judgement of the House, but he has no power to censure or punish the member without the direction of the House.

The powers of the Speaker over members of the House of Representatives find an echo in those of the British Speaker over the House of Commons. Until the 1880s the balance struck between the immediate authority of the chair and the ultimate authority of the House was the same at Westminster as in Washington. Moreover the same powers that the Speaker of the House of Representatives has are still held to reside in the Speaker of the Commons 'under ancient usage'.[1] In the 1880s, however, to curb the obstruction of the Irish Nationalists the House of Commons found it necessary to endow the Speaker under standing order with instant authority to enforce its rules. These powers (described above) have virtually superseded the powers 'under ancient usage'. The House of Representatives has not found it necessary to reinforce the authority of the chair in the same way.

Other differences between the two Speakerships stem from the second feature of the American Speakership, that its incumbent is a party leader as well as a presiding officer. The style and perquisites of his office reflect his closer involvement in the active and partisan life of the House. Instead of a state coach for ceremonial occasions, he has a Cadillac and chauffeur for everyday occasions. He does not wear special robes to preside over the House of Representatives nor is the mace borne before him in procession as he enters or leaves the chamber to open or close a sitting. It is already in the House, being placed on a pedestal on the right of the chair when the Speaker enters, and removed to a lower position when the House goes into a committee of the whole House.[2] Nor has he felt the need to isolate himself from other members of the House as does the British Speaker. These differences reflect the essentially different nature of the American Speakership and its position in the centre of the party political life of the House, rather than that of the high officer who presides

1. They are described in Erskine May, 18th ed. (1971), pp. 425–7.
2. In adopting its original rules in 1789 the first House of Representatives rejected a proposal to follow the practice of the House of Commons in placing the mace on the table and, in committee of the whole House, below the table.

in disengaged, aloof spirit over proceedings of the House of Commons.

The need to combine the fairness expected of a presiding officer with the duty of a party leader to help forward his party's policies and programme calls for political judgement and sensitivity of a high order. As Dr Riddick has observed:

> there is a world of play in the system which will permit the Speaker to act within certain bounds and still work on behalf of his party . . . in the twilight zone a large area exists where . . . he has many opportunities to apply the rules to his party's advantage.[1]

A classic example of the Speaker's use of both the rules and the opportunities offered by the twofold nature of his office is the action taken by Speaker Sam Rayburn (1941–46, 1949–52, 1955–62) to secure the enlargement of the Rules Committee in 1961. Without this reform it was believed that the conservative alliance of two Southern Democrats with the four Republican members of this Committee of twelve could hold up indefinitely the 'New Frontier' legislative programme to which President Kennedy was pledged. An enlargement of the Committee would allow the addition of 'liberal' members to tip the balance. To achieve this object, Speaker Rayburn personally supervised, and took part in, the intense canvass of members of both parties to ensure a majority for his proposal; postponed the vote from one week to another—and in particular till after President Kennedy's inaugural address—to make sure that the majority was solid; in the interim tried and failed to work out a compromise with the Chairman of the Rules Committee who was fighting the Speaker's proposal tooth and nail; and finally, at the end of the debate on the motion, left the Chair to make the winding up speech from the floor. This sustained effort was rewarded with a favourable vote of 217 to 212 votes.[2]

All this activity, it should be emphasized, the House accepted as being within the proper bounds of the Speaker's authority.

1. F. Riddick, *Congress: Organization and Procedure* (1949), p. 67.
2. For a comprehensive and lively account of this political crisis, see Neil MacNeil, *Forge of Democracy* (1963), pp. 412–48. An inside account by a close collaborator of the Speaker in this struggle is given by Richard Bolling, Representative of Missouri since 1948, in *House out of Order* (1966), pp. 209–20.

Not only can he take the floor, but he can vote, though he does not usually do so. Like the British Speaker he is required to vote in order to break a tie. Unlike the British Speaker he is also required to vote if, by his vote, he could bring about a tie; in American practice an unbroken tie means that the question is decided in the negative.[1] In both instances, unlike the British Speaker, he votes as he thinks right on the merits of the matter.

On occasion the proper bounds of an American Speaker's authority have been exceeded. Once when the Democrats had taken advantage of a thin attendance of Republicans to bring forward a bill they wanted passed, Republican Speaker Joe Cannon asked the clerk as a delaying tactic to call the roll not only twice (which accorded with the Rules) but a third time. When the Democrats angrily objected and asked how such an unprecedented action could be justified, the Speaker calmly answered: 'The chair is hoping that a few more Republicans will come in'. This candour caused much merriment and the Democrats acquiesced in the eventual defeat of their bill.[2] During the Speakership of Cannon, the powers of the office which had grown steadily in the nineteenth century, reached their apex. The Speaker had power to nominate members of legislative committees; to select the members of the Rules Committee and (from 1858) personally to preside over it; and to exercise his unlimited power to call or not to call upon members to speak so as virtually to extinguish minority rights. With this degree of control over the membership (and so the action) of standing committees and over the order of business in the House, the Speaker was not only able to decide upon a complete legislative programme but was also virtually certain of being able to carry it through.

In 1910 the House rebelled against this ascendancy. 'Czar' Cannon, as the Speaker had become known, was stripped of his membership of the Rules Committee and his power to appoint members of the standing committees. At the same time his unrestricted power over calling members in debates was curbed by a number of innovations, notably by granting certain members at certain times (such as those reporting bills from committees) an absolute entitlement to be called. But the Speaker's powers have remained considerable. He has retained much influence over the

1. House Rule I, 6.
2. Neil MacNeil, op. cit., p. 78.

timing, and so the viability, of controversial bills, especially when a Congress is drawing to a close. He still appoints members of select committees and House members of conference committees (though these are usually the chief committeemen concerned). He no longer appoints members of legislative committees, but as the leading member of the caucus, he can make sure that his views are known. Moreover some recent Speakers, while being scrupulously fair in their dealings with the House, have tended to develop an inner cabal of advisers and lieutenants —comprising usually the Majority Leader, one or two key committee chairmen and one or two close friends—to map out strategy and tactics in relation to the House's business. These gatherings—known in Speaker Rayburn's time as 'the Board of Education'—have gone far to re-establish the power and thrust of the Speaker's leadership without giving rise to criticism of an overblown authority vested in the chair.

The Speaker can nominate any member to carry out the duties of the chair for up to three days, or ten days if illness is the cause. If he is absent for a longer period or fails to provide for a substitute, the House elects a Speaker pro tempore (with the Clerk acting as presiding officer (see below)) who acts until the Speaker returns.[1] Almost invariably the Speaker calls on members of the majority to substitute for him, though on rare ceremonial occasions members of the minority are designated. But the post of Deputy Speaker, appointed to act as required on behalf of the Speaker as at Westminster for a whole parliamentary term, is unknown to the House of Representatives.

Presiding Officers of the House of Lords and the Senate

The Speaker of the House of Lords is a unique phenomenon. As Lord Chancellor chosen by the Prime Minister, he is a member of the cabinet and the government's chief legal adviser, and he takes the speakership of the House of Lords ex officio. He is not necessarily a peer, though in modern times he has invariably been raised to the peerage. This combination of executive and legislative functions is found in other parliamentary assemblies and notably in the Senate of the United States. The Lord Chancellor's uniqueness lies in carrying a third responsibility: he is

1. House Rule I, 7.

head of the judiciary and when possible presides over the House of Lords when it sits in its capacity as the highest British court of appeal. In his absence the senior Lord of Appeal presides.

His duties as a cabinet minister and as head of the judiciary overshadow his function as Speaker of the House of Lords. Few, if any, presiding officers can have less power. He puts questions to the vote and declares the results. But he is not addressed by members (who address each other: 'My Lords' is the beginning of every speech); he does not call speakers (the order of speaking is usually pre-arranged: if there is a dispute the Lords settle it themselves). He cannot entertain or arbitrate upon points of order; again the Lords themselves settle any problems of order. Still less can he adjourn the House or take any other action without its consent. The House has authority over its own proceedings: its Speaker has no more than any other member. Conversely he enjoys the same rights as any other member. He takes part in debates, stepping a foot or two away from the woolsack[1] to address the House, and votes. But he has no power to settle a tied vote; in that event the motion is not carried. In speaking and voting he is openly partisan. As a cabinet minister it would be pointless for him to act otherwise.

In the House of Lords the Lord Chancellor is essentially a political leader, and he collaborates for political purposes with the Leader of the House and the Chief Whip. This close linkage between the chair and the floor leadership suggests an analogy with the House of Representatives. The difference lies not in this linkage but in the composition of the two Chambers. The Conservatives have a perpetual majority in the House of Lords, so that when the Labour Party is the party of government, the Lord Chancellor, and the Leader and Chief Whip, are leading a minority party in the House of Lords.

If the Lord Chancellor is absent, one of several Lords appointed by the Crown presides in his stead. The first on the list of these Lords is the Lord Chairman of Committees, who also takes the chair in committee of the whole House and any other committee

1. The woolsack, on which the Lord Chancellor sits as Speaker of the House of Lords, is traditionally held to have been placed in the House in the reign of Edward III. In 1938 it was restuffed with a blend of British and Commonwealth wool. See *The Houses of Parliament* (1958) by K. R. Mackenzie, p. 41.

of which he is appointed a member unless the Lords direct otherwise.

'The Vice-President of the United States shall be President of the Senate, but shall have no vote, unless they be equally divided.' The Constitution makes clear that the presiding officer of the Senate owes his position—as does the Lord Chancellor—to his having gained an extraneous office. He may or may not have been a member of the Senate, and certainly owes no obligation to the body of senators for his position as their presiding officer. Moreover he may be (in the 91st Congress (1969–70) was) of a political colour different from that of the majority controlling the Senate. But even if the political colour is the same, there remains a gulf fixed between the Vice-President and the senators. He is not accountable to them (except by the device of impeachment, and no Vice-President has ever been impeached), and there is about him the whiff of executive power. Even Vice-President Lyndon Johnson, after enjoying the confidence of senators for over thirty years, was unable to bridge this gulf. His expectation, on moving in 1961 from the position of Majority Leader to the chair, that he could carry on business as usual as effective leader of the Democrats in the Senate, was rebuffed within the Democratic caucus.

No such inhibitions surround the position of President pro tempore with whom the Vice-President shares the powers of the Senate's presiding officer. Until 1890 a President pro tempore was elected on each occasion that the Vice-President was absent. Since that date he has enjoyed a permanent tenure, and is usually elected with the Vice-President present at the beginning of a Congress or whenever the majority changes. Unlike the Vice-President, the President pro tempore is 'one of the family'. He is generally the senior senator of the majority, being elected first by the majority party caucus and then by the Senate. But his opportunities are limited. In practice neither the Vice-President nor the President pro tempore preside very often. The chair of the Senate is usually taken by more junior senators appointed by the Vice-President or the President pro tempore 'to perform the duties of the chair'.[1] Only when the Vice-President succeeds to the Presidency (up to 1970 eight Vice-Presidents had become President in this way) is there an opening for the President pro

1. Senate Rule I, 4.

tempore to make an important and continuing contribution to the leadership of the Senate. Whether he does so depends on his personal qualities.

The presiding officer of the Senate, unlike his opposite number in the House of Lords, has the usual powers of a presiding officer. Besides putting questions to the vote and declaring the results, he calls members to speak, ensures that proceedings are conducted in an orderly manner and gives rulings on points of order as they arise subject to an appeal to the Senate. In practice however he has less discretion than the Speaker of the House of Representatives in that he has to call senators in the order in which they rise, except the Majority and Minority Leaders who are by custom accorded precedence. His powers to keep order are much the same as the Speaker's, though there has been little need to apply them. The Vice-President, not being a member of the Senate, takes no part in debates, and votes, as the Constitution says, only to settle a tie. But the President pro tempore is usually as well the chairman of an important legislative committee of the Senate, so that he is likely to intervene on Senate business within that committee's province.

CLERKS, PARLIAMENTARIANS AND OTHER STAFF

The status and functions of the officers of Parliament and Congress largely reflect the nature of the assemblies that they serve. In both the relationship between the Speaker and the officers is especially close, so that over the years the duties laid upon the Speakership have come to influence the functions and activities of the officers. To illustrate this point, the chief officers of the House of Commons first will be contrasted to those in the House of Representatives.

Officers of the House of Commons

The chief officer of the House of Commons is the Clerk of the House. This is an ancient office, tracing an unbroken succession to Robert de Melton in 1363; in 1970 the incumbent was the 39th to hold the position. He is appointed by the Crown for life. In making the appointment the Crown is advised by the Prime Minister of the day, the practice—now of at least fifty years' standing—being to designate the successor to the office from the Clerk's department. The clerks of the House of Commons are recruited through open competitive examinations for the highest grade of the civil service. But as from their entry into the Clerk's department they become servants of the legislature.

The object of appointing the Clerk of the House and recruiting the officers of his department in this way is to safeguard the department's independence and ensure the impartial discharge by the clerks of their functions. The chief duty of the Clerk is to advise the Speaker and members of the House (including ministers) on the practices, procedures and privileges of the House. For this purpose he sits at the table of the House below and a little to the right of the Speaker's chair when the House is sitting. He gives the same service to committees of the House appointed to inquire into any of these subjects, and often appears as the first witness to help a committee to chart its inquiry. His department consists of two clerks assistant and forty-three other clerks organized in six offices dealing with the main branches of the House's business, namely, the Public Bill Office, the Journal (or records) Office, the Committee Office, the Table Office (dealing chiefly with Questions to Ministers), the Private Bill Office and the Overseas Office (first created in 1968 to deal with the press of business arising from the Clerk's relations with Commonwealth Parliaments and international parliamentary assemblies).

Of these offices the Committee Office provides most obvious contrast to the staff structure of Congress. The clerks serving committees of the House of Commons are largely provided by the Committee Office; they comprise twenty-two out of the total establishment of forty-six. Yet they remain under the direction of the Clerk of the House, like the clerks in the other offices; they are not appointed by the committees themselves. The basis for this staffing is that each committee is served by an officer recruited into the highest grade of the public service. Equally important is that the duty of giving impartial advice and assistance should be standard, and should be seen to be standard, throughout the Clerk's department. Thus the Clerk himself works closely with the Speaker in formulating the chair's approach to the business of the House. He brings the same impartiality to the advice he gives to ministers, opposition leaders and other members. A clerk in the Public Bill Office will give an equal service to a member wishing to bring forward a bill as to another who wants to cut its throat. The clerk of a select committee will undoubtedly work closely with the chairman in planning the inquiry and suggesting witnesses; but he remains the servant of the committee as a whole, and if requested to do so will draft advice or a dissenting opinion, for any member unwilling to accept the majority's view.

This has not always been the tradition. Orlo Williams has recorded how the Goldsboroughs and Paul Jodrell, Clerks of the House from 1661 to 1726, were directly paid by the Treasury for seeing the Crown's business through the Commons.[1] Under Hatsell and John Henry Ley, who between them held the office of Clerk of the House from 1768 to 1850, a larger measure of independence developed based on fees which were charged to members and outsiders dealing with Parliament and which multiplied prodigiously throughout the eighteenth century. In 1800 an Act of Parliament established the Commissioners for the House of Commons Offices—of whom the most important members were the Speaker and the Chancellor of the Exchequer— who brought parliamentary fees under their control and created a salaried basis for the Clerk and his two assistants. This statutory innovation, which survives to this date, protects the position of the Clerk as the House's chief adviser, since under its provisions he is publicly remunerated for his services to itself and no other. The Act of 1800 was completed by further reforms in the 1830s which established the structure and organization of the House of Commons offices largely in their modern form. The committee initiating these latter reforms provides the link between the new establishment of the Clerk's department and the modern, impartial Speakership of the Commons: on the committee sat Shaw Lefevre and Denison, who were to be Speakers from 1839 to 1872, and who are generally accounted the first two Speakers of the present day pattern.

Besides his functions as procedural adviser to the Commons and head of the Clerk's department the Clerk of the House is also the accounting officer for the House of Commons Vote. In other words he is responsible for the House's estimates of expenditure, and he is accountable for that expenditure to the House's Public

1. O. C. Williams, *Clerical Organization of the House of Commons* (1954), p. 44.

Accounts Committee. This gives him a measure of financial oversight of the four other departments of the House. First there is
the department of the Serjeant at Arms. It is he who carries the
mace in the Speaker's procession, keeps order in the galleries and
the lobbies, controls the staff of doorkeepers, porters and mes-
sengers, directs the police on duty at the House and acts as general
housekeeper, in particular allocating committee rooms. The
department of the Speaker includes the Speaker's Secretary and
the Speaker's Counsel (legal adviser), the Editor and staff of the
official report (Hansard), and the Vote Office which circulates
official papers to members. The department of the Library
comprises the Librarian who, with a deputy librarian and
eighteen other librarians, directs the Library and carries out
research projects at the request of members. Finally there is a
small Administration Department under the Clerk Administrator,
who serves the House of Commons Services Committee and
directs the Fees Office. The officers and officials of these departments are variously appointed, but the impartiality of their
service to the House and its members is common to all of them.

Officers of the House of Representatives

A clerk visiting the House of Representatives from the House of
Commons is at once struck by several differences between the
staffs of the two Houses. The first is that the functions coming
together in the office of the Clerk at Westminster are in Washington divided between several independent officers or offices.
Secondly, the staffs serving committees of each House are
entirely separate from the staffs serving the House itself. Thirdly,
with the exception of the Parliamentarian and his assistants, the
tenure of office of the staffs serving the House and the committees
is dependent on the majority party. Conversely none of the staff
of the House or the committees owes his position to competitive
examination for the public service. This general statement of
difference does, however, call for qualification in respect of each
category of office.

The Clerk of the House of Representatives is appointed for the
two-year life of a Congress, though he may be, and usually is,
reappointed. To a limited extent he has a continuing function: on
the first day of a new Congress he acts as presiding officer until

the Speaker is elected. The House's first business after the Speaker's election is to decide whether its clerk should continue in office or not, a decision which turns primarily on the political colour of the majority. At Westminster the Clerk also acts as presiding officer while the House chooses its Speaker; but his continuity of tenure bridges the gap between one Parliament and another, and there is no need for the House of Commons, in the words used by Hinds about the House of Representatives, to endeavour 'to perpetuate its authority beyond its own existence'.[1]

The Clerk of the first House of Representatives in 1789 was John Beckley of Virginia. The Clerk of the 92nd Congress (1970–71) was Mr Pat Jennings, who not only comes from Virginia but also represented a constituency of that state in the House for six Congresses (1954–66). Defeated in 1966, he was nominated as Clerk by the Democratic caucus and first elected by the House in the 90th Congress (1967–68). His political origin and nomination differentiate him principally from the Clerk of the House of Commons.

Some of his duties, however, find a parallel in the office of the Clerk of the Commons. For example the keeping of records of House proceedings, the reading to the House of messages, bills and other documents, the handling of bills throughout their passage in the House, the preparation of daily calendars of business and taking of roll calls all come within the overall responsibility of the Clerks of the House in both countries. On the financial and administrative side, the Clerk prepares the annual budget[2] for the House of Representatives and defends it before the Appropriations Committee. In this sense his duties are cognate to the responsibilities of the Commons Clerk as accounting officer for the Commons estimate. But they go much wider. He also has direct responsibility for the House's recording studio, the finance office (paying members and staff), supplies, the internal telephone system and electrical installations (notably computers to handle records of all kinds). In general he does

1. Hind's Precedents 1, 235.
2. The estimates for the House of Representatives and Senate are first submitted—like any other estimates coming before Congress—to the President's Office of Management and Budget. The object is to include them in the national budget, not to submit them for amendment by the executive branch.

many of the housekeeping duties which at Westminster would be done by the Administration Department and the department of the Serjeant at Arms.

The chief responsibility for advising the Speaker and members on procedure, however, rests not with the Clerk of the House but with another high officer, styled the Parliamentarian. Unlike the Clerk, the Parliamentarian is a permanent officer appointed by the Speaker, though he has been styled Parliamentarian and enjoyed permanent status only since 1900. The present incumbent has been in the post since 1929 which gives him a lead of many years over any Clerk or Secretary General in Europe occupying a nonpartisan post of comparable importance. His duties correspond broadly to the procedural responsibilities of the Clerk of the House of Commons, allowances being made for the different legislative systems. For example he refers bills in the name of the presiding officer to the appropriate standing committee, a task replete with borderline problems, as a cursory glance at the House rules and Cannon's *Procedure in the House of Representatives* shows. He also advises on how a bill should be drafted if it is to be referred to one committee rather than another. He, or one of the two Assistant Parliamentarians, sits in the House on the Speaker's right hand during sittings and is at the disposal of the Speaker, the party leaders and individual members to give guidance on the detailed legislative processes. He also advises committees as required on legislative procedure, and in particular he attends the Rules Committee and drafts the rules to govern the progress of bills on the floor. Whenever necessary he drafts amendments to the Rules of the House.

Two other officers serving the House of Representatives and elected by it, the Serjeant at Arms and the Doorkeeper, may be more briefly noticed. The Serjeant, like his opposite number at Westminster, is the executive arm of the chair in preserving order and decorum in the House; as at Westminster the mace is the symbol of this authority. But other duties belonging to the Serjeant at Westminster have come for historical reasons to be shared in Washington between the Serjeant and the Doorkeeper. The Serjeant for instance attends all sittings of the House to maintain order when requested to do so by the presiding officer, while the Doorkeeper is responsible for security of the Chamber, controlling access to the floor and the galleries. The Doorkeeper is the custodian of the House's property and of committee rooms, and is generally responsible for supplying members with papers and other conveniences. Some measure of the importance of this official is gained from the fact that in the absence of the Clerk and the Serjeant, he has presided over the House on the opening day of the Congress until the Speaker was elected.

Finally there are the staffs of House Committees. These staffs are directly employed by the committees themselves, not as at Westminster furnished to the committees from the general staff of the Clerk of the House. The scale and two-fold nature of this staff—professional and clerical—are discussed in a later Chapter on Committees (pp. 244, 245). Here reference need only be made to the fact that in practice appointments are made by the Committee chairmen. On most committees, however, staff to serve the minority party are appointed by the chairman in consultation with the senior (ranking) minority member. When the control of the House changes from one party to the other, the staff are likely to remain, though some posts may change hands as a consequence of the change in the majority of the committee. The growing complexity of the work and the need for experienced staff to suggest areas for study, to advise on the appropriate witnesses and to draft the necessary bills and reports, are enough to account for the desire of committees—leaving aside the desires of the staff themselves—to keep the turnover of staff to a minimum.

What kind of service do all these officers and officials serving the House of Representatives seek to give? The comparison being struck is with the impartial service accorded to members of the House of Commons by clerks recruited by open competition for a professional career within the House. This is by definition not the status of the Clerk of the House of Representatives nor the Serjeant at Arms nor the Doorkeeper. These officers aim to give a fair service to all members; but they remain officers appointed by, and indebted to, the majority. Indeed, there is a skeleton establishment of Clerk, Serjeant and Doorkeeper of the minority in existence, paid out of public funds and expecting to take over these posts when control of Congress changes hands.

The method of appointing most of the committee staff is in the same tradition. In many instances they are in a post for half a lifetime and build up a formidable experience of their committee's subject matter. Yet appointment by the chairman, with the implied degree of obligation to the majority, has led some committees to demand staff with a special duty to the minority. This is the weight behind the recommendation of the Joint Committee on the Organization of Congress, 1965–66 and the provision in the Legislative Reorganization Act 1970 that the number of professional staff on each committee should be raised from four to six in order that two of them may be made available to advise the minority members. The provisions of the Act of 1970 make clear, however, that the appointment of additional staff is optional, at the wish or discretion of the minority. It also provides that all committee employees, including minority employees, must be approved by the majority vote of the full committee, thus preserving the final and full authority of each committee to employ and dismiss its own staff.

The position of the Parliamentarian and the Assistant Parliamentarians lies somewhere between that of the majority officials in the House of Representatives and that of the clerks in the House of Commons. They have a permanent status. They are the expert custodians of the procedures, precedents and practices of the House. Their prime allegiance is to the chair: they are appointed by the Speaker and the location of their offices, adjoining his, underlines the direction of their service. The difference from Westminster lies less in them than in the Speaker that they serve. He is a party leader as well as a presiding officer, and in the nature of things the expert advice tendered both to the Speaker and to other members is given against the background of these constitutional arrangements.

Officers of the House of Lords and Senate

Between the House of Lords and the Senate the differences of staff, compared with those of the first chambers, are broadly differences of nomenclature and scale. The officer in the House of Lords corresponding to the Clerk of the House of Commons is styled the Clerk of the Parliaments. This grander description goes back many centuries. It may be merely the appropriate description of the Clerk of successive Parliaments; or it may derive from the splitting of the English Parliament into two Houses. When the Commons met separately for the first time they took with them the 'under Clerk of the

Parliaments'; to this day the patent of the Clerk of the House of Commons so describes him.

The Clerk of the Parliaments personally appoints the clerks of his department; they are not recruited through open competitive examinations for the administrative grade of the civil service. In addition to serving the House of Lords as a legislature, these clerks staff its judicial work. The Judicial Office administers this business. Otherwise the Clerk's department and other departments in the House of Lords are smaller replicas of those in the Commons.

In the Senate its chief administrative officer, styled the Secretary of the Senate, is selected by the majority party and approved by the Senate. The Secretary continues in office from one Congress to another for as long as the party which nominated him remains in control of the House. In this respect he is like the Clerk of the House of Representatives and he has many of the same administrative duties. But there are differences. Within his jurisdiction is the Chief Clerk, the senior career official of the Senate—there is no exact equivalent in the House—whose responsibilities, discharged with the help of other clerks, include the reading to the Senate of bills and resolutions and amendments proposed to them and the calling of yea and nay votes and of quorums. Also under the Secretary's administrative jurisdiction, but operating independently on the floor under the Vice-President and President pro tempore, is the Parliamentarian whose chief duty, discharged with two assistant Parliamentarians, is to give advice directly to the presiding officer on the rules, procedure, practice and precedents of the Senate. Like the Parliamentarian of the House of Representatives, he has a permanent status. If there are differences in the relative freedom and discretion of the two Parliamentarians in carrying out their advisory functions, they may be attributed to the very different functions, powers and prestige of the Vice-President of the Senate and the Speaker of the House when acting as presiding officers of the two chambers. The Senate combines the post of Serjeant at Arms and Doorkeeper and has two other officials not found in the House, the Secretary for the Majority and the Secretary for the Minority. They are located on the floor of the Senate during sittings, helping and advising senators of their party and in some degree carrying out the duty of information and liaison done by whips in the larger House.

CHAPTER TWO

MEMBERSHIP

OVER the centuries those belonging to the first chambers of Parliament and Congress have successfully pre-empted the style and title of 'Member of Parliament' and 'Congressman'. Members of the House of Commons have been designated as 'Members of Parliament' since the Restoration,[1] and members of the House of Representatives have been referred to as 'Congressmen' by custom of long standing. Yet members of the House of Lords and of the Senate are just as much members of Parliament and of Congress as members of the other two Houses; and in both countries the statutes—on such subjects as qualification or disqualification for public offices—endorse this principle by referring when appropriate to members of the House in question. The customary usage could be seriously misleading if it conveyed that the second chambers were in some sense not an integral part of Parliament and Congress.

This chapter describes and compares the constitutional framework in which a member of Parliament and a member of Congress do their work. It deals successively with the composition of the legislatures, their duration and sessions; with qualifications, privileges and immunities; and finally with the ethical standards and remuneration of their members. Under these heads the membership of all four Houses within Parliament and Congress is treated. If more emphasis is laid on the first chambers, it is because their proceedings are, on the whole, more politically contentious than those of the second chambers, with the result that their constitutional and organizational problems, arousing great challenge inside and outside the legislature, have tended to be given more prominence.

COMPOSITION OF HOUSES

How large is the membership of each House of Parliament and Congress, and what factors govern its size? The simplest answer

1. Erskine May, 18th ed. (1971), p. 7.

is for the Senate of the United States. The Constitution entitles each state of the Union, regardless of its acreage or population, to two Senators, so that the Senate's membership has grown *pari passu* with the number of states in the Union. The first Congress (1789) convened with only eleven states and a maximum membership of twenty-two—somewhere between a large and a small Senate committee today. The steady expansion of the United States brought the Senate's membership up to ninety by the end of the nineteenth century. The addition of five further states in the present century—Oklahoma (1907), New Mexico and Arizona (1912), Alaska (1958) and Hawaii (1959), has meant that today the Senate has 100 members.

The House of Lords has developed according to very different but equally recognizable principles. Its two basic categories of membership are the temporal lords and the spiritual lords. In 1968 the temporal lords comprised 736 hereditary peers by succession; 122 hereditary peers of first creation; 155 life peers; 23 serving or retired law lords; and the spiritual peers, 26 archbishops and bishops; making a total House of 1,026 members.[1] It has not always been so large. Up to the civil war (1642–49) the number summoned fluctuated between 70 and 150—on average something like the size of the modern Senate of the United States. There was a marked increase after the Restoration, especially arising from the union with Scotland (1707) and Ireland (1801); and there were regular additions to the peerage throughout the eighteenth, nineteenth and twentieth centuries. No hereditary peerages have been created since 1964, but the number of life peerages created since the Life Peerages Act 1958 has inflated still further the House's membership.

The two first chambers reflect the size and distribution of the population of the two countries. The original House of Representatives in 1789 had only 65 members. Since 1912 the number of seats has been fixed by law at 435. If the Resident Commission for Puerto Rico, elected for a four-year term to a seat in the House with the right to speak but not to vote, and the Delegate from the District of Columbia, to be elected for a two-year term with the

1. These figures for 1968 are taken from the government's white paper on House of Lords Reform, Cmnd. 3799 (1968), and are used again in Chapter IV. The total number of members in 1971 was not significantly different.

same rights, are included, the total membership is 437. The number rose steadily throughout the nineteenth and twentieth centuries as decennial censuses measured the rising population. Following a census, the reapportionment of representatives to each state is made automatically. An Act of 1929 (amended in 1941) lays on the President the duty of submitting to Congress every ten years a statement of population and a scheme for the reapportionment of members among the states. The scheme has to respect the method of 'equal proportions'; that is, the average number of people to each representative—the electoral quota— has to differ as little as possible as between any two states. Congress determines the size of the quota, which in practice is about 450,000. The result is that Alaska, Delaware, Nevada, Vermont and Wyoming, with the smallest populations, have only one representative[1] (though they each have two senators), while New York and California, with the largest populations, have forty-one and thirty-eight (and also two senators each).

A decennial redistribution can cause upheaval in the House of Representatives. Following the census of 1960, for example, the representation of twenty-five states, with a total delegation in the House of 325 representatives, was altered, so that the re-election of each representative depended on how the boundaries were redrawn. Congress works out the quota, but the drawing of the boundaries of districts (constituencies) is the duty of each state legislature, subject to any general guidance given by Congress. At one time Congress provided, for example, that districts should be composed of 'contiguous and compact territory containing as nearly as practicable an equal number of inhabitants'. Since 1929 this has not been a statutory requirement. The way in which the various state legislatures have discharged their responsibilities for 'districting' has varied.[2] In 1963 the Supreme Court intervened for the first time in the reapportionment of population within districts, and has since on several occasions sought to enforce the broad principle of 'equal representation for equal numbers of people'.

1. Where the population of a state is too small to be divided into separate constituencies (districts), its representative in the House is described as being 'at large'.

2. The term 'gerrymander' is of American origin, being linked since 1812 with the name of Elbridge Gerry, a governor of Massachusetts, who had overseen the redrawing of electoral districts to favour his party.

The House of Commons in modern times has always been a more numerous body than the House of Representatives. Under the early Stuarts it had little short of 500 members, a number which rose to 558 after the Union with Scotland (1707), 658 after the Union with Ireland (1801), and reached a peak of 707 in 1918. Even after the partition of Ireland in 1922, leaving only Northern Ireland represented in the Commons, the number was still as high as 615, and after more fluctuations has been 630 members since 1955.[1] There are 511 members for England, seventy-one for Scotland, thirty-six for Wales and twelve for Northern Ireland. The total of 630 is close to half as large again as the number of members of the House of Representatives and about a hundred more than the total membership of the House and the Senate.

Even when due allowance has been made for the representation of the American people in state legislatures as well as in Congress, the size of the House of Commons remains something of a curiosity. A smaller House would enable a higher proportion of members to speak in important debates and would ease the pressure on the limited space and other facilities in the Palace of Westminster. But it could have disadvantages. A larger House is more likely to mirror the variety of opinion in the country than a smaller one. The two largest political parties are both in some sense coalitions, each bringing together within its compass a wide range of view and attitudes. Given the structure and behaviour of parties under the British system, a marked reduction in the size of the House of Commons could lead to sterner discipline and less tolerance for the unorthodox. On the government side it might be that a higher proportion of members would be office holders. These may be some of the reasons why there have been few moves to reduce the size of the House of Commons.

It is laid down by law that the electorate of each constituency is to be as close as possible to an electoral quota established by dividing the total electorate for Great Britain by the number of constituencies. The quota is thus determined by reference to the electorate whereas in the United States it is by reference to population. The result in Britain is a quota of about 62,000

1. At the general election after that held in 1970, 635 members will be elected, five more seats having been added for England in the redistribution to which effect was given in October 1970.

(1970) over the whole country (compared with the quota of about 450,000 for the House of Representatives). Constituency boundaries are reviewed at intervals of ten to fifteen years by four permanent Boundary Commissions—one each for England, Scotland, Wales and Northern Ireland—who are required to adjust boundaries to the shifting populations in accordance with certain statutory rules and in particular with respect for the electoral quota. The object of setting up these independent commissions was to secure that boundaries were redrawn without political bias. The Speaker of the House of Commons is the chairman of each commission, and all other members of Parliament are expressly excluded from membership. Nevertheless the Commissioners can only recommend schemes for readjusting boundaries. It is then for the Home Secretary, who receives the recommendations, to lay Orders in Council before both Houses of Parliament who have to approve the recommendations before they can come into effect. At this stage political considerations come into the picture. If the Home Secretary does not like the recommendations, he introduces a bill embodying a different scheme of redistribution. The House of Commons (Redistribution of Seats) Bill 1969 was such a bill. It passed the House of Commons after intense controversy. The House of Lords amended it so as to give effect to the recommendations of the Boundary Commissions; and as no further action was taken by the Commons on the Lords amendments, the bill died at the end of the session. In the next session, the Home Secretary laid the orders before Parliament, as he was bound to do by statute, but invited the government majority to vote against them, which it did. The election of 1970 was accordingly fought with the same boundaries as the election of 1966. After the election of 1970 the new government invited Parliament to accept the proposals of the Boundary Commission. This time they were agreed to.

In neither country therefore is the drawing of constituency boundaries of the popular House removed from politics. The boundaries of the House of Representatives are subject to majority opinion of the legislature in each state; those of the House of Commons are ultimately subject to the opinion of the Home Secretary and the majority view of the Commons, and if necessary the agreement of the House of Lords. In the United States the Supreme Court has had to intervene to secure in some instances a fair reapportionment of populations to constituencies. In Britain appeal to the courts against alleged defects in reports made by the Boundary Commissions has evoked the reaction that Parliament, not courts, is the judge of whether the reports are defective.[1] Under these arrangements differences of opinion within Parliament on a matter so close to the rights of every elector can be expected to give rise—as in 1969—to prolonged and bitter controversy.

DURATION

What authority decides when elections are to be held for Congress and Parliament, thus putting a term to their lives?

For Congress this question is tidily answered by the Constitution. The House of Representatives 'shall be composed of members chosen every second year by the people of the several states'.[2] The Senate 'shall be composed of two senators from each state elected by the people thereof, for six years'.[3] While the House of Representatives is elected in its entirety every second year, the Senate is elected partially and periodically, only one-third of its membership being subject to election every second year.[4] In that sense the Senate, unlike the House, is a continuing body; never being elected in its entirety, it has been in continuous existence since 1789. Terms of office of senators and representatives elected for a full term run from 3 January of the year following their election. Congress is required to meet at 12 noon on that date, unless they appoint another day by law. Terms of office expire with the Congress on the same date two years later.[5]

Two points of special interest to a comparison with Parliament need to be made about these arrangements. The first is that elections for Congress are separate from the election of the President as Chief Executive, though they coincide with it on every second occasion. The President is to 'hold his office during the term of four years'.[6] Every fourth year, therefore, the President,

1. Hammersmith Corporation and others v. The Boundary Commission for England, *The Times*, 15 December 1954.
2. Article I, 2.
3. Amendment XVII.
4. Article I, 3.
5. Amendment XX, 1 and 2.
6. Article II, 1.

the whole of the House of Representatives and one-third of the Senate is elected, the other two-thirds of the Senate being unaffected. Every second year the whole of the House and a different third of the Senate go to it, while the President and the other two-thirds of the Senate look on. In no year do the people of the United States cast their votes 'across the board', that is, for both the President and the whole of the two Houses.

This careful spacing of the electorate's efforts is deliberate. Foremost in the minds of the Founding Fathers of the Constitution was the need 'to afford as little opportunity as possible to tumult and disorder' at election time.[1] This reservation about the value of elections expressed itself in the requirement that the President and senators should be elected indirectly: the former was to be chosen by an electoral college, the latter by the state legislatures. Both these barriers against a direct expression of the popular will have since been thrown down. Citizens elected to the electoral college have come (as a rule) to regard themselves as pledged to cast their votes for presidential candidates in accordance with the majority vote in their own states;[2] and since the Constitution was amended in 1913 senators have been directly elected by the people. Nevertheless the elections of the President, the Senate and the House remain separate and distinct, so that at no time can the American people make a clean sweep of their elected representatives at national level.

The second point is that the terms of office of senators and representatives are fixed by the Constitution and owe nothing to the executive power. The President does have power to convene either or both Houses in special session.[3] But today when Congress meets on 3 January every year, with a regular session often spanning the whole of the year, this power has lost much of its importance. In 1968 when Congress concluded its session on 14 October President Johnson considered calling the Senate in special session to discuss the nuclear non-proliferation treaty, but did not do so. The last special session was in 1948.

1. See e.g. *The Federalist* (1788), No. LXVIII.
2. An amendment to the Constitution providing for the direct election of the President and the elimination of the electoral college passed the House of Representatives in 1970 but failed to secure the agreement of the Senate before the end of the 91st Congress (1969–70).
3. Article II, 3.

In both these respects the constitutional arrangements for Parliament are very different. National elections in Britain are less frequent than in the United States: since 1945 there have been eight, giving an average of one in just over three years. But when they happen they are comprehensive. The whole of the House of Commons—including the Prime Minister as chief executive and his cabinet colleagues in the Commons—has to be renewed, which means that the majority of the House, and so the identity of the next government, is in question. The House of Lords, though exempt from popular election,[1] reflects the result of a general election in the political colour of the ministers appointed on the advice of the incoming Prime Minister to lead it and in the seating arrangements for its membership.

Secondly the influence of the executive over the arrangements for convening and dissolving Parliament differentiates them markedly from those in Washington. In principle Parliament can only be convened by an act of the Sovereign. On the only two occasions when the Lords and Commons have met on their own authority—before the Restoration of Charles II in 1660 and at the 'glorious revolution' of 1688—the two Houses were subsequently declared by statute to be a Parliament notwithstanding the irregularity of their mode of assembly.[2] It follows that the Sovereign has power to determine the period between one Parliament and another, though under an Act of 1694 a new Parliament has to be summoned within three years of a dissolution. In practice the regular provision of money for the public services in annual bills and the need for the Houses to review annually the authority for maintaining an army and air force make it obligatory for the Sovereign to summon Parliament to meet every year. In practice, too, the royal proclamation dissolving a Parliament appoints a day for the meeting of its successor, thus implicitly recognizing the need for continuity.

The statutory life of a Parliament is limited to five years,[3] though in both world wars it was extended by further Acts of Parliament. If it lasts for five years, it is dissolved automatically.

---

1. It cannot meet during a dissolution except for the hearing and determination of appeals, for which the Appellate Jurisdiction Act made provision in 1876.   2. Erskine May, 18th ed. (1971), p. 53.
3. Parliament Act 1911 s. 7. From 1715 to 1911 the statutory limit on the life of a Parliament was seven years.

But before that term is reached, it may be dissolved by an exercise of the royal prerogative. In dissolving (as in summoning) Parliament, the Sovereign takes advice from the Prime Minister of the day. It is possible to imagine theoretical situations in which the Sovereign could refuse, or at least delay an answer to, a request by the Prime Minister for a dissolution. But in practice, as Jennings has pointed out, no monarch since the middle of the nineteenth century has refused advice to dissolve.[1] The effective power to dissolve has long been regarded as one of the strongest weapons that the Prime Minister has at his disposal. It can bring solid advantages which the chief executive of the United States does not enjoy.

The chief advantage is that he can choose the moment most favourable to himself and his party to hold a general election. This has for long been the practice. The 'Khaki' elections of 1900 and 1918 are famous instances, but the same practice has occurred in peacetime. Since 1945 the growing governmental power over the economy, the greater accuracy of economic forecasting and the more sophisticated techniques of opinion sampling have enabled Prime Ministers to judge with increasing confidence (though not always with success) the most favourable moment for dissolution.

A lesser advantage is that the threat of a dissolution helps a Prime Minister to maintain party discipline. As a positive power the threat of a dissolution may not be as potent as is sometimes suggested. If he uses it purely from motives of maintaining discipline, the Prime Minister is likely to forfeit the greater advantage (just described) of being able to choose the most favourable moment for dissolution. But as a negative weapon, it remains significant; supporters of the Prime Minister will be reluctant to defeat him in the House of Commons on a matter of confidence lest he should be forced to resign and then be obliged to go to the country at a moment not of his own choosing.

The recognition of this substantial advantage to the government in power has led to proposals for introducing in Britain the American concept of a Parliament with a fixed term.[2] The sense of these proposals is that the Prime Minister would not have the

1. I. Jennings, *Cabinet Government* (1947), pp. 317–18.
2. In *The Times*, 8 May 1969 (Ronald Butt); 22 April 1970 (Ian Gilmour); and 11 July 1970 (Roger Fulford).

right to ask the Sovereign for a dissolution unless he had lost the confidence of the House of Commons. Matters involving confidence for this purpose would be restricted to the main financial bills (Consolidated Fund and Finance) of the year and any general vote of confidence in the government. A vote of confidence on finance bills would probably be necessary in Britain to preserve the constitutional principle of the primacy of the crown in matters of finance and to assure the money for the Government to be carried on (though the American Administration does not enjoy this assurance[1]). But the convention of confidence would not extend to other legislation, so that both government and opposition would be freed from the straitjacket of their party political attitudes to bills and would be encouraged to seek a more genuine consensus view on legislative proposals. Under some such system, it is argued, a government would still get most of its bills because it would be supported by its own party. Other bills, on which its party was not unanimous, it would get with the support of the opposition. If a bill were defeated because not enough of the government's supporters or the opposition were willing to vote for it, then its defeat would probably be deserved and desirable. The defeat of a government bill could, if necessary, be followed by a general vote of confidence which the government would almost certainly win.

From the standpoint of a comparison between Parliament and Congress, the interesting aspect of the proposal for a fixed parliamentary term is that it would enhance Parliament's independence of ministers and to that extent mark a stage towards the equality, if not towards a separation, of legislature and executive. It would no doubt reduce the number of votes on party lines. The results would probably be seen chiefly in the committee stage of bills, because the tendency of members in committees to work towards a compromise would find a larger outlet for expression. For the same reason governments could be expected to regard the proposal with apprehension. A more flexible approach to legislation could quickly become infectious. Too regular a search for compromise or consensus might blunt the edge of a government's programme and, it could be argued, might muffle the message or mandate conveyed by the electorate in giving its approval to that programme. Above all a fixed date for dissolution would limit the options at

1. See Chapter VII.

present open to a Prime Minister in seeking to perpetuate himself and his party in power. It is true that governmental controls over the economy could as well be directed to a fixed date as to a date to be decided by the Prime Minister. But other factors at home or abroad might well lessen the attractions of the fixed date from his standpoint. All these reasons suggest that the present arrangement is deeply entrenched and unlikely to be changed.

SESSIONS

A 'session' in both Congress and Parliament describes the period between the opening of two Houses for business and their closing. In both countries the session is of indeterminate length, though as a rule it spans most of the twelve months, with several recesses or adjournments.

Congress is required by the Constitution to assemble at least once in every year and that meeting has to be on 3 January unless a different day is appointed by law. The effect is that a session beginning on 3 January cannot be longer than one year, since the next session must start on the following 3 January. There are normally two regular sessions in a Congress, its term being limited to two years. These requirements are laid down in the twentieth amendment made to Constitution in 1933. Before that date Congress held a third regular session from December to 3 March, which was then the prescribed date for the expiry of the congressional term of office.[1] As that session was held after the elections in November but before a new Congress (and in every fourth year a new President) took office, it was known as the 'lame duck session'. This short twilight period invited the obstruction of legislation. Some of the most famous filibusters in congressional history were carried out during 'lame duck' sessions. It is still sometimes necessary—as in 1970 for example—for Congress to sit in November and December after elections have taken place but before the new Congress opens.

The modern session begins on 3 January and has to end around 31 July, unless Congress provides otherwise.[2] Nowadays it almost invariably continues to sit beyond that date. Only two sessions

1. Constitution, Article I, 4.
2. Section 132 of the Legislative Reorganization Act of 1946, as amended by section 461 of the Legislative Reorganization Act of 1970. This provision makes an exception for time of war or 'during a national emergency'.

(1952 and 1965) since World War II have ended by 31 July. The rest have continued, some through the summer months, others through the autumn, several to December and two (1950 and 1971) to 2 January, the eve of the next session. The session ends when Congress adjourns *sine die*. But before that Congress usually adjourns to a stated date for a 'recess' on several occasions during a year.[1] In the session of 1967 both Houses recessed on the same dates. They can and often do recess at different times, though not for more than three days without the consent of the other House.[2] In the session of 1967 the Senate sat on 200 days and the House of Representatives on 189. The arrangements for bringing a session of Congress to a close, like those for its assembly, are thus in practice independent of the executive power, though if the two Houses were to disagree upon their time of adjournment, the Constitution empowers the President to adjourn them to such time as he thinks proper.[3]

In Britain a new Parliament meets on the day appointed by the Sovereign in the royal proclamation dissolving the previous Parliament. After a Speaker has been chosen and members have taken an oath of allegiance, the Queen opens the first session of the new Parliament a few days later. The opening date of the first session is thus part of the regular pattern of events when a general election is held. The dates of subsequent sessions are decided by the Sovereign on the advice of the Prime Minister, but here he has room for manoeuvre. The normal session is opened, usually by the Queen in person and with high ceremony, at the end of October. It continues until the following October when it is closed (prorogued) by the Queen either by royal proclamation or more usually by an announcement made in the House of Lords by a peer (normally the Lord Chancellor) acting on her commission. But the Prime Minister can tailor the length of a session to political necessities as he sees them. His choice of a date for a general election will obviously affect a session's length. The session of 1965–66 began in November 1965 and ended in March

1. In the first session of the 90th Congress (1967) which lasted until 15 December, Congress recessed from 23 March to 3 April (Easter), 29 June to 10 July (over Independence Day), 31 August to 11 September (over Labour Day), and 22 to 27 November (over Thanksgiving).

2. Constitution, Article I, 5.

3. Constitution, Article II, 3.

1966, a general election being held in that month. The next session began in April 1966 and continued until October 1967. Again, a shorter session of little more than one month, like that in 1948, may be held in order to expedite the passing of legislation in successive sessions and enable the Commons to override what the Lords have done.[1]

Within the span of the sessional period each House of Parliament has the right to adjourn[2] itself. It does so on motion moved by the Leader of each House, the terms of the motion respecting well-established practices of adjourning at regular and recognized intervals. The House of Lords adjourns, also on motion moved by the House Leader, for more or less the same periods.[3] During the summer adjournments of 1968 the Speaker and Lord Chancellor convened the two Houses on 26 and 27 August to debate the invasion of Czechoslovakia (the two presiding officers are authorized by standing order to take this action if, after representations by the government, they are satisfied that the public interest so requires). The two Houses sat again in October for a few days to conclude the session's business. The session was then ended (prorogued) and the new session was opened shortly after. In the session of 1967–68 the holiday adjournments of the two Houses coincided. In 1967–68 the House of Commons sat on 176 days and the House of Lords 138 days (the Lords frequently sitting on only three or four days a week).

By and large the session in Congress and Parliament follows the same pattern of timing. With recesses or adjournments taken into account the two first chambers tend to sit for around 160–180 days a year. The Senate sits more and the Lords less than this figure. But there is one fundamental difference. In the United

1. The powers of the Commons to override the Lords are described in Chapter IV.

2. A difference of terminology has to be noted. The period between sessions is known in Congress as an adjournment, in Parliament as a recess. The period within a session when a House is not sitting is known in Congress as a recess, and in Parliament as an adjournment. This is strict usage, not always observed in every day reference in either country.

3. In the session of 1967–68 the House of Commons adjourned from 21 December to 16 January (Christmas), 11 to 23 April (Easter), 31 May to 11 June (Whitsuntide) and 26 July to 14 October (Summer). The Lords usually rise a day earlier and return a day later than the Commons. Sometimes if there is a heavy programme of legislation, the Lords will sit a week longer than the Commons before rising for the summer adjournment.

States the unit of time for legislation is not a session but a Congress, covering a period of two years. Though all legislation pending at the end of a Congress dies, bills not passed by the end of the first session can be taken up again at the same stage in the next session. In Britain, by contrast, the slate is wiped clean at the end of each session. The government and other members must secure the passage of legislation under the penalty of losing it and having to go through the whole legislative process afresh in the next session.[1]

QUALIFICATIONS AND DISQUALIFICATIONS

Whatever other differences are to be found between Congress and Parliament, the legal qualifications required of their members might be expected to be similar. In fact they differ in almost all respects except the obvious one, that a member cannot belong to both Houses at the same time. Even the basic nomenclature suggests a different approach. The American textbooks and constitutional commentaries speak of qualifications, the British equivalents of disqualifications. Parliament has a range of statutory disqualifications—such as treason, lunacy and bankruptcy—which are not found in Congress. The reason is that it has always been regarded as doubtful whether Congress can by law add to the qualifications prescribed by the Constitution. It is as doubtful whether either House of Congress could alone establish such qualifications. Even under the stress and provocation of civil war, both Houses acted on the assumption that they did not have this power.[2]

If the more extreme British disqualifications are left on one side, the basic rules of qualification can, with one exception, be said to have been more restrictive in Congress than in Parliament. The single exception is sex; and even this exception is more technical than real. The Constitution of 1789 made no reference in terms to the eligibility of women. But it was generally assumed that they were not eligible until they had obtained the right to vote. This right was given to them by the nineteenth

1. Arrangements are usually made as required to carry over private bills (see p. 274) from one session to another in order to spare the promoters and opponents undue expense.

2. *House Rules and Manual* (1971), para. 12.

amendment to the Constitution which came into force in 1920. The first woman was elected to the House in the 65th Congress (1917–18) shortly before that amendment came into force, while the first woman to sit in the Senate began her service in 1922. In Britain by contrast it needed the passion and violence of the suffragette movement and World War I to bring about the removal of this sexual discrimination. The Parliament (Qualification of Women) Act 1918 enabled women to stand for membership of the House of Commons. In the following year the first woman member took her seat in the Commons. Women had to wait until 1957 to enter the House of Lords. Until the passing of the Life Peerages Act in that year, a woman might be a peeress in her own right; but, in Anson's words, 'the privilege of acting as an hereditory counsellor to the Crown [was] confined to the male sex'.[1] The first life peeresses were appointed in 1958, and the first peeress in her own right was seated in 1963, under the authority of the Peerage Act of that year.

The restrictive qualifications for members of the House of Representatives and the Senate are laid down in the Constitution. A representative must be at least twenty-five years of age, a senator at least thirty. A representative must have been a citizen of the United States for seven years, a senator for nine years.[2] According to *The Federalist*:[3]

> the propriety of these distinctions is explained by the nature of the senatorial trust which requiring greater extent of information and stability of character, requires at the same time that the senator should have reached a period of life most likely to supply these advantages; and which, participating immediately in transactions with foreign nations, ought to be exercised by none who are not thoroughly weaned from the prepossessions and habits incidental to foreign birth and disposition.

The same restrictions have not been thought necessary in Britain. Twenty-one (the age of majority until changed in 1969 to eighteen) is the age qualification for membership of both Houses of Parliament. For the Commons this has been a statutory requirement since 1695, though there were several instances of its breach in the eighteenth and early nineteenth centuries, notably by

1. Anson, *Law and Custom of the Constitution*, 5th ed. (1922), p. 227.
2. Article I, 2.
3. Everyman Edition (1965), p. 315.

Charles James Fox who was returned, sat and spoke before he was of age.[1] In the Lords the matter is regulated by a standing order which dates back (earlier than any Commons standing order) to 1685. Aliens are disqualified by common law and by statute law for membership of either House. But an alien who has been naturalized is not disqualified. The process of naturalization takes a minimum of five years. Once naturalized he can stand for election without having to be a citizen for a given number of years. So this qualification is in practice much less exacting than those for the two Houses of Congress.

A more significant restriction on a member of either House of Congress is that, when elected, he must be an 'inhabitant' of the state in which he is chosen.[2] 'Inhabitancy', it should be noted, is less exacting than residence, which is not a constitutional requirement. There is also room for play with the words 'when elected'.[3] But the practical effect is that, with a two-year term between elections and although there is no constitutional requirement on them to do so, most members of the House of Representatives maintain a residence in their own districts (constituencies) or at least in another district of the same city. With a six-year term, and representing a state, senators have more flexibility, but the result is very much the same.

This 'locality rule' is often contrasted to the British practice. Not since 1774 has there been a statutory requirement that a member of the House of Commons shall reside in his constituency, and even before that it had fallen into disuse. Today it is by no means unknown for a candidate to bow to pressure to live in the constituency. Often it will help his prospects if he does so. As a general rule, however, non-residence is acceptable. Non-resident members are sometimes described as 'carpet-baggers'; but, in recalling the Northerners who went South after the American civil war in search of political spoils, the term can hardly be taken, in a context of a comparison between Parliament and Congress, as a precise description.

The locality rule in the United States and its absence in Britain make several points about the two parliamentary systems. The

1. Erskine May, 18th ed. (1971), p. 35.
2. Article I, 2.
3. The case history on this complex subject is summarized in the *House Rules and Manual* (1971), paras. 11 and 35.

rule reflects the strong local pressures with which American legislators, and particularly members of the House of Representatives, have continually to contend. It reflects, too, the belief—already studied in Chapter I—that the obligation to a constituency or a state often has to be accorded priority over a national programme as conceived by the President or the national committee of a party organization. Politics is a balancing and melding of those local interests. By contrast Parliament has benefited by the more flexible system. A cabinet minister, unseated at a general election by a swing against his party, can often secure readoption at the other end of the country and be returned at a by-election, so that his talents and experiences are not lost to the House of Commons. Churchill who sat successively for seats in Lancashire, Scotland and Essex and Mr Harold Macmillan who, displaced from Durham, found refuge in Kent, are two Prime Ministers whose political careers would have suffered seriously from a strict locality rule.[1] This flexibility is possible because Britain, unlike the United States, is a compact and reasonably homogeneous political unit. A member of Parliament can and does think primarily in national terms. It is natural for him to combine the strongest efforts on behalf of his constituents with a determination to remain free to speak and vote on national issues as he thinks right, subject to any stance he may have taken or pledge given at election time. Burke's classic address to the electors at Bristol in 1774 is too well known a statement of the freedom and obligation of a member of Parliament to need quotation. The same point was made more succinctly by Mr Duncan Sandys, Member for Streatham since 1950: 'I was elected to represent Streatham in Parliament, not Parliament in Streatham.' A congressman would think twice before uttering such a statement.

The last and most important restrictive qualification for congressmen is the basis of the separation of the legislative from the executive power. According to the Constitution:

1. Not only established politicians would suffer from a strict locality rule. Sir Denis Brogan has pointed out that a parliamentary aspirant in the United States who has 'the misfortune to live in a district safely dedicated to the immortal principles of the other side' cannot enter Congress at all. He would have to change either his party or his residence. *An Introduction to American Politics* (1954 ed.), p. 337.

No senator or representative shall during the time for which he was elected be appointed to any civil office under the authority of the United States . . . and no person holding any office under the United States shall be a member of either House during his continuance in office.[1]

These statements have been scarcely modified by subsequent case histories in both Houses. A tolerance has been extended to members-elect holding incompatible offices (in view of the two-month period between the election of a member in November and the meeting of Congress in January). But the division between executive and legislature in this respect remains absolute. By derivation it has been extended to the office of governor—the executive head of each state—which has been held to be incompatible with membership of Congress.

The contrasting position in Britain, in which ministers of the Crown are members of one or other House of Parliament, is today so generally understood that it takes an effort to recall how close the English once came to a separation of legislature and executive on the American pattern. Historically the law on disqualification has reflected the struggle of the House of Commons to win independence of the Crown and under the later Stuarts to resist a systematic attempt to bind individual members to the royal interest by distributing offices and places of profit under the Crown. The reaction against these methods of management led to the passage in 1701 of the Act of Settlement which excluded all office holders, including ministers, from the House of Commons. The Act made statutory in England precisely the same separation of legislature and executive that the Founding Fathers were to write into the American Constitution later in the same century.

But even before the Act of 1701 came into force, the House changed its mind. In debate on later bills the value of having ministers in the House, and the difficulties that would flow from their removal, were recognized. Yet the key Act of 1707, usually known as the Statute of Anne, revealed in full measure Parliament's ambivalence on this subject. One section of this Act provided that no persons holding an office or place *under* the Crown which had been created before October 1705 should be able to

1. Article I, 6.

sit in the Commons. But another section said that if any person, being a member of the Commons, accepted an office of profit *from* the Crown, his seat would be vacated, though he could submit himself for re-election. The apparent conflict between the two sections was resolved by requiring the holders of offices created before as well as after October 1705 to stand for re-election, though there was no express authority for so doing. The position was modified by later statutes; and there remained much doubt in what was and what was not an office of profit under or from the Crown. Nevertheless the basic inconvenience—to the country and to the individuals concerned—of requiring ministers to submit themselves for re-election lasted throughout the the eighteenth and nineteenth centuries. It was not finally eliminated until the Re-election of Ministers Act passed in 1926. That it lasted so long was the measure of Parliament's suspicion of the Crown's ability to undermine its independence by corrupt gifts.

Erskine May has pointed out that the veto embodied in the Statute of Anne on the capacity of office holders to sit in the House of Commons could have produced a government most of whose members were outside the House. In fact the reverse process took place. In May's words:

A movement had begun which was destined ... to change the House from being a body united, or almost united, in opposition to the Crown into a body of which only the minority are opponents, while the majority are supporters, of a ministry whose chief members are necessarily also members of the House of Commons.[1]

It was a movement which spelt the end, even before it had begun, of that separation of the membership of legislature and executive which was to provide the ground rules in the United States.

The historical obscurity of the law on disqualification extended beyond ministerial offices to most other kinds of public office. Attempts to regulate the question of disqualification ad hoc as new statutory offices were created only added to the law's complexity. As late as the 1950s Parliament was having to pass hastily bills to indemnify individual members of the House of Commons found to be holding offices—in some instances of a purely advisory nature and without salary—which might have involved

1. Erskine May, 14th ed. (1946), p. 201.

penal consequences for them under statute or common law. Not until the House of Commons Disqualification Act 1957 was the law comprehensively reformed and clarified.

Under the new Act most of the persons disqualified under the law as it had been before 1957 were still disqualified. What the Act of 1957 did was to repeal over one hundred old statutes and substitute a simple and clear list of the offices that were incompatible with membership of the House of Commons. It includes the holders of a specified list of judicial offices, members of the civil service, any police force maintained by a police authority, the armed forces of the Crown (though not reserve and auxiliary services), and a large number of commissions and tribunals—including the boards of all the major nationalized industries. The list is long. But if an office is not expressly included in it, the Act says that a member shall not be disqualified by being appointed to it. Secondly the Act provides that only a certain number of ministers may be in the House of Commons as members. A statutory limit of seventy (since amended to ninety-one)[1] and within that limit a maximum of twenty-seven ministers of higher rank, are entitled to sit in the Commons at any one time. Thus on the one hand a large number of non-political offices of profit under the Crown were specifically declared incompatible with membership and on the other a stated number of ministerial office-holders were expressly located on the floor of the House. The Act of 1957 also preserved the legally fictitious offices of Steward of Her Majesty's Chiltern Hundreds of Stoke, Desborough and Burnham; Bailiff of the same; and Steward of the Manor of Northstead. Acceptance of one of these offices, which formerly were actual offices of profit under the Crown, is the time-honoured method of leaving the Commons. While a member of Congress can resign if he wishes, a member of the House of Commons, once elected, cannot. But he can be appointed, for practical purposes at his own request, to one of these disqualifying offices, and then have to leave the House.

The Disqualification Act of 1957 has been successful. Since its passage the House of Commons has not been plagued with problems about disqualification for office holding. There remains the sanction in the Act that a member of the public may apply

1. In December 1970 there were sixty-seven ministers with seats in the House of Commons.

to the Judicial Committee of the Privy Council for a declaration
that a member is disqualified, and the Judicial Committee may
direct the issue to be tried.

For the House of Lords the offer by the Crown of places of
profit did not pose a comparable threat. Succession by heredity
and life tenure have militated in favour of independence. Today
the only restraints on members of the House of Lords are of a
practical kind. Under civil service rules a peer who is a civil
servant may attend the House but may not take part in debate or
vote until he has resigned or retired. Peers who are in the armed
services may not indulge in political controversy but otherwise
may speak and vote. Peers who are chairmen, board members or
employees of public corporations or nationalized industries are
inhibited from speaking or voting on matters affecting those
bodies. This last restraint is analogous to a conflict of interest, a
topic which is discussed later in this chapter.

PRIVILEGES AND IMMUNITIES

A legislative assembly can carry out its constitutional functions
only when its members come together as representatives of the
people for deliberation and decision. As Cushing has pointed out,[1]
legislative power and authority reside in the collective body, not
in the individual member. This is the foundation of the privileges
accorded to members of Parliament and of Congress. The most
important privileges are freedom from arrest and freedom of
speech. The first is essential to allow members to come together
and remain together to constitute the legislative body; in principle
they should not be prevented from attending or be withdrawn
from attendance. The second follows from the first: the right of
attendance to make up the assembly must be complemented, if it
is to be effective, by the freedom to speak, to debate and to decide.
These principles are personal to each individual member. But
they vest in him as a member of the legislative body, not in any
other personal capacity. He can look for their protection when
carrying out his duties as a member, not when doing other things
extraneous to those duties.

In Britain the Speaker of the House of Commons at the beginning of each Parliament lays claim 'by humble petition' on behalf

1. *Legislative Assemblies in the United States* (1856), paras. 529-30.

of the Commons 'to their ancient and undoubted rights and privileges', of which freedom from arrest and freedom of speech are the chief. He does so after being elected Speaker, when he goes to the House of Lords to seek the Royal approval of his election (see p. 50). On behalf of the Sovereign, the Lord Chancellor replies to this petition that 'Her Majesty most readily confirms all the rights and privileges which have ever been granted to or conferred upon the Commons by Her Majesty or any of her Royal predecessors'. This time-honoured proceeding suggests that the privileges of the House of Commons are subject to royal favour, unlike those of the Lords who 'have ever enjoyed them simply because they have place and voice in Parliament'.[1] But in practice the House of Commons does not rely on the royal grant in response to its request as the sole basis for its privileges. As long ago as 1604 the Commons claimed that the request was 'an act only of manners' and that their right to these privileges was, and had long been, prescriptive.[2] Since then the two major privileges of members—freedom from arrest and freedom of speech—have been virtually confirmed by statute, thus placing them beyond the reach of the Crown. The custom of requesting these privileges is retained, like several other customs in Parliament, as a reminder of the prolonged struggle of the Commons to assert and establish their privileges against the Crown.

Freedom from arrest, though of great antiquity, traditionally extended only to arrest in civil proceedings. The crimes of treason, felony and breach of the peace had always been exempted from its ambit. During the eighteenth century various statutes extended those exemptions to all other statutory offences. But the freedom of members of both Houses from arrest in civil cases was for long of first importance because of the ready resort to imprisonment which the law made in civil cases. This basic protection for members was reaffirmed in the Parliamentary Privileges Act 1770 which also stripped the servants of members of the same protection. The passage of the Judgements Act 1838 and later Acts virtually abolished imprisonment in civil process, with the result that this privilege has become less important.

1. Erskine May, 18th ed. (1971), p. 66, citing W. Hakewel, *Modus tenendi parliamentum* (1660).
2. Erskine May, 18th ed. (1971), p. 67.

The privilege of freedom of speech finds its classic statement in the Bill of Rights 1688:

> . . . freedom of speech, and debates or proceedings in Parliament ought not to be impeached or questioned in any court or place out of Parliament.

declared section 9 of that statute. The reason for this restatement of the privilege was the attempts by the Crown to intimidate members of the House of Commons. A peak of pressure was scaled in 1629 when a judgement was obtained in the courts against Sir John Eliot, Denzil Holles and Benjamin Valentine for their speeches and conduct in Parliament. This famous judgement was in 1641 declared by the Commons to be against the law and privilege of Parliament; and following a conference between members of the two Houses in 1667, the House of Lords in the following year formally reversed the judgement, upon a writ of error. A select committee of the Commons has expressed the view that the declaratory words in the Bill of Rights would cover:

> everything said or done by a member in performance of his duties as a member in a committee of the House or a joint committee of both Houses, as well as everything said or done by him in the House in the transaction of parliamentary business.[1]

By the time the American Constitution came to be written, therefore, the two major privileges enjoyed by members of the two Houses of Parliament had been established both by custom and by statute. As the language of the Constitution makes clear, the Founding Fathers of the American Constitution drew consciously from this common historical background in making the same two provisions for members of both Houses of Congress. Senators and representatives, says Article I (6):

> shall in all cases except treason, felony and breach of the peace be privileged from arrest during their attendance at sessions of their respective Houses and in going to or returning from the same.

This provision corresponds broadly to the position in Britain in the eighteenth century.

1. Report of the Select Committee on the Official Secrets Act, House of Commons Paper 101 of 1938–39, pp. 4–5.

Today, as in Britain, the privilege of freedom from arrest has for practical purposes lost much of its importance. In both countries a member of either House can be pursued by all lawful means except, in legal language, the attachment of his person. This protection extends to a subpœna issued by a court of law. Both Parliament and Congress regard it in principle as a breach of privilege for a court to summon their members to attend and give evidence while the House is sitting; with reason, as Jefferson put it, 'because a member has superior duties to perform in another place'.[1]

In both countries, however, the application of this privilege has been much attenuated. While consistently upholding the principle that they have the paramount claim to the attendance and service of their members, both Parliament and Congress have authorized their members in individual cases to comply with the summons of particular courts of law. There has been no general waiver of this privilege, however, because it remains such an important protection for the legislatures. In a recent case in the United States the courts reaffirmed that a senator engaged in legitimate legislative activity was protected by privilege from the results of that legislation and from the burden of defending himself in court for the part he had played in its enactment.[2] This important case raised issues relevant not only to immunity from the service of a subpœna but also the other major privilege of freedom of speech.

The privilege of freedom of speech, too, is enshrined in the Constitution. According to the same Article I (6):

for any speech or debate in either House, they [senators and representatives] shall not be questioned in any other place.

This is substantially the language of section 9 of the Bill of Rights. As in Britain, this privilege is held to cover anything said or done by a member of Congress in the exercise of his functions. In the words of Cushing:

whether the member is in his place within the house, delivering an opinion, uttering a speech, engaging in debate, giving his vote, making a written report, communicating information either to a house

1. *House Rules and Manual* (1971), para. 290.
2. Drombrowski v. Eastland 387 U.S. 82 (1967).

or to a member, or whether he is out of the house sitting in a committee, and engaged in debate or voting therein, or in drawing up a report to be submitted to the assembly.[1]

The common historical language and background of privilege in both countries is important. In neither was it the intention of Parliament or the Founding Fathers of the Constitution to place members of the legislature above the ordinary law of the land. In both it was to protect them from possible depredation by other branches of government—the Crown or executive—or indeed the courts of law. This end was to be achieved by ensuring not that a member of the legislature could speak without any restraint or inhibition whatever, but that the legislature alone, through its own procedures and practices, should have the power to question and if necessary proceed against a member for what he had said or done in carrying out his duties.

A jurisdiction of privilege implies a power of enforcement. As Cushing has pointed out:

> the privileges of a legislative assembly would be entirely ineffectual to enable it to discharge its functions, if it had no power to punish offenders, to impose disciplinary regulations upon its members, or to enforce obedience to its commands.[2]

Nevertheless, while the power of the legislature to enforce its privileges is common to Parliament and Congress, there are differences in the origin and scope of that power.

The power of each House of Parliament to protect its privileges and punish their violation is described by Erskine May as 'akin in nature and origin to the powers possessed by the courts of justice to punish for contempt'.[3] The origin of the power is imprecise. It owed much to the medieval concept of Parliament as a High Court which gave 'judgements' on the petitions submitted by individual citizens complaining of wrongs done to them. When the unitary medieval Parliament divided into two Houses distinct from the Crown, the Lords as original members of the King's Court had as clear a title as any other superior court to punish for contempt. The rights of the Commons as a separate House were

1. Cushing, *Legislative Assemblies in the United States* (1856), para. 603.
2. Ibid., para. 533.
3. Erskine May, 18th ed. (1971), p. 112.

less certain. But an important step forward was taken in 1415 when the Commons obtained from the Crown the services of a Serjeant at Arms. With this officer, to execute its orders and carry the royal mace as the symbol of its corporate authority, the House of Commons could and did develop its judicial jurisdiction. By the middle of the sixteenth century the power to commit offenders was being exercised with the same freedom by the Commons as by the Lords.[1]

There have since been innumerable precedents for its exercise. In the case of Kielley v. Carson (1842)[2] this power was recognized by the courts. Edward Kielley had used threatening language and gestures to a member of the Newfoundland House of Assembly. He was arrested under the Speaker's warrant, brought to the bar of the House of Assembly and committed to prison for the alleged contempt. When eventually the case reached the Judicial Committee of the Privy Council, the Committee allowed Kielley's appeal on the ground that the powers of a colonial assembly did not include the power of arrest in order to adjudicate upon a contempt committed out of the House. The Judicial Committee contrasted this limited authority to that of each House of the British Parliament in which the power to punish for contempt inhered, not because it was an assembly with legislative functions but because of its origin and legal status as the High Court of Parliament and by virtue of the law and custom of Parliament.

The analogy with the courts of law is apparent also in the scope and extent of the power to punish. It is a general power which can be applied to any contempt offered to either House; it is not restricted to the enforcement of the individual or collective privileges of the two Houses. In the words of Halsbury:

any act or omission which obstructs or impedes either House in the performance of its functions, or which obstructs or impedes any member or officer of the House, in the discharge of his duty, or which has a tendency to produce such a result, may be treated as a contempt even if there is no precedent of the offence.[3]

1. A useful note on the early history of the royal Serjeants, to which this account is indebted, is found in the Report of the Select Committee on Parliamentary Privilege. House of Commons Paper 34 of 1966–67, pp. 155–157.
2. 4 Moore P.C. 63.
3. Halsbury, *The Laws of England*, 3rd ed. (1959), p. 465.

This right to punish for contempt has been exercised in modern times chiefly by the House of Commons, perhaps because its higher political content and temperature have tended to provoke more reaction from those beyond the precincts of Parliament. For the same reason its actions have often proved controversial. It has dealt with contempts falling clearly within the field of its own privileges such as a witness's wilful misleading of a committee, or the refusal of a witness to answer or produce documents. But it has also travelled beyond the strict boundaries of its privileges and proceeded against speeches or writings in public prints or journals which reflected on the House or on individual members in their capacity as members. The principle followed in these cases has been that speeches or writings of this kind diminish the respect in which the House is held and lower its authority, thus tending to obstruct its effective working. If the contempt is not regarded as serious or if an apology is made, the House normally takes no further action. But if an allegation of corruption or improper behaviour by members or of partial conduct by the chair is made the House is likely to proceed against the offender. In the most widely noticed case of recent years, the editor of a Sunday newspaper, which had alleged that members of Parliament were giving themselves special treatment at a time of petrol rationing, was summoned to the bar of the House and formally reprimanded by the Speaker.[1]

This is the point at which American practice parts company from the British tradition. In 1800 the editor of an American journal included some passages defamatory of the Senate and, having failed to appear on the order of the Senate, he was then ordered to be committed. At once the question whether Congress, or one of its Houses, possessed an inherent power to punish for a contempt of this kind was raised and debated. The arguments for and against are succinctly summarized in Jefferson's manual.[2] Those in favour appealed to the practice of the British Parliament and to every state legislature, all of which punished for contempt; without it, the argument ran, proceedings in Congress would be perpetually disturbed. Those against pointed out that Parliament had this power by express provision of British law. State legislatures have the same authority because all power

1. *Commons Journals* (1956–57), pp. 50, 66.
2. *House Rules and Manual* (1971), paras. 297–9.

resides in them except to the extent that their constitutions expressly deny it to them. But Congress has no power except that given to it by the Constitution. Expressly it gives to Congress freedom from arrest, freedom from question anywhere for what is said, and power over its own members. It also gives power to 'make all laws necessary and proper for carrying into execution' the powers vested by the Constitution in them;[1] so that Congress could provide by law for the punishment of any contempt which might disturb its proceedings. But until that law was passed, it was argued, the power did not exist. This second view has carried the day. Jefferson himself suggested that Congress could usefully pass a law defining the offence of contempt and so 'hang up a rule for the inspection of all'. But in 1837 the House declined to proceed with a bill both defining the offence and prescribing punishments, and it has not done so since then. Today a member of either House may rise to a point of privilege, calling attention to a paper writing reflecting on the House or its members, but unless it plainly involved one of the privileges given by the Constitution, nothing is done about it.

Nevertheless from its earliest days Congress has exercised the power to deal with contempts so far as necessary to protect its exercise of legislative authority expressly granted by the Constitution. In 1832 the House of Representatives affirmed its freedom of speech by censuring a citizen for an assault on a member for words spoken in debate. In 1870 it asserted its freedom from arrest by arresting and imprisoning a person who had assaulted a member on his way to the House. Within these constitutional limits the House's action has been approved by the Supreme Court. In 1818 when a person was arrested, tried and censured by the House for the attempted bribery of a member, he appealed to the courts, and eventually the Supreme Court upheld the right of the House to punish for contempt, because 'public functionaries must be at liberty to exercise the powers which the people have entrusted to them'. Late in the nineteenth century the Supreme Court refined its statement of congressional authority. In 1876 it found against an attempt by the House of Representatives to coerce a witness in an inquiry which, it held, was not within the constitutional authority of the House. In this finding the Court made clear that the House had no general power to

1. Article I, 8.

punish for contempt; and it specifically made the point that no support for such a proposition could be drawn from the precedents and practices of the two Houses of the English Parliament nor from the cases in which English judges have upheld these practices. In 1894, however, in another case involving a contumacious witness, the Supreme Court affirmed the undoubted right of either House of Congress to punish for contempt on a matter to which its power properly extended under the Constitution.[1] In short, Congress has power:

> to prevent acts which in and of themselves inherently prevent or obstruct the discharge of legislative duty and to compel the doing of those things which are essential to the performance of legislative functions.[2]

The difference between Parliament and Congress in this field is, then, clear. Both enjoy broadly the same privileges. But in Britain a further power of immunity resides in each House of Parliament, namely, the power to arrest a person and punish him for contempt. Even if the order or warrant on which he has been arrested does not state the cause of his arrest, the courts of law will not look behind it or inquire into the reasons why he was found guilty of the contempt. In such cases it is presumed that the order of warrant has been duly issued unless the contrary appears on the face of it.[3] In the United States by contrast each House of Congress is circumscribed by the grant of powers in the Constitution, and such action as it takes has to be within the scope of those powers. The power to punish for contempt is restricted in this sense.

Yet the modern attitude of each legislature to its privileges and immunities is probably very much the same. In 1967 a Select Committee on Parliamentary Privilege made a thorough review of the law of parliamentary privilege as it affected the Commons. It recommended a number of changes in the law and in the practice of the House on matters of privilege. In particular it proposed that the House should exercise its penal jurisdiction

> only when it is satisfied that to do so is essential in order to provide

1. This power is considered further in Chapter V on Committees, p. 236.

2. See official commentary in *House Rules and Manual* (1971), paras. 294–96, in which these and other cases of contempt are reviewed.

3. Halsbury, op. cit., Vol. 28 (Parliament), para. 918.

reasonable protection for the House, its members or its officers from such improper obstruction or attempt at or threat of obstruction as is causing, or is likely to cause, substantial interference with the performance of their respective functions.[1]

Debates in the House[2] on the Committee's report showed differences on how effect could best be given to this general principle but none as to the principle itself. In the United States, the Joint Committee which in 1965 and 1966 looked into all aspects of the organization of Congress made no recommendations on the existing law and practice of privilege. Nor was there any provision on this subject in the Legislative Reorganization Act of 1970 which gave effect to many of the Joint Committee's recommendations. It seems a fair deduction that in Parliament as in Congress there is a growing tendency to lean upon the protection of privilege as little as possible, and to exercise with restraint their considerable powers against public criticism of their membership and activities.

POWERS OVER CONSTITUTION OF LEGISLATURES

The choice of candidates for Congress and Parliament, the electoral campaign and the methods of election lie outside the scope of a book dealing with the practice and working methods of those assemblies. It is necessary however to advert briefly to the procedure by which vacancies in Congress and Parliament, whether arising from resignation, death or other cause, are filled, to the manner in which disputes arising from elections are settled and to the exclusion or expulsion of members, because these two matters touch the powers of the Houses concerned over their constitution.

Vacancies

In Congress the filling of vacancies in both the House of Representatives and the Senate is regulated by the Constitution. If a vacancy occurs in the House, the executive authority of the state whose representation is affected is required to issue a writ for an election to fill the vacancy. In practice the state governor may either call a by-election (special election) or, if Congress is well

1. House of Commons Paper 34 of 1966–67, Report paragraph 48.
2. On 4 July 1969 and 16 July 1971.

advanced towards its two-year term, the seat may be left vacant. This is within the governor's discretion: no time-limit is laid down in the Constitution, though he would be open to criticism if the seat were left vacant for too long.

For the Senate the requirements are different. The Constitution authorizes the executive authority to issue a writ for an election to fill a vacancy, in the same way as for the House of Representatives. But it also authorizes the state legislature to empower the state governor to make temporary appointments until the next election that the legislature may direct (in practice it is the next scheduled election). Most states have given this authority to the state governor who does not exclude political considerations in making his appointments. For example, after the assassination in June 1968 of Robert Kennedy, elected Democratic Senator for New York State in 1966, the Republican state governor of New York, Mr Nelson Rockefeller, who had been duly authorized by the state legislature of New York, appointed Republican Congressman Charles Goodell, then representing the 38th District of New York in the House of Representatives, to fill the vacancy created by Senator Kennedy's death. In making this appointment Governor Rockefeller fulfilled the requirements of the law. An appointment is made provided that the outstanding period of the term is not more than two years. On this occasion there would not have been enough time to nominate a person for election and complete the electoral process, and still leave two years to be served. In the House of Representatives Congressman Goodell's seat was left vacant, as 1968 was an election year. Thus as the direct result of an appointment by the state governor, the overall Democratic majority in the Senate was reduced by two, while the Republican minority in the House lost one of its members.

Both for the House and the Senate local considerations thus bulk large in the procedure for filling vacancies. In Britain the House of Commons retains control over the filling of casual vacancies. The most usual reasons for a vacancy are death, elevation to a peerage (membership of the other House) or resignation by appointment to the Chiltern Hundreds or the Manor of Northstead. If a vacancy occurs, the House on motion orders the Speaker to set in train the process of issuing a writ authorizing a fresh election to fill the vacancy.

This motion is customarily moved by the Chief Whip of the party to which the member whose seat is vacated belonged. It is the usual practice for that party to choose the moment most politically favourable to its interest, provided that the constituency is not left unrepresented for too long. On occasion, however, delay has been criticized as unreasonable, and bills have been introduced to limit it, though none has passed into law. A recent example, in the session of 1969–70, would have set a limit of four months. In fact, however, under the existing law members can ensure that in most instances vacancies are filled in due time, if need be against the wishes of the political party chiefly concerned. For during a recess or an adjournment the Speaker is required by statute[1] to set in train the electoral process if he receives from any two members of the House a certificate specifying the cause of the vacancy. He must then insert a notice in the *London Gazette* and six days later cause the writ for a fresh election to be issued. Since recesses or adjournments occur at regular intervals (Christmas, Easter, Whitsuntide and summer), there is no reason why most vacancies need to be prolonged. Except where the vacating member has resigned or in the rarer case of lunacy (specific statutory exemptions), any two members of the House can by this means secure that the electoral process for filling a vacancy is set in train.

In the House of Lords a hereditary peer on death (or disqualification) is succeeded by his eldest son.[2] On the spiritual side, if one of the sees of Canterbury, York, Durham or Winchester becomes void, the vacancy is filled by the issue of a writ of summons to the bishop appointed to that see. To fill a vacancy caused by the voiding of any other see, a writ of summons is sent to the next senior bishop, that is, the longest serving among the bishops not in the House.

Disputed Returns

In 1604 the House of Commons established its right to decide cases in which the election returns of its members are disputed.

1. The Recess Elections Act 1784 as amended by the Elections in Recess Act 1863.
2. Since there is no limit to the number of life peerages, appointments to them are in no way related to the death of individual life peers.

In that year, as a step in its struggle for independence, it successfully asserted its sole and exclusive jurisdiction against the attempt by the Crown to confer that jurisdiction on the Court of Chancery. Having won this battle, the House remitted cases of disputed returns at first to a committee on privileges and elections, later to the Committee of the whole House, and finally from 1770, to a select committee. But on a subject so close to the sensitivities of contending factions, it proved impossible to secure an objective form of inquiry into the merits of the disputes. In 1868 the House frankly recognized its own impotence. The Parliamentary Elections Act of that year transferred the jurisdiction to the High Court. Since that date election petitions alleging irregularity have to be considered not by the House of Commons but by two judges of the High Court. The judges report their findings to the Speaker who lays their report before the House. If they decide that a candidate other than the sitting member was duly elected, the House makes the necessary order to give effect to that decision. Over the last hundred years this method of inquiry and decision has proved satisfactory.

Mindful of the need of an assembly to have ultimate control of its own composition, the Founding Fathers wrote into the Constitution the jurisdiction which the House of Commons had asserted for itself under James I. 'Each House' says Article I (3) 'shall be the judge of the elections, returns and qualifications of its own members'. This clear statement of authority has been the ground for several consequential decisions by both the Houses of Congress. For example the House of Representatives has decided that it is debarred from handing over its jurisdiction—as the House of Commons has done—to another tribunal. The House of Representatives has also asserted its right to investigate relevant electoral activity under state law. As state law largely governs the election of both senators and representatives, this assertion was essential to make the House's jurisdiction effective. The House has held that the certificate of election issued by an official of a state in strict accordance with state law does not prevent the House investigating the voting and reversing the return.[1]

Elections resulting in disputes are not uncommon in the United States. In most Congresses there are a few cases, initiated either

1. *House Rules and Manual* (1971), para. 47.

by an aggrieved elector in the district or state concerned or on the motion of a senator or representative. They are referred in the Senate to its Committee on Rules and Administration and in the House of Representatives to its Committee on House Administration. The results of their inquiries are reported to the parent House which as a rule accepts them and takes any necessary action. In the last half of the nineteenth century, the flagrant partisanship brought to the settlement of the results of disputed elections became a public scandal. Congress, however, responded to the volume of criticism, and since World War I the arbitration by committees of these disputes has proved acceptable and effective.

Thus the two Houses of Congress for constitutional reasons proceed differently from the House of Commons on disputed elections. But although its jurisdiction over disputed elections has passed to the courts, the House of Commons—like the Houses of Congress—has retained its rights over the qualifications of its members arising from other causes. In 1950 for instance it appointed a select committee to consider whether the election of a priest of the Church of Ireland was valid under the existing law governing disqualification.[1]

Expulsion and Exclusion

The House of Commons also has the right to discipline and if necessary to expel a member whom it thinks unfit. The House of Lords on the other hand cannot exclude a member of the House permanently by its resolution as a legislative body.[2] Here again the Constitution of the United States is specific: each House of Congress is given the power to punish and expel,[3] though a majority of two-thirds of the votes cast is specified for the expulsion of a member.

In neither country does the expulsion of a member create a disqualification: his constituents may decide to return him at the next opportunity. The case of John Wilkes established this pro-

1. The Select Committee was unable to make up its mind. The House, after taking advice from the Judicial Committee of the Privy Council, decided that the election was void.

2. Acting in its judicial capacity, if one of its members were impeached, the House of Lords can create a permanent disqualification unless overruled by the Crown's prerogative or pardon.

3. Article I, 5.

position beyond further argument in Britain. Expelled by the Commons in 1764 for publishing a 'false, scandalous and seditious libel' against ministers of the Crown, he was returned at the next general election in 1768 and again expelled. He was subsequently re-elected for the same seat on three occasions, each time the same House of Commons declaring him ineligible and refusing to seat him. In 1782 the Commons gave in. They ordered the resolution of 1769 declaring him 'incapable of being elected a member to serve in this present Parliament' to be expunged from the Commons Journal as 'subversive of the rights of the whole body of electors'. Exactly a hundred years later the Commons remembered this experience. When Charles Bradlaugh was expelled from the House in 1882—one of a series of incidents in his dispute with the Commons over the taking of the oath—and he was immediately returned by the electors of Northampton, no question was raised about the validity of his return.

The case of Powell v. McCormack has lately raised similar issues in the United States. During the 89th Congress (1965–66) a committee of the House of Representatives inquired into expenditure incurred by its Committee on Education and Labour, of which Congressman Adam Clayton Powell was chairman. The report of the inquiry concluded that the chairman (and others) had deceived the House authorities about their travelling expenses. In November 1966 Powell was re-elected for the 18th Congressional District of New York. But when the 90th Congress (1967–68) met in January 1967, the administration of the oath to Powell was deferred, and another committee of inquiry was appointed. Eventually in March 1967 the House voted to exclude Powell from the Congress and to notify the governor of New York that the seat was vacant. On 11 April Powell was re-elected to the House of Representatives at a special election called to fill the seat. But as he had already initiated action in the courts, he did not again present himself to the House or seek to take the oath. After much litigation the Supreme Court finally ruled that Powell had been unlawfully excluded from the 90th Congress.[1]

Erskine May described the Commons action in the Wilkes case as 'an excess of their jurisdiction . . . for one House of Parliament cannot create a disability unknown to the law'.[2] In deciding that

1. Judgement given on 16 June 1969.
2. Erskine May, 13th ed. (1924), p. 67.

Powell should not have been excluded, the Supreme Court cited Alexander Hamilton's words 'that the people should choose whom they please to represent them'. Both legislatures have learnt by hard experience that they are without power to exclude members-elect who meet the constitutional requirements for membership.

CONFLICTS OF INTEREST

It sometimes happens that a member's personal financial interest may run counter to his public duty. Techniques for policing conflicts of interest vary according to the nature of the public office. In an organization where each person is directly answerable to and overseen by another, the direct lines of responsibility simplify the problem. But this is not the position of a member of a legislative assembly. To resolve conflicts of interest which he may have, most western Parliaments have relied either on a code of conduct which he is expected to apply himself or have required him to declare when he has a personal financial interest which may influence him.

Historically the rules in Parliament and Congress regarding the financial interests of members have been remarkably similar. In the House of Commons no member who has a direct, financial interest in a matter is allowed to vote on that matter when it comes before the House. But to be enough to debar him from voting, that interest must be direct and personal, not the interest of a class to which he belongs or a matter of state policy. Members may, for example, vote on their own salaries, a farmer-member may vote on farming subsidies or a doctor-member on improved salaries in the national health service. In practice, on matters of public policy there is no obligation on British members to refrain from voting.[1] The House of Lords have no specific rule as in the Commons. Peers speak and vote 'on their honour'. In practice, however, the approach of the two Houses to questions of direct, personal and financial interest is much the same.

The basic ruling on what constitutes a financial interest for purposes of voting was given to the House of Commons by

1. This was the conclusion of the Select Committee on Members' Interests (Declaration), House of Commons Paper 57 of 1969–70, paras. 26 to 28.

Mr Speaker Abbot in 1811. Abbot referred to the practice as having been established two hundred years before and then spoken of as an ancient practice.[1] It is not surprising, therefore, to find Jefferson writing in his Manual (1797–1801) that 'where [a private] interest has appeared, [a member's] voice has been disallowed even after a division' and describing it as 'a rule of immemorial observance'.[2] The House of Representatives adopted a specific rule in this sense during the first Congress (1789), and it has since been interpreted in much the same way as Speaker Abbot's ruling in the House of Commons; that is, the interest must affect the member personally and not as one of a class.[3] The Senate's rule is different. A senator is required to vote for or against a question, even with a conflict of interest, unless he is specifically excused by the Senate.[4]

The only difference historically in the British and American traditions is that in both Houses of Parliament there has grown up a practice that a personal interest should be frankly avowed during a debate. In Congress there is no such practice. It is not easy to say how the British practice of declaring an interest during debate originated. It is a relatively modern practice: as a behaviour invariably expected of members, it is a development of the twentieth century.[5] This is a purely verbal declaration, to be made when appropriate by the member in debate. It is true that written declarations of interest are also known at Westminster, but they are made only by members of committees, which are to consider an opposed private bill (see p. 225). Here members arbitrate on petitions for and against the granting of special powers, and it is thought right that they should establish before the committee sits that they have no local or personal interest. In the public sphere there is no requirement of this sort.

The rules and practices handed down to the Congresses and Parliaments of the 1960s were general and imprecise. In that decade both legislatures were obliged by particular circumstances and events to consider whether those rules and practices were

1. Parliamentary Debates (1811), 20 cc. 1001–12.
2. *House Rules and Manual* (1971), para. 376.
3. House Rule VIII and para. 659.
4. Senate Rule XII.
5. See Report of Select Committee on Members' Interests (Declaration), House of Commons Paper 57 of 1969–70, Appendix XXV.

exacting enough to ensure or maintain the proper ethical standards of their membership. Both appointed select committees to inquire and report on these matters. But the reasons for appointing them were different. In setting up a select committee on members' interests in May 1969 the House of Commons was concerned with the growing tendency by public relations and other bodies to employ members of Parliament for a salary or a fee to represent pressure groups at home or overseas, sometimes without their fellow members being aware of these interests. One specific connection of this kind had recently come to light which, taken with a number of earlier incidents involving benefits in kind from foreign governments, seemed to the House to warrant an inquiry not into cases of individual misconduct but into the general principles and practices which ought to govern the *declaration* of an interest. In the United States, by contrast, a select committee was appointed by the Senate in 1964 and a standing (legislative) committee by the House of Representatives in 1968 in the wake of widespread public criticism[1] of alleged unethical activities by several members and employees of Congress. There had also been prolonged congressional inquiries into three highly publicized cases, namely, the case of the Secretary for the Majority who resigned in 1963 after a civil suit had been filed charging him with using his influence to obtain contracts in defence plants for one of several firms in which he had an interest; the case of a senator who was censured by the Senate in 1967 for the misuse of political funds; and the case of a member-elect of the House of Representatives who was excluded in 1967 from the House for misusing committee funds and abusing the rules governing the employment of House staff.

Before the inference is drawn that congressmen, as compared with their British opposite numbers, are born with more than their due allotment of original sin, note has to be taken of the constitutional framework in which members conduct themselves in Parliament and in Congress. Many of the basic legal provisions are similar in both countries. In Britain the acceptance by any member of either House of a bribe to influence him in his conduct as a member or of any fee, compensation or reward in connection with a bill, resolution or other matter coming before

1. See for example, Drew Pearson and Jack Anderson, *The Case Against Congress* (1968).

either House or one of its committees has for centuries been treated as a contempt.[1] Analogous provisions for congressmen are laid down in statute law and read as follows:

> Whoever . . . directly or indirectly receives or agrees to receive, or asks, demands, solicits, or seeks, any compensation for any services rendered or to be rendered either by himself or another
> (1) at a time when he is a member of Congress . . . or
> (2) at a time when he is an officer or employee of the United States in the . . . legislative . . . branch of the government . . .
> in relation to any proceedings, application, request for a ruling or other determination, contract, claim, controversy, charge, accusation, arrest, or other particular matter in which the United States is a party or has a direct and substantial interest, before any department, agency, court-martial, officer, or any civil, military, or naval commission . . . shall be fined not more than $10,000 or imprisoned for not more than two years or both; and shall be incapable of holding any office of honor, trust, or profit under the United States.[2]

Nevertheless there are broader constitutional differences, the effect of which is to give greater protection to the British member. The financial initiative within Parliament resides in the House of Commons. That House works under a standing order, now over 250 years old, that no petition for any sum relating to the public service and no grant or charge upon the public revenue is to be proceeded with unless recommended by the Crown. This is straightaway a large limitation on the power of a member to confer some financial benefit on a constituent or other person. The reasons for the adoption by the House of Commons of this self-denying ordinance are discussed later (pp. 309–10). Its effect is to leave the initiation of all proceedings on public grants and charges in the hand of ministers who dispose of the Crown's recommendation in financial matters. Ministers themselves operate under a strict code of conduct drawn up and reviewed from time to time by successive Prime Ministers. A minister must so order his affairs that 'no conflict arises, or appears to arise, between [his] private interests and [his] public duties'.[3]

1. Erskine May, 18th ed. (1971), p. 138.
2. U.S. Code: 203(a).
3. The most recent guidance was published in 1952. See House of Commons Debates (1951–52) 496, cc. 701–3.

Specifically he is required, on assuming office, to resign director-ships, whether paid or honorary; to divest himself of a controlling, or even a non-controlling holding of shares, if there is any danger of a conflict of interest; and to avoid scrupulously speculative investments in securities about which he has, or may be thought to have, early or confidential information likely to affect the prices of those securities. Ministers are advised by a civil service bred in a long tradition of impartiality and incorruptibility. These two traditions of discipline come together in every ministerial recommendation for expenditure or taxation, and in the framing of every bill initiated by the cabinet. These constitutional arrange-ments have gone far to eliminate corruption from public life in Britain. In this context the repeal by Parliament in 1957 of the existing legislation, disqualifying a member of the Commons on his becoming a public contractor, should be noted. It made this provision in the House of Commons Disqualification Act 1957 after a committee had ascertained that there had been no corrup-tion found affecting members of the House in this field for more than a hundred years.

A congressman does not enjoy this protection. The standing order under which the House of Commons operates is not apt for the composition and legislative function of Congress. There are no ministers in Congress. Nor does the right to initiate a bill or a grant of money belong to them. That right is vested in each individual member of Congress. No guidance was given to congressmen in either the Constitution or in Jefferson's Manual on a congressman's relationship with the departments and agen-cies of the executive power or with members of the public. Until 1968 his actions were bounded only by the provisions of the criminal code and by the unwritten rules of good behaviour. Yet with less constitutional protection than his British counter-part, he is exposed to much greater pressure. The working of the 'locality rule', with its remorseless expectations of, and demands for, local and state advantage tends to make politics much more a matter of business negotiation than in Britain, where a member is freer to concentrate upon national issues. Moreover congressmen, especially in the House of Representa-tives, are above all specialists in the particular fields of govern-ment to which their legislative committee assignments have led them. To that extent it is easier than at Westminster for the

interested pressure groups to pinpoint the particular congressman who could exert a crucial influence on a bill or resolution.
It is also easier for such a congressman to exert influence on the
action of the departments or agencies to which his committee
assignment relates. The perils inherent in the position of a congressman have been well summed up by George Galloway:

> The mere fact of being a member of Congress bestows upon the
> individual a measure of power that probably is unmatched in any
> other sphere of public or private life. The temptations and the induce-
> ments are almost incalculable. With the minimum exertion and
> hardly any risk of censure a member can bring tremendous pressure
> to get a contract awarded to a favourite firm, to win approval of a
> government loan . . . to squeeze concessions out of regulatory agencies
> or to affect the course of countless administrative decisions that may
> spell fortune or disaster for various interested citizens.[1]

The constitutional differences in the status and functions of
members of Congress and Parliament have largely directed the
search in the two countries for a solution of these problems. Both
Houses of Congress took action in 1968. The Senate had appointed a Select Committee on Standards and Conduct in 1964
—comprising three members of the majority and three of the
minority—to draw guidelines for ethical conduct and investigate
cases of misconduct. At the instance of this Committee the Senate
in March 1968 adopted two new rules of conduct for its members
and officers. The first regulates the acceptance of contributions
from individuals or organizations for political campaigns, and
requires the disclosure of any gift of more than 50 dollars. The
second deals with the personal finances of each senator and
officer.[2] He is required to disclose for public inspection every
honorarium of more than 300 dollars, and to show both its value
and source. In addition, he must file annually with the U.S.
Comptroller General a sealed envelope containing a copy of his
income tax return, or that of himself and his wife jointly, and
further information about specific fees, interests in property
and trusts and liabilities over stated levels. This information
remains confidential unless the Senate Select Committee on

1. *The Legislative Process In Congress* (1955), p. 389.
2. Senate Rules XLIII and XLIV.

Standards and Conduct decides to send for it as part of an investigation.

In the same month the House of Representatives adopted two new rules, the first setting out a code of official conduct with eight stipulations and the second requiring a two-part disclosure of certain financial interests.

Among the eight points covered in the code of official conduct are a general requirement for conduct which is to reflect creditably on the House of Representatives and adherence to the spirit and letter of the rules of the House; specific requirements with respect to honoraria, campaign funds and the employment of staff; prohibitions against the direct or indirect receipt of gifts of substantial value from persons having an interest in legislation before the Congress; and a reaffirmation of the ban against conflict of interest. The rule requiring financial disclosure was then adopted in order to monitor the conflicts of interest. Under this rule a member is required to disclose for public inspection any business holding which he owns worth 5,000 dollars or more, or from which he receives annual income of 1,000 dollars if that holding is one that does 'substantial business with the government or is regulated by the government'. In addition a member must list sources of certain items of income which may be relevant to a conflict of interest. But the exact amounts, which above a stated, minimum level have to be filed with the House Committee on Standards of Official Conduct, remain confidential in sealed envelopes unless the Committee decides to examine them as part of an investigation into the conduct of a member. This Committee, comprising six members of the majority and six of the minority, was set up by the House as a permanent legislative committee to police the observation of the code, to recommend improvements as required, to receive members' statements of financial interests and to give advice to members, on request, on the propriety of current or proposed conduct.[1]

Declarations of interest by members of both Houses of Congress under the new rules were made for the first time in 1969 and published in the *Congressional Quarterly* of 23 May 1969. But pressure for a greater degree of disclosure has continued.

1. A convenient summary of Congress's rules and practice is given in the Report of the U.K. Select Committee on Members' Interests (Declaration), House of Commons Paper 57 of 1969–70, App. XXIV.

In the Senate a move by Senators Case and Clark in 1969 to require detailed public disclosure of the full range of the assets, liabilities and business relationships of members and officers of the two Houses was defeated by the narrow majority of forty-four votes to forty. Bills to give effect to the senators' proposals have since been introduced in both Houses of Congress. In March 1970 the House's Committee on Standards of Official Conduct itself proposed to strengthen the rules by requiring, in addition to the material already published, the annual publication by each member of the sources of all honoraria of 300 dollars or more and the identity of creditors to whom 10,000 dollars or more was owed for ninety days or longer without the pledge of specific security. The Committee made this recommendation after reviewing the working of the House's resolution of 1968 requiring a measure of disclosure. At the same time it set its face against the principle of total disclosure, contending that disclosure should be confined to areas in which it was reasonably possible for a member's private interest to conflict with his public duties and need not extend to every financial detail about a member and his family or associations, much of which would be irrelevant to those duties. The Committee's recommendations were accepted by the House.

The same approach to disclosure is found in the report of the House of Commons Select Committee on Members' Interests (Declaration).[1] Here again both views were expressed. One member of the committee took his stand on the principle of total disclosure. Membership of Parliament, he argued, implied a deliberate choice 'to live in a glass bowl'; a member could no longer expect the same degree of privacy as a private citizen. What was needed was a full declaration to enable the House and the public to judge how far a particular outside interest might influence his action as a member on any issue that might come up. He thought the most convenient method of registering this information was to publish tax returns of Members of Parliament. The other eight members of the Committee disagreed. They believed that the object of a member's declaring a financial interest was to inform other members and the public if it touched an issue

1. The report of the House of Representatives Committee No. 91–938, pp. 2–3, cites with approval a key passage in the Commons Committee's report.

which was currently the subject of a member's speech or action. They objected to most kinds of public register of financial interest because much more information would be exposed to view than was relevant to a member's discharge of his duty as a member. They preferred to rely on the code of conduct which over the centuries the House had laid down in the form of various resolutions and conventions. This they thought more appropriate to the constitutional function of a British member than the more elaborate and strict rules of conduct governing the conduct of ministers and others at national and local levels with executive responsibilities.

The Select Committee did, however, recommend that the traditional code of conduct should be strengthened. That code has two chief elements: the first (already described), which affects all members, is that any relevant personal, financial interest should be declared in the course of debate; the second, which affects fewer members, that nobody should advocate in the House any measure in connection with which he may have acted professionally for a fee or reward. The Select Committee proposed that both parts of the code should be clarified and extended. They recommended that the declaration of interest, hitherto restricted to debate in the House or in its committees, should extend to *any* transaction or communication that one member might have with another or with a minister or a civil servant; also that 'benefits of whatever nature' should be disclosed, a phrase designed to cover journeys abroad and benefits received overseas. They further recommended that the prohibition on advocacy, which had hitherto seemed to apply only to barristers, should now extend to *any* member taking a 'fee, payment, retainer or reward, direct or indirect'. In recommending this stiffer code of conduct, the Select Committee expressed the view that a serious breach should be treated as a contempt of the House.

Lobbies and Pressure Groups

Perhaps because of the constitutional differences just described, Parliament, unlike Congress, has no machinery for checking upon the many organizations, firms and companies which seek to press their interests with members. The House of Commons committee on the declaration of members' interests took the view that the activity of lobbyists was outside their terms of reference except to the extent that the personal, pecuniary interests of members were involved. Its recommendations did not touch the problem of how the lobbyists, who seek with increasing skill to penetrate most Parliaments, should be controlled.

Congress grappled with this problem in the Federal Regulation of Lobbying Act 1946. It laid down that any person who directly or indirectly solicits, collects or receives money 'to be used principally' to aid or influence the passage of legislation in Congress must formally register this activity with the Clerk of the House and the Secretary of the Senate. Registration means the lodging of full details about the employer or interest that he represents and the benefits he is obtaining. Once registered, he has to report quarterly on how the money received by him for this work has been spent, to whom and for what purpose it was paid, the legislation that he is supporting or opposing, and the names of any publications in which he has caused material to be published. Finally the name and address of any person who has contributed more than 500 dollars or has been paid more than ten dollars for the relevant purposes must be included in the report. All this information is open to public inspection.

The weakness in this machinery was pin-pointed by the Joint Committee on the Organization of Congress 1965–66 which reviewed the working of the Act of 1946. It was that the phrase 'to be used principally' had been interpreted in a manner exempting altogether many organizations with obvious legislative interests. This had certainly not been the intention of Congress in passing the Act of 1946. The most recent move to close this loophole has been by the House of Representatives. In May 1970 it empowered its Committee on Standards of Official Conduct to conduct inquiries from time to time into the 'laws, rules, regulations, procedures, practices and activities' of lobbyists in order to help Congress to frame the necessary remedial legislation.[1]

SALARIES AND REMUNERATION

Few contrasts between Parliament and Congress are more striking or more frequently made than of the salaries paid to their

1. House Resolution 1031 of 1970.

members. The bare figures, as they have increased over the years, are instructive.

In the early Congresses members of both Houses received an allowance of six dollars a day, raised to eight dollars in 1817. These payments were consolidated into an annual salary for the first time in 1855. Since that date the salary—which is the same for members of both Houses—has moved as follows:

	Dollars	
1855	3,000	
1865	5,000	
1907	7,500	
1925	10,000	
1946	12,000	(£3,125)
1964	30,000	(£10,720)[1]
1969	42,500	(£17,700)[1]

In Britain before the nineteenth century such payment as a member of the House of Commons received was held to be the responsibility of the constituency that he represented. Many members were lucky if they received anything. Not until 1895 did the House of Commons itself accept the principle that some kind of payment for members ought properly to be a charge on national funds; and not until 1904 was an annual salary paid. From that date the salary has moved as follows:

	£
1904	400
1937	600
1946	1,000
1954	1,000 plus £2 for every sitting day (except Fridays)
1957	1,750
1964	3,250

In 1957 for the first time an expenses allowance was introduced for peers attending the House of Lords. In 1970 peers could draw up to a maximum of £6.50 for each day of attendance in respect of expenses they incurred.

1. These two conversions take account of the devaluations of the £ in 1949 and 1967.

To give a precise evaluation to the figures in this comparison it would be necessary to take account of the extent to which each member is dependent on his official salary, the amount he receives from other, sponsoring sources, the balance between the full-time and the part-time activities of members in each House and the allowances and tax liabilities of each individual member. All these (and other) factors are beyond the scope of this book. For present purposes it is enough to point out that the criteria according to which the salary is fixed have not been the same in both countries. The salary of a member of the House of Commons, in the view of the most recent independent committee on the subject, should be:

> such as to enable a man with no external means to become a member of the House without financial embarrassment but to allow him to discharge the proper expenses of conscientious and efficient membership and to live at a level consistent with the dignity of the service.[1]

The point was put in a different way by the Prime Minister in a debate in 1937:

> The salary [should not be fixed] so high that it becomes an inducement to people to enter the House for the purpose of earning more than they would outside and . . . so low that men or women who could give valuable service to the House should be prevented from doing so merely by the fact that they have not sufficient means to avoid it.[2]

In the United States a different note has been struck. Here the objective has been seen as to enable Congress to compete efficiently with other enterprises in attracting men and women of calibre and ability. In debate in the House of Representatives on the Salary Bill of 1967, which set up a commission to conduct periodic reviews of congressional and other governmental salaries, it was argued:

> If we want a strong federal government, if we want people doing their jobs rather than having hacks and bureaucrats . . . we have to compete with private enterprise.

1. Report of the Committee on the Remuneration of Ministers and Members of Parliament, Command Paper 2516 of November 1964, para. 29.
2. Op. cit., para. 16.

Another congressman defined the objective as 'a fair, reasonable and comparable salary for all who serve the American public'.[1]

Comparability with other salaries may in future figure more prominently in assessing the right salary for the British member. In December 1970 the government decided to refer the salary and emoluments of members and ministers to one of three independent Review Bodies already set up to advise on the remuneration of certain groups for whom ordinary negotiating machinery and procedures were not appropriate. The Review Body in question was one already advising on the remuneration of boards of nationalized industries, the judiciary, senior civil servants and senior officers of the armed forces. Its 'knowledge and experience based on looking at other salaries in the community as a whole' said the government spokesman, would make it 'better placed than any specially constituted body to study this difficult question. . .'[2]

A bare statement of the salary of a Commons member ignores the fact that something like one-eighth of the total membership are paid salaries higher than £3,250. As ministers of varying grades of importance they receive salaries ranging from £3,000 to £8,500 a year (or £14,000 if the Prime Minister is included). Whatever his grade a minister does not receive a salary as a member of Parliament in addition to his salary as a minister, but he does receive an extra £1,250, so that the effective range of ministerial salary is from £4,250 to £9,750 (or £15,250).[3] This is also true of the three members who are officers of the House of Commons—Speaker, Chairman of Ways and Means and Deputy Chairman—as well as of the Leader of the Opposition and the Opposition Chief Whip. The effect of these salaries is markedly to raise the *average* salary paid to a member of the House of Commons. In 1970, under the incoming administration this figure was £3,671; in 1969, with more ministers in the previous administration, the figure was £3,757.[4]

1. Congressmen Udall (Dem) and Clausen (Rep), Congressional Record, 11 October 1967, pp. 28642, 28644.

2. House of Commons Debates, 4 December 1970, cc. 1723–4.

3. In the House of Lords ministers, the chairmen of committees and the Leader and Chief Whip of the opposition are entitled to claim reimbursement of expenses, like any other peer, up to £6.50 a day, in addition to their salaries.

4. House of Commons Debates, 21 July 1970, c. 83.

The salary, however, is only part of the picture. A much more significant contrast is found in the staff available to a member of Parliament and to a congressman. Since 1 October 1969 members of the House of Commons have been able to claim an allowance of up to £500 a year for secretarial expenses incurred on parliamentary business. Until that date no specific payment was made from public funds for the staff of members. Any member has been free to employ whom he wishes to help and advise him in his parliamentary duties; and in recent years a possible scheme for research assistance for a few individual members has been ex-explored.[1] But none of this work is paid for out of public funds.[2] Nor is an additional allowance paid to members of the House of Lords for this purpose.

By contrast every member of Congress is entitled to a basic allowance paid by the United States Treasury to enable him to hire staff. The size of the allowance is determined according to a formula which takes into account the scale of his representative function. In the House of Representatives a member who represents fewer than 500,000 people receives an allowance of 140,000 dollars and is entitled to employ up to eleven persons at any one time. A member representing more than 500,000 people (there were 114 in 1970) receives 148,000 dollars and may employ up to twelve persons. Population is also the basis for computing the allowance paid to senators for employing staff. But as a senator represents a whole state, the figures are correspondingly larger. In March 1969 the maximum annual payment to senators for this purpose varied from 217,905 dollars if the population of his state was less than 3,000,000 to 365,165 dollars if the population was more than 17,000,000. Within that total sum a senator may fix the number and rates of compensation of the employees in his office. In practice the staff of senators varies from seven or eight up to more than twenty-five persons. On the staff of a representative one, sometimes two will be of high grade and

---

1. See M. Shaw, Institute for Social Research, Oct. 1964: *Assistants for Members of Parliament*; Anthony Barker and Michael Rush, *The Member of Parliament and his Information* (1970), pp. 326–32.

2. Research assistance for individual members has lately been said by a government spokesman to have a lower priority than the staffing of the House of Commons committees: House of Commons Debates 18 November 1970, c. 1229.

highly paid; on the staff of a senator employing twenty-five persons, two or three will be of this calibre.

This comparison points to one conclusion: it is that senators and congressmen are doing an essentially different job of work from that of their opposite numbers at Westminster. The difference (if the relative scope of the United States and British responsibilities throughout the world is left on one side) is two-fold. The first is a simple difference of scale. It is implicit in the formula according to which the allowances paid to congressmen for staff are calculated. A representative has a responsibility for a population of 450,000 on average. A senator has anything from three million in a small state to upwards of forty million in the largest state. A British member has an average electorate of 62,000 (1970). Even when it is recalled that the American people are represented in a state as well as a national legislature, the difference in scale of representation at national level is still great. The second is a difference of function. An American member plays a continuing part in a governmental exercise. To mention only his law-making duties, he takes part in a range of inquiries and consultations with outside interests and staff of government departments which in Britain would be conducted within the executive organization under ministerial control. These activities will be noticed and contrasted with the British equivalent in subsequent chapters on Committees, on Legislation and on Finance. Here it need only be pointed out that the salary, allowances for staff and other larger allowances and privileges such as those for stationery and franking in some degree reflect this difference of function.

The same difference is apparent in the material facilities made available to congressmen and to members of Parliament. The Senate has two office buildings, the House of Representatives three—all within easy reach of the Capitol and connected to it by private underground railway. These buildings contain suites of two or three rooms in which every congressman can bring together his staff and do his work. It has been different in Parliament. The traditional approach has been that essential business is despatched not in an office but in the debating chamber. An office, and still more an office block separated from the Palace, has been regarded with suspicion as tending to withdraw members from the debating chamber; and an individual telephonic link with the outside world has been resisted lest the public should press too closely and directly upon members of Parliament. Since World War II this approach has been changing. By the end of the 1970s the Commons hope to obtain an office building across the road to the north of the Palace of Westminster. Some idea of the pressure on existing accommodation in the Palace can be gained from the official estimate that at least 400 rooms will be required for members in the new building. This figure was based on the assumption that ministers, chairmen of committees and about 130 other members would have rooms in the Palace itself when the new building is ready and some of the present occupants of the Palace can move into it.[1] It is a measure of the general acceptability of the traditional approach that change has taken, and will take, so long to come about.

1. Report of the Select Committee on House of Commons (Services) House of Commons Paper 295 of 1969, p. 5.

CHAPTER THREE

FIRST CHAMBERS

THE first two chapters of this study have described the links between the electorate and the two legislatures, the political and party organizations and groupings within them and the constitutional setting in which a member of Congress or Parliament goes about his business. Later chapters will consider the way in which Parliament and Congress carry out their functions of making law, controlling finance and overseeing the government. Each of these functions entails the use of committees, and these too are the subject of a chapter. But before these more detailed descriptions, two chapters are interposed describing and contrasting the first and second chambers of each legislature. They deal in particular with the size and seating arrangements of each chamber, the nature of its debates, the basic procedures and practices and the methods of reaching decisions and of voting. Their broad object is to compare the general workings and practices of each pair of chambers, regardless of the type of business under debate at any particular moment. This chapter is primarily devoted to the House of Commons and the House of Representatives, though some of its material will be seen to apply also to the House of Lords and the Senate and will not be repeated in the next chapter which is devoted to those chambers.

SIZE OF CHAMBERS AND SEATING OF MEMBERS

House of Commons

The chamber of the House of Commons has seats for only about two-thirds of its membership.[1] The chamber of no other legislative assembly has been constructed on this principle. Yet the size of the Commons chamber is no mere accident of history or tradition. The chamber built in 1852 had only 437 places for its 658 members (and had between 1918 and 1922 to accommodate

1. The official estimate is that 437 out of 630 members can be seated.

707 members). When the House was destroyed by fire-bomb in 1941, it could easily have been redesigned to provide enough seats for all. The House, however, deliberately chose to stay with the size of the former chamber. More seats were provided for the public and the press, but the area of the floor of the new chamber (a mere 68 feet by 45 feet 6 inches) was the same as before.

The House's decision to work in a room that is, in one sense, too small was born of a conviction that that is best suited to the prevailing style of debate. In a small chamber there is less need for speakers to raise their voices. Debate in consequence tends towards conversation rather than rhetoric. There is an intimacy about the exchanges in the House of Commons that would be difficult to achieve in a larger forum. After the bombing of 1941 the Commons moved into the chamber of the House of Lords until their new chamber was ready for occupation in 1952. The Lords chamber was only 12 feet 9 inches longer than the destroyed Commons chamber. Yet the Commons committee appointed in 1943 to consider the plans for rebuilding recorded their belief that even this slight difference in length had produced a 'noticeable diminution of intimacy'. The committee was closely divided on whether the width of the new House might be increased to accommodate one more bench on either side, but finally they agreed to recommend exactly the same dimensions as in the bombed chamber.[1]

This arrangement makes allowance for a cardinal fact of parliamentary life—that for much of every sitting, most members will be absent from the chamber. Attendance in committees, the demands of constituents, and the need to prepare for future parliamentary business combine to keep many away from the floor of the House. If the chamber had been made large enough to provide a seat for every member, it would for much of the time give an impression of emptiness. As it is, at peak parliamentary hours and at times of tension, the House rapidly over-fills. All the seats on the benches get taken, and members sit on the floor in the gangways between the blocks of seats on either side of the chamber. Other members come in and form a standing crowd at both ends of the rectangular chamber, either facing the Speaker or behind his chair. This pressure, often quick to occur and as quick to

1. Report of the Select Committee on the House of Commons (Rebuilding), House of Commons Paper 109 published in October 1944.

dissipate, adds to the drama of major parliamentary occasions. There is, Churchill once said, a 'sense of crowd and urgency'.

The shape of the chamber is oblong. Five benches with green leather upholstery, broken in the middle by a gangway, rise on steps on either side of the narrow well of the room and stretch nearly the full length of the rectangle. The government and its supporters sit on one side, on the Speaker's right; the opposition sits on his left. On the first or front bench on either side sit, facing each other, the government ministers and the opposition shadow ministers; in the benches behind them sit their supporters (hence a 'frontbencher' has come to mean a member who speaks officially for his party, while a 'backbencher' speaks for himself). There is a strong sense of confrontation.

At one end of the chamber, equidistant from the two front benches, on a throne raised up from the well of the floor, sits the Speaker. He sits, as it were, at right angles to the political contest and on a different plane from it. He alone among the 630 members wears special clothes: a full-bottomed wig and a long black gown over court dress. The effect is to set him apart from the others, to stress his removal from their political activities.

In front of the Speaker sit the Clerk of the House and two assistant clerks, also in wigs and gowns. Stretching out before them is the book-strewn table of the House that separates the two front benches and invites their occupants to put their feet up while leaning back in their seats. The table is an extension of the Speaker's neutrality, and perhaps it has another function: Disraeli was once led to give public thanks for the substantial piece of furniture that kept him at a safe distance from Gladstone's fury. At the end of the table, farthest from the Speaker, rests the mace (see also p. 49) on two brackets; when the House goes into committee, the mace is placed on other brackets below the level of the table. The mace's custodian, the Serjeant at Arms, sits at the opposite end of the chamber from the Speaker.

On each side of the table, near the end further from the Speaker, are the two despatch boxes. These heavy metal-bound boxes are the two focal points of this debating chamber, symbolizing Her Majesty's Government and Her Majesty's Opposition. Rising from the front benches, the leading spokesmen address the House standing at the despatch boxes and resting their notes on them. All other members speak from where they happen to be sitting. The layout and furniture of the chamber thus provide the setting for the dialogue between ministers and members which is the core of debate in the House of Commons.

House of Representatives

The chamber of the House of Representatives is, like the Commons House, oblong in shape. But it is much larger: it measures 139 feet by 92 feet, and is therefore about four times the area of the Commons chamber. The larger size has had its effect on debate. Members frequently address the House, not from where they are sitting, but from one of two lecterns set on either side of the reporter's table in the well of the chamber. The reason is that despite recent improvements in the amplifying system members have a better chance of being heard if they speak facing their audience from lecterns close to a microphone. Perhaps for the same reason the presiding officer, unlike his counterpart at Westminster, uses a gavel to reinforce his appeals for order.

The layout of the chamber is also different from the Commons. The Speaker's rostrum is set against the wall in the centre of one of the long sides of the rectangle. From this centre-piece eight rows of seats are drawn round in semi-circles, with the vestiges of a ninth and tenth row behind them. The semi-circles are split into six segments, with aisles radiating from the centre like spokes in a wheel. The centre aisle is known as the line of division. There are 444 seats—much the same as in the House of Commons, but here available for 435 members only. The rostrum is occupied by the Speaker. One step lower than his seat sit the Parliamentarian and the Serjeant at Arms, on his right, and the Clerk of the House to his left. Other assistants, including the Journal Clerk, Tally Clerk, Reading Clerk and Time Keeper, sit just in front of the Speaker's dais. In front of the rostrum is a table at which the official reporters of debate sit to take a record of debates. In the House of Commons the reporters can work from the gallery above the Speaker's chair, but in the larger House of Representatives a place on the floor, closer to the speakers, is necessary to achieve accuracy; even so, the reporters may need to move up close to a speaker when necessary. Behind the semi-circular rows of seats, there is a space where members and officials can perambulate and smoke.

The House of Representatives first occupied its chamber in the Capitol in 1807. It was burned by the British in 1814, entirely reconstructed and subsequently much expanded. It has to be large enough to accommodate both representatives and senators at the joint meetings and sessions which are always held in the House. The present chamber was first occupied by the House in 1857 when its total membership was 237. It remains large enough today to accommodate the full membership because in 1913, when the total had already reached 435, the individual desks for members were removed. Now the only facility of this kind is provided by the four tables in the third row from the front.[1] At these tables traditionally sit the party leaders or their representatives, and the members in charge of the business which the House is considering. Microphones are available at the tables, so that many of the leading speeches are made from there.

Members do not have individual seats assigned to them, but Democrats sit in the seats on the right-hand side (viewed from the presiding officer's chair) while Republicans sit on the left. Members of the majority party are entitled to sit on, as it were, the 'wrong' side of the line of division to the extent necessary to accommodate all of them; usually however this is unnecessary, since the attendance is not so great as to warrant it. While the House of Representatives does not share with the House of Commons the occasional problem of over-crowding, it often, like that House, gives an impression of under-occupation, and for the same reasons. As interest in the debate increases, the tendency is for the chamber to fill up from the front.

Contrasts

In both first chambers, then, members are seated in a particular area appropriated by custom to their party. In both, members do not have the right to a particular seat; within the part of the room appropriated to their party, they may in general sit where they like. In the House of Commons convention restrains them from sitting on either of the front benches unless invited by their party leadership; and in the House of Representatives the seats at the tables in the third row back are, as

1. Each table takes up the space of three or more seats. They are placed on either side of where the second and fourth aisles transect the third row of seats.

mentioned above, reserved for the party leaders and the members in charge of business. In neither House may a member reserve a seat for a debate, though in the House of Commons a member may reserve a place for the prayers which precede each day's sitting, and custom allows him to continue to occupy the same seat for the rest of the day. (This not unnaturally has had the effect of encouraging far more members to pray on the day of an important debate than on another; which is perhaps as it ought to be.)

The House of Representatives provides, as the House of Commons does not, for distinguished visitors to address it from the rostrum. There is for example the joint session[1] of Congress at which the President delivers his message on the State of the Union. The Speaker presides, the Vice-President sits on his right hand and the first three rows of seats are reserved for senators. The President is escorted to the rostrum by a small committee of each House and addresses the joint session from there. When the House of Representatives decides by resolution to receive other distinguished visitors or guests of honour, they too address the House from the Clerk's desk. In the House of Commons by contrast visitors, however distinguished, are seated in one of the galleries. When President Nixon visited the House of Commons in 1969 he sat in a special gallery, below the ordinary public galleries and slightly above the level of the floor, facing the Speaker. Many members on the floor were outside his field of vision there, and he of theirs.

Longstanding tradition dictates that no notice is taken in debate in the Commons of what is happening in the galleries or who is sitting there. Since 1933 the House of Representatives has had a similar rule.[2] But its willingness to receive, and be addressed by, distinguished strangers, suggests a less sacred attitude towards 'the floor' than in the House of Commons. So too does the permission given to members and officials to perambulate and smoke in the area behind the semi-circular rows of seats, and to cabinet ministers and former members to come on to the floor of the chamber. Representatives with young children are also sometimes permitted to bring them on to the floor.

1. Any other occasion on which distinguished visitors address the Congress is referred to as a joint *meeting*.
2. Rule XIV, 8.

In practice it is easier for members of the Commons to ignore the public galleries. Inclining towards the chair to address the House, they see the public galleries only from the corner of their eye. In the House of Representatives, the great floor area, the semi-circular seating, and the public galleries on all four sides of the chamber, make members more aware that they are not the only people present.

A DAY'S SITTING AND REPORTS OF DEBATES

Before going more deeply into the working of both Houses it is perhaps convenient at this point to draw in brief outline the pattern of a day's sitting in each case. The House of Representatives' normal working week is from Monday to Thursday, but it occasionally sits on Friday as well. A typical day's sitting begins at 12 noon; there is no provision for terminating the sitting at a given hour. After prayers have been said, members are able to make brief speeches of up to one minute in length. These may be concerned with such things as the member's views on an affair of state, or may relate to some matter affecting his constituency; they may refer to business coming before the House at a later stage, or correct the record of what has happened before; they may be used for the purpose of seeking permission to insert extraneous matter in the Congressional Record. Members may also take this opportunity to seek unanimous consent to a proposal about the future of a piece of business.

When these mainly routine items have been disposed of, the House proceeds with the consideration of legislation. This is likely to take up the main part of the sitting, and may be interrupted by the usual devices of opposition—quorum calls, parliamentary inquiries to the Speaker on matters of procedure and order, and requests for roll-call votes.

At the conclusion of the legislative business for the day, members who have previously been granted a special order for the purpose by unanimous consent raise matters for the period of time specified in the order. These special order speeches may relate to any matter, and provide the opportunity for members to publicize their views on national or local issues. There may well be a number of special orders on each day, and some of them may last for an hour or half an hour each; they are on the whole a series of unilateral statements.

With the completion of the special order speeches and any other formal business, the House adjourns. An average hour of adjournment is 6.30 p.m.

The sequence of a day's business in the House of Commons is not dissimilar, though the time span is very different. The normal sitting week runs from Monday to Friday. After prayers at 2.30 p.m. (11 a.m. on Friday) the first major business is (except on Fridays) Question Hour, in which a number of points are dealt with briefly. There follow any statements by ministers on matters of public policy, and on Tuesdays and Wednesdays private members can at this time introduce new bills under the ten-minute rule (see page 268). The main business of the day then follows. At the end of it, usually around 10 p.m., there may be debates on rules and instruments made by the government under powers delegated by Parliament. The day's sitting ends with the half-hour adjournment debate, in which a member raises some matter of importance to himself, and hears a reply to it from a minister. An average hour for the rising of the House is around midnight (Fridays, 4.30 p.m.).

In both Houses an official report of the day's debates is published on the following morning, as is the case too in the House of Lords and the Senate. In Britain the report is colloquially known as Hansard—the name of a family of printers and publishers associated with parliamentary papers throughout the nineteenth century. Each day's Hansard includes, in addition to a transcription of the previous day's debates, the answers to parliamentary Questions which had been put down for written reply. The report breaks off at about 10 p.m.; the report of debates continuing after that hour is bound up with the following day's publication. A Hansard is also published of the proceedings in Standing Committees. In each House of Parliament there is an Editor of the Official Report. A member may make verbal alterations to the published report only if, in the opinion of the Editor, these do not substantially alter the meaning of anything said in the House.

In Congress the daily Congressional Record reports the debates in the House of Representatives and in the Senate. In addition it incorporates other material. At the back it prints a Daily Digest, a brief report of proceedings in each House and in their committees, including a note about the programme for the next day's business. A considerable part of the Record is taken up with Extensions of Remarks—an Appendix containing material, often taken from local or national newspapers, which members wish to draw to the attention of their fellow-congressmen or the public at large. Furthermore the report of the day's debate is not confined to what is said by members; it is permitted for members to incorporate in the report of their speech matter which, for reasons of time or otherwise, they did not include in their speech. It is not therefore possible for the reader of the Record to know how much of it was spoken in the debate. There is an added possibility of confusion. Members of the House of Representatives who address the House under the one-minute rule often wish to enlarge their remarks in the Record. If the extension is less than 300 words, it appears in the Record at the place where it might be expected—the place corresponding to the moment during the sitting when the speech was made. But if the extension is more than 300 words, it and the speech itself are printed, not in the record of the debate, but in the Extensions of Remarks.

A Member of Congress is allowed a wide discretion to alter the reporters' record of his speech before it is printed. He is permitted to strike out any portion of it, or omit it in its entirety if so wished—provided that in doing so he does not place a different aspect on the remarks of a colleague. The practice of revising and extending remarks is subject to a number of limitations. While a member may revise the reporter's notes of his speech with the approval of the Speaker, he may only extend his remarks with the express consent of the House. Sometimes however the Majority Leader will move that leave be given by unanimous consent to all members who have taken part in a debate to extend their remarks—such remarks being confined to the bill. In extending a speech, members may not introduce words or matter that they would not have been allowed to use in the House; they cannot for instance refer to proceedings in the other House, or criticize members of that House. The extension of remarks, like the remarks themselves, must remain within the rules of order. Where the extension is very lengthy, the request to print it must be accompanied by an estimate of the cost, prepared by the Public Printer, and announced at the time when leave to print is secured.[1]

1. Cannon's *Procedure in the House of Representatives* (1963), pp. 327-30.

THE PURPOSE AND FORMS OF DEBATE

In all legislatures the proceedings consist of talking about a proposition and then deciding about it—debate, followed by decision. The acuity of the process and the drama lie in the fact that on any matter of controversy the majority are more ready to come to a decision than the minority, who by extending debate may hope to defer or avoid a decision. Procedure in other words is the agreed, or the imposed, balance of opportunity open to the two sides.

So much is common to Parliament and Congress. A glance at the two first chambers shows the difference. In the House of Commons the majority contains ministers who expound government policy, while the minority comprises one or more groups who challenge, criticize and oppose what ministers are trying to do. Debate is, and in a sense always has been, the process by which this exercise is carried out. From its origins Parliament was never merely a 'speak-in', a conversation of unlimited length between its members. It was a dialogue between the monarch and his subjects. In modern times the powers of the monarchy are exercised by ministers with seats on the government front bench in the House. But the debate is the same—a dialogue between the government and, through their elected representatives, the governed. The object of the debate, then as now, is for the government to state and justify its needs and decisions. Equally it is for individual members and groups of members and in particular the official opposition (see pp. 8–9) to force adequate exposure and explanation, and to record their dissent and the reasons for it.

This direct confrontation with the executive branch is missing from Congress. In the absence of ministers, the contest is different. Bills before the House of Representatives may have originated in, and been sent to the House by, the executive, but they are introduced by individual members. Debate there is not primarily a conversation, even at one remove, with the President. The object of debate is rather to form combinations of members, unrelated more often than not to the major grouping of Republicans or Democrats, and bring them to decision. This exercise of a constitutional authority separate and distinct from that of the President is something quite different from the object of debate as understood in Britain.

Nor is debate related, as in Britain, largely to matters of ministerial responsibility. In the House of Commons speeches are made in the expectation of being answered or at least noted by ministers or by other members. In the House of Representatives much time is taken up by speeches made by members without reference to what came before and what will come after them. That latter House offers its members a personal podium from which they can catch the public ear, with anything from their views on the state of the nation to an unabashed recital of the charms of their constituency. Parliament, which has relegated the consideration of private and local bills almost entirely to smaller committees, and has ceased to debate petitions, has lost much of the parochial character it once was able to assume. Congress, being an amalgam of state and local interests as well as a national assembly, has not.

There is another difference. Parliament, and especially the House of Commons, provides individual ministers for every administration. The floor of the House is their training ground; as ministers they will stand and fall primarily by the capacity they show for debate. Success in debate secures the reward of a place, or a better place, in the government. By contrast, it is rare for a member of the House of Representatives (or the Senate) to be taken into the administration. There are no government members and no governmental prizes. Within Congress itself, most of the best jobs are allocated on seniority. There are in other words fewer personal rewards in Congress than in Parliament for those who shine in debate.

Debate in the Commons is more personal than in Congress. Political success or failure can be easily (if not always wholly fairly) assessed by what a man achieves in Parliament. But the congressman's success often has to be measured elsewhere—in his home state, in obtaining his party's nomination for a seat, in his job, or sometimes in running for other public offices. Congress is part of a much broader system of government than Parliament, and this is reflected in the different way each legislature conducts its debates.

Forms of Debate

When analysed, debate in Parliament is observed to have three distinct phases. First a motion is proposed. Secondly the presiding officer proposes a question based on that motion, and the House debates the question. Thirdly he puts the question to the House, and the House, by voting or otherwise, comes to a decision. Since the end of the seventeenth century[1] these have consistently been the essential components of all parliamentary debate, whether on a stage of a bill, or on a motion. The only exceptions, the only occasions in a parliamentary day when none of these is taking place, are at Question time and afterwards when ministers may make statements on matters they wish to draw to the House's attention. When such a statement provokes discussion, the Speaker or a member may point out that there is no question before the House and that an extended discussion would be therefore out of order. It is the essence of parliamentary debate, in other words, that it leads inexorably to a decision.

The need to base every debate on a proposition can raise difficulties. Sometimes it is advantageous to discuss a matter in general terms, without members' taking sides on the issue. Sometimes the House wishes to debate matters of such breadth (for example, foreign affairs) that any meaningful proposition is likely to put undesirable limits on the debate. In these circumstances, rather than abandon the traditional basis of debate, members debate a motion that means little or nothing: 'That this House takes note of such-and-such', 'That this Committee has considered the matter of such-and-such'. Pre-eminently in these circumstances they use the traditional motion—'That this House do now adjourn'—but a number of different procedures takes advantage of this formula, so that the phrase 'adjournment motion' is ambiguous[2] and may confuse the layman.

Several rules circumscribe the use of motions in the House of Commons. Motions must not anticipate business which the House has set down for future debate. They must not reopen matters already decided earlier in the session. They must not

1. Campion, *Introduction to the Procedure of the House of Commons* (1958), p. 20.

2. It is used (1) for general debates, when it is wished that their scope should be broad; (2) for the half-hour debates at the end of each day's sitting, when a private member raises a matter of his own choosing (see pp. 371–2); (3) for the emergency debates held under Standing Order No. 9 (see pp. 372–3); (4) as a delaying tactic in a debate; and (5) as a genuine proposal that members shall be allowed to go home.

refer to matters which are before the courts. Criticism of members of Parliament, and of certain high dignitaries of the state, can only be made in straightforward, positive motions, and not for example by means of an amendment to a motion. Motions do not need to be seconded, although on formal occasions they sometimes are. After a motion has been debated, the member who moved it must obtain unanimous leave if he wishes to withdraw it before a decision is taken on it. A number of motions, designed to delay the progress of business (see below), can only be employed in certain circumstances.

In Congress there are three types of resolution. A *joint resolution* is a resolution which, if passed with identical wording in both Houses and signed by the President, becomes law, just like a bill in simple form (see also p. 275).[1] A *concurrent resolution* when agreed to by both Houses expresses their views or intentions, usually on matters affecting their own operations. This kind of resolution is distinguishable from a legislative measure in that it does not require the President's signature or risk his veto. ('Concurrent' in this sense does not mean that the resolution is introduced and considered by each House simultaneously, but that each House concurs in it.) A *simple resolution* of the House (or Senate) affects matters which are entirely within the competence of one House—such as the setting-up of a special House committee—or expresses the opinion of the House on a particular subject.[2]

In contrast to Parliament Congress devotes a certain amount of debating time each day to business in which there is no question before the House or Senate. As already noted, at the start of every day's sitting in the House of Representatives members are able to make one-minute statements about matters of their choice. At the end of the day members may again be recognized by the Speaker for a period of up to one hour—time which has been granted to them by previous, unanimous consent of the House— for the purpose of making speeches on various subjects. In each case the speeches are self-sufficient; they need not relate to what comes before or after them.

1. Joint resolutions designed to amend the Constitution are sent to an official called the Administrator of General Services for transmission to the states legislatures and not to the President.

2. Riddick, *Congress: Organization and Procedure* (1949), pp. 19–22.

Advance Notice of Business

The difference between business in the House of Commons and in the House of Representatives is shown most clearly by the fact that the former works off a daily, prearranged order paper and the latter does not. The daily order paper of the Commons tells, in a certain amount of detail, what will take place in the House on the day in question. Even when the time of the House is to be taken up by private members with matters which do not lead to a decision (Question time, or half-hour adjournment debates), the subject matter is generally set out on the order paper. A prerequisite of debate in Parliament is that, as a general rule, notice of it has to be given in advance. In practice this means that the text to be debated, whether a motion or an amendment, has to be handed in at the latest on the previous day so that it appears printed on the order paper for the day of debate.

The practice of the House of Representatives is different. In the absence of a formal, officially produced order paper, the two whip notices, issued by the parties and based on the announcements made to the House by the Majority Leader at the end of the previous week, are widely circulated and in general use as guides to the business to be taken on each day. In addition, the Daily Digest at the end of the Congressional Record mentions briefly the main business to be taken on the day on which it is published.

Bills and resolutions coming before the House are available in print. But there is no requirement that advance notice of amendments must be given. As a rule an amendment is offered to the House during a sitting; on the demand of a member it may be put in writing there and then and read out to the House by one of the clerks.[1] Sometimes, if the amendment is long or complex, a member will circulate it informally to other members before the debate in order to improve its chances of acceptance.[2]

It is possible to find out from the published documents of the House of Representatives what business is pending before the

1. House Rule XVII, 1 and Cannon, op. cit., p. 5.
2. Alterations made in 1970 to the rules of procedure have improved the prospects of an amendment's being debated if its author circulates it first (see p. 298).

House. All bills and resolutions reported by committees are listed on one of the calendars,[1] and together comprise the pending business. On certain stated days the business on a particular calendar automatically comes before the House; and on two of the calendars, the Consent Calendar and the Private Calendar (both containing relatively non-controversial matter), the business is read through and may be passed in the order in which it reached the calendar. But with that general exception, the listing of a piece of business on a calendar does not determine the timing nor the manner of its subsequent consideration by the House. The Rules Committee may at any time use its privilege of requiring the House to give immediate consideration to a bill or resolution. Many bills on the Union or House Calendars are never acted on by the House, and remain there to die at the end of a Congress.

There is thus much less assurance in the House of Representatives than in the Commons about what is likely to be achieved on a particular day. In a House where there are no ministers pressing the government's business on the attention of members, and where members are less susceptible to the blandishments of party, this feature is not surprising. The consequent inconvenience to the leadership is mitigated to a considerable extent by consultations between the Majority Leader and the chairmen of the various committees, especially the Rules Committee, on when and how a particular bill or resolution is to be brought before the House. The leadership is also helped by several rules (discussed below) limiting the length of the debate. The confusion that might result on the floor of the House from the absence of an official order paper is reduced partly through the known order of precedence accorded to various items of business[2] and partly by the information disseminated by the party leaders through the whips.

Amendments

The object of moving an amendment—to alter the terms of a motion or bill—is the same in the House of Representatives and

1. The various kinds of calendar are described in Chapter VI on Legislation.
2. Cannon, op. cit., pp. 253-76.

the House of Commons. In both chambers debate on an amendment takes precedence over debate on the motion or bill which it seeks to amend. There are differences however in the forms of amendment that may be offered.

In the House of Representatives an amendment may seek either to strike out existing words, or to insert new words, or to do both. There can be as many as four different amendments, each of a separate type, to a text at any given moment. The types of amendment are:

(a) a straightforward amendment to the proposition before the House;

(b) a substitute amendment, put forward as an alternative to (a) above;

(c) an amendment to amendment (a); and

(d) an amendment to the substitute amendment (b).

Complicated rules specify the order in which these four types of amendment are disposed of.[1] Amendments put forward by members of the standing committee which had studied the motion or bill are considered before other amendments.

In the House of Commons the handling of amendments is less complex. There, too, an amendment may seek to leave out words; to leave out words and insert other words; or simply to insert words. Whatever the form of the amendment, the question usually proposed on it is 'That the amendment be made' and debate takes place on that question. A substitute amendment, as used in the House of Representatives, is not known as such in the Commons nor treated differently from any other amendment. In both Houses an amendment has to be relevant to the text it seeks to amend. But if an amendment is offered to replace the entire text, it frequently runs the risk in the House of Commons of being held by the presiding officer to be 'wrecking' and thus to be out of order.

The rule requiring that amendments should be relevant or germane was adopted by the first House of Representatives in 1789 and introduced a principle not then known to parliamentary law and practice.[2] Today most assemblies consider it fundamental to the conduct of business. But it is worth noting that the

1. Cannon, op. cit., pp. 5–6.
2. *House Rules and Manual* (1971), Rule XVI, 7 and para. 794.

House of Commons did not consent to be bound by it until the 1880s,[1] and that the American Senate has never adopted it.

Several other rules governing amendments are found in the first chambers of both countries. In applying the rules, however, the House of Commons has allowed greater power to its presiding officer. For example in both Houses an amendment has to be consistent with an amendment already agreed to. But whereas in the House of Commons the presiding officer arbitrates on consistency, the House of Representatives has retained that power for itself.[2] Another important constitutional difference is that a member of the House of Commons, unlike his counterpart in Washington, may not propose an amendment which would have the effect of increasing expenditure or taxation, unless it is authorized by the appropriate money resolution.[3]

In accordance with the general practice of the House of Commons, advanced notice of amendments is normally required. Like motions, amendments must be handed in by members in time to be printed on the order paper, so that their effect can be studied before the debate begins. By this means the presiding officer can operate the power given to him by standing order[4] to 'select' amendments, that is, to choose for debate only those amendments which he thinks important and effective. He may also group for a single debate a number of similar or related amendments and perhaps, at the end of the debate, allow separate votes on some or all of them. There is no limit to the number of amendments that may be tabled, but all of them are subject to the presiding officer's scrutiny and selection. 'Manuscript' amendments, that is, amendments offered without notice in the course of debate, are only accepted in exceptional circumstances. In general, if notice of an amendment has not been circulated at latest on the previous day, it is unlikely to be selected. This is in contrast to the House of Representatives where there is no requirement for amendments to be circulated in advance of discussion and where the power of the chair to select amendments is unknown.

1. Erskine May, 18th ed. (1971), p. 381. It is affirmed for the first time in the 9th edition of this work (1883), p. 325.

2. *House Rules and Manual* (1971), para. 466.

3. See p. 269. The rules governing financial procedure are treated in Chapter VII.

4. Standing Order No. 33.

RULES AND PRACTICES

In 1789 when the first Congress was convening, the House of Commons had only four standing orders to regulate its proceedings. They all related to the use of public money, the control of expenditure and taxation. For the rest business was done according to time-honoured usage. Accepted practices such as that a bill should be read three times and committed to a committee for the consideration of amendments, that debate on a motion should take the form of a question being proposed to the House and subsequently put to it for decision, or that members had equal rights to speak and vote, had no authority save a general and long standing acceptance. Where these precepts needed to be interpreted or applied in particular instances, the presiding officer would give a ruling. Collectively these precedents formed, and still form, a body of case law and have always been regarded as binding with the same force as a standing order or a statutory provision.

The House of Representatives began life in 1789 with a few simple rules. By coincidence there were four of them, the same number as in the contemporary House of Commons, though they were not about the use of public money. All four rules smacked strongly of contemporary Westminster. One defined the duties of the Speaker as presiding officer. Another regulated the handling of motions, the methods of voting, and decorum in debate; in particular, a member had to confine himself to the question under debate,[1] and he could not speak more than once to the same question. The third and fourth rules dealt with bills. These were read twice before being committed; debated clause by clause and subjected to amendment in a Committee of the whole House or a select committee; reported to the House; and given a third reading. These few rules set the House of Representatives advancing, as it were, from the same starting line as the contemporary House of Commons.

As at Westminster the rules of the House of Representatives were not intended to be a complete code of practice. From the first they were expected to be supplemented by interpretations and rulings from the chair. Between 1797 and 1801 Thomas Jefferson, then presiding officer of the Senate, prepared his famous manual

1. This was a procedural innovation (see above, p. 139).

of parliamentary practice. Today it is still bound up and re-published with the rules of both the Senate and the House of Representatives. This authoritative work was 'made up wholly of collations of English parliamentary practice and decisions', said a House Committee when recommending in 1880 a revised set of rules. According to the official commentary on the House rules, 'the Manual is regarded by English parliamentarians as the best statement of what the law of Parliament was at the time Jefferson wrote it.'[1] Given the constitutional differences between the two countries, the rules, practices and precedents of the two popular Houses at the end of the eighteenth and the beginning of the nineteenth centuries were markedly similar. In both Houses the individual member had opportunities to raise any matter of public interest that took his fancy; and in both his powers to delay or oppose any measure with which he disagreed were very considerable.

Since that time the procedures of the two first chambers have developed very differently. In the United States the pressures making for change in the House of Representatives were essentially two. The first was the steady rise in the number of members, reflecting the massive increase in population and the admission of new states. The House membership of sixty-five, for which the original rules were designed, had become 237 by 1850 and 435 (the present number) by 1910. With more and more members seeking to take part in debate, time became an increasingly scarce commodity. The other constant pressure was the changing nature of the business that confronted the House. In something less than 200 years the simple agrarian and trading society of the original thirteen states has been transformed into an advanced industrial complex of over 200 million people with responsibilities and commitments extending far beyond its continental frontiers. For Congress, and especially the House of Representatives, the perennial problem has been to trim the procedures, while preserving the right of minorities, so as to cater for an ever increasing work load and to keep pace with its constitutional duties *vis-à-vis* the executive branch which has itself expanded as fast as the Republic.

In Britain the pressures for change were different. The number of members remained more or less constant at about 660 throughout the nineteenth century (see p. 76). But the type of member

1. *House Rules and Manual* (1971), para. 284.

returned to the reformed House of Commons from 1832 onwards, with business and industrial interests not previously represented in Parliament, pressed steadily for more efficient and systematic procedures. More important, successive governments drawing strength from a larger and more articulate electorate made increasing demands on the time of the House to give effect to the policies and programmes to which they were publicly pledged. Here the difference from the United States is noteworthy. While the increased work load in the House of Representatives bore equally on the opportunities of all members and generally restricted debate, in Britain the government, leading an increasingly coherent majority of the Commons, was able to secure an increasing share of the available time for its business. Whoever else suffered in the process, the government did not.

Restriction of Debate in the House of Representatives

In both first chambers, then, the freedom of debate was curbed during the nineteenth century. This is not the place to review in detail the stages by which this process was accomplished, or to chart the trail of rules and standing orders which inexorably penned in members.[1] But it is worth indicating the milestones along the road in order to make intelligible the differing ways in which debate today in both chambers came to be confined.

In the United States the four rules adopted by the first House of Representatives were soon found to allow an unlimited tolerance for obstruction, and the gentle art of killing a bill by debate was quickly mastered. The 'filibuster', made famous by the American Senate, in fact found its earliest practitioners in the House of Representatives. The most renowned was Barent Gardenier, a Federalist from New York who once spoke continuously for twenty-four hours to block a bill and eventually provoked one

1. The best accounts of developments in the standing orders of the House of Commons are to be found in Campion, *Introduction to the Procedure of the House of Commons* (1958), Chap. I, and an essay by Sir Edward Fellowes in *The Commons in Transition* (ed. Hanson and Crick) (1970), pp. 26–40. For the House of Representatives the same service has been done at length by D. S. Alexander in *History and Procedure of the House of Representatives* (1916) and in a short, lively account by Neil MacNeil in *Forge of Democracy* (1963), Chap. 3.

of the floor leaders to challenge him to a duel. Though severely wounded, Gardenier recovered and returned to the House with his verbosity undiminished.[1] The first limit on debate was imposed in 1811 when the 'previous question'—for which provision had been made in the original rules of 1789—was made an instrument for bringing a debate to a close. As from 1811 the effect of moving and carrying the previous question was to cut off debate and bring the House immediately to a vote on the main question. The previous question was an effective form of closure; but it could not be moved while a member was on his feet in possession of the House, and so did not touch the personal filibuster.

This latter indulgence was outlawed by the House in 1841, after several abortive attempts. The effect of rules adopted in that year was to limit a speech on any question in the House or Committee of the Whole to one hour.[2] Efforts were made to escape the grip of this rule by putting down innumerable amendments to a bill. This move was met by the introduction in 1847 of the five-minute rule,[3] which confined a speech made on an amendment to five minutes. Even these two severe restrictions on debate did not stop determined opponents filibustering for weeks, sometimes months, against controversial measures. Only in 1860, when the House armed the majority with the power to close *all* debate on amendments, was the filibuster finally crushed.[4]

The circle of controls to prevent obstruction was completed in 1890 by the adoption of the 'Reed' rules, named after Thomas Reed who was elected Speaker of the 51st and later Congresses (1890–91, 1896–97 and 1898–99). He began his first Speakership by declining in January 1890 to accept a motion for the adjournment—notwithstanding the priority to which it was entitled under current practice—on the ground that it was 'dilatory' or obstructive. At the same time he announced his intention of refusing to put to the House any motion which, though within the ambit of accepted parliamentary practice, he considered to be dilatory and offered solely for purposes of delay.

In the same month Speaker Reed struck with equal determina-

1. Neil MacNeil, op. cit., 45.
2. House Rules and Manual (1971) Rule XIV, 2.
3. House Rules and Manual (1971) Rule XXIII, 5.
4. House Rule XXIII, 6.

tion and success at another deeply entrenched minority practice, known as the 'disappearing quorum'. The Constitution lays down that the House cannot do business unless a quorum is present. The quorum (half the number of members, plus one) had traditionally been determined by reference to the number of members voting. When a yea and nay vote was taken, the minority members though present on the floor could refuse to answer their names. The effect was often that the total number voting was less than a quorum. A quorum call then took place automatically to summon the 'absent' voters, and when in due course a quorum was made up, the vote was taken again, often with the same result. Sometimes whole days were consumed as quorum calls were alternated with votes. Speaker Reed's solution was simple and dramatic. Faced with a 'disappearing quorum' he directed the Clerk of the House to record the names of members who were present but had not voted, and then declared the quorum present. The uproar was intense, but Reed successfully rode it. When his right to count as present a member who had refused to vote was challenged by that member, he replied 'The chair is making a statement of fact that the gentleman . . . is present. Does he deny it?'[1] This inescapable logic carried the day. In the following month—February 1890—both Reed's reforms were embodied by the House in its revised rules.[2]

These two changes removed from the minority two of its most potent weapons for delay. But Reed made a third and important lasting contribution to the procedure of the House by establishing the Rules Committee as a body controlling the business to come before the House. Though appointed regularly since the first Congress in 1789, the Rules Committee had been concerned only with preparing and recommending a body of rules for adoption by the new House in each Congress. Now, under the forceful leadership of Reed in 1883, the Committee gave a new meaning to the word 'rule': it was to mean a recommendation setting out in detail how a bill (chosen by the Rules Committee) was to be handled on the floor, and in particular settling how much time (if any) was to be allowed for amendments.[3] Under the direction of Speaker Reed the majority supported this procedure which

1. Neil MacNeil, op. cit., p. 52   2. Rules XV, 3 and XVII, 10.
3. House Rules and Manual (1971), para. 717. An example of a 'rule' is given on p. 283.

amounted in British terms to a 'guillotine' on each bill (see p. 148) and a detailed programme for that guillotine—all rolled into a single resolution. Not unnaturally the acceptance of these rules gave to the Rules Committee and its chairman a large measure of control over what passed on the floor of the House. Later reforms have affected the chairmanship and membership of this Committee (see p. 24). But since its transformation by Speaker Reed, it has remained one of the major centres of power in the House of Representatives.

Restriction of Debate in the House of Commons

Over the same period the corresponding story of the House of Commons makes a striking contrast. Both first chambers, it will be recalled, started the nineteenth century with broadly the same ground rules and practices. But the House of Commons was much slower to change its procedure and impose limits on debate. Between 1832 when the first reformed House began work and 1880, seven major inquiries were held by House committees into its procedure and practice. As a result of these recommendations many useful, organizational changes were made, many of them with general agreement. Sittings of the House, for example, became more systematic; the order paper began to reflect the sequence of business that would be taken; the number of questions to be put on the various stages of bills, excluding questions on amendments, was reduced from eighteen in 1848—the highest figure ever—to four or five in 1880.[1] There were some important casualties. The right of the subject to petition the House to remedy a grievance was emasculated in 1842 by standing orders, passed on government initiative, to end all debate on them. The ever increasing flow of petitions had threatened to engulf all other debate, but the solution found to this problem was drastic and offset only in part by the development of the procedure of questioning ministers on the floor of the House. In the same period the government was able to secure that the one day a week reserved since the beginning of the nineteenth century for government business became two days in 1837 and three days in 1852. But the government's control of time on these days was by no

1. Campion, op. cit., p. 29, and Fellowes, op. cit., p. 28.

means complete because various procedural devices still enabled private members to pre-empt or delay government business with which they disagreed.

The extensive tidying operation conducted steadily between 1832 and 1880 left abundant opportunities for debate. On the whole those opportunities were used with restraint. There was an understanding, amounting to a convention, that after reasonable time had been given for objection or opposition, the government should be allowed to have its business. This restraint was the chief reason why the House of Commons by 1880 had not been obliged to restrict debate, as the House of Representatives had done by introducing the closure (previous question) and the one hour and five minutes limits on speeches.

The introduction by standing order in the new Parliament of 1880 of a summary method of disciplining disorderly members marked the crumbling of this traditional restraint. Moreover the Irish Party, intent on forcing attention to their major policy of home rule, made a calculated move to obstruct government business by exploiting the available procedural opportunities. Strathearn Gordon has calculated that in the session of 1881, which lasted 154 days, fourteen Irish members delivered 3,828 speeches, a daily average of twenty-five speeches from that group alone.[1] This scale of obstruction invited drastic counter-measures. The first and most famous came not from the government but from the chair. On the morning of 2 February 1881, after five days' debate on the second reading of a government measure, the Protection of Persons and Property (Ireland) Bill, concluding with a continuous sitting of forty-one hours, Mr Speaker Brand—his papers fluttering in his hand like a trapped bird, according to an eye witness—directed the House, on his own initiative, to vote at once on the motion before them, although Irish members were still rising to continue the debate. In this way the closure was instituted. Speaker Brand's coup was comparable in importance for parliamentary proceedings with that of Speaker Reed in extirpating the 'disappearing quorum' from the House of Representatives. So great was the relief of the House of Commons at the Speaker's example that in the following session it embodied the measure in standing orders as a permanent part of the procedure.

1. *Our Parliament* (1952 ed.), p. 101.

Further restrictions were soon required. After five days in Committee on the same Protection of Persons and Property (Ireland) Bill, little progress having been made, the House agreed to a motion that the committee should, at a given hour, put all outstanding questions to the vote in order to conclude the committee stage. This was the first 'guillotine' of a bill. A similar motion later applied the same procedure to the report stage of the bill. Other Irish bills were treated in the same way, but the motions passed curtailing debate on them became more elaborate, specifying time-limits for the various parts of each bill.

The introduction of the first guillotine was followed by other restrictive measures. Dilatory motions—including attempts to adjourn the debate or the House and equivalent delaying motions in committee—were made subject to acceptance by the presiding officer: if he thought them an abuse of the rules, he was not to call them. Moreover debate on such a motion had from now onwards to be strictly confined to the subject matter of the motion: on a motion to adjourn, for example, a member is restricted to a statement of the reasons for and against adjournment and may not canvass the merits of the bill under consideration or any other extraneous matter. In 1902 further measures adopted permanently by the House on the initiative of Balfour, then its leader and soon to be Prime Minister, gave the government effective control over the lion's share of the House's time and, by applying the closure to the business of supply, restricted the traditional opportunities for criticizing the executive. By so doing, they substantially altered the balance within the Commons in favour of the official opposition as a whole and against the individual private member.[1]

By the end of the nineteenth century, then, both the House of Representatives and the House of Commons had found it necessary to arm the majority with a number of procedural weapons to ensure the eventual passage of its business. Some of these restrictions of debate were similar in both the first chambers—for example, the reduction in the number of questions on which debates and votes must be held; the restriction on the power to disrupt business by moving dilatory motions; and the use of such drastic devices as closure (or previous question in the House of

1. This balance, and the present procedure on the business of supply, are discussed in Chapter VII on Finance.

Representatives) and guillotines (special orders or 'rules' in the House of Representatives). But there are significant differences. The first is that a 'rule' applied to a bill on the floor of the House of Representatives is a far greater invasion of a member's right to debate the bill than a guillotine of the committee and subsequent stages in the Commons, because the moment at which a bill is subjected to a 'rule' is the first opportunity that the House of Representatives as a House has had to consider it. All the preceding work on it has been done in a committee. In the House of Commons, by contrast, the debate on second reading—taking place before it is sent to a committee—is the most important stage, at which the House debates the principles underlying the bill. In the 1880s and for many years afterwards, second readings of bills later subjected to guillotine would take up several days, so that the meaning of the measure was fully understood and debated by the House.

The other difference is that the House of Commons has never accepted any general restriction on the time for an individual speech in the House or in committee.[1] Individual members have pressed for some such limit, committees of the House have recommended it, but the House itself has never countenanced it.[2] Undoubtedly a one-hour rule, if introduced in 1841, as it was in the House of Representatives, would have seriously abridged the Commons tradition of great debate. Palmerston, defending Don Pacifico in 1850 in a historic speech of four and a half hours—said by Gladstone to have lasted from dusk of one day to the dawn of the next—would have been cut off before he had warmed to the business; every Chancellor of the Exchequer since Gladstone would have found himself in difficulty; and the wartime philippics of Churchill (to come no closer to the present day) would have been truncated. A five-minute rule, of the kind applied by the House of Representatives to debate on amendments, would crucially have affected the quality as well as the amount of scrutiny and argument that a member could bring to

1. The 'ten-minute' rule which gives a private member an opportunity of introducing a bill with a short speech (see p. 268) and a similar restriction in respect of motions to recommit a bill are *particular* limitations placed on the length of speeches.

2. *Parliamentary Reform* (Cassell, for the Hansard Society), 1967, pp. 81–84.

the consideration of a bill. These important differences have to be borne in mind in any assessment of the relative claims of the two Houses to have remained effective chambers of debate, despite the need to fortify the majority against unlimited or obstructive speech.

THE BALANCE OF STRENGTH BETWEEN
MAJORITY AND MINORITY

By the end of the nineteenth century the broad pattern of proceedings in both the first chambers was set. In the twentieth century, the cutting edges of the restrictive devices have been honed finer. In both chambers the rules and standing orders have been extended and refined in an effort to meet every imaginable contingency. While the pattern set by the beginning of the century has not been disturbed, it is necessary to look at the kind of restrictions that apply today to debate, in order to assess in each first chamber the balance of strength between majority and minority.

In the House of Commons

Debate in the House of Commons takes place under conditions which make it feasible for the government to plan how much business shall be decided in a session, in a week, in a day. The government's plans may in the event be frustrated; but it provides the framework for all the activities of the House, so that there is at all times a clear legislative programme before the Commons. This is a result of the fact that the time *not* at the disposal of the government—the time available for the official opposition, and for private members—is itself largely controlled by standing orders or accepted usage, and therefore predictable in its incidence.

The government control the length of sessions, and may prolong a session until its legislative programme is completed. In practice a session generally lasts about 160 sitting days. Among the three contenders for the initiative on those days—private members, official opposition and government—the allocation of time to the first two groups is broadly as follows:

Private Members

		Days
1.	Bills	12[1]
2.	Motions	10[1]
3.	Financial business (when private members, by agreement, have the initiative)	3
4.	For Adjournment debates (on the day the House rises for each recess)	4
	Total	29

Official Opposition

1.	Supply days (on which by convention the opposition chooses the subject of debate)	29
2.	Votes of Censure (for which the government by convention find time), on average	2
3.	Amendments to the Address in reply to the speech from the throne (when the Opposition at the start of a session can focus attention on matters of their own choice)	5
	Total	36

To these sixty-five days have to be added a total of about ten days which the government may concede for debates, either because it is required under standing order (for example, an urgency debate) or because it is expedient so to do. The effect of all this is to leave the government with about eighty-five days for its own business.

This calculation does not by itself give an accurate picture of the extent of the government's control of time in the Commons. For example, while the official opposition chooses the subject of debate on a supply day, the government decides when there is to be a supply day—or, put another way, whether or not a supply day is to be included in the business for a particular week. Again, though the standing orders say that private members' bills are to be considered on Fridays, the government proposes to the House which Fridays these shall be. The government, in other words, largely controls the framework within which the session's business is taken.

1. The balance of time given to private members' bills and to private members' motions, though laid down by standing order, has often been varied by sessional resolution.

Similarly the length of each day's sitting is to some extent within the government's control. Standing Orders bring the main business of the day, with the exception of certain financial bills,[1] to a conclusion at 10 p.m. (or 4 p.m. on Fridays)—when the government may move a motion to allow the House to take further specified business after that hour. With its controls over the length of the session and the sitting, the government can forecast how many decisions will be reached by the House in a given period of time, and the probable rate of progress on each legislative measure.

The taking of decisions by the House is helped by a number of procedural devices whose historical background has already been referred to. There is, first, the closure. As it is now operated, any member may rise during a debate (whether a speech is being made, or between speeches) and claim to move 'That the question be now put'. The Speaker or chairman (and there are rules stipulating who must be in the chair at the time) has instantly to decide whether a closure is justified—whether, in other words, minorities have had the requisite opportunity to put their point of view. He need not state any reasons for his decision. So the first limitation on the use of the closure is that the presiding officer must believe that it is justified. If he does, the House proceeds to vote at once on whether or not the debate should be brought to a conclusion. At this point the second limitation comes into play: a simple majority is not enough to make a closure effective; it must be a majority with at least a hundred members voting in support of it.[2] If such a majority is obtained, the House proceeds to vote on the question which was under debate when the closure was claimed, and on any other questions necessary to bring the matter to a decision.

The frequency with which the closure is used in the House of Commons depends on political factors such as the controversial nature of a party's legislation, and the size of its majority. Some idea of its impact on parliamentary debate is given by the fact that it was employed on 525 occasions in the period 1950–70;

1. Some other classes of business are allowed by Standing Order to continue for a specified period after 10 p.m. See for example p. 384.

2. Standing Orders Nos. 30 and 31. In a Standing Committee, the majority necessary is at least a quorum of the Committee—Standing Order No. 65.

that is, on average, nearly once every sitting week. A picture of the role played by the chair in refusing to allow an indiscriminate use of a closure is given by the fact that over the same period a public request for closure was refused on 106 occasions, or once in every six applications.

The 'previous question', used in the House of Representatives to bring debate to a sudden end, has been available to the House of Commons since the seventeenth century. It can be moved by any member in the form 'I move the previous question'. The Speaker then puts to the House the question 'That the question be *not* now put'. If that motion is carried, the Speaker is prevented from putting the original question, the House having put off the matter to a later date. If the motion is negatived, the effect is to require the original question to be put straight away, thus closing the debate. But the previous question in the Commons is itself a debatable motion, so that it is not as effective a means of bringing the House to a decision as the closure (described above) which, if accepted by the presiding officer, must be put to the vote without debate. Until 1888 the form of the previous question in the Commons was 'That the question be now put'. In that year the Speaker for the first time put it to the House in the form 'That the question be *not now* put', because the original form was akin to the closure which had lately been embodied in the standing orders.[1] The original form is still valid in the House of Lords, though the previous question is used in that House solely for the purpose of denying a decision to the House and not as a closure. In the Commons the previous question has not been moved since 1943, and is now more a procedural curiosity than a device of practical utility.

The second procedural device leading to decision of the House is the allocation of time order, usually known as a guillotine. In their modern form these orders are highly complex and are designed to ensure that all parts of a bill receive some consideration,[2] and that within the time allotted there is no room for the insertion of obstructive motions or other business. The standing orders of the House now provide for two kinds of guillotine.

1. Erskine May, 18th ed. (1971), p. 372.
2. This object is not always achieved. An extreme example was the guillotine on the Industrial Relations Bill 1971. In the result 111 out of the 150 clauses in the bill as introduced were not specifically debated on either committee or report stage.

Under the older form, the House first agrees to an allocation of time order, saying that a specified time is allotted to each stage of the bill. Then a 'business committee', consisting of all members of the chairmen's panel (see also p. 29) together with five other members who act as party spokesmen, decide how much of the allotted time shall be spent on each part of the bill at each of its stages. Their decisions are then put to the House, which votes to accept or reject them without debate.[1] If accepted, as they regularly are, they become orders of the House and regulate the debates on the bills.

A more recent form of guillotine[2] presupposes that attempts have been made by the government to get the opposition to agree voluntarily to an allocation of time. When these attempts have failed, the government brings forward a guillotine motion providing that each stage of the bill must be completed by a certain date. This motion has to be decided by the House after two hours' debate. The business committee then decides, within the dates laid down by the House, how much debating time should be given to each part and at each stage of the bill. The committee's recommendations are put to the House which votes without debate to accept or reject them. The newer procedure gives an advantage to the government, in that debate on the guillotine motion is restricted to two hours; the older procedure has invariably required a full day's debate before the House could accept the guillotine. On the other hand it has the disadvantage from the government's point of view that the business committee may recommend more days for the completion of a stage than the government is willing to provide.

The use of the business committee to decide the details of debate under a guillotine is an attempt to ensure that its application will be as reasonable as possible. 'If it was necessary to have a guillotine', said a former Leader of the House who had much to do with the development of the procedure, 'what the government wanted was a fair guillotine'.[3] There have, however, been

1. Standing Order No. 43. If a guillotine is imposed on a bill which is already before a Standing Committee, a business subcommittee is formed to fulfil a role similar to that of the Business Committee in the House (Standing Order No. 74).

2. Standing Order No. 44.

3. Herbert Morrison, *Government and Parliament*, 3rd ed. (1967), pp. 224–5.

occasions when the government have themselves preferred to prescribe the detailed allotment of time to the various divisions of the bill in the original order imposing the guillotine.

Since 1945 guillotines have been imposed at an average rate of about one bill a year by governments of all political complexions. Unlike the other restrictive procedures introduced as a result of the Irish obstruction in the late nineteenth century, the guillotine has never been accepted by the House as a normal process of government. It is 'the extreme limit to which procedure goes in affirming the rights of the majority at the expense of the minorities of the House',[1] and each application of it raises considerable protests. For this reason, it seems, a guillotine was not used to ensure the passing of the Parliament (No. 2) Bill in 1969 to alter the powers and composition of the House of Lords (see p. 294); some of the majority which supported the bill would not have supported the use of a guillotine to aid its passage.

The more modern form of guillotine is grounded on the fact that frequent attempts are made by governments behind the scenes to get the opposition voluntarily to enter into agreement as to the total time to be spent on a particular piece of business. Oppositions, whose public reputation may depend on the fierceness with which they oppose, are often unwilling to be seen to enter into such agreements, but they nevertheless do so to an extent that is not generally recognized. Paradoxically it is in the shadow of the guillotine, the extreme negation of the parliamentary idea, that useful exercises of toleration and accommodation sometimes take place.

There are other provisions in the standing orders of the Commons which, though not within the control of the government, tend to ensure that the deliberations are not unduly protracted. Principal among these is the Order[2] requiring debate to be relevant to a motion and forbidding a member from indulging in 'tedious' repetition of arguments already advanced. In the House too (as opposed to Committee of the whole House) it is forbidden for a member to speak (except in certain limited circumstances) more than once to a motion.[3] When amendments are offered to a bill or motion, there is the formidable power given to the chair to select which amendments shall be debated and which shall

---

1. Erskine May, 18th ed. (1971), p. 437.
2. Standing Order No. 22.   3. Erskine May, op. cit., p. 408.

not.[1] This power, first given to the chair in 1909, has far-reaching effects. It moderates the multiplication of amendments as a means of slowing down the progress of business, and it places on the chair the unenviable duty of deciding which points are most worthy of discussion. In so doing, he in effect decides the extent to which the minority shall be muzzled in the overall interests of the House. A similar power is given to the chair, in committee, to forbid debate on a clause as a whole if its principle has been adequately covered in debate on amendments to the clause.[2]

A recital of the weapons in the government's armoury and in the rules of the House which together circumscribe the ordinary member's freedom of action might lead to the conclusion that scales are weighted all too heavily in favour of the majority and against the minority. But it should not be assumed that the art of obstructing the government's business, within the existing rules of procedure, has become a dead art. A study of proceedings on the Parliament (No. 2) Bill in 1969 shows how an intelligent use by a minority of the rights open to them, in circumstances where a guillotine could not be applied, can succeed. The tabling of many amendments raising serious problems; the making of lengthy but relevant speeches; keeping debates going to a late hour when the supporters of the bill may not stay the course; raising countless points of order, each of which has to be ruled on by a patient chairman, on whose every pronouncement further points may be raised for a while—all these tactics were skilfully employed and eventually forced the government to abandon a bill which had been favoured by the leaders of the three main parties in the House and given a second reading by a substantial majority.

In the House of Representatives

The absence from the House of Representatives of a dominating government party to drive debates forward to the point of decision imports the danger that a minority might occupy more than its appropriate share of the time of the House. To avoid this danger the rules have been gradually tightened over the years, and various limitations imposed on debate. The main

1. Standing Orders Nos. 33 and 65.
2. Standing Orders Nos. 48 and 65.

reasons why debate today in the House of Representatives is kept within manageable bounds are the limits imposed on the length of speeches; the limits of time on certain types of business; unanimous agreements to limit the length of debate; and the procedures for bringing debate to a conclusion.

Limits on Length of Speeches

The rules of the House prescribe for different circumstances limits on speeches of one minute, five minutes and one hour. Each morning, after the saying of prayers, members by unanimous consent may make speeches of up to *one minute* in length on any subject they choose. This, coupled with the right of extending his remarks in the Congressional Record, enables a member for example to draw attention to a matter of public interest, to clarify something he has said or done, or to give publicity to a matter affecting his constituency. The time limit is strictly applied, and the Speaker will decline any requests for extending it,[1] or for yielding it in part to another member.

On an amendment to a bill in Committee of the Whole, speeches are limited to *five minutes*. Only one speech for and one speech against each amendment is allowed; though, if no one opposes, a second speech in favour of the amendment is in order. Any unused time in the first speech may not be used in the second. Nor may a speaker yield part of his five minutes to anyone else,[2] although he may yield for a question or remark by another member. The advantages of the rapid progress with bills which the five-minute rule allows to the Committee of the Whole have led the House to adapt the procedure for its own use. To save the need for a bill to be considered first in Committee of the Whole and then in the House, it can sometimes proceed with a single consideration in 'the House as in the Committee of the Whole'. To achieve this mid-way position, the House needs to make a special rule or to give unanimous consent. Once in 'the House as in the Committee of the Whole', the rules of order are that a quorum of the House (i.e. a majority) must be present, and the Speaker remains in the chair. There is no general debate, and the

1. Cannon, *Procedure in the House of Representatives* (1963), p. 146.
2. Ibid., p. 147.

five-minute rule applies to amendments. When these are disposed of, the bill can go forward to its final stages.[1]

In general debate, whether in the House or in Committee of the Whole, no member may occupy more than *one hour* in debate on any question. The one exception is that, if general debate continues for more than one day, the member who began the debate by reporting a measure from a committee may occupy a second hour in closing the debate. A member may yield a specified part of his allotted time to another member (see below); or he may reserve a part of it for a later intervention by himself. Having spoken an hour in the House on the main question, a member may speak there for another hour on an amendment[2] (but in Committee of the Whole he is, as mentioned above, limited to five minutes on an amendment).

Limits of Time on Certain Types of Business

Besides limits of time on speeches, the rules of the House impose a time limit on certain kinds of business. There is no debate on the previous question (see below) except in special circumstances, when it is limited to forty minutes. Debate on any motion to suspend the rules is also limited to forty minutes. In each of these kinds of debate twenty minutes is allowed to each side, though the length of time may on occasions be increased by unanimous consent.[3]

Unanimous Agreements to Limit Length of Debate

In both Houses of Congress the effect of many of the rules is frequently negated by agreements to proceed in some different way. Agreements can be made by unanimous consent, and it would be a matter for wonder in Parliament to realize how often the opponents of a measure concur in such voluntary agreements. It frequently happens that before entering on an extended debate the House will arrange by unanimous consent for the debate to be limited in time, and for that time to be controlled by two members (generally the chairman and the ranking minority

1. Riddick, *Congress: Organization and Procedure* (1949), pp. 212–13.
2. Cannon, op. cit., p. 145.
3. Cannon, op. cit., pp. 147, 457–8; and House Rule XXVII (3).

member of the committee concerned), one favouring and one opposing the bill. Sometimes, too, unanimous consent will diminish the one hour that is ordinarily allowed for each speech. Agreements can be made by the House to affect not only its own debates, but those in Committee of the Whole.[1]

Procedures for Bringing Debate to a Conclusion

The House, but not the Committee of the Whole, is able to closure debate by means of the 'previous question'. When a member demands the previous question (he says 'I move the previous question', the exact form of words used for the previous question in the House of Commons), the Speaker at once puts the matter to the vote. He has no discretion—unlike the British presiding officer when a closure is claimed—as to whether he should accept it or not. The motion is carried if a simple majority of members vote in favour of it. If it is unsuccessful, the House resumes the debate; but control of time, the opportunity to offer amendments and the right to be the next mover of the previous question pass to the other side.[2]

The successful use of the previous question brings the House to a vote immediately, without further amendment or debate. It is frequently invoked by the member in charge of a bill, but can be employed by any member having the floor. He can seek it in respect of the single question under discussion, or of a specified series of questions, so that it may in practice cut out all amendments to a bill. It can be moved before debate on a question has begun; but in that case forty minutes (which can only be increased by unanimous consent) of debate is allowed, half the time being allotted to those favouring and half to those opposing the question.[3]

As noted earlier, the House may agree to a motion which will bring a general debate in Committee of the Whole to end at a stated hour; the Committee cannot impose such a restriction on itself, except by unanimous agreement. The Committee can however impose a time-limit on itself once it has begun debate under the five-minute rule.[4]

1. Cannon, op. cit., p. 146.
2. *House Rules and Manual* (1971), para. 755.
3. Cannon, op. cit., pp. 277–81, and House Rule XVII.
4. Cannon, op. cit., p. 111.

A different procedure for bringing the House to a decision is that under which motions may be made to suspend the rules on the first and third Mondays of each month and on the last six days of a session.[1] If the rules are suspended, bills may be passed with unusual despatch and possibly without a chance for amendments to be offered to them. It follows that permission to move the suspension, which is within the discretion of the Speaker, cannot be lightly given, and is in practice reserved for matters which are meritorious, urgent, and likely to be supported by a two-thirds majority. For if the Speaker's permission is granted, a member opposing the suspension may demand 'a second'. In that event a vote takes place, and a simple majority of those voting can ensure that the motion for suspension is seconded. Two speeches of twenty minutes each, one favouring and the other opposing, the suspension of the rules can be made; then the House votes. A two-thirds majority at this stage successfully abrogates the rules which may have been holding up the progress of the item of business.[2]

This account of the various restrictions on debate in the House of Representatives will have misled if it has left a picture of debate consisting of formal set speeches, cut off by the clock after stated intervals. There is less rigidity about the speeches than might appear from an account of the rules which control them. For instance, a speaker under the five-minute rule may always be allowed to extend his time by unanimous consent. Furthermore a great deal of fluidity is introduced by the practice under which members yield the floor to each other, perhaps to enable questions to be asked about what is being said, to let in corroborative views, or to allow additional time to a like-minded member who has already exhausted his own quota of time. When member A, who controls time, yields to member B, B may himself yield it to member C, and the granting member may increase the allotment of time when it elapses.

Nor are the restrictions placed on the length of speeches as absolute as may seem, because members are frequently given permission by the House to publish in the Congressional Record matter which they were unable to deliver, or did not choose to

1. House Rule XXVII, and see p. 282.
2. Cannon, op. cit., pp. 454–8.

deliver, when in possession of the floor. The permission of the House may go further; it may allow the member to revise the speech he made, going so far as to strike the whole thing out if he wishes, so long as he does not put a different aspect on the remarks made by his fellow members. This device, which seems to some to catch *l'esprit de l'escalier* so well, has been defended by Clarence Cannon:

> Especially important, though often decried, is the right to extend remarks in [the] record. In large legislative bodies where time is necessarily at a premium, it affords members opportunity to explain their attitude on pending questions and so give constituents a basis on which to approve or disapprove, and at the same time apprises colleagues and the country at large as to local sentiment the member is elected to represent.[1]

In a House where debate is so limited by the rules, it is not surprising that the Speaker is prohibited from entertaining any dilatory motion.[2] But opinions may differ as to what is or is not dilatory, and there is in fact a rich variety of obstructive devices available to members who wish to slow down the progress of business. In addition to the procrastination which a committee can show with regard to a measure committed to them, there are many opportunities open to members on the floor. Most popular perhaps is the practice of drawing attention to the lack of a quorum. The presiding officer is then required to order a roll call of members. Since the quorum of the House is 218 (half plus one of the total membership) or 100 in a Committee of the Whole, it often takes time to gather it together. An average quorum call could take thirty minutes. But the Legislative Reorganization Act of 1970 provides that the call may be discontinued as soon as the requisite number have answered. This will undoubtedly save time in future; but it remains a fact that as a delaying tactic, a quorum call is effective and can be repeated before long. By contrast the House of Commons has a quorum of only forty out of 630 members. A 'count' by the chair of members present is in order only at certain times and not at all after 10 p.m.; and in any event there is no roll call, or division. In general, with tighter

1. Cannon, op. cit., p. 325.
2. C. J. Zinn, *American Congressional Procedure* (1957), p. 11.

party discipline, more members and a smaller quorum, the problem of 'keeping a House' bulks much less large at Westminster than in the House of Representatives.

Up to the end of the 91st Congress (1969–70) the business of each legislative day in the House of Representatives used to begin with the reading and approval of the previous day's Journal. Often the Journal was read in abbreviated form, which took only a few minutes, when approval was given by unanimous consent. It was legitimate however for a member who wished to delay the progress of later business on that day to insist that it should be read in its entirety to question its accuracy, to offer amendments to it and force these amendments to a vote. Under the Legislative Reorganization Act 1970 the reading of the Journal is dispensed with unless the Speaker so orders or the House, by agreeing without debate to a motion, so requires. Here too the opportunity to delay has been trimmed but not eliminated.

In committee the strict limit on the time spent considering an amendment has been alluded to but there are no limits to the number of amendments which may be offered, and these if need be can be multiplied. A popular device is the use of 'pro forma' amendments. A member moves to omit, for example, the last word of a particular section of a bill. After five minute speeches have been taken on that amendment another member will move to strike out the last two words. Later amendments will seek to leave out the last three words, and so on.

With these obstructionist devices available to the minority, and the restrictive devices available to the majority, a balance is struck in House debate; and there are times when the bargain is driven hard. Yet there is an unexpected degree of accommodation between both sides, partly because the 'sides' are not invariably the two political parties, but often coalitions of members joining together on a particular issue. Party loyalties, instead of separating the two sides, may well be bringing parts of each of them together. Nor is there, as in the House of Commons, a confrontation between a government and an alternative government. On the contrary, both sides comprise a single arm of government, and there may be an impulse to make a common front against the executive. Whatever the cause, the result is a degree of accommodation and of tolerance that is not always found at Westminster.

METHODS OF VOTING

In the House of Representatives there are five methods of voting, of which only four are used in the Committee of the Whole.[1] First there is the voice vote. The presiding officer puts the question and judges, from the volume of the shouts of Aye and No that successively answer him, which side is in the majority ('The Ayes (Noes) seem to have it, the Ayes (Noes) have it'). This is the way in which each vote is ordinarily taken in the first instance.

If the result of a voice vote is doubtful, the presiding officer calls for a division; and any other member may demand a division provided that he does so before the result of the voice vote is announced. For a division the Ayes are called on to stand and are counted. The Noes are then counted in the same way, and the presiding officer announces the result of the vote.

If the presiding officer is still in doubt, or if at least one-fifth of a quorum—that is forty-four in the House or twenty in the Committee of the Whole—demand it, a teller vote is taken. In that event the presiding officer appoints one teller on each side of the question being voted upon. He then directs the Ayes to pass between the tellers, who stand on either side of the central aisle and count them. One teller announces the number in the affirmative, and the presiding officer then directs the Noes to act likewise. The count is similarly announced by a teller and the presiding officer declares the result.

When a teller vote has been demanded, but before tellers are named, it is possible for a member, if supported by a fifth of a quorum, to request 'tellers with clerks'. In that case the procedure outlined in the previous paragraph is followed, but in addition the names of those voting on both sides, and of those not voting, are recorded by the clerks (or electronically, if the House should go over to electronic voting), and afterwards published in the Journal.

Finally there is the yea and nay (or 'roll-call') vote, which can be demanded[2] in the House but not in Committee of the Whole. A demand for this vote has to be supported by at least one-fifth

1. There was also voting by ballot, last used in 1868; see House Rule XXXVIII.

2. The right to demand a yea and nay vote is laid down in the Constitution, Article I, 5.

of the members present (compared with one-fifth of the quorum for a teller vote). If this support is forthcoming, the clerk calls the roll of members, who answer Yea or Nay as their names are called out. The clerk then reports the result to the Speaker, who announces it to the House.

In both Houses of Congress a member may 'pair' with an opponent and so contract with each other to be absent for a period. The names of pairs are registered and published with the published list of every yea and nay vote.[1] A member who is present, though paired, counts towards a quorum.

Four of the five types of vote mentioned above are in use in the House of Commons or its committees in some form or other; but only the first and fourth (in American parlance, the voice vote and the teller-with-clerks vote) are in common use on the floor of the House. When, in both the House and the Committee of the whole House, the presiding officer puts the question at the end of a debate, he uses virtually the same phrases as his opposite number in the House of Representatives, and the Ayes and Noes successively respond. But if his view of the result ('I think the Ayes (Noes) have it, the Ayes (Noes) have it') is challenged, the House or Committee proceeds at once to a division. Here a difference in terminology has to be noticed. In the House of Representatives (and the Senate) a division means a vote by standing and sitting. In the House of Commons (and the House of Lords) it means something closer to the teller-with-clerks vote in Congress. But there are important differences. In the Commons members leave the chamber to vote and pass through one of the division lobbies on either side of it. The lobby on the Speaker's right is the Aye lobby and on his left is the No lobby. Towards the end of each lobby their names are recorded by clerks. At the end of each lobby stand two tellers who count the votes and report the result to the House. The four tellers are members appointed by the Speaker for each division, one for each side of the question, to count the votes in each lobby. In effect the British division is similar to the teller-with-clerks vote, but with both sides casting votes at the same time.

Voting by standing and sitting is still provided for in the standing orders of the House of Commons.[2] It can be used if, in the opinion of the presiding officer, a division is unnecessarily

1. House Rule VIII, 5.   2. Standing Order No. 36.

claimed—when for example only a handful of members challenge his verdict. But this method of voting is rarely used. Voting by roll call is not used in the House of Commons or Committee of the whole House, but it is the usual method of voting in Standing Committees and select committees.

The pairing of members is as familiar a part of life at Westminster as in Washington. But in the House of Commons pairs are arranged privately, within the control of the party organizations. They are not known to the officials of the House or published in the official records. In Washington where the quorum is relatively large (218 in the House and 100 in Committee of the Whole, out of 435 members), the recording of pairs is an essential part of establishing that a quorum is present. In the House of Commons, with a quorum of only forty out of 630, this point is not so important.

All questions in the House of Commons are decided by majority vote, though for a closure there is the additional requirement that at least a hundred members must be in favour to make the vote effective. In the House of Representatives by contrast several matters require a favourable vote of two-thirds of the members voting (a quorum being present). Sometimes this requirement is laid down in the Constitution, as when the vote is to expel a member, or to override a veto;[1] sometimes it is laid down in the Rules of the House, as when the vote is to suspend a rule or to consider immediately a report from the Rules Committee.[2] A vote to over-rule a presidential veto must always be by yea and nay vote. Otherwise any method of voting may be used, though unless the required majority is easily seen to back such a proposition, it is customary to proceed at once to a teller vote or a yea and nay vote.

Neither legislature has an electronic system of voting. Other parliamentary assemblies, notably in Belgium, Finland, France and India, have shown that this kind of system can be operated reliably and can save time consumed in recording votes by traditional methods. But the electronic systems pose problems in assemblies such as the House of Commons and the House of Representatives where no member has a personal desk or seat. For that reason the conventional electronic system, dependent on every member's being able to activate a switch fixed to his own prescribed seat in the chamber, is impracticable.

1. Constitution, Article I, 7.   2. House Rules XXVII, 1 and XI, 23.

For the House of Commons it is arguable whether such a system would over a session save much time. The time taken on a division is between eight and eleven minutes.[1] Of this time six minutes from the Speaker's first putting the question is allowed for members to reach the chamber from wherever they may be in order to cast their votes. Even if an electronic system were to be installed, some period of this kind would have to be preserved, so that a large saving of time would only be achieved on the comparatively rare occasions when two or more divisions are taken in quick succession.[2] An electronic system might also lose one of the advantages of the present system of divisions which brings debates to a conclusion by sending members out of the chamber in like-minded groups, who then have the chance of discussing the debate in a relaxed manner before returning for the next business.[3]

In the House of Representatives the present methods of voting are deeply entrenched. Roll calls for the yea and nay vote date back to the first Congress in 1789.[4] Over the years, moreover, the delays which they impose have been seen to have their own value. It has been noticed how various obstructive devices play a characteristic part in congressional debate. The demand for a vote and the call for a quorum, with ensuing delays, are powerful weapons of the minority in its negotiations with the majority. As a delaying tactic the demand for a vote is in one sense especially effective: being a right conferred on each member by the Constitution, it cannot be declared dilatory by the presiding officer, whereas he can, and often does, declare dilatory a quorum call and decline to entertain it.

A mechanical system of voting could make a substantial saving of time for the House of Representatives. In a yea and nay vote

1. Report of the Select Committee on Procedure, House of Commons Paper 283 of 1966–67, Qn. 9. The Committee saw so little prospect of significant savings that they did not even recommend a feasibility study of an appropriate mechanical system.

2. Such a system would however have made a spectacular difference on the morning of 24 March 1971, at the conclusion of the report stage of a guillotined bill. Members then spent nearly twelve hours going through the lobbies in a series of consecutive divisions.

3. *Parliamentary Reform* (Cassell for the Hansard Society) (1967), pp. 89–90.

4. House Rule XV, 1.

the roll is called twice, those failing to respond to the first call
being called a second time. At the end of the second call there is
an opportunity for members who have not yet voted to give their
votes individually to the clerk from the well of the House. The
average number of names called is 600, and the total voting time
is between twenty-five and forty-five minutes.[1] Even if allowance
is made for the time a member would need to reach the chamber
(and most of their offices are some distance away), and on reaching
it to decide how to cast his vote, the use of an electronic device
would result in considerable savings. George Galloway has estimated that the House of Representatives could save about one
month of sitting time in every session by such an installation.[2]
Having balanced this large saving against the wider implications
of voting by roll call, the House in the Legislative Reorganization
Act of 1970 has authorized the use of electronic voting if the
technological problems associated with its installation can be
overcome. An inquiry into those problems is in progress.

1. Riddick, op. cit., pp. 299, 385.
2. George Galloway, *Congress and Parliament* (1955), p. 63. This is
supported by evidence given to the Joint Committee on the Organization
of Congress (27 May 1965, p. 518), where a witness calculated that in
1958–63 the House spent the equivalent of 111 full legislative days on
roll-call votes and sixty-nine days on quorum calls. This gives an average
of thirty days a year.

CHAPTER FOUR

SECOND CHAMBERS

'UPPER HOUSES' or 'Second Chambers'? In Britain both usages are known, neither is objectionable. The Lords pre-dated the Commons as members of the King's Council and so are 'upper' in time as well as degree. But preponderant power has long since been surrendered to the Commons, and their representative function has established them for practical purposes as the first chamber. In the United States the issue is more delicately balanced. One view[1] is that the Senate was designated the upper House solely because in the original Hall of Congress in New York the Senate occupied the first floor and the House of Representatives the ground floor. Defenders of the House's claims point to the Constitution which deals first with the House of Representatives. It was the only directly elected assembly until the Constitution was amended in 1913. Even with the present-day prestige and authority of the Senate, the House retains its primacy in such important duties as the control of the purse. For all these reasons the phrase 'second chambers' has been preferred to 'upper houses' as the title of a chapter making a comparison between the Senate and the House of Lords.

ORIGINS AND PURPOSES

On the face of it, the differences between these two assemblies seem so great as to make any comparison far-fetched. The House of Lords is not an elected body; the Senate is. The House of Lords has over a thousand members, the majority being there solely because their fathers were there before them. A large number do not wish to take part in the work of the House, and on average a quarter of them have at any one time gone so far as to seek formal leave of absence from taking part in the proceedings of the House. By contrast the 100 members of the Senate have

1. Expressed by Mr Speaker McCormack and cited in MacNeil's *Forge of Democracy* (1963), p. 12.

achieved their position there against fierce competition, and are anxious by their activities to maintain the prestige of membership.

In power too there is a great difference between the Lords and the Senate. The House of Lords, as a result of periodic clashes with the Commons, is now much the less powerful chamber. The passing of the Parliament Act in 1911 not only confirmed the exclusive right of the Commons to control the nation's finances, but also ensured that Commons legislation passed in the earlier years of a Parliament could not be indefinitely rejected by the Lords. The Senate is barred by the Constitution from initiating taxation bills and by practice from introducing general appropriation bills; but there are no limits to the amendments it can make to such bills coming from the House of Representatives, and its concurrence is necessary if the bills are to pass. The Constitution further gives the Senate an executive power, which the House of Representatives does not have, of advising and consenting to nominations for public office and to treaties.

By the nature of its composition the Senate can claim to be the voice of the Union. While the House of Representatives may reflect more directly the attitudes of the population as a whole, in the Senate fifty states, with two senators each, speak to each other as equals, and this gives the Senate a role of its own. By contrast the House of Lords is demonstrably less powerful than the Commons, to the extent that the government in the United Kingdom stands or falls by its majority in the Commons. It is true that the House of Lords has one function which the House of Commons does not possess, of being the highest court in the land. But since the American Constitution sedulously separates both Houses of Congress from the exercise of judicial power (other than impeachment), this function of the House of Lords only emphasizes further the difference between it and the Senate.

Yet the origins of the House of Lords and the Senate have some similarities. The House of Lords, like the House of Commons, developed out of the King's Court. But the Lords were 'the great men of England', operating from spiritual as well as temporal bases, who had traditionally advised the King on the government of the country. The assertion by William the Conqueror of feudal overlordship made this relationship close and systematic. From now on, as his feudal vassals or tenants-in-chief across the whole of the country to which he had successfully laid claim, the Lords owed the King the duty to attend the royal court and to give advice. The history of the House of Lords is the story of how this feudal relationship was worked out and how the balance of power was struck first with the King and then with the Commons.

A similar concept lay behind the creation of the Senate. The intentions of the Founding Fathers of the American Constitution were clear. They wanted a bicameral system, giving to each House separate and distinct powers, so that each would check the other and both, together or separately, could check the President. But the Senate was to have special, additional responsibilities. Its members were to be ambassadors from their states, the 'great men' from the four corners of the country, who collectively would comprise a council with specific powers to 'advise and consent', in particular to share with the President the responsibility for the conduct of foreign policy and appointments to the executive and judicial branches of the government. Even today the Senate's authority owes much to the discharge of its special responsibilities as an executive council.

In its early days the Senate largely restricted its interests and activities to these special duties. The first Senate convened in 1789 with a membership of twenty-two representing the eleven states then in the Union. The proceedings of this small body took place for several years behind closed doors.[1] But its duty to participate in the legislative process gave it scope enough to develop, when it chose to do so, along the same lines as the House of Representatives. In 1816 it followed the House in creating the standing committees which from then on characterized its system of working. As new states joined the union, the membership of the Senate expanded. Finally, in 1913 the seventeenth amendment to the Constitution made it a directly elected body; and the six-year span of office, combined with the far greater size of constituency, gave to each senator a detachment from the electorate which the congressman, bound to fight an election every two years, might envy.

While the Senate has developed in that way, the most significant characteristic of the House of Lords has been its ability to survive with so little change in its composition. The clamour for more popular representation in Parliament that led to the

1. Bryce, *The American Commonwealth* (1889), p. 109.

Reform Act of 1832 left the Lords unchanged. The prolonged constitutional crisis that led to the Parliament Act 1911 called in question both the composition and the powers of the Upper House; the Act severely limited its powers, and its preamble said specifically:

> ... whereas it is intended to substitute for the House of Lords as it at present exists a Second Chamber constituted on a popular instead of hereditary basis, but such substitution . . . cannot be immediately brought into operation . . .

These words were written into the British statute book only two years before the Senate of the United States was made a directly elected second chamber. Yet in Britain the intended conversion to a popular basis has still not come about; and the likelihood of its happening has receded. Two hundred and sixty-eight hereditary peerages were created in the period 1912 to 1964. When at last in 1968–69 the leaders of the political parties drew up and agreed upon a plan for gradually eliminating the hereditary element in the House of Lords, they did not attempt to create 'a second chamber constituted on a popular . . . basis'. In 1968–69 there was less disposition than in 1911 to set up a body which might prove to be a serious rival to the House of Commons. Instead the party leaders agreed to propose a chamber nominated by themselves. But in spite of this agreement, the government was unable to secure the passing of the Parliament (No. 2) Bill. Some of the bill's critics found fault with the eventual extinction of the hereditary principle in favour of a virtually nominated chamber. Others, recalling the effect of the reform of 1913 on the authority and prestige of the American Senate, feared to strengthen the House of Lords by approving the much more modest reform proposed by the party leaders. The critics from their several standpoints combined, and the government abandoned the bill to ensure enough time for the remainder of its legislative programme.

Even as at present constituted, the House of Lords has not lacked vitality or self-confidence. In the same session that saw the Parliament (No. 2) Bill fail, the Commons passed a bill dealing with constituency boundaries. As a non-elected House the Lords were not affected by the bill; yet they radically amended it, and the government did not use its majority in the Commons to force the bill through against the Lords' opposition.

COMPOSITION AND CONSTITUTION

The House of Lords

In August 1968 the House of Lords consisted of 1,062 peers, made up of the following categories:

(a) 736 hereditary peers by succession;
(b) 122 hereditary peers of first creation;
(c) 155 life peers (excluding law lords);
(d) 23 serving or retired law lords; and
(e) 26 bishops.[1]

It should be noted that only category (e), the bishops, and the serving law lords in category (d), are limited in number. The other categories vary from time to time in number, so that the House does not have a fixed total membership. Its *effective* membership is, in any case, considerably reduced by factors to be considered later (see p. 174). Membership of the House of Lords automatically disqualifies a person from membership of the Commons. Until 1963 it was thus impossible for a member of the Commons, on inheriting a peerage, to remain in the Commons. But under the Peerage Act of that year, it became possible for such a person to disclaim his peerage for life. The peerage remains in abeyance and in due course, on the death of the disclaiming peer, passes to his heir.

Hereditary peers by succession or creation—categories (a) and (b) above—were until 1876[2] the only men, other than bishops, who could sit in the Lords.[3] Their titles are of different degrees—dukes, marquesses, earls, viscounts and barons—but the distinctions do not affect their rights or powers as members of the House of Lords. Peerages are created by the Sovereign; but under

1. These figures, and others in this chapter and in Chapter II, have been taken from *House of Lords Reform*, Command Paper 3799 of 1968, which is the most recent, comprehensive analysis of the composition of and attendance in the House of Lords. Except for category (b)—89 instead of 122—and category (c)—203 instead of 155—the corresponding figures for July 1971 are not significantly different.

2. When an Act of Parliament brought Lords of Appeal in Ordinary into existence as life peers (see p. 173).

3. The Lord Chancellor is Speaker of the House of Lords ex officio, though it has long been the custom to make him a peer.

the constitutional system in Britain, the Sovereign must act on the advice given by the Prime Minister. It is thus effectively the government of the day which creates hereditary peerages. At times of constitutional crisis a government can create enough new peerages to ensure a majority in the House of Lords sympathetic to its legislation. By this use of the royal prerogative the Tories carried the Treaty of Utrecht in 1713; and by the threat of its use the Whigs secured the passage of the Reform Bill of 1832 and the Liberals the Parliament Bill of 1911.

The passage of the Life Peerages Act 1958 has affected the number of hereditary peerages. In each year from 1958 to 1964 the number of new hereditary peerages was not significantly different from previous years. Since 1964 however it has been the policy of successive governments not to recommend the creation of hereditary peerages.

The Peerage Act 1963 allowed the few holders of hereditary peerages who were women to have the same rights of membership as their male counterparts. It also allowed the holders of such Scottish hereditary peerages as have survived (none has been created since 1706) full membership of the House of Lords. Before 1963 these peers balloted amongst themselves for the right to fill sixteen seats in the House.

Under the Life Peerages Act 1958 the Sovereign can grant baronies for life, without any limit in number, to persons of either sex. Grants are made on the recommendation of the Prime Minister who in practice includes names put forward by the leaders of the Opposition parties. Life peers together with the first holders of hereditary peerages comprise the majority of those who undertake the work of the House. About one in eight of the life peerages have been granted to women.

The law lords—category (d) above—are those peers who are entitled to act as Lords of Appeal when the House of Lords is acting in its judicial capacity (see p. 187). They include the Lord Chancellor and former Lord Chancellors; other peers who hold or have held high judicial office, such as the Lord Chief Justice; and up to eleven serving 'Lords of Appeal in Ordinary', together with Lords who have retired from that office. The function of Lord of Appeal in Ordinary was created by an Act of 1876 in order to strengthen the House in its judicial role. Lords of Appeal in Ordinary are appointed for life, with the rank of baron.

Finally there are the 'lords spiritual'—the two archbishops, and twenty-four bishops of the Church of England who make up category (e) above. Unlike the lords temporal who have tenure for life, they quit the House on retiring from the bishopric which brought them into it, unless they change to another bishopric with a seat in the House.

The ease with which a Prime Minister can create new peerages, the desire to reward faithful supporters and the government's need to keep a strong political force in the House of Lords have combined to result in a steady increase in the size of that House. It has nearly doubled in size in the first seventy years of this century. But its unwieldy numbers have in practice been considerably reduced as a result of an administrative innovation in 1958. In that year a standing order was introduced by which, in effect, peers have to decide whether or not they will take part in the business of the House. A peer who decides not to take part or fails to make the choice is given leave of absence. At any one time, something like a quarter of the potential members of the House thus do not take part in its activities. Of the remaining three-quarters some have not proved their claim to a writ of summons and many choose to attend the sittings of the House only when they feel they can take a useful part in its debates. There is not the compulsion that exists in the Commons to be available whenever a vote is taken. Figures for 1967–68 show that of the 679 members (i.e. two-thirds of the total eligible) who attended at any time during the session, 291 attended more than one sitting in three; 216 attended between one sitting in three and one sitting in twenty; and the remaining 172 attended less than one in twenty.[1]

The average daily attendance in the House of Lords in 1971 was 265; this compared with a figure of ninety-two in 1955. One cause of this increase has been the influx of life peers since 1958. Another has been the introduction of payments to peers who attend. Although no salary is attached to membership of the Lords, travelling expenses for peers who attend at least one-third of the sittings of the House were instituted in 1946; and in 1957 a fixed sum was allowed for the expenses, in addition to travelling expenses, of each day's attendance. Since 1957 the sum has been twice increased and in 1971 stood at £6.50 a day.

1. *House of Lords Reform*, Command Paper 3799 of 1968, p. 5.

An important aspect of the composition of the House of Lords in this century has been political. Since the hereditary peers are mainly Conservative, the House of Lords has been predominantly Conservative, and has posed a threat to governments of a different colour. The size of the Conservative majority has in recent times been reduced because so many Conservatives are among those who have been given leave of absence; and many more do not attend frequently. Nevertheless the Conservatives have remained preponderant. Of the 291 members who attended more than one sitting in three in 1967–68, 125 took the Conservative whip, ninety-five the Labour whip and nineteen the Liberal whip. This Conservative majority could be reinforced, when necessary, by the large number of Conservatives who did not attend frequently.

Of the 291 most frequent attenders in 1967–68, fifty-two took no party whip. Known as cross-bench members, they sit on the benches facing the throne, with government supporters to one side of them and opposition supporters to the other. They are a special feature of the House of Lords, bringing a wide range of experience to match their detachment from party political allegiance. They do not act together as an organized group: they make up their minds as individuals on the issues that come before them. On occasion their votes can be decisive. Politically speaking, the Lords as at present composed can be seen as a House with a potentially overwhelming Conservative character, but one which, in its normal day-to-day working, especially when dealing with matters of middling or less political content, acts and speaks with a persuasively independent style.

Finally there is the element of ministerial representation in the House of Lords. There are never less than two cabinet ministers—the Lord Chancellor (see also pp. 61–2) and the Leader of the House—and in some recent administrations there have been several more. The duty of answering debates or Questions on the affairs of particular departments falls on more junior ministers, of which there are generally about fifteen in the House of Lords. Following the general election of 1970, the government were represented in the House of Lords by three cabinet ministers out of eighteen, and thirteen out of the sixty-four ministers outside the cabinet.

The Senate

Compared with the House of Lords, with its categories of member and its ranks of precedence, its indeterminate numbers and diffuse political composition, the Senate is simple to describe. Its 100 members, two from each state, are directly elected and serve for six years, with elections taking place in rotation so that one-third of the Senate is renewed every two years. The Constitution requires that a senator should be at least thirty years old, should be an inhabitant of the state for which he is elected, and should have been a citizen of the United States for at least nine years. A senator receives a salary of 42,500 dollars (about £17,700), and is supported by a personal staff on average of thirteen to fourteen employees.

The allocation of two senators to each state regardless of size was decided upon by the Founding Fathers of the Constitution after argument had run high between the larger and the smaller states. The larger states claimed that their greater resources and financial contribution entitled them to greater representation; the smaller states feared domination by the larger states. The resulting compromise was a House of Representatives related to the size of population and a Senate with equal representation for each state. The Senate, rather than the House, thus has the essentially federal function.[1] The fears expressed in 1787, that this arrangement would cause conflict between the larger and the smaller states, has not been realized.

Yet election by states of unequal size, rather than by constituencies of approximately equal size, has inevitably given a hostage to the statisticians, for it is easy to show that the seventeen per cent of the nation who live in the twenty-six smallest states can command a majority of the seats in the Senate.[2] But the fear that legislation coming from the House might be nullified by an unrepresentative combination of senators from the small states has proved a chimera. In the great divisive issues it has been the geographical location and grouping of the states— west coast, rocky mountain, middle west, New England, deep

1. On the debates in the Federal Convention on the composition of the Senate, see George H. Haynes, *The Senate of the United States* (1938), Chapter 1.
2. Lewis A. Froman, *The Congressional Process* (1967), p. 4.

south—rather than their size or population which have dictated their points of view.

As matters were first arranged, the senators formed a link between the national and the state legislature, the latter nominating members of the Senate from among their number. The method of nomination by the state legislatures was made uniform by Congress in 1866. But the link was broken in 1913 when the seventeenth amendment to the Constitution removed from the caucus in power in each state the right to nominate senators, and placed it in the hands of the people at large. This change immeasurably strengthened the hand of each senator. No longer reliant on the votes of a transient majority in the state legislature, he could himself claim to represent the will of the state as directly as the legislature itself. The change also played its part in diminishing the influence of the national political parties in the states. Before 1913 the parties had to work hard to gain control of the state legislature in order to increase their representation in the Senate. Since 1913 this compulsion has been removed.

A senator's six-year term of office is a major factor in any analysis of the Senate's functioning. A period of this length, compared with the two years served by members of the House of Representatives before seeking re-election, gives a relative security of tenure. At each election new faces appear in the Senate, but two-thirds of its members have been undisturbed. It is they, rather than the new members, who set the tone of its proceedings.

The Senate's system of rotating elections means that, unlike the House of Representatives, it is a continuing body. Its 'permanence' is in practice qualified: with each new Congress, it acts as a fresh legislative body. As in the House of Representatives all legislation lapses at the end of a Congress. Specific rules[1] of the Senate provide that proceedings on treaties die at the end of a Congress and that proceedings on nominations die at the end of a session. All these matters have to be reopened in the new circumstances. The only difference is that the President does not have to submit treaties again, though he does have to submit nominations. Nevertheless the Senate, unlike the House,

1. Senate Rules XXXVII and XXXVIII.

has the hallmark of a continuing body. Its rules, first adopted in 1789, are assumed to continue in force with such amendments as it may make from time to time. Whereas the House adopts its rules anew at the beginning of each Congress, the most recent occasion on which the Senate adopted a revised code of rules was 11 January 1884.

The authority of an elected ambassador for the home state; the special responsibilities, in addition to legislative duties, for foreign policy and for the composition of the executive and judicial branches of the government; the sense of belonging to a continuing body; and the longer term of office; all these factors have combined to enhance the prestige of the Senate and to make its membership more coveted than that of the House of Representatives. The proof is the steady flow of members from the House to the Senate. In the 91st Congress (1969–70) no fewer than thirty senators had been members of the House, but no member of the House had been a senator. State governors wishing to enter politics at national level as a rule choose to run as senators: in the 91st Congress, eighteen senators had been governors or lieutenant governors. Especially in recent years the Senate too has proved a nursery for presidential candidates. President Nixon was elected to the Senate in 1950 and served as Vice-President (President of the Senate) from 1953 to 1961; President Johnson served as Majority Leader from 1953 to 1961 and as Vice-President from 1961 to 1963; and President Kennedy was a member of the Senate when elected President. These political opportunities have added to the Senate's drawing power at the expense of the House. The point can be stressed by considering the relative position of the second chamber in Britain. Here there is a steady flow from Commons to Lords. But the reasons are either the inheritance of a peerage or, more frequently, the reward for long and useful political service.[1] If political advancement is being sought, the flow is in the other direction. Four members of the House of Commons of 1966 to 1970 had taken the advantage of the Peerage Act 1963 and disclaimed their peerage in order to remain, or to become, members of that House.

1. It has been suggested that one function of the House of Lords has been to keep down the average age of members of the House of Commons. See Ian Gilmour, *The Body Politic* (1969), p. 301.

POWERS AND FUNCTIONS

The powers and functions of the House of Lords and the Senate are so greatly at variance that a different method of comparison suggests itself at this point. The powers and functions of the second chamber are compared with those of the first chamber in each country so that a general picture of the relative strength of the two second chambers emerges.

House of Lords

Descriptions of the powers of the House of Lords often tend to be negative in character; they stress the limitations on the powers rather than describe the powers themselves. This is because the two Houses once exercised equal powers, but the passing centuries have placed limits on the powers of the Lords, though not on those of the Commons. Originally, legislation was a joint act between equal partners, the clothing of ideas in a form to which both Houses could give their assent, much as it is in Congress today. As in Congress, too, the second chamber, sometimes even more than the first, could reject proposals made to them by the Sovereign or his ministers. The Sovereign likewise owed no responsibility to the two Houses and, as does the President of the United States, could accept or reject the bills put up to him. The legislative functions of the House of Lords were gradually restricted, first by the development of other elements in the constitution. The Privy Council and later the cabinet supplanted the Lords as chief advisers of the King; the House of Commons won control over finance and later secured that ministers, acting on the royal behalf, should stand or fall by the will of the majority of that House only. Today a defeat of the government in the House of Lords may be embarrassing; it can never, as in the House of Commons, be fatal.

If the change in the relationship between the two Houses was ratified by the Parliament Act 1911, it was foreshadowed much earlier. Once the King had acknowledged the compelling nature of the advice given by ministers with authority rooted in a majority of the House of Commons, the government was able to ensure that in the last resort the House of Lords gave way to the will of the Commons. The ultimate sanction was that the government would advise the King to create new peers, sympathetic to the views of the Commons' majority, in such numbers as to ensure the passage of legislation through the House of Lords. It has been shown (p. 173) how such an action in 1713 and its threat in 1832 and 1911 were enough to secure measures of major importance.

The powers of the House of Lords have for long been inextricably bound up with its composition. During the debates in both Houses between 1907 and 1911 on the powers of the House of Lords, much of the attack was directed against the composition of that House. 'Six hundred men chosen accidentally from among the unemployed' was a typical sally of Lloyd George. But although this kind of attack was made on the composition of the Lords, the result was to cut the power of the Lords without altering that composition. The preamble to the Parliament Act 1911 spoke of the need to change the composition; the actual changes made by the Act were limitations on the powers which an unchanged House of Lords could employ.

The same pattern has appeared in the succeeding sixty years. Although the two strands were so knotted, Parliament continued to try to deal with each in isolation. The Parliament Act 1949 further limited the powers of the Lords. The Life Peerages Act 1958 and the Peerage Act 1963 dealt only with its membership. Not until the Parliament (No. 2) Bill of 1968–69 was a comprehensive change attempted in which the powers and the make-up of the House of Lords could be debated together. The failure of that bill may have deepened the traditional reluctance to tamper with so intractable a constitutional problem.

The Parliament Acts

The powers of the House of Lords over public bills were restricted by the Parliament Act 1911 and further restricted by the Parliament Act 1949. These Acts distinguished two kinds of public bills, namely, money bills and other bills.

Money bills are defined by the Act as bills containing *only* provisions dealing with certain financial matters specified in the Act. In practice this definition chiefly extends to the annual Consolidated Fund Bills voting money to the government and some taxation bills. The Act makes the Speaker of the House of

Commons the sole judge of whether a bill falls into this category. He must, if practicable, seek the advice of two senior members of the House nominated for the purpose at the start of each session. But the final decision is his, and it may not be questioned in a court of law. If he certifies a bill as a money bill, it is almost invariably passed rapidly by the Lords without amendment.[1] If, on receiving the bill, the Lords were to take no action, it would nevertheless go forward for royal assent a month after it had been sent to them.

This virtual exclusion of the Lords from the consideration of money bills was not altogether an innovation of the Parliament Act 1911. It gave legal definition to a principle that originated several centuries earlier and which extended to a wider range of bills. In 1671 and 1678 the Commons had passed Resolutions denying the right of the Lords to alter bills of 'aids and supplies' (whose modern counterparts are the Finance Bill for taxation and the Consolidated Fund Bill for expenditure), and claiming that such bills ought to originate in the Commons. Any *amendment* of such bills by the Lords has been regarded by the Commons as intolerable. But Lords amendments to other bills having a financial effect, though equally a breach of the Commons' privileges, have been considered by the Commons on their merits. The Lords however could still *reject* financial bills without infringing the privileges of the Commons. When in 1860 they rejected the Paper Duty Repeal Bill, the Commons restated their privileges and resolved to include all the financial schemes for a year in one bill. They included the paper duty provision in a general financial bill in 1861, which the Lords agreed to, and from then on adopted the practice of incorporating their main financial proposals each year in a single bill. When therefore the Lords rejected Lloyd George's Finance Bill of 1909, they were rejecting the entire financial provision for that year.

The Finance Bill of 1909 was not a simple taxation bill. It contained elements of social reform that paved the way for what, in the 1940s and 1950s, would be called the welfare state. That was why the Lords rejected it. The government of the day could

1. The Commons are not debarred by the Act from considering an amendment made by the Lords to a certified bill, and there are a few instances of such amendments being made in the Lords on the proposal of the government and later agreed to by the Commons.

not tolerate this handling of their financial plans, and so set about the task of excluding the Lords, for all practical purposes, from the consideration of money bills. The Lords eventually passed Lloyd George's Finance Bill in 1910, before the Commons had achieved the statutory power to insist on its passing. The irony is that the Speaker of the day (Lowther) later gave it as his view that, had he possessed in 1909 the power which he was given in 1911 to certify a bill as a money bill, he would not have so certified the Finance Bill of 1909 because it contained provisions that were not 'money' provisions.[1] Since that date other finance bills for the same reason have not been certified as money bills,[2] and in theory the Commons could not have insisted on their passage within one month as money bills.

Bills other than money bills comprise the second category of public bills dealt with in the Parliament Acts 1911 and 1949. Here the restriction imposed on the Lords was not a virtual exclusion from the legislative process but a limit on the time in which the Lords could delay the passage of a bill sent to them by the Commons. The limits laid down in the 1911 Act were shortened in the 1949 Act. Consequently if a bill now passes the Commons in two successive sessions (whether of the same Parliament or not) with a minimum period of one year between the Commons giving it a second reading for the first time and a third reading for the second time, it may be submitted for royal assent without the approval of the Lords, provided that it has been sent to them at least one month before the end of each session. If in the second session the Lords reject the bill, it must go direct to the Queen for enactment, unless the Commons direct to the contrary. There is thus an effective minimum time-lag of thirteen months from the original second reading of the bill in the Commons before it passes into law. But not all of this is a delay imposed by the Lords on the passing of the bill, because some of the time is taken up by its normal legislative progress through the Commons. The effective delay therefore, the period for which the Commons are being prevented from getting their bill on the statute book, is likely to be between six and nine months.

This delay may not at first glance seem excessive, bearing in mind that the second House must be able to exercise restraint

---

1. Ullswater, *A Speaker's Commentaries* (1925), Vol. II, p. 103.
2. More finance bills fail to be certified as money bills than the contrary.

of some kind if it is not to be a rubber-stamp. But the requirement that the bill must pass in two successive sessions means that in the final session of a Parliament a government cannot be assured of passing its legislation through the Lords. To that extent the mandate given to it by the electors is limited by a non-elected body. It can be argued that a government should not introduce controversial legislation towards the end of a Parliament, when it may no longer possess the confidence of the electorate. But governments of the left point out that in practical terms it is only they who are liable to be thwarted in this way in the last year of their five years in office; Conservative governments are not likely to be frustrated by opposition from the House of Lords because the majority in that House is politically sympathetic.

The powers of the Commons to insist on the passing of legislation opposed by the Lords have not often been employed. In the aftermath of the political disputes that had led to the passing of the 1911 Act, the powers were used to ensure the passing of the Welsh Church Act 1914, and the Government of Ireland Act 1914. They were used again in 1948–49 to pass the Parliament Bill restricting further the powers of the House of Lords. Three uses of a power in more than fifty years do not suggest that the House of Lords has been delaying Commons bills to any great extent. Today it seems to be generally recognized that the Lords would only use their powers to reject a bill on matters of 'great constitutional and national importance'.[1] But the power cannot for that reason be disregarded. Scarcely less important than the formal power to delay a bill by rejecting it is the influence which the possession of that power enables the Lords to exert. Because governments do not want bills to be delayed for the period which a formal disagreement with the Lords would entail, they are the more ready to agree to the amendments which the Lords propose to bills. Because a government may not wish to be embroiled in a constitutional clash between the two Houses, which could in time provide an election issue that it may not desire, it may refrain from insisting on the progress of a bill which is rejected by the Lords. It is here, in the largely unchartable field of influence, rather than in the formal use of its legislative powers, that the effect of the Lords' delaying power is most felt.

1. House of Lords Debates, 16 February 1967, 280, c. 418.

Delegated Legislation

The Parliament Acts of 1911 and 1949 do not apply to any of the various kinds of Statutory Instruments which comprise delegated legislation.[1] Unless they are financial, Instruments require the approval of both Houses before they can come into or be continued in force (the affirmative method) or can be annulled by a resolution of one House (the negative method). The displeasure of either House is, in other words, enough to reject an Instrument subject to these methods. Recent years have seen an increase in the volume and importance of delegated legislation so that the potential of the Lords for opposing the will of the government has increased to that extent. The Lords did not use their powers to reject an Instrument until June 1968 when they rejected an order giving effect to the decision of the United Nations to apply sanctions to Rhodesia. They did not, however, persist in their opposition and when an equivalent order was later introduced, it passed. But the earlier refusal of the Lords was enough to cause the government to break off the all-party talks then going forward on the powers and composition of the House of Lords. A provision of the Parliament (No. 2) Bill, introduced later in the same year, would have given the Commons the power to override the rejection by the Lords of an affirmative order. But the bill did not pass, and the power of the Lords over Statutory Instruments remains intact.

Power to Initiate Bills

Though virtually excluding the House of Lords from the legislative process on money bills and restricting their powers to delay other bills, the Parliament Act said nothing about the practices which have traditionally restricted the rights of the House of Lords to initiate certain kinds of bills. The Acts were silent about those rights because they were not then in contention. They are nevertheless crucial to the efficient allocation of business between the two Houses.

Most government bills begin in the Commons for one of two reasons. The first is the financial privilege of the House of Commons, the exclusive right of that House to impose and appropriate charges on the people and to grant supplies. The second is

1. Delegated legislation is discussed in Chapter VIII.

that government measures which arouse political controversy are more appropriately debated by the elected House in the first instance.[1] How far do these limitations restrict the Lords in practice?

The resolutions of the House of Commons of 1671 and 1678, governing the financial privileges of that House in regard to 'bills of aids and supplies' (for example the annual Finance Bills and Consolidated Fund Bills) have already been noted. But in practice Commons privilege has prevented the government from introducing in the Lords a much larger class of bills, namely, bills whose *main* object is to create a public charge. If the Lords were to pass such a bill and send it to the Commons, it would be formally 'laid aside' by that House and not considered. Consultation between the authorities of the two Houses usually aims to forestall a public rebuff of this sort.

With other bills, in which the creation of a charge is *subsidiary* to the main object, the House of Commons does not rigidly enforce its privileges. Indeed if the exclusion of the Lords from financial matters were to be total, only a minute proportion could start in the Lords, for most of them have some financial content, however minor. As things are, the Commons co-operate in several devices which avoid this inconvenience. When the Lords have agreed to pass a bill containing financial matter, they formally decide to delete all such matter and send the bill to the Commons with gaps in it to indicate where the financial matters came. (In practice the relevant words remain in the printed bill that goes to the Commons, but are placed within brackets and underlined, so that there is no doubt about the purport of the bill.) The Commons, with their privilege thus inviolate, can then formally put back into the bill the words which the Lords had formally excluded from it. Another device is for the Lords to insert in the bill a subsection declaring that the bill does not impose a charge. When the bill reaches the Commons, the subsection is removed, and any charge can then become effective.

These devices, it should be emphasized, are available only where the financial aspects of the bill are subsidiary. When they are primary, the bill has to originate in the Commons. But, if the bills of aids and supplies are left on one side—bills like the annual Finance and Consolidated Fund Bills which as essentially taxing

1. Erskine May, *Parliamentary Practice*, 18th ed. (1971), p. 453.

and spending bills must always begin in the House of Commons—
the distinction between a bill whose financial content is major and
one where it is minor is a matter of degree. The restriction on the
Lords' right to initiate bills of major financial content seriously
impedes the efficient distribution of legislative business between
the two Houses. In modern times, when the powers of the Lords
are closely confined by statute and the government is accountable
to the House of Commons alone for its administration of the
national finances, the restriction seems unnecessary. The House
of Commons could abolish it at any time by passing a standing
order waiving their privilege in respect of any bill introduced
in the Lords by the government except a bill of aids and supplies.

The other reason for starting bills in the Commons is that
bills arousing political controversy are more appropriately considered first in the elected House. But this again is a matter
of degree. In every session there may be as many as ten bills of
high controversy—bills nationalizing or denationalizing industries or regulating prices and incomes are obvious examples—
which any government will wish to submit first to the elected
House. Sometimes, too, there are bills of less controversy but
equal public importance, like the series of Agriculture Bills,
which may be the main legislative contribution of a particular
department in the lifetime of a Parliament. The ministers concerned will want to be associated from the outset with these bills
in Parliament; and most ministers are in the House of Commons.

Besides these measures of high controversy or public importance, there is in every session a much larger number of
government bills of less importance but still arousing political controversy in varying degree. In most sessions twice as many bills
in this category are introduced first in the House of Commons
as in the House of Lords. Yet there appear to be no constitutional
or practical reasons militating against a more balanced allocation.
There has been no evidence that the House of Lords would
amend such bills wholesale in a manner unacceptable to the
government of the day. If they did so it would be open to the
government to restore the bill to its original form when it reached
the Commons, and to press its amendments as it does under the
existing procedures—almost invariably with success. It is true
that the limitations imposed on the delaying power of the Lords
by the Parliament Act do not apply to bills originating in the

Lords. But if a bill were to be heavily amended or rejected in the Lords, the government could always reintroduce it in the Commons. In any case the Lords are not likely to use their delaying powers on bills which are not of major political or constitutional importance.

Judicial Functions

To the general powers of the House of Lords must be added one which the House of Commons does not have. The House of Lords is the supreme appellate court in the United Kingdom. It has, in other words, a judicial function which the other parts of Parliament—the Commons and the Sovereign—do not.

The mixing of legislative and judicial functions in the House of Lords—personified in the Lord Chancellor as head of the Judiciary, member of the Cabinet and presiding officer of the legislature—is more apparent than real. In its judicial aspect the House of Lords has little if any resemblance to the House as a legislating body. As a court its membership is in practice confined to the law lords.[1] They are judges first and last, whose elevation to the House of Lords marks a step in the continuation of an exclusively legal career. It is true that Lord Chancellors, present and past, serve as Lords of Appeal when the House is acting judicially, and that they usually have been politicians. But even if they were to bring political considerations into their judgements, which is unthinkable, they are always outnumbered by those whose careers have been exclusively legal. Other members of the House do not take part in judicial deliberations. The converse does not apply: the law lords can take part in the debates of the House of Lords. By tradition they do not take sides in partisan politics.

The role of the House of Lords as part of the judiciary is a relic of the constitution as it existed in medieval times. Other aspects of the role have been specifically repealed or fallen into desuetude. The right of a peer accused of treason or felony to be tried by his fellow-peers was exercised as late as 1936, when the House resolved that it was a costly and obsolete procedure and should be abolished. The Criminal Justice Act 1948 eventually gave legal effect to that resolution. The right of the House of

1. The law lords are described above, p. 173.

Lords to judge persons impeached by the House of Commons has not been used since 1805. It can now be considered a dead letter.

The Senate

If a study of the powers of the House of Lords inevitably turns into a study of the way in which these powers are limited as compared with the powers of the other House of Parliament, such a progression is inappropriate to the powers of the Senate. The Senate's powers are largely the same as those of the House of Representatives. The balance between them is something like that between the House of Lords and the House of Commons in the seventeenth and eighteenth centuries, a relationship on which the Founding Fathers consciously drew in framing the American Constitution. Neither House of Congress can dominate the other, except to such extent as the power of its personality or the respect accorded to it by public opinion allow. In the exercise of the powers which any legislature employs—passing bills, overseeing the administration, influencing public opinion—the Senate plays a full part. If the following pages concentrate on the differences between the two Houses in Congress, as the preceding pages did on those in Parliament, the effect will not be to show them as being of a fundamentally different kind. Though important, the differences do not amount to a difference in status, and they do not take long to spell out.

The Constitution lays down differences in the powers of the Senate and the House of Representatives with regard to five matters: the initiation of revenue bills; the election of President and Vice-President; nominations for the public service; treaties; and impeachments. These apart, the powers are equal. Each of the five matters may be considered separately.

Taxation and Appropriation

There seems at first sight to be a parallel of a kind between the Senate and the House of Lords in the matter of financial bills. The Constitution gives to the House of Representatives alone the initiation of revenue bills. 'All bills for raising revenue shall originate in the House of Representatives', it says: but it goes on to say that '. . . the Senate may propose or concur with amendments as on other bills'.[1] This latter phrase mitigates the former, and to a considerable extent modifies the analogy with the House of Lords. Although all bills to levy taxes must originate in the House of Representatives, there is no limitation on the extent to which the Senate may try to alter them. Similarly the Senate in practice ranges comprehensively over the whole field of appropriation. By long standing custom all general appropriation bills originate in the House of Representatives, so that the House has the advantage of declaring first its view on the appropriate level of expenditure. But once the bill is sent to the other House the jurisdiction of the Senate's Appropriation Committee, and subsequently of the Senate itself, is as wide as at the corresponding stages in the House. It is left to the Conference between the two Houses to iron out the differences, as on any other bill.

Election of President and Vice-President

The complex system laid down for electing the President and the Vice-President of the United States is beyond the scope of this book. It has to be noted, however, that the Constitution gives the two Houses of Congress specific functions in the election of the chief officers of the Executive. Congress has first to determine the time at which the members of the electoral college (for whom, rather than for the President and Vice-President themselves, votes are cast at a presidential election) are to be chosen.[2] It has fixed the Tuesday after the first Monday in November in every fourth year. The electoral college itself meets on the Wednesday after the first Monday in December to cast its votes. On the following 6 January the presiding officer of the Senate counts the votes cast in the electoral college.[3] He does so in the House of Representatives in the presence of the members of both Houses; it is the only occasion when the Vice-President presides over a sitting of the two Houses. As a rule this count is a formality. The votes cast for members of the electoral college in November have usually decided who the President and the Vice-President are to be, because the practice is for each member of the college to consider himself, regardless of personal or party preference, as

1. Article I, 7. 2. Article II, 1.
3. Twelfth Amendment (1803) to the Constitution.

pledged to vote for the candidates who have won the majority of votes in his state.[1]

If no candidate for President or Vice-President wins a majority of votes in the electoral college, the two Houses of Congress have an important reserve function. For the office of President, the election is thrown into the House of Representatives which chooses by ballot between the three candidates who have won the highest number of votes. For this choice representatives vote by states, the representatives from each state having one vote between them, and the requisite majority is a majority of all the states. For the office of Vice-President the election is thrown into the Senate which chooses between the two candidates who have won the highest number of votes. For this choice senators vote as individuals, and the requisite majority is half the total membership of the Senate.[2]

The House of Representatives elected Thomas Jefferson President in 1801 and John Quincy Adams in 1825. The Senate elected Richard Johnson Vice-President in 1837. A special procedure was devised in 1877—a commission consisting of five senators, five representatives and five judges of the Supreme Court—to settle the claims of Hayes and Tilden to the Presidency: its award was to Hayes, although Tilden had received a majority of the popular vote.[3] Since that date the electoral college has always chosen a President and a Vice-President. If a strong third party were to emerge, as it appeared to have done in the election of 1968, this record could be in jeopardy.

Nominations and Treaties

The procedure relating to nominations for public office is detailed elsewhere in this book (see pp. 398-9), as is that relating to treaties (see pp. 405-8). In each case the Senate has the duty,

1. A proposed Amendment to the Constitution to abolish the electoral college, thus providing for the direct election of the President and Vice-President, passed the House of Representatives in the 91st Congress but failed to pass the Senate.

2. Twelfth Amendment (1803) to the Constitution. The quorum laid down in the Twelfth Amendment for the House is one or more members from two-thirds of the states and for the Senate two-thirds of the total membership.

3. An account of this historic election is given in Morison and Commager, *Growth of the American Republic*, 5th ed. (1962), Vol. II, pp. 73-77.

not given to the House of Representatives, of advising on and consenting to propositions put to it by the executive.[1] This is the Senate's executive function of which there is no equivalent in the House. In consenting to nominations, a simple majority suffices; in consenting to treaties, two-thirds of the senators present must concur.

Impeachment

Impeachment is a proceeding of British origin. It is the only way in which the Senate exercises judicial power, and this the only point at which in this respect it compares with the House of Lords. Impeachment is a weapon given to Congress by the Constitution.[2] It can be directed against the President, Vice-President, the federal judiciary and all federal officials including those in independent administrative agencies. It does not extend to the armed forces. Its use is limited to cases of 'Treason, Bribery or other High Crimes and Misdemeanours' and it has never been clearly settled whether this last phrase means something broader than violations of the criminal law for which the person could be tried in court. The fact that President Andrew Johnson was impeached on political grounds suggests that at least in 1868 'other high crimes' were thought to extend beyond the criminal code. But the President was not convicted and the issue remains in doubt.

The procedure for impeachment is similar to that which was used in the British Parliament. The House of Representatives alone has the right to bring a charge; the Senate alone has the right to try the impeachment.[3] The procedure is set in train by charges made on the floor of the House on a representative's own responsibility, or by charges preferred in a message from the President, or from a state legislature or a grand jury. A direct proposal to impeach is a matter of high privilege and supersedes all other business. The charge is always referred to an investigating committee. On its report, if the House votes for impeachment, the case is tried on the floor of the Senate, sitting as a court in private, after each senator has sworn or affirmed that he will

1. Constitution, Article II, 2.   2. Article II, 4.
3. Constitution, Articles I, II and III.

act according to the rules of law. If the President of the United States himself were to be tried, the Chief Justice would preside over the Senate. Two-thirds of the senators present need to vote in favour if a prosecution is to succeed. In the case of President Andrew Johnson, after the House had successfully accused him, the Senate's vote on the matter was one vote short of the necessary two-thirds majority; and the President duly completed his term of office. The result of a successful prosecution is removal from office.

Impeachment could be a major weapon at the disposal of Congress in its oversight of the executive if its scope can be construed as going wider than the criminal law. In practice it has rarely been employed. In the whole history of the Union, the House of Representatives has impeached only twelve men—one President, one secretary of war, one senator, one judge of the Supreme Court and eight judges of other federal courts; and the Senate acquitted all of them except four judges (dismissing the case against the senator for want of jurisdiction). The last impeachment to be voted by the House was in 1936; and although threats are uttered from time to time, enthusiasm for this procedure, at least in the Senate, seems to be dwindling. The Lords found that the right of a peer to be tried by his fellow peers on the floor of the House consorted ill with the requirements of a legislature. The Senate has reached the same conclusion about impeachment. Today it can no longer easily interrupt its congested schedule to sit as a court, nor can busy senators easily be kept on the floor. Impeachment today may be less significant as a positive deterrent than as a constitutional statement of Congress's duty to ensure that persons elected or appointed to high public office are not corrupted by the temptations of power. Congress, like Parliament, has found other ways to assert its powers over the executive.

PROCEDURES AND WORKING METHODS

With procedures and working methods, as with powers and functions, the differences between the Lords and the Senate are greatly at variance. The comparison struck is again generally with the first chambers. Some of the material in the preceding chapter, for example on the nature and form of debate, applies equally to the second Houses and, as foreshadowed there, is not repeated here.

The House of Lords

Like the House of Commons, the House of Lords is rectangular in shape; but the red benches, the gilded furnishings, the stained glass windows and the Victorian ornamentation combine to give the House of Lords a more sumptuous appearance than the modern, reconstructed House of Commons. One end of the Lords chamber is dominated by the throne from which the Sovereign reads the speech that opens each new parliamentary session. In front of it is the woolsack—a red divan, as it were, with a backrest—on which sits the Lord Chancellor, or whoever is deputizing for him, as Speaker of the Lords. Benches for peers are arranged along the other three sides of the rectangle. On the two longer sides, on the Lord Chancellor's right and left respectively, sit ministers and supporters of the government, and the members of the opposition. The front bench immediately to the right of the Lord Chancellor is reserved for the bishops. The seats facing the Lord Chancellor are the cross-benches for peers who are not committed to the main parties. In the centre of the hollow square is the table of the House, where the Clerk of the Parliaments and his assistants sit.

The quorum of the House is three; but if a division on any stage of a bill or on subordinate legislation reveals that there are less than thirty peers present, the matter remains undecided and further debate on it is adjourned until another sitting. Procedure is basically similar to that of the House of Commons, in that the process of debate consists of proposing a motion, debating a question based on it, and deciding the question by collecting the voices, or if that method is challenged, by a division of the kind used in the Commons.

All speeches must be relevant to the question under discussion. There are rules, as in the Commons, to forbid allusions to debates in the other House, to eschew personal and offensive remarks, and not to comment on matters before the Courts. No peer may speak twice to the same question (except in committee and in some other special circumstances) but the peer who moves a motion may reply at the end to the debate on it. Speeches are made not to the chair as in the Commons and elsewhere but to the other peers—'My Lords', are the opening words of each speech. The order of speaking is not left to be decided by the presiding officer.

A list of speakers is usually drawn up beforehand, outside the chamber, by discussions among the interested persons. It is not binding and may be varied, though it is commonly followed. As explained elsewhere (see Chapter I), the powers of the chair in the Lords are strictly limited. It is left to individual peers to keep to the path of order, and for the House as a whole to discipline those who stray from it, often on the initiative of the Leader of the House.[1] Nothing can be more dispiriting for a peer than to have his speech interrupted by a colleague rising to move, 'That the noble lord be no longer heard'. This is a possible, though a very rare, motion.

As an exceptional procedure, debate can be closured by a peer's moving, 'That the Question be now put'. The chair does not have the power, as in the Commons, of refusing to accept the motion. If it is pressed the question has to be put; and if the closure motion is carried, the original question is put without further debate. Before he puts the question, the occupant of the chair has to remind the House of what an exceptional procedure it is, thus giving the peer who is moving the motion a chance to withdraw it before the question is put on it. It has been used only twice in the last fifty years, in 1926 and 1961.

Debates continue until all those who wish to speak have spoken for as long as they care to. No power resides in the chair, comparable with that in the Commons, for the presiding officer to select which amendments are debated; they are taken in turn. The House of Lords seems to have time at its disposal to hear all the speeches its members wish to make, though recently pressure to speak has been mounting, and could lead to formal restraints if the traditional 'self denying ordinance' of the peers is not observed. In practice much of the business is disposed of under informal agreements reached through 'the usual channels' (see p. 31), which though not binding, are generally accepted by the House.

The Lords do not need to refer bills very often to public bill committees. There have been recent experiments with the use of

1. The main recommendation of a Select Committee on Procedure reporting to the House of Lords in August 1971 was that the House should continue to exercise self-discipline and should not institute a speakership on the pattern of the Commons to control proceedings. House of Lords Paper 227 of 1971, paras. 3 to 7.

ad hoc committees off the floor; but the normal practice is for the committee stage of bills to be taken in committee of the whole House. Decisions are reached by voice vote, or if necessary by a recorded vote taken by walking through division lobbies, as in the Commons. When the question is put, the Lords call out, not Aye and No, but Content and Not-Content. There is no official or unofficial system of 'pairing' in the Lords.

The House meets on Tuesdays, Wednesdays and Thursdays and, if necessary, on Mondays and Fridays as well. It usually meets at 3 p.m. on Thursdays and 2.30 p.m. on the other days, but it can meet at any pre-arranged convenient hour. If there is judicial business in the House, it is usually taken in the morning;[1] after it, the House 'adjourns during pleasure' until its sitting in the afternoon.

Each sitting begins with prayers read by one of the Bishops, or the Lord Chancellor or one of the deputy speakers. There follows, if needed, the picturesque ceremony in which a new peer in scarlet robes, supported by others similarly clothed, takes his seat for the first time. Private business (business on private or local bills)—largely formal at this stage—follows, after which is the time for starred Questions to ministers. These are limited to four a day, so do not amount to anything like Question time in the Commons; nor are the Questions themselves so rigidly contained within rules of order. The exchanges in both Houses are however not dissimilar. Starred Questions seek information only, and are not designed to start a debate, although they are pursued at greater length than in the Commons. Supplementary Questions are in order but not speeches.

After these Questions business that does not require notice is taken: for example, Questions are asked by private notice, and announcements made about future business. Ministerial statements are usually synchronized with the equivalent statement in the Commons, but when a statement is made by a minister in the Lords who is head of a department, it is made immediately after Questions. The main business of the day then follows. With some exceptions items are taken in the order in which notice of them was given, though the order may be varied by

1. The main judicial business is now transacted outside the House in the room for Appeal Committees.

agreement. Except on Wednesdays proceedings on public bills have priority. Government business has no precedence over other items but as most public bills are government business, the government in practice has precedence, by and large, on all days except Wednesdays.

Included among the business at this stage are motions and unstarred Questions of which notice has been given by peers. Unlike starred Questions (see above), unstarred Questions are designed to initiate a debate. A peer frequently adds at the end of his Question the words 'and to move for papers', as an indication that he intends to exercise his right to reply to the debate. Motions and unstarred Questions cannot be put down for a day more than four weeks in advance, though they may be put down for 'no day named'.

It can be seen that business in the Lords, unlike in the Senate, follows a certain order. To this extent it resembles business in the Commons. But it differs from the Commons, first of all, in not being subject to time rules; items are taken as briefly or as spaciously as their lordships desire. Time is not nearly such an important consideration as might be expected in a chamber which has to carry through a programme of government bills. There is no set hour for the rising of the House or the ending of a debate, and virtually no closure. But there is no history of obstruction. It is the restraint with which the Lords make use of their opportunities that is most striking. There is also more flexibility about the Lords proceedings: the order of business, for example, can easily be changed 'by leave of the House'.

Debate in the House of Lords is rarely as boisterous as in the Commons, and the rules of order are not such as to bring the chair into conflict with whoever is speaking. The pre-arranged order of speaking, too, removes the element of the unpredictable which sometimes breathes life into a debate in the Commons. But debates in the Lords have a quality of their own, with down-to-earth differences being clothed in courteous language. Some of the compulsions which drive members of the Commons to make speeches—such as headlines or votes—do not exist to the same degree in the Lords. Instead a higher proportion of the speakers are knowledgeable people who are both interested in, and objective towards, the matter under debate.

The Senate

Like the House of Lords the Senate chamber is oblong in shape. Unlike the peers senators sit in armchairs, each at a personal desk, in rows that form a semi-circle enclosing a dais on which the presiding officer sits. As in the House of Representatives Democrats sit on his right hand and Republicans on his left, the dividing line between them moving in accordance with the result of each election. Behind the seats is an open space where the staffs of senators can be seated. Large galleries open off the chamber for the use of the public. As a rule a senator speaks from his own place, though he may on occasion move about and speak from another place if convenient.

In both second chambers the rules of procedure are simpler and less restrictive than in the first chambers. But there is a special feature of proceedings in the Senate which marks it as much more like the House of Lords than the House of Commons. In the Senate the rules are frequently dispensed with by unanimous consent. This important qualification has to be made in advance of any description of the Senate's procedure. The rules are there, but at any time the Senate is likely by unanimous consent to depart from them.

The reason is that the Senate is a body with a comparatively small number of members, each of them very busy. A senator represents a whole state rather than a constituency or district within the state. He will belong to more committees and subcommittees than his opposite number in the House of Representatives. With the difficulty that senators find in attending so many meetings it often happens that a very small group, even a single senator, will handle most of the work on a given bill. Every senator is therefore tolerant of the convenience of other senators and confident that equal tolerance will be shown to him when his convenience is in question. As a general rule business is taken at such a time and in such a way as to meet the convenience of senators most concerned with it. More than in the House of Representatives there is co-operation between the parties to forward the individual's convenience.

An example of this tolerant approach is the procedure on bills when they return to the floor from committee. In general the procedure is less elaborate than in the House of Representatives. Although there is a Senate Committee on Rules and Administration, it does not, as does the House Rules Committee, provide 'rules' to control the consideration of a bill on the floor (see p. 283). The Senate has two calendars only. The Executive Calendar consists of nominations and treaties. The Calendar of Business lists, under the sub-heading 'General Orders', legislation that has come from committee. Every sitting day except Mondays, at the conclusion of the 'Morning Hour' (described below), the Senate proceeds to consider bills on the calendar. Important bills are usually brought forward on a motion moved by the Majority Leader and agreed to by a majority vote. On Mondays the rules provide for the Calendar of bills to be called over during the Morning Hour. Bills not objected to are taken up in order, each senator being entitled to speak once and for five minutes only. If objection is made, the bill is either passed over or it may be considered—provided that a motion to that effect is agreed—without the five-minute rule applying. There is, however, nothing sacrosanct about the Monday call of bills. It may be unanimously dispensed with to suit the general convenience. Alternatively it may be made on other days and at other times by unanimous consent.[1]

As a general rule the day's proceedings in the Senate depend from the outset on whether it adjourned at the end of the previous day's sitting, or whether, with business unfinished, it recessed with the intention of carrying on with the same business the next day. In either case proceedings begin at noon (unless otherwise pre-determined) with prayers and the reading of the Journal of the previous day's proceedings—the latter being frequently dispensed with by unanimous consent. If the Senate has adjourned overnight, the day's business starts with the Morning Hour. In this time petitions can be presented, reports made from committees, bills and resolutions introduced, agreements made that certain material should be published in the Congressional Record. The Morning Hour can be used to dispose of uncontroversial matters; it is the time when senators can rid themselves of a number of commitments. Senate committees may sit during the Morning Hour, but not later. As an example of the far-ranging and disjointed nature of proceedings during Morning Hour, a day chosen at random in July 1969 may be taken. Among the seventeen matters recorded as being raised were:

1. Senate Rules VII and VIII.

the American way of Life;
oil pollution on the coast of California;
the President's moving expenses;
world peace;
the retirement of an editor in Wisconsin;
the price of pesticides;
the problems of American businesses overseas;
the history of Wyoming;
the need for a national park in Texas;
the workings of the Joint Economic Committee;
the costs of medical treatment;
rural housing; and
the dangers of cigarette smoking.

It frequently happens that the Senate, wishing to continue a debate on the following day, will not adjourn at the end of the day, but 'recess', that is, suspend its proceedings so as to be able to continue on the next day. Dr Riddick records that once a whole regular session was thus reduced to five legislative days.[1] If the Senate has recessed overnight, a Morning Hour will not take place except as a result of unanimous agreement, in which case recent practice is to limit speeches at this stage, by unanimous agreement again, to three minutes. At 2 p.m. the unfinished business of the previous day is again broached—unless of course, by unanimous consent or on motion, it is decided to take up some quite different bill. There is a volatility about debate in the Senate which is quite foreign to that in Parliament, and distinctive from that in the House of Representatives. Unlike the House, for instance, the Senate may have several bills before it at a given moment.

This volatility is encouraged, rather than restrained, by the rules and practice of debate. A senator may speak twice, without leave, upon any question in debate on one day. He must not use disorderly language, not address another senator in the second person, and not refer to the actions of the House of Representatives. At any given moment one senator alone retains the floor; he has been recognized by the presiding officer for that purpose. But he can, as it were, sub-let his lease of the floor to his colleagues

1. Riddick, *Congress: Organization and Procedure* (1949), p. 341. The Senate's practice has varied. In the last five years its practice has almost invariably been to adjourn from day to day.

without himself losing the floor. Under the rules he can yield only to be asked a question. But he will often allow a brief speech to be made, though in so doing he risks being called to order by the presiding officer or another senator. Once speaking, a senator cannot be interrupted against his will unless, as rarely occurs, he transgresses the rules of debate.

Within this thin framework, debate can range almost without limit. There is little need for relevancy in speeches. A Senate rule, adopted in 1964, requires speeches to be germane to any legislation under discussion for a period of three hours after each Morning Hour; but this rule is frequently broken, either with the consent of all present, or *sub silentio*. This apart, senators can speak about whatever they wish and, provided that the Senate has not adopted a rule to the contrary, for as long as their inclination takes them and their stamina allows. Nor do the amendments which they propose need to be germane to the bill in question (except to general appropriation bills or once the cloture (see below) has been invoked).

This remarkable latitude of debate, and the extent to which senators take advantage of it, is undoubtedly the best known feature of the Senate's proceedings. While both the House of Representatives and the House of Commons were confining debate increasingly by such devices as previous questions, closures and guillotines, the Senate was holding to its chosen course of unrestricted debate. The original meaning of the word 'filibuster' —an engagement in unauthorized warfare against a foreign state—has long been overshadowed by the meaning given to it by the Senate, namely, obstruction to the point of killing a measure under debate.

There is one exception to this lack of restriction. To protect the Senate against obstruction on too great a scale and to assure progress in legislation when necessary, a majority has been armed since 1917 with a power to apply a form of closure. The cloture[1] can be invoked on a motion signed by sixteen senators. On receiving this motion, the presiding officer at once states its terms to the

---

1. The term used by the Senate shows its French derivation. The closure introduced into the House of Commons on the personal authority of Speaker Brand in 1881 (described on p. 147) was also of French inspiration, but the English translation—closure—was later preferred. See Eric Taylor, *The House of Commons at Work*, 8th ed. (1971), pp. 115–16.

Senate. Debate can continue on the measure through that day and the next. But on the second calendar day after the motion was filed, one hour after the day's proceedings have begun, senators vote on the cloture. If two-thirds of those present and voting are in favour, the cloture is carried. No senator may then speak for more than one hour on the measure and amendments thereto, while points of order are decided without debate. As amended in 1949 the cloture rule required support of two-thirds of the whole membership before it could be invoked; but motions to change the Senate's rules were specifically put beyond its reach. As a result of further amendments in 1959, it now applies to all motions, and requires two-thirds of those present and voting.

This form of closure cannot be described as a particularly harsh device. But, mild as it is, it offends so much against the tolerance that marks the Senate's proceedings that it was successfully invoked on only eight occasions between its inception in 1917 and the end of the 90th Congress in 1968.[1] So it does not loom over every debate in the way that similar procedures do in other legislatures. Instead the Senate prefers self-discipline. A timetable can be imposed on proceedings as a result of unanimous consent; and senators frequently and voluntarily agree to forgo their rights in this way. Time limits imposed by unanimous consent have become something of a standard practice, and many of the agreements include a requirement that motions and amendments should be germane to the matter under consideration.

It is unlikely that a proposal for unanimous consent to a timetable will be sprung on the Senate without a great deal of pre-arrangement between the leadership on the two sides. It is one of the characteristics of the Senate that its superficially casual processes generally disguise the hard bargaining and earnest planning that have preceded them.

Agreements can be made inoperable by the dissent of a single senator. He can also with propriety hold up progress on a matter to which he is opposed. The power of the individual senator is thus considerable. Yet paradoxically that power serves to underline the strength of community expression in that House. Again

1. *Limitations of Debate in the Congress of the United States*, a compendium including a select bibliography issued by the Legislative Reference Service of the Library of Congress (revised edition 1970), pp 48–53.

and again a senator will voluntarily concur in a proposal to throw bounds around his dedicated opposition to a measure. The most remarkable feature of debate in the Senate is not so much the latitude given to individual senators as the toughness of the communal self-discipline it constantly displays.

The quorum of the Senate is fifty-one, a majority of the House. Senators frequently ask for the roll to be called in order to establish that a quorum is present. This is an effective delaying tactic. It is also a method of recalling senators to the floor to hear what is going on, to make up the numbers necessary for some procedural move, or possibly to prevent subsequent complaint that an unwelcome proposal had been agreed to unanimously in their absence. It is not wholly effective however, since senators are counted as they enter the chamber and they may then depart immediately.

Voting takes place in one of three ways; either by voice, when the volume of support and opposition is readily ascertainable; or by division, when senators stand to be counted; or by roll-call, when each senator's vote is recorded. A vote by roll-call is taken if at least one-fifth of senators present (assuming a quorum present) demand it. Votes by roll-call are frequently planned and announced in advance. When a vote has been taken by one method, a different kind of vote can be requested (as in the House of Representatives) at any time before the result of the first vote has been announced. It is however possible for a senator who has voted for the winning side, or who did not vote, to require at any time within the next two days that the matter be reconsidered in another vote. This can happen only once, and since the winners may not be confident of retaining their majority on a later occasion, one of them may as a precaution demand a reconsideration immediately after the principal vote has been taken. In practice this motion to reconsider can be made immediately by another senator moving that it be 'tabled'. A motion to table the reconsideration motion has to be decided without debate; if carried, it disposes of the reconsideration motion, which cannot be raised again.

As in the House of Representatives, the 'pairing' of senators is an officially recognized process. A single pair is in effect a contract between two members on opposite sides not to take part in a particular vote. They cancel out each other's absence. There are other kinds of pairs. A general pair occurs when two absent senators contract not to vote, without disclosing how they would have voted. Then there is a 'live pair', when a senator who is present withholds his vote in order to honour an obligation to an absent senator on the opposite side. Pairs are recorded and published, and they count towards the quorum necessary for a vote.

GENERAL CONTRASTS

Almost every nation with a large population and a democratic form of government has a two-chamber Parliament. Experience has shown the advantages of this system. The volume and complexity of present-day legislation and the gradually increasing power of executives everywhere provide too much material for a single chamber to digest easily, and carry with them so many possibilities of error going unchecked as to compel the need for a second look at most decisions.

This compulsion, when considered in relation to the House of Lords and the Senate, has clearly had widely divergent results. When the Senate was born, the resemblances to the House of Lords may have been greater than the differences. To John Dickinson, representative of Delaware at the Philadelphia Convention, 'the Senate should be as much like the House of Lords as possible'. The Constitution of 1789 responded to this desire in authorizing two chambers of more or less equal powers—as in Britain at that date—and in grafting on to the Senate advisory and executive duties (over treaties and patronage) redolent of the House of Lords of a much earlier epoch. Constitutional development has been very different in the two countries. The Senate has retained its powers—even increased them if prestige is to be read in conjunction with written powers—in relation to the House of Representatives; the House of Lords lost ground as the spread of popular representation, and the doctrine that the government stands or falls by its majority in the House of Commons alone, made that House politically and constitutionally the dominant partner.

The difference is apparent in the way in which the Lords and the Senate carry out their legislative function. The Lords reject a bill only on rare occasions; in principle theirs is a revising function. Government departments prepare a bill carefully before its presentation to Parliament and every effort is made to consult and appease interested parties, unions and associations. None of this work has removed the need for meticulous and public inspection of bills by the second chamber. The time available for the drafting of important measures is often inadequate, with the result that the draftsman works under extreme pressure. Debate on bills in the House of Commons is often curtailed by the congested state of business; and any government may have to resort to a guillotine to enforce the passage of its most controversial bills through the Commons, with the consequence that some clauses are not discussed there at all. Some idea of the contribution that the revising chamber has made can be gained from the session of 1946–47 in the course of which a total of 996 amendments were made by the Lords to public bills, of which only fifty-seven were rejected by the Commons. These bills included measures to take under public control road and rail transport and the gas and electricity supply industries.[1] Less controversial bills of a more technical character on such subjects as company law, water resources and weights and measures, for example, are often considered first by the Lords whose thorough scrutiny enables the Commons to consider the bills with many of their imperfections removed.

By contrast the approach of the Senate to legislation befits an assembly which for practical purposes shares power equally with the other House. Here too the revising function is important. The limited nature of debate on the floor of the House of Representatives, leaving the processing of bills in practice to a small group of appropriate committee men, and the speed with which, consistent with the rules, bills can be taken through that House, make it essential, in the eyes of senators, to take a close second look at bills. But their legislative duty takes them much further than mere revision. With the exception of general appropriation and taxation bills, the Senate initiates legislation as freely as the House of Representatives, and it rejects or amends without inhibition.

For these purposes their relative freedom from the tyranny of the clock gives the Lords and the Senate an advantage over the

1. Constitutional and Parliamentary Information, 3rd Series, No. 70 (April 1968). Article on the House of Lords by the Clerk of the Parliaments.

other Houses. The Lords are not subject to the pressure of constituents, nor to the demands of local party organization. As
shown above they do not spend time on the annual Finance and
Consolidated Fund Bills; nor do they inquire into or debate such
related matters as estimates of expenditure that flow from the
enactment of public bills. If the Lords are obliged towards the
end of a session to work against the clock, it is because the present
allocation of business between the two Houses enforces it, not
because of their own rules of procedure. Unlike peers, senators
have large, representative duties, and they play a full part in
scrutinizing financial (as well as other) legislation. Yet the Senate
has held fast to its tradition of virtually unlimited debate as the
only certain way of checking the claims of the other two elements
in the legislative process, the President and the House of Representatives. In preferring self-restraint and personal independence
to the clamp of strict rules and standing orders, in settling for
conditions where it is left to fellow members rather than to the
chair to insist on the niceties of order, the second chambers in
the United States and Britain have much in common.

Yet, as with the first chambers, the basic difference remains.
The House of Lords is a chamber of debate, of which the essence
is a dialogue between ministers on the one hand and peers on the
other. As a debating chamber it is less a scene of drama than the
Commons because the ultimate sanction is lacking: the government stands or falls by what happens in the Commons, not in the
Lords. But whether raising a matter of individual grievance or
high political significance, the peers evoke a reply, a comment or
a point of view from the government. Within the constitutional
limitations, the House of Lords, able as it is to call upon a wide
range of experience from among its large membership, shows to
its best advantage in confronting the government in debate on
the floor. The Senate has no government spokesman; and it is
open to question whether it is any longer primarily a debating
forum. It has a long tradition of great debates. The speeches of
Webster and Clay and Calhoun are part of the embodied memory
of every American schoolboy. Filibusters have been equally
notable: according to George Galloway, twelve famous filibusters
of the past occupied on average thirty days each of the Senate's
time. Today the debate continues. But the search for consensus,
and the fragmentation of power among the chairmen of important

committees as well as the official leaders of the two parties means that debate on the floor tends to be overshadowed by the bargaining and compromise in the committees and the lobbies.

The Senate is above all the chamber of Union, its hundred members bringing together the fifty states on a basis of equality. The House of Lords as at present constituted does not exercise a unifying influence of this kind. Yet its origins lie in just such a local or regional representation since each peer, in the eyes of the Sovereign, carried a territorial responsibility for the area of which he was the feudal lord. In recent years proposals have been advanced for a House of Lords elected by regions of the United Kingdom.[1] If such proposals were to fructify, the House of Lords would regain the near federal function of its early days. It would never, unlike the Senate, have powers comparable with the first chamber, because the primary responsibility of the British government to the House of Commons and to that House alone is too deeply entrenched. But with powers as at present, the House of Lords, so reconstituted, could recover its pristine function as a unifying institution. In that regard, the Senate could be a model for a future British second chamber.

1. A scheme with this object was put forward during the committee stage of the Parliament (No. 2) Bill 1969 (as New Clause 22) by a group of Conservative and Labour backbench members; but the government abandoned the bill before the scheme could be debated.

CHAPTER FIVE

THE COMMITTEE SYSTEMS

IN no way is the difference between Parliament and Congress more marked than in the use each makes of committees. Congress has chosen to operate through a number of autonomous committees, and has shown how these can successfully be used to carry out its constitutional functions. Parliament on the other hand has never agreed to allow its committees much scope or power; they have always had to operate in the shadow of the House that created them. A picture of Congress today is of a great number of self-contained machines operating independently of each other. Parliament is itself one machine, of which its committees form a component part—a vital part, but one which has little utility except when fitted into place.

This chapter will consider how the two systems diverged so far, and will then describe various aspects of them today. It will be looking at committees as machinery, concerning itself principally with how they work. Their fruits, the products of their activities, are considered at other appropriate places in this book—in the chapters on legislation, finance and the scrutiny of government in particular—but this chapter concludes with a comparison of the work done by two committees, one in each legislature.

It is necessary at the outset to make clear a point of nomenclature. It would be logical to call every permanent committee a 'standing committee', and that is the practice in the United States. In its American context a standing committee is a legislative committee which continues its operations from one session to another and one Congress to another. But in Britain the phrase today has a different meaning; a Standing Committee is the name given to an ad hoc body which debates public bills and whose membership is nominated afresh for every bill. The epithet 'Standing' is therefore misleading; in a sense it could more appropriately be applied to the small investigatory committees (the 'select' committees) which do have a continuing function, and which are set up anew every session. This is, not unnaturally, a fruitful cause of confusion to minds coming fresh to a comparison of the two legislatures. The difference should be clearer after the various types of committee have been described in detail in this chapter. But from the outset an attempt will be made to mitigate the confusion by describing the British legislative, debating committee as a Standing Committee—thus, with capital letters—and the American permanent committee as a standing committee—thus, without.

DIFFERING ORIGINS OF COMMITTEES

In Britain there were already signs of a permanent committee system developing in the sixteenth-century House of Commons. Five committees came in time to be appointed regularly in every session.[1] They were to consider, respectively, election returns and matters of privilege; religion; griefs and petitions; trade; and courts of justice. Such committees were better equipped to consider matters of detail and individual cases than was the House itself, and by the early seventeenth century they played an important part in the work of the House. They consisted of a nucleus of thirty to forty members, to whom were added other specified classes—privy councillors, knights of the shire—and they existed to consider all matters that fell within their scope. In addition smaller, 'select' committees, consisting of three to fifteen members, were used for other matters, including the consideration of bills.

If there are similarities between this arrangement and the system of committees that has come to exist today in the United States, it is possibly because in Britain then there was more of a separation of powers than exists today. But this separation was more apparent than real; the Crown's influence was present in the Commons in the persons of the Speaker, who at that time acted as a business manager on behalf of the King, and of privy councillors, who had the King's interests at heart. Since it was the Speaker and 'those nearest the chair' (probably privy councillors) who nominated the members of the small committees, and since privy councillors became ex officio members of the larger

1. Campion, *Introduction to the Procedure of the House of Commons* (1958), pp. 25–29.

ones, it was through committees that the Crown's influence was most effectively exerted.[1]

In the seventeenth century, as the King's representation in the Commons dwindled and as the House sought to diminish his influence, it is hardly surprising that the Commons turned to the creation of larger committees. Members were allowed to attend the bigger committees, even though they had not been nominated to them—at first without, and then with, a vote. Then it was affirmed that bills could be committed to the whole House even when the Speaker was absent; later his absence was a necessary condition for the committee to proceed. Not only did this remove the King's most powerful agent, but it also enabled his other supporters to be outnumbered; it denied to the grandees the power to make important decisions in small groups which they could dominate. It was an attempt to ensure that from then on members would always be equal in status, that decisions would be communal, that no small privileged group would control the functions of the House. It threw open to the whole House such secrets as had hitherto been reserved to committee members only.

In retrospect it would seem that the House's mounting dislike of small committees at this time had an effect on it that was traumatic, and left it with an ineradicable prejudice against them, a fear of what they could effect, and the assumption that they would get up to mischief if they could. This attitude showed itself most clearly in the practice by which for many years the House allowed committees on bills to be composed only of members who were in favour of the bill in question. It was, in other words, not thought to be the function of a committee to prejudice the fate of a bill whose principle had already been endorsed by the House as a whole. It showed itself, too, in the Commons' continued use of the clumsy Committee of the whole House. Something of its effect is felt to this day, in the continuing restraints which the House imposes on its small committees.[2]

Limitations were placed on Committees of the whole House as well as on smaller committees. As late as the eighteenth century, resolutions of a Committee of the whole House had to be in the form 'That it is the opinion of this committee . . .'. A

1. Campion, op. cit., pp. 26–27, 43.
2. Ibid.

committee, in other words—even a Committee of the whole House—could only express opinions and could not presume to take effective decisions; those had to await the endorsement of the House itself.[1] In the same way the amendments made to a bill by a Committee of the whole House were all reconsidered by the House at the report stage.

In the United States when the first House of Representatives assembled, it had a great deal of business, especially financial business, to transact. It had no official (government) members; it therefore lacked within its membership—what Britain possessed —ministers who were able to put before it the results of all the routine work, done by the executive, which was necessary before the House could usefully debate proposals, motions and bills. In the circumstances the gradual growth of small bodies capable of doing the groundwork is understandable; a select committee was raised in order to consider each bill or matter as and when needed. At this stage there were still affinities with the British system. Most important matters were first considered in a Committee of the whole House in order to lay down guiding principles, before bills were referred to smaller, select committees which established the facts and went into the details. These smaller committees were expected to be sympathetic to the proposals committed to them; they were given specific instructions as to their authority and duties. Some of the select committees dealt with matters (such as elections) of recurrent concern and the House saw the virtue of making permanent or 'standing' committees of them. With more standing committees—there were five by 1802—and more authority being assumed by their chairmen, the House began to lose the initiative to them, and in 1822 ruled that they should have sovereignty in their respective fields.[2] From then on the committee system expanded rapidly. Standing committees were set up to meet particular needs. George Galloway has shown how, with a little imagination, a chronological list of standing committees can be seen as an outline of American history.[3] By mid-century there were thirty-four standing committees in the House and by 1900 the number was fifty-eight. It

1. Erskine May, 17th ed. (1964), p. 722.

2. Galloway, *History of the U.S. House of Representatives* (Printed for the House Committee on Administration, 1962), pp. 68–70.

3. Ibid., pp. 60–61.

seems that industrious congressmen were keen to take part in committee work not only because it made the work of the House more effective but also because it enabled them to influence decisions at an early stage.

In the Senate, the development of legislative committees was much slower. Its smaller size gave individual members greater influence in debate. Moreover the Senate, unlike the House, was charged by the Constitution with much of the executive's work in dealing with appointments and treaties; while the House, again by constitutional requirement, had the larger burden of legislative work in raising and appropriating funds. Not until 1816 did the Senate first appoint standing committees. Thereafter they developed apace; by 1888 there were forty-one and by 1909 the number was seventy-two.

A British observer of the scene in the late nineteenth century noted the immense amount of work which committees were doing in Congress:

> It is as a committee man that a member does his real work. In fact the House has become not so much a legislative assembly as a huge panel from which committees are selected.[1]

But he observed too that the Americans at large did not themselves seem to have noticed to what extent the committees had grown in importance; the deliberations of committees were generally secret, and the newspapers rarely reported either the evidence given or the decisions reached. He summed up:

> It is through these committees chiefly that the executive and legislative branches of government touch one another. Yet the contact, although the most important thing in a government, is the thing which the nation least notices, and has the scantiest means of watching.[2]

Meanwhile, in Britain, the general pattern set in the seventeenth and eighteenth centuries continued into the nineteenth. Both Houses continued to transact much of their public business through the medium of Committees of the whole House and select committees, appointed for a given limited purpose and subject to the strict control of the House. Each House continued to discuss legislative and financial projects twice over—once in

1. Bryce, *The American Commonwealth* (1889), Vol. 1, p. 155.
2. Ibid., p. 154.

the House, and once as a Committee of the whole House. In the nineteenth century, the small committees on public business were important but auxiliary bodies, preparing material for the information for the House and investigating concrete questions of fact or law to which the House required an answer. In the Commons seven of these committees sat from session to session, as five of them (Privileges, Public Accounts, Public Petitions, Selection and Standing Orders) still do. In addition there were on average thirty-four select committees set up in each session in the 1880s and twenty-eight in the 1890s. Although circumscribed by the conditions laid down by each House, these select committees were well armed to carry out the job they had been given. They could require the attendance of witnesses and examine them on oath; they could send for documents relevant to their inquiry, and insist upon the production of papers by witnesses. With such powers select committees had for many years been able to collect valuable material, digest it and place it before the House.

But by the end of the century the importance of these committees was declining. More and more the government employed royal commissions as the means of conducting major public inquiries. A royal commission could prolong its work over several years without regard to parliamentary sessions and holidays, and could include appropriate experts who would ensure an impartial treatment of the subject. As a result the royal commission, rather than a select committee, became the usual vehicle for large-scale inquiries. Royal commissions have often included members of Parliament in their number, but they are created by government, not Parliament.[1]

A new kind of committee was set up by the Commons in 1882 at a time of acute parliamentary stress. The House set up Standing Committees on legal matters and on trade matters. The Standing Committee was much bigger than the traditional select committee. It had a nucleus of between sixty and eighty members, to whom another fifteen members could be added in respect of each bill; and its quorum was twenty. Its procedure was to be that of a select committee, rather than that of a Committee of the whole House; but in practice it assumed from the start the character and

1. Redlich, *The Procedure of the House of Commons* (1908), Vol. II, Chap. VI.

practices of the latter. The Standing Committees were intended to relieve the Committee of the whole House of the need to look at particular fields of legislation. Seven bills were referred to them in the first two sessions. They lapsed after 1883, but were revived in 1888 and continued to exist until 1907. In twenty years they dealt with over 200 bills.

In 1907 the House decided to extend the system further. It set up four Standing Committees, but with the significant difference that they were no longer to specialize in particular fields of legislation. It was now to be the rule that all bills (with a few stated exceptions, such as taxation or supply bills) would be automatically sent to Standing Committees for their committee stage, unless the House specifically resolved otherwise.

At the same time the House altered its standing orders to ensure that the Standing Committee worked as a committee for *debate*—as a miniature of the Committee of the whole House— rather than as a select committee for *inquiry*, as the nineteenth century select committees had been, and as it had been contemplated that the early Standing Committees would be. Later alterations—in 1919, 1925, 1947 and on several occasions since— progressively reduced the size of Standing Committees, concentrating the membership on those interested in the bill. But the essential nature of the modern Standing Committee was effectively decided in 1907. It was to be a committee for processing bills; it was not to specialize in bills of a defined subject matter; and it was to be a committee of debate, not of inquiry. From then on, the committee systems of Parliament and Congress could never be alike.

In the House of Lords the practice of referring public bills to a Standing Committee as well as to a Committee of the whole House was much discussed and given a long trial between 1889 and 1910. After that it was abandoned. But Standing Committees came to be an essential part of House of Commons machinery. Their value today is shown by the way in which the House has been able to off-load more and more of its work on to them. In particular they have been used as a device for regional devolution.

One of the four Standing Committees set up in the Commons in 1907 was earmarked as the Scottish Standing Committee. It was to contain the members for all the Scottish constituencies and was to consider bills relating exclusively to Scotland. It was no more specialized as to subject matter than the other three Standing Committees; and like them it was a committee for debate, not for inquiry. But it developed a character and style of its own which later encouraged the House to devolve other Scottish matters to it. Since 1948 certain Scottish estimates have been referred to the Scottish Standing Committee for debate on up to six days in each session. These debates have not replaced those of supply days in the House, they have been an addition. But they marked the start of a new process. For since then Standing Committees have been used as deliberative bodies, and not just for the committee stages of bills. In the same year the practice began by which the Scottish Standing Committee was empowered to discuss the 'principle' of certain Scottish bills, in debates which were designed to replace the debates on second reading in the House. This step proved very popular, though for different reasons, with both Scottish and English members. Its success was recognized by changes made in 1957. From then on the committee stage of Scottish bills could be taken by a smaller Scottish Standing Committee (increased later to two such committees). A bigger committee, still containing members for all Scottish constituencies together with a few others, and now called the Scottish Grand Committee, could undertake various deliberative tasks, debating not just the estimates and the principle of bills, but also other matters of general concern to Scotland— 'Research in Scotland' and 'Tourism' for example. With this development the Grand Committee was able to act as something like a specifically Scottish House of Commons. Without claiming this title, it nevertheless acts as a forum for Scottish affairs, though a forum limited to deliberation. It can do little more than consider matters of interest; it cannot for instance come to any resolutions about them. The development of a Welsh Grand Committee followed naturally—incorporating, amongst others, members for all Welsh constituencies; if it has not operated to the same extent as its Scottish counterpart, this has largely been because of the scarcity of legislation dealing exclusively with Welsh problems.

The establishment of the Grand Committees marked the formal acceptance by the House of Commons of the principle that some of its work could and should be delegated to bodies smaller than itself. The logical development came in the period 1965–67. It then became possible to send some bills to a Standing

Committee for debate on their second reading and to a slightly larger committee on their report stage. Since at the same time the House removed the need for debates on the third reading of bills in some circumstances, the position was reached that a bill could pass through all its stages in the Commons without ever being debated on the floor of the House.

This picture of the House devolving its functions on to its Standing Committees needs to be qualified in two major respects. First, it applies to bills which are, by common consent, uncontentious. Secondly, the devolution only takes place in each instance by leave of the House; there is no automatic dispensation of the House's authority. It only needs ten members to stand up at one time to prevent a bill or a subject from being referred to the Scottish Grand Committee; while twenty members can prevent a bill's report stage or second reading being taken in Standing Committee. It is rare that members avail themselves of these safeguards,[1] but their existence conforms to what has already been shown—that is, that the House is always suspicious of its own committees.

In recent years the Lords have experimented with bodies similar to a Standing Committee, though known as 'public bill committees off the floor of the House'. Bills have been referred to such committees when it has been desired to save time on the floor of the House. The motion to refer the bill to the committee includes instructions 'that the procedure of the committee shall be, so far as possible, that of a Committee of the whole House . . . that the report of the committee's debates and the minutes of the committee's proceedings be published from day to day . . .'[2] After the committee has reported, the bill is recommitted to a Committee of the whole House, but proceedings there are considerably abbreviated.

In the House of Commons the procedural changes of 1965–67 also had a major effect on other types of committee. While the House had handed over business to Standing Committees, something of the reverse process took place in regard to Committees of the whole House. Financial matters which had for centuries

---

1. In practice the Government Whips try to ensure in advance that each use of this procedure will prove acceptable to the Opposition.

2. See e.g. motion to refer the Gaming Bill, *Lords Journals* (1967–68), pp. 408, 736.

been taken in such committees were now to be taken in the House itself. The Committees of Supply and Ways and Means, together with the committees on the money resolutions which authorized expenditure in connection with bills, were all abolished; debates which had previously been held in them were now to be held in the House. This change, however, was more one of form than of substance. As its name suggests, the Committee of the whole House has always been a committee only in name. Under the new dispensation as under the old, all members could continue to take part in debates on the financial matters on the floor of the House, so neither the convenience of members nor the time of the House was affected in any way. There were procedural reasons which favoured the change but its effect on the committee system can be ignored.

Of rather more moment were the changes that took place in 1965–67 with regard to select committees. In the first place they were allowed to travel abroad in pursuance of their inquiries. Some of them (notably the Estimates Committee) had always been empowered to 'adjourn from place to place', which enabled them to pursue their inquiries on site away from Westminster; and on occasion a committee had been allowed to travel abroad by special dispensation of the House. But by a resolution of 3 February 1966 it was conceded that they could travel, if necessary to the inquiry they were pursuing, whenever they wished to seek foreign experience of the matters under review. This change was moderate in its effect; the Estimates for 1970–71 show a sum of only £12,000 being allowed for it. But the principle that committees should be allowed to operate outside the limits to which the House's authority could reach was recognized.[1] Secondly the House resolved to authorize committees to pay for the expert assistance that they might need in assessing the evidence—often of a technical nature—put before them. The effect of these changes, and of others affecting the publicity given to committees' proceedings, was enough to transform the style of select committees' operations. It was not long before select committees, which had for so many centuries operated under the shadow of the House, were recommending that their proceedings should be televised.[2]

1. For an account of the stages by which this principle was established, see article by Sir Barnett Cocks in *The Parliamentarian*, Vol. LII, No. 1.
2. House of Commons Paper 196 of 1968–69.

At the same time changes were made in the number and scope of select committees. The increase in number was limited at first by shortage of staff and accommodation in the House of Commons, and it had to be accompanied by a reduction in size of the Estimates Committee; but the total effect was to increase the number of select committees (excluding ad hoc committees set up for particular limited inquiries) from an average of eleven in the period 1963–66 to sixteen in 1966–69. Some of the new committees were designed to range over the same area as a government department (Agriculture, Overseas Aid), but others (Science and Technology, Race Relations and Immigration) went wider than that. (The new committees were colloquially known as 'specialist committees'. If the name persists, it will add a new confusion to an already misleading nomenclature. The new committees are merely new select committees which, like many continuing select committees, specialize in some topic.)

The expansion of the Commons system of select committees had long been advocated as a means of increasing its efficiency and raising it in the general esteem. The arguments which accompanied it went deep. It was accepted that change was necessary in some form or other, but there was no agreement on whether the change should come in the House's committees or on the floor of the House itself. In the end changes were made in both; but while the argument lasted, while the House balanced its mistrust of committees against the possible good they might do, the cadences of a debate that has gone on in the House of Commons for three or four centuries could be heard once again.

No such doubts or hesitations characterized the growth of the congressional system of committees. Its development in parallel with the expansion of the country and with the experience Congress gained of their usefulness has been noted. In the House of Representatives sixty-five standing committees had emerged by 1920. With the consolidation in the twenties of a number of appropriations and expenditure committees, offset by the creation of a few more new committees, there were forty-eight in existence in 1946. In the Senate by the same date there were thirty-three.

That year saw a major rationalization by Congress of its whole committee system. By statute Congress laid down what committees it needed, what part of the public domain they should concern themselves with and what results it expected them to achieve. The Legislative Reorganization Act of 1946 left the Senate with fifteen committees, and the House with nineteen. The terms of reference were deliberately drawn to correspond as closely as possible to the departmental structure of the executive power. Each committee, the Act said, in addition to its normal legislative role, was to show 'continuous watchfulness' of the appropriate part of the executive; and the means of doing so—in the decade, a doubling of committee staffs in the Senate, and a tripling in the House—was granted to them. The effect of this has been to increase greatly the number of investigations which Congress committees carry out into the activities of the executive. Although most of the committees spend the bulk of their time considering bills, the Government Operations Committees (through their subcommittees), and certain other subcommittees set up by their parent legislative committees for the purpose, now have the oversight of the executive as their principal function.[1]

With these changes Congress prepared itself for what was needed in the third quarter of this century. Later inquiries into the functioning and role of committees—such as that of the Joint Committee of 1965-67—did not feel called on to question the fundamentals of the system as it had been operating over the previous twenty years. The matters they considered, such as the seniority rule, were important enough. But they were incidental to the main question of whether Congress now had the committee system it needed. That question, it seems, did not need to be asked.

The picture drawn by Woodrow Wilson and Bryce[2] of Congress in the 1880s is easily recognizable today. There have been changes in detail, administration, style perhaps—Bryce's observations on the lack of publicity given to congressional committees no longer ring true, and the role of chairman has changed—but by and large the committees are today what they were then: industrious, self-contained, numerous, permanent and influential.

The contrast with committees at Westminster over the same period—the financial committees of the whole House abolished,

1. Cf. Galloway, *History of the U.S. House of Representatives*, p. 77.
2. Wilson, *Congressional Government* (1885); Bryce, *The American Commonwealth* (1889).

select committees transformed, and a new dimension of Standing and grand committees created—is striking. The contrast is all the greater when it is recalled how each of the major changes in Parliament's committee structure has been made only after much heart-searching, endless inquiries and fierce controversy. Meanwhile the Americans have experienced the expansion of their country, the onset of worldwide responsibilities, the spread of federal responsibility throughout the states, and the vast technological problems of the present century with much the same system that had emerged by 1825 at the latest. The curiosity is that the American system had been derived (via the colonial assemblies, especially those in Pennsylvania and Virginia)[1] from the system as it had existed earlier in the House of Commons.

TYPES OF COMMITTEE

Types of Committee in Parliament:

(i) *Standing Committees*

Enough has been said about British Standing Committees to make clear that they have no counterpart in the American system of committees, and that they must not be confused with the standing committees of Congress. The British Committees were designed in the first place to take the committee stage of bills, and this remains their principal function today. But as has been shown, there has been a trend in recent times to employ them for other, broader purposes. Generally speaking the committees have diminished in size over the years, although they may have a larger membership when conducting their broader debates than when going through a bill.

Perhaps their most notable characteristic is their lack of initiative. They are set up by the Commons to perform a particular task—the conducting of the committee stage of a bill or a second reading, for instance—and that is all they can do. Furthermore in carrying out their prescribed task, they do so in a formal, pre-ordained manner. They never have to ask, What is the best way of carrying out the job that the House has given us? They have no choice in the matter.

1. Galloway, op. cit., p. 59.

The next thing to note is their impersonality. Such Standing Committees as are in existence at any one moment are distinguished from each other alphabetically—they are called Standing Committee A, Standing Committee B, etc. But it would be meaningless to try to establish any continuing thread in the work done by, say, Standing Committee A over a session, because the composition of that Committee on one bill is likely to be different from its composition on the next; it is nominated afresh for every bill. Its traditions are those of the Standing Committee system as a whole, not those of Standing Committee A.

Thirdly Standing Committees are designed to be useful, rather than decisive. They do not (except in extraordinary circumstances) defeat a bill. They can amend a bill, and sometimes they do so drastically; but the bill then goes back to the House, which may undo what they have done. Very rarely a Standing Committee has disagreed to all the clauses, or the key clause, in a bill, and has made a special report to the House to that effect; but in general its task is to improve a bill rather than defeat it. When not taking the committee or report stage of a bill, the possibilities open to a Standing Committee are even more limited; they can only vote yes or no to a motion saying that they have done what the House asked them to do.

The size of a Standing Committee is now fixed by standing order at between sixteen and fifty members, of whom roughly a third make a quorum. For report stages the size is fixed at between twenty and eighty members. The Scottish Grand Committee consists of the members for all seventy-one Scottish constituencies, with ten to fifteen other members.[1]

Standing Committees are nominated by one of the House's 'machinery' committees—the Committee of Selection, a small committee of eleven members. It tends to nominate to the Standing Committee on a bill many of the members who spoke in the debate on the second reading of that bill—members who will have specialized in the subject at issue. When the appropriate ministers and opposition leaders on the matter have been added, the committee can be seen to be well versed in the subject matter of the bill. But apart from nominating these members who can be especially effective in committee, the Committee of Selection has to ensure that the party strengths on the committee reflect

1. Standing Orders Nos. 60 to 74 relate to Standing Committees.

those in the House itself. This has two considerable effects. In the first place it means that the small parties in the House, and the independent members, may not qualify for a place on the committees which interest them. Secondly it means that when the party numbers in the House are fairly equally divided, the government majority on a Standing Committee will only be minimal; it may not be enough to prevent bills being amended in a manner disagreeable to ministers. Accordingly, in a Parliament where the government does not have a sizeable majority, there may be practical limits to the number and importance of the bills that can be sent to Standing Committees.

A chairman for each Standing Committee is appointed by the Speaker from the Chairmen's Panel—a group of about eighteen senior members who are chosen at the beginning of each session for the purpose of chairing these Standing Committees and the Committees of the whole House. The chairman specifies the date and time for the first sitting of a Standing Committee on a particular bill or matter, but the Committee makes its own arrangements for further sittings. The norm is for meetings to be held on Tuesdays and Thursdays from 10.30 a.m. to 1 p.m. But a long or contentious bill will require more frequent meetings than that, and the Committee will need to meet on Wednesdays, or in the afternoons as well.

A Standing Committee on a bill normally begins with the first clause in the bill. It debates any amendments which may be proposed to that clause, and decides the fate of each. It then debates whether or not the first clause (amended, perhaps, as a result of their consideration of amendments) should remain part of the bill. Having decided that, it passes on to clause 2, and in a like manner works its way through the whole bill. When a Standing Committee is considering a matter, or estimates, or the principle of a bill, debate is conducted as in the House, with members from either side making speeches in turn.

The Standing Committee, being essentially a committee for debate, resembles the House in miniature. Members sit in rows down either side of a rectangular room, facing each other across a narrow well, with the chairman and his advisers sitting on a dais that runs along a third side of the room. There are a number of seats along the fourth side of the room for the public. Members speak standing. Their words are taken down (generally by shorthand writers, but sometimes mechanically), so that a record of what has been said can be published by the following day. There is a considerable formality about proceedings—perhaps too much. It may be significant that when the Lords experimented recently with a committee similar to a Standing Committee, their members remained seated while they spoke. It could be that the future development of the Standing Committee will be, not in any further reduction in size or quorum, but in a lessening of formality.

(ii) *Select Committees*

Select Committees are small committees used by both Houses, but more frequently by the Commons, either to hold a watching brief on a subject or to solve a problem. Their function is to consider the matter allotted to them, and then to make a report on it to the House. They cannot present a minority report. From a study of the minutes of the committees, it is possible to deduce that a minority of members would have preferred to make a different report—but the majority report is the one report that the committee may make.

Very rarely a bill is committed to a select committee. When examining it the committee may go through it clause by clause and amend it, in which case the amended bill is their report; they may, and usually do, make a special report as well. But the bill will still have to go through a committee stage in Committee of the whole House or Standing Committee. Examination by a select committee is additional to the normal legislative process.

Select committees vary to a great extent in their subject matter. Six categories may be distinguished. They may be:

financial—to examine government accounts (the Public Accounts Committee) or to look at the value obtained for government expenditure (the Expenditure Committee);

investigative—to find out the facts of a matter and make recommendations to the House. A recent example of this has been a select committee on the declaration of members' interests;

overseeing—either of a department, such as the recent committees on Education, Agriculture, and Overseas Aid, or of a general subject (the Committees on Nationalized Industries, Science and Technology, and Race Relations);

quasi-judicial—to consider a case of privilege (the Committee of Privileges) or, rarely, to appraise the conduct of a member;

domestic—to make arrangements for the greater convenience of members (the Services Committee); or finally

legislative—to examine the implications of a bill (such as the Obscene Publications Bill 1959) or to study all delegated legislation (the Statutory Instruments Committee).

The hallmarks of a select committee are its non-partisan approach, its examination of detail, its disclosing of the facts of a case, its ability to advise the House on the best course of proceeding. It does work for which the House, a body of over 600 persons, is unsuited, and it does so in a manner which tends to mute party differences, so that one of the main features of select committee reports is the extent of cross-party agreement they reveal.

Some of these select committees, such as the Expenditure and Public Accounts Committees, exist by virtue of standing order. Others are sessional, being set up regularly at the start of each session.[1] They include the Committee on Privileges, the Committee on Nationalized Industries, the Committee on Statutory Instruments and the Services Committee. Others are also set up at the beginning of the session, but without the expectation of continuing indefinitely into the future. Some of the new departmental committees for instance, like the Agriculture Committee and the Education Committee, lasted in practice for two years or so. Finally there are the ad hoc select committees which are set up from time to time to consider a particular problem or matter. They can expect to disband as soon as they have completed their inquiry.

A select committee may not consist of more than fifteen members without special authority. The House gives authority if there are good reasons for it, but most select committees have ten to fifteen members. The quorum ranges from three to six. Select committees are nominated by motion in the House, and it is possible for members to seek to alter the proposed names. It is rare, however, for such an alteration to be made; as a result

1. The Government in 1970 promised that certain sessional select committees would continue to operate throughout the lifetime of the Parliament—(Command Paper 4507).

most select committees contain the members whom the party whips wish them to contain. The parties are in most Commons committees represented so as to reflect party strengths in the House.

Unlike the Standing Committees, select committees are largely masters of their own proceedings; at their first meeting they decide how to set about the task they have been given, and they can do this in any way that seems to them profitable, provided that they do not transgress the terms of reference the House gave them when it set them up. They meet perhaps weekly, though more frequently if their inquiry is urgent, or if they wish to complete it quickly. If meeting in one of the committee rooms of the House, they sit round a horse-shoe table, with their chairman in the centre and the clerk of the committee normally sitting beside him. The witnesses sit at a small table along the base of the horse-shoe, with a shorthand writer between them and the chairman. Meetings are frequently open to the public, and the evidence is almost invariably published, but when the committee deliberate amongst themselves and consider their report they always do so in private.

(iii) *Joint Committees*

Where a matter concerns both Houses of Parliament equally, a joint committee is sometimes appointed to consider it, consisting of an equal number of members from each House. A joint committee acts in a manner similar to a select committee; the chairman may be chosen from either House. Joint committees are generally ad hoc (a recent one considered the need to revise the law relating to censorship in the theatre), but there is one sessional joint committee, that which considers all bills designed to consolidate the law on a particular matter.

(iv) *Committees of the whole House*

Committees of the whole House are now used only for the committee stage of certain bills.[1] They meet in the chamber of the House, in the course of a sitting of the House, and a spectator might have difficulty in distinguishing between the House and a

1. For the criteria which determine whether a bill should be sent to a Committee of the whole House, rather than a Standing Committee, see p. 270.

Committee of the whole House. There are two visible points of difference. In the committee the Speaker's chair is empty, the committee being chaired by a deputy of the Speaker or a temporary chairman who sits at the clerk's seat at the table of the House; and the mace rests on rungs below the level of the table, rather than in its normal resting place a little above the table. The rules of debate are rather more relaxed in committee, members being allowed to speak more than once to each question for instance; but there remains a strong resemblance to proceedings in the House itself.

(v) *Private Bill Committees*

Private legislation is described in the chapter on Legislation. Here it is only necessary to note that both Houses use a distinctive type of committee to consider private bills. In the Commons it consists of four members if the bill is opposed by people affected by it, or five members if unopposed; in the Lords five members comprise an opposed bill committee, while unopposed bills are committed to the Lord Chairman, sitting as a committee of one. Proceedings on opposed bills are much more prolonged, and a committee may sit for perhaps four hours, day after day, hearing evidence put before them by counsel for and against the bill. Attendance by members of these committees is compulsory. They act as judge and jury, deciding whether the need for the bill has been proved or not, and if so, whether amendments should be made in it to meet the objections of its opponents. For unopposed bills the process is much more rapid. Two or three bills will be considered in the course of a single meeting which may last two hours. These committees are likely to meet weekly through spring and summer, when the flood of this type of legislation is at its height.

Types of Committee in Congress

At the outset two general points differentiating congressional committees from those in Parliament must be made. First, committees of the same kind are used to the same extent by both Houses of Congress (whereas in Parliament, only the House of Commons uses committees to any great extent). In what follows, except where otherwise stated, reference is made to committees existing in similar form in both Houses of Congress. Secondly, many of the congressional committees are set up by law. Although they have to be nominated at the start of every Congress, their status is wholly different from committees in the Commons, which are set up by that House alone.

The categories of committee in Congress are as numerous as in Parliament, but their functions, as already shown historically, are largely different.

(a) *Standing Committees*

Since the system of standing committees was recast by the Legislative Reorganization Act of 1946 there have been a few additions. Following a similar Act of 1970 there are seventeen standing committees in the Senate, and twenty-one in the House. These are:

HOUSE	SENATE
Agriculture	Aeronautical and Space
Appropriations	Sciences
Armed Services	Agriculture and Forestry
Banking and Currency	Appropriations
District of Columbia	Armed Services
Education and Labor	Banking, Housing and
Foreign Affairs	Urban Affairs
Government Operations	Commerce
House Administration	District of Columbia
Interior and Insular Affairs	Finance
Internal Security	Foreign Relations
Interstate and Foreign Commerce	Government Operations
merce	Interior and Insular Affairs
Judiciary	Judiciary
Merchant Marine and	Labor and Public Welfare
Fisheries	Post Office and Civil Service
Post Office and Civil Service	Public Works
Public Works	Rules and Administration
Rules	Veterans' Affairs
Science and Astronautics	
Standards of Official Conduct	
Veterans' Affairs	
Ways and Means	

These committees are permanent and are nominated at the start of each Congress. Most Senate standing committees have between 12 and 17 members, though the Appropriations Committee has more (24), while the Rules and Administration Committee, the Committee on the Post Office and Civil Service, the Committee on Veterans' Affairs (9 each) and the Committee on the District of Columbia (7) have less.[1] House standing committees are bigger, consisting of 25 to 41 members, though here again the Appropriations Committee is larger (51), and the Rules Committee (15), the Committees on Internal Security (9) and Standards of Official Conduct (12) are smaller.

A majority of a committee constitutes the quorum which must be present if reports are to be filed, though not necessarily when hearings are held. If a majority is present, and so far as the committee's rules allow, a proxy vote can be cast by a member on behalf of an absent member. In all committees the ratio of members from the majority and minority parties is approximately the same as in their respective Houses.[2] The nominations are made on behalf of each party by its Committee on Committees[3] and are then agreed to by each House. Conventions in each House limit the number of committees on which members may serve.[4] Since a member's career may depend on the committees to which he gets assigned, this is a sensitive point in the congressional system, and there is intense activity by congressmen, especially

1. The Legislative Reorganization Act of 1970, in specifying these numbers, made certain arrangements which may result in the numbers being exceeded for a transitional period.

2. The Committee on Standards of Official Conduct, however, has six members from each party; while the House Rules Committee has ten members from the majority party and five from the minority.

3. In the Senate the Democratic Committee on Committees consists of that party's Steering Committee, which is chosen and chaired by their party leader; while the Republican counterpart is composed of such members as are chosen by the party. In the House the Democratic members of the Ways and Means Committee, and a Republican from each state, comprise their respective Committees on Committees.

4. In the House, about sixty per cent of members serve on one standing committee only; the rest serve on two. In the Senate in 1970, about thirty per cent served on three standing committees; the rest served on two. However, the Legislative Reorganization Act of 1970 specified that in future senators would in general serve on no more than two major and one minor committees.

at the start of each Congress, to get assigned to the committees of their choice.

Since all bills and resolutions have first to be considered by a committee, it falls to the presiding officer of each House, on the advice of the Parliamentarian, to refer them to the committee that is appropriate. The terms of reference of each committee are precisely stated in the Act which created it, and a vast case-history charts the borders between the various committee jurisdictions.[1] The decision to send a particular bill to one committee rather than to another is sometimes of considerable moment to the bill. It is well known that committees vary in the sympathy they show towards certain causes, and bills are often drafted in such a way as to ensure that they go to a committee which is likely to favour them. The presiding officer's allocation generally raises no problem but it can be voted on and altered if strong objection is taken to it.

Committees may sit when their House is not sitting—in the recesses or after either House has adjourned. With the exception of the Committees on Government Operations, Rules and Internal Security, they may not sit without special permission while the House itself is meeting. Each committee has its own committee rooms either in the Capitol building or in the House or Senate office buildings; but committees undertaking studies or investigations may be empowered to meet at other places. Hearings are generally held in public, but executive (closed) sessions, to which departmental officials are sometimes invited, take place when the committees are deliberating on a bill or making their report, or dealing with confidential or secret matters.[2] Members sit at a table in order of seniority, Democrats on the chairman's right and Republicans on his left, with witnesses and the public sitting in front of them. Compared with meetings of parliamentary committees, the impression given is one of far more bustle and movement. Many more people seem to be involved in the hearing than is the case at Westminster. There are more staff for the committee, their counsel may do some of the

1. Cannon's *Procedure in the House of Representatives*, pp. 344–409. For a description of the process of referring bills to committees, see Goodwin, *The Little Legislatures* (1970), pp. 35–38.

2. Closed hearings are held as a regular practice by the House Appropriations Committee, but not by its Senate counterpart.

questioning, the witnesses are sometimes accompanied by their own counsel, the press (and sometimes television and radio operatives) are more active, other members more often exercise their right to attend if they wish.

While it is difficult to generalize about these committees, because of their diversity and the differing use they make of sub-committees, the amount of work they get through is impressive by any standards. In a recent (two-year) Congress some fifty committees, the great majority of which were standing commit-tees, held over 5,000 subcommittee meetings and 3,000 full committee meetings.

(b) *Select and Special Committees and Subcommittees*

Select and special committees are occasionally created by resolu-tion in either House for some particular purpose and for a limited amount of time. They are investigative rather than legislative, and are useful for drawing attention to urgent public issues. In the Senate the resolution which creates them says how their members are to be nominated, whereas in the House the Speaker appoints the members and the chairmen.

Four reasons have been identified for the creation of select committees in the House, all of them the result of difficulties created by standing committee boundaries.[1] They have been formed to accommodate interest groups which feel they lack access to a standing committee; to help solve problems of a nature personal to an individual legislator; to evade standing committees which are believed to be inadequate for a particular task; or to perform specific duties in areas of overlapping jurisdiction.

Standing committees sometimes appoint special subcommittees to obtain information about some aspect of their responsibilities. Generally they investigate a matter rather than consider an item of legislation. The fact that these special committees and sub-committees start as it were from scratch, that they are limited in time and possibly in funds, that they frequently deal with matters of great public interest and therefore operate in a blaze of publicity, means that they rely to an even greater extent than usual on the initiative and ability of their chairmen. A man who

1. By V. S. Vardys in *The Midwest Journal of Political Science*, August 1962; cited by Goodwin, op. cit., p. 41.

makes a success of chairing one of these committees can become a national figure, and it can lead him to the heights. Senator Truman, who chaired a special committee looking at the National Defence Programme during World War II, and Senator Kefauver who led an investigation into organized crime in the 1950s, are two examples.

(c) *Joint Committees*

These are committees consisting of members of both parties in both Houses, and they have at times played an important part in the work of Congress. Some of them are set up after a concurrent resolution to that effect has been passed by both Houses; but others, like the Joint Committees on Atomic Energy, Internal Revenue Taxation, Defence Production, and Printing, and the Joint Economic Committee, have been created by statute and have achieved particular influence in their fields. Their members are appointed by the presiding officers of each chamber.

Problems of precedence and protocol inevitably arise when Joint Committees are created. They have to decide in which House to hold their meetings, and from which House their chairman should come. But where the will exists to make a go of such committees, they have proved to be of great value.

Joint Committees do not normally consider and report bills. The Joint Committee on Atomic Energy is an exception. It drafts and considers legislation which it then reports in identical terms to both Houses.

(d) *Conference Committees*

A different kind of joint committee is the conference committee appointed to resolve matters in disagreement when a bill or a resolution has been amended in the second House. (Conference committees were used in Parliament for similar reasons up until the middle of the nineteenth century.[1]) In Congress the Senate members of a conference committee are appointed in the way specified in the resolution agreeing to the conference, while the House members are nominated by the Speaker. In both Houses they are in practice generally chosen from the senior members of the standing committees which considered the matter in question.

1. Erskine May, 17th ed. (1964), p. 625.

They vary in size, having perhaps a minimum of three members from each House. They meet in secret, and the agreements they reach can be rejected by either House—in which case either the conference reconvenes or the bill is lost. The work of these committees is considered in Chapter 6.

(e) *Committee of the Whole*

In the House of Representatives a Committee of the Whole considers bills and resolutions on the Union Calendar[1] after they have been considered by a standing committee, and after the Rules Committee has proposed a special rule to govern debate on them. By these means the business can be expedited, for there will be a time-limit on speeches and the debate will be controlled by the chairman of the standing committee concerned and a floor manager for the representatives of the minority party on the committee. The Committee of the Whole is chaired, not by the Speaker, but by a chairman appointed by him; and whereas the quorum of the House is 218, that of the committee is 100. Amendments can be moved and made, and the bill can be rejected if necessary. If the committee reports favourably, the House resumes, and further amendment and debate is possible before a final version is agreed to—provided that the Rule does not disallow it, and that the previous question is not moved.

POWERS OF COMMITTEES

In Parliament

The House of Commons will not concern itself with what takes place in any of its committees until the committee has reported to it. But in other respects it is difficult to generalize about the powers of Commons committees as a whole. It has been noted above that the House of Commons Standing Committees exist to carry out certain duties (chiefly legislative) on behalf of the House in a fixed way and without the power to display initiative of any kind. They are in a sense internal, domestic committees, so that the question of their jurisdiction hardly arises. The

---

1. Its full title is consequently 'The Committee of the Whole House on the State of the Union'. The different kinds of Calendar are described in Chapter 6.

same is true, *a fortiori*, of the Committee of the whole House, which is today exclusively concerned with legislation, again without the need to show initiative; its powers stem from the House, and not from the fact that it is a committee. But select committees fall into a different category. They have to decide their own course of proceeding. They have to deal with people and organizations outside the House. The House moreover distinguishes between one select committee and another in deciding how much freedom of action each should have. For all these reasons an analysis of the powers exercised by select committees can be useful.

The principal power given to almost all select committees is the power 'to send for persons, papers and records'. This is the power which enables a committee to investigate, to hear witnesses, to assemble facts and generally to conduct the inquiry with which they have been charged. It enables a committee to send for anyone who it thinks can help it; and if a person refuses to attend or to give evidence, he can be reported to the House, treated as guilty of contempt and punished by the House. The need to enforce the committee's powers by subpoena has however rarely been necessary in recent times. In addition witnesses can be examined on oath, and perjury under these circumstances attracts statutory penalties; but witnesses are on the other hand protected by the privileges of the House, in respect of the evidence they give, from such consequences as actions for slander.

The power to send for persons does not include a right to require members of either House to attend and give evidence. They can, however, be invited to do so (a peer can only be invited after the House of Lords has given express permission for him to attend, if he so wishes). Evidence about departmental matters is traditionally given to select committees by senior civil servants; but a recent practice has been for the minister concerned himself to submit to examination.

The power to send for papers and records is rather more limited. It is confined to such departmental documents as are not of an internal kind; in other words, departmental files and minutes cannot be demanded. Nor are matters involving national security likely to be often disclosed. Faced with an official refusal to disclose information, a committee's only redress is to report to the House, where the refusal would in the last resort be upheld by the government's majority. Witnesses, official or otherwise, can however be asked to produce memoranda on the matters in question and this, coupled with the information that can be extracted by cross-examination, is enough to ensure that most committees get the information they need.

Other powers which are, when appropriate, given to select committees are the power to adjourn from place to place, allowing them to travel in order to see things for themselves; the powers to set up subcommittees and to have the assistance of expert advisers in their inquiry—both of which will be considered in the context of the organization of committees; and the power to sit while the House is in recess. But of rather more importance is a limitation which the House has on many occasions applied to select committees. It has sought to confine the activities of some of them to matters of administration, and deliberately to exclude from their attention the policies of the government of the day. This bar on the discussion of policy in some select committees is a fundamental limitation on their freedom of action, and, since it reflects an attitude which the House frequently adopts towards its committees, needs to be looked at in some detail.

Some select committees are excluded from the consideration of policy as a natural consequence of their function. The Public Accounts Committee, for instance, exists in order to examine departmental accounts, and these naturally are matters of administration. The Select Committee on Statutory Instruments looks at delegated legislation, which is generally administrative in character. Since the Ombudsman is a parliamentary commissioner for administration, the select committee which considers his reports is not concerned with policy. But other committees do not have this intrinsic limitation; the character of their work would enable them to look equally at policy and administration. It is some of these committees which the House has at various times attempted to hobble, by specifically including in their terms of reference a bar on the consideration of policy. It is instructive in this respect to look at the history of two important select committees, the Estimates Committee[1] and the Nationalized Industries Committee.

1. The Estimates Committee was appointed in most sessions from 1912 to 1970. Since 1971 it has been replaced by the Expenditure Committee (see also p. 322).

The terms of reference of the Estimates Committee for many years limited it to examining current expenditure and reporting what, if any, economies *consistent with the policy decided by the Government* could be effected. In other words the committee was debarred from considering the policy that caused the expenditure. This reflects the deep-seated belief that policy is a matter for the House, while committees should be concerned only with the effects of policy. Members of Parliament do not always accept that the role of committees should be secondary in this manner, and a number of attempts were made to allow the Estimates Committee greater latitude. As the result of one attempt, the terms of reference were widened in 1960 so as to allow it to report on the principal variations between the Estimates and those of the previous year; to this extent it could discourse on policy. But the main function of the committee was still to do with administration and with the search for economy and efficiency. However, when the Government announced in late 1970 their plan to replace the Estimates Committee by the Expenditure Committee they made clear that the new committee would not be barred from the consideration of policy.

Something of the same battle on the subject of the policy bar had to be fought when the House of Commons set up in 1955 a select committee to consider the industries which had been nationalized. The terms of reference were drafted so as to prohibit the committee from investigating the day-to-day activities of the industries on the one hand and government policy on the other.

The committee held a number of meetings, took advice from the Attorney-General, and then decided that they could not operate within those terms of reference. They may have felt that the parameters imposed upon them would have made it too easy for witnesses to ride off the awkward questions. So they made no progress. In the following year a new committee was set up to consider 'the Reports and Accounts of the nationalized industries'—just that, without any restrictions being laid upon them. In moving the motion to create the Committee with these new terms of reference, the government spokesman said he hoped the Committee would not touch on those matters which had been specifically excluded from its earlier terms of reference, even though it was now empowered to do so. The Committee has responded to the extent of not concerning itself with the industries' quotidian problems, but has felt free to criticize ministers and suggest new policies whenever appropriate.

The setting-up of the Nationalized Industries Committee may have marked a turning point in the history of Commons select committees. The numerous so-called specialist committees created since then have had no policy bar placed on them. This is shown by the way they have been able to take evidence direct from ministers, and not only from civil servants. While civil servants can talk about administration, what the minister says is more likely to be policy.

Select committees are given a power to report; or, if they are intended to continue in existence, to report from time to time. In the former case the report concludes the committee's proceedings; in the latter it concludes a particular investigation, or used to do so. However, it is now the practice for certain committees which have been looking at aspects of government administration to evoke a reply to their report from the government department under scrutiny. The reply shows the extent to which (if at all) the department have met the committee's criticisms.

Some select committees exercise something like a direct control in their limited fields. If for example the Statutory Instruments Committee find fault with a particular piece of delegated legislation, the Instrument may be withdrawn and another issued in its place. The decisions of the Services Committee about matters within the Palace of Westminster—though technically the Committee is only advisory to the Speaker—are in practice often put directly into effect. But for major positive results to flow from a select committee's endeavours, it generally needs the House specifically to endorse the committee's conclusions. Left to themselves select committees have a certain influence but little power. Power remains in the House, and committees remain its creatures.

In Congress

In their origins the same could be said of the committees of Congress. Jefferson, writing in the period 1797 to 1801, notes in his Manual the limitations on a committee's handling of a bill or a resolution or an address:

Even if they are opposed to the whole paper, and think that it can not be made good by amendments, they can not reject it, but must report it back to the House without amendments, and there make their opposition.[1]

It was the gradual increase in the demands on the time of Congress in the nineteenth century that led, as described above, to the situation today wherein the committees have come to play a leading part in policy-making. Their powers have been increased in order to enable them to do so, and the powers given to them in each case are appropriate to their function, be it primarily investigative, legislative or both.

The power to send for persons and papers, derived from the House of Commons, was one of their earliest rights. It is usual to require witnesses to file written statements of their testimony in advance. As in the House of Commons the power to call witnesses cannot be used to enforce the disclosure of internal matters of administration. This is the field of 'executive privilege', the defence of which has led to rather more conflict in Congress than in Parliament. When the Senate Committee on Government Operations asked in May 1954 for information about certain discussions, a ukase from President Eisenhower forbade his officials to give it on the ground that to do so ran counter to the separation of powers. For a time it was believed that the President's order could justify almost any refusal of information to Congress, but later Presidents have redressed the balance by promising that the privilege would only be claimed after they have themselves specifically authorized it. There has never been a definitive judgement on whether a committee can compel an official to give it information in the face of a directive from the President not to do so. Congress has power to commit intransigent witnesses, but this power has never been invoked against officials.[2]

All Senate standing committees, and four standing committees of the House, are given power to subpoena witnesses. This power made for instance the House Committee on un-American

1. *House Rules and Manual* (1971), para. 412.
2. *Extent of the Control of the Executive by Congress* (1962), by C. J. Zinn, printed for the use of the House Committee on Government Operations.

Activities[1] particularly formidable. Yet witnesses who appear before congressional committees cannot thereby be deprived of their constitutional rights. In particular the Fifth Amendment to the Constitution enables witnesses to sidestep questions, unrelated to the matter under investigation, which the committee have asked in order to expose them to social pressure or ridicule. Nor can a witness be required to incriminate himself.

A measure of the autonomy of standing committees is that they have a budget of their own, and can spend money within certain limits as they think fit. They hire their own staff, who work for them rather than for the House or the Senate. Their rules are the rules of the House they belong to, but they can add to these rules so long as they are not inconsistent in doing so. Certain House committees can report at any time on certain stated matters within their terms of reference, and their reports receive expedited treatment in the House.[2]

Under the Legislative Reorganization Act of 1946 standing committees were charged with the duty of exercising 'continuous watchfulness' over the administrative agencies operating in their field. This empowers them to oversee everything that the agencies do; they can investigate everything that goes on within the administration, whether or not it relates to any legislative project. They are thus able to exercise considerable influence; but it is their handling of legislation, discussed in Chapter VI, that shows most clearly to British eyes the extent of their powers. A handful of members, comprising a majority of a committee or sometimes only of a subcommittee, can effectively destroy a bill which may be favoured by a majority of Congress. For a committee will only report a bill favoured by a majority of its members. They can bury bills they dislike, and it is only rarely that the House will extract from them a bill which they do not wish to release.

In the result it is the standing committees which effectively decide the agenda of Congress, for Congress deals with such bills and matters as the committees report to it. Further, the proceedings on the floor on matters reported from committees are largely controlled by the chairman and senior minority member of the committee and, in the House, it may only be the committee's

1. Now called the Committee on Internal Security.
2. House Rule XI, 22.

amendments which will be considered. Nothing shows more clearly the relationship between Congress and its committees than the fact that the two Houses have surrendered to their committees so much of the power to decide what shall be considered on the floor of the House, and how the debates there should be organized.

ORGANIZATION OF COMMITTEES

Committees as a rule adapt themselves to the world in which they work. Any two committees may have the same powers, yet choose to use them differently. Each committee may adopt its own rules and evolve its own style and traditions. While it is possible to generalize about the way in which committees function both in Parliament and Congress, allowance has to be made for the individuality that each one will often display.

Role of the Chairman

In Congress it is the chairman of each committee who usually determines its agenda, and some committees have a history of meeting only on the call of their chairman.[1] From amongst the many bills which are referred to it, he decides which shall be considered and in what order. By so doing he can expedite one bill, retard another, and perhaps stifle a third. He probably decides how many, if any, subcommittees the committee should set up, and nominates their chairmen and members (perhaps after consultation with the senior minority member of the committee). He may be able to refer a bill to a particular subcommittee, and by so doing ensure that it make progress or fails to do so. He has a dominant say in the recruiting and organizing of committee staff, and controls the committee's expenditure. He in effect decides which witnesses shall be heard by the committee[2] and leads the questioning of them; he can punish breaches of order and decorum by censuring witnesses and excluding them

1. The Legislative Reorganization Act of 1970, however, requires each Committee to fix regular meetings. Additional meetings can be summoned by the chairman, or by three members acting jointly.
2. Under the Legislative Reorganization Act of 1970, the minority side of a committee are permitted to call witnesses during at least one day's hearings.

from further hearings. When the inquiry is complete, he either supervises the writing of the committee's report or nominates the member who will do so. When the report is considered on the floor, and the bill is controversial, it is he who manages the debate; otherwise it is managed by another member of the committee whom he has chosen. He is also either in charge of, or helps to select, the members of his committee who will take part in the conference committee which will decide the final shape of a bill.

In practice each chairman generally consults the ranking (i.e. senior) minority member of the committee before taking decisions; but there are exceptions, and, even with that qualification, the extent of a chairman's influence is immense. In a much-quoted remark Woodrow Wilson described the American system of government as 'a government by the chairmen of the standing committees of Congress'. Though written over eighty years ago (in his *Congressional Government*), it remains largely true today. The lore of Congress is full of stories of high-handed actions by which chairmen have diverted the stream of congressional business in a manner satisfactory to themselves. Some of these stories may be over-stated. It takes a majority of a committee to decide many of the rules under which their chairman acts; and when a chairman appears to be acting in particularly cavalier fashion, he may well be doing so with the silent approval of a majority of his committee.

Even with this possible qualification, it is obvious that every chairmanship of a standing committee is highly sought after, and particular interest attaches to the way in which chairmen are chosen. The chairman of each committee is a member of the party having a majority in the House, and he is elected by the House at the start of each Congress. The choice of each House is however subject to a powerful convention that he is always the member of the majority party having the longest unbroken service on the committee. The implications are obvious. The convention ensures that the chairmen, perhaps the most powerful men in Congress, are always people of long congressional experience, are generally elderly, and never come from the more volatile constituencies. They are bound, through their long service on the committee, to be specialists in the subject-matter of their committees, and they are likely to have a clear picture of what the role of a congressional committee ought to be. But their personal ability will not be a factor in their election, nor will their prejudices (if any) be a bar to it.

At first sight nothing could be further from this picture of an all-powerful congressional chairman than a description of his nearest equivalent in the House of Commons—the chairman of a select committee, who is appointed not by seniority but by the committee itself at its first meeting. He takes the chair, and a discussion then takes place on how the committee's inquiry should be conducted. It is the committee, in other words, which decides on its agenda, on what witnesses should be called and on the time-scale of the inquiry. At each meeting the chairman will start the questioning of each witness, but he may be interrupted by the other members wishing to pursue his points, or to place a different gloss on them. At the end of the inquiry the chairman puts a draft report before the committee for their consideration. But there is nothing to prevent any other member doing the same. If he does so, the committee can vote on which draft they will accept as the basis of their report. In one respect the chairman could be said to have less power than the other members of the committee: he does not have a vote in the committee unless the voting numbers are equal, in which case he gives a casting vote.

Chairmen of select committees do not always come from the majority party in the Commons. It is traditional that the chairmen of certain committees likely to prove critical of the administration —the Public Accounts Committee, the committees on Statutory Instruments and on the Parliamentary Commissioner—should always come from the official opposition. But these committees, like all other select committees, contain a majority of members from the majority party, so that there is little likelihood of a partisan opposition viewpoint being adopted.

It is clear from this recital of facts that the authority of a select committee chairman is very much less than that of a standing committee chairman in Congress. But there are a number of practical reasons why the difference is not so great as might be assumed. Although a select committee appoints its own chairman, it invariably chooses the member who has been pre-selected for the job by the government (or in appropriate cases the opposition) whips and who has been nominated to the committee for that particular purpose. These nominees are not chosen because of their long previous service on the committee. That would be impractical in a parliamentary system where members become ministers from time to time, and thereby relinquish membership of most committees. But they are always people of long parliamentary experience, frequently ex-Ministers and seldom young.

Furthermore, although the powers of a select committee chairman are circumscribed, in practice a forceful member can exert considerable dominance over a select committee which he chairs. By working closely with the committee staff, he is probably better briefed than the other members of the committee; and he probably gives more time to the committee's problems than they do. The authority of his office may not be great in theory, but in practice his fellow-members defer considerably to him, and he is able to stamp his personality on the committee's activities.

The seniority system in Congress is not a particularly old tradition. In the House of Representatives it was formally instituted in 1911 as one of the steps taken to break the power which had come to reside in the Speaker of the House of Representatives, although the tradition of granting posts by seniority dates further back than that.[1] (The Speaker of the House still nominates chairmen of select committees.) In the Senate it is an older tradition, dating from the mid-nineteenth century. It has been justified in that it offers an attainable ambition for many members of Congress; it prevents internal strife, which would come if members were jockeying all the time for chairmanships; it rewards experience, and ensures that each chairman is well schooled in the subject-matter of his committee; and it prevents too much centralization of power. Its drawbacks are that it has resulted in a feudal system where a few men have great power without the corresponding responsibility. It can make chairmen unresponsive to the views of their colleagues on the committee. It enables an individual member to block action favoured by a majority of the House. It allows no means of getting rid of an ineffective, arbitrary or senile chairman (although the majority of a committee can diminish the powers of an arbitrary chairman by changing the committee's rules, and on occasion has done so). It means that the qualities of leadership are not taken into account when choosing leaders of committees (though they may be when choosing leaders of subcommittees; see below); and, it is argued, it tends to make Congress an isolated, ingrown institution, since there is

1. Galloway, *History of the U.S. House of Representatives* (1962), p. 62.

no incentive for gifted and experienced men to seek a career in Congress in middle or late life after they have reached positions of power elsewhere.

These arguments for and against the seniority system were amongst those put to the Joint Committee on the Organization of Congress by Congressman Udall in 1965. (His suggested solution was that the chairman of each standing committee should be chosen, by secret ballot of all members of the majority party, from among the three senior majority members of the committee.) Whatever view is taken of the seniority system, it is successful in removing from Congress much of the internecine struggling that would otherwise take place. For practical reasons it would be hard to change, for at any given moment the great majority of members will have made dispositions some years earlier in the expectation of benefiting from the system in the years to come. Perhaps an election bringing a landslide change in the membership of the House could create the conditions in which the seniority rule would be abandoned. Without it, for better or for worse, Congress would be a very different place.

The Use of Subcommittees

In the House of Commons a select committee cannot set up subcommittees unless the House has given it specific authority so to do. In other words, in setting up a select committee, the House takes a view on how it should organize its work. If it decides that a committee would benefit from this power, it grants it, sometimes specifying the number of subcommittees permitted, but sometimes leaving it to the committee to decide how many subcommittees it needs, and what their size should be; in all cases the committee decides who the members and chairmen of each subcommittee should be. In practical terms the number of subcommittees is dictated by the width of the committee's remit and the time available to deal with it, by the work-load which individual members are willing to take on, and by the number of staff available to service the committee. All subcommittees report to the full committee, which goes through the report, perhaps only formally, and then issues it as its own.

One select committee, the Expenditure Committee, being a much larger committee than normal, operates through a highly organized system of subcommittees, one of which contains all the subcommittee chairmen and acts as a steering subcommittee. Other committees have developed their own organization; in 1969, eight select committees were working through twenty-eight subcommittees, while ten select committees did without.

In Congress subcommittees are used far more extensively. In 1970, thirty-seven standing committees had between them two hundred standing subcommittees, forty-seven subcommittees and two ad hoc subcommittees. Only four of the thirty-seven standing committees operated without subcommittees. Each representative is likely to be on two subcommittees at the most; but each senator is likely to be assigned to at least six.[1] Many of the subcommittees are permanent and bipartisan features of the committee system, and some of them have been allotted by their parent committee a permanent staff and a sizeable budget of their own. Their existence, each with a specified jurisdiction, increases the specialization within the committee system. It results in a bill's being initially considered by people with special expertise in the subject; and by this means, most public hearings are conducted by members with special knowledge of the detailed point under discussion. A subcommittee can recommend amendments to a bill, or can recommend that a bill be 'tabled'—that is, that no action be taken on it. Since the reports of subcommittees on less controversial bills are frequently accepted without question, first by the committee and then by the parent House, it can be seen that the few members of the subcommittee exercise considerable influence in their fields.

The power to create subcommittees, to nominate their members and to refer bills to them, has been noted above as one of the strongest weapons in a chairman's armoury.[2] However, some committees have successfully countered this by adopting rules which spell out the jurisdiction of subcommittees, and thereby make automatic the referring of bills to the appropriate subcommittee.

Apart from the advantages which chairmen can reap from the subcommittee system, there are advantages for others as well. For the practice of setting up numerous subcommittees, of which the

1. Goodwin, *The Little Legislatures* (1970), p. 48.
2. When the right of a Senate chairman to establish subcommittees was challenged in the courts, a Federal Court of Appeals confirmed that he was acting within his powers—see Goodwin, op. cit., p. 56.

chairmanship is not allocated according to seniority, broadens opportunities for newer and younger members to display their abilities and their leadership. Opportunities of this kind are sometimes created for promising young men—especially in the Senate, where the combination of a small overall size and multiple assignments has given to many an able young senator the chance to make a national reputation by his handling of a subcommittee.

Committee Staff

The principal difference in this field has already been noted. It is that congressional committees employ their own staff, while the staff of parliamentary committees are assigned to them from the Clerk's Department by the Clerk of the House. The former are employees of the committee, the latter of the House. Another important difference is of scale. Each congressional committee may engage a staff which includes six professional members (other than the two Appropriations Committees, which employ such staff as they deem necessary); while each parliamentary committee (together with any subcommittees) is unlikely to be served by more than two clerks.[1] (An exception is the Expenditure Committee which operates differently from other committees and has a clerk for each of its subcommittees.) In addition each congressional committee may employ six clerical staff, while parliamentary select committees are aided by one or two secretaries. Both congressional committees and parliamentary select committees are frequently aided by officials from their respective libraries.

The House of Commons gives authority, when appropriate, to its select committees to employ expert advisers from outside the House. These advisers are especially useful in giving the committee an independent view on the evidence and memoranda given to them by government witnesses. They are chosen by the committee and employed on a contractual basis for the duration of a particular inquiry. Congress on occasion gives similar power to its committees to employ consultants on a temporary basis.[2]

1. It is significant that one of the first reports of the Expenditure Committee advocated the establishment of a small, permanent, qualified secretariat, within the establishment of the Clerk of the House, to assist it in its work—House of Commons Paper 436 of 1970–71.

2. Legislative Reorganization Act of 1970, Sec. 303.

If the work-load of a congressional committee increases, each House may allow it to appoint additional staff on an ad hoc basis. As a result each committee shows considerable flexibility in the organization of its work. The same is less true in the House of Commons, where the staff are mostly permanent, need to be fitted into a career structure, and can be required to give help to the House in matters quite removed from committee work. It follows that a decision on whether or not to set up a new committee is far more affected by considerations of staffing in the Commons than in Congress.

The present scale of committee staff in Congress is of comparatively recent origin. Only in the second half of the nineteenth century were regular funds made available for this purpose. This enabled some committees to operate with very satisfactory results; but it has only been since the Legislative Reorganization Act of 1946 that all committees have been potentially able to employ high-grade, specialist staff. Of particular importance is the work of the staff director who is responsible for assigning duties to the other staff and often acts as the personal representative of the chairman. He helps in the planning of the committee's programme, and maintains formal and informal contacts with the various executive departments and agencies.[1]

There are still three sensitive points in the organization. First a distinction is made between professional and clerical staff which is not always easy to sustain. In general, professional staff either specialize in a particular area of the committee's work, or are allocated to a particular subcommittee; the clerical staff handle the committee's correspondence and stenographic work. In practice, however, on many committees the distinction bewteen the two is blurred, and the rules of the House of Representatives show that the pay of both branches may range up to the same peak.[2]

Secondly, there could be a danger in the trend towards allotting staff members exclusively to one side of the committee or the other. Professional staff are recruited 'without regard to political affiliations and solely on the basis of fitness to perform the duties of their respective positions'.[3] There seems, however, to be a

1. Lees, *The Committee System of the United States Congress* (1967), pp. 27–8.
2. House Rule XI, 28 (c).
3. Legislative Reorganization Act of 1970, section 301–2.

growing belief that the staff should be deliberately assigned to the majority or minority party. This is sanctioned by the Legislative Reorganization Act of 1970 which, in increasing the professional staff from four to six persons, specifies that two of them may be selected, and carry out work assigned to them, by the minority. One member of the clerical staff may function similarly. This, it is sometimes argued, improves the overall quality of the staff's work—there is, it is said, a 'creative tension'. But the strength of a staff often lies in their sharing of information and advice; there are obvious hazards when the staff may be set to oppose each other.

Thirdly there is the bureaucratic danger that staffs who are given or achieve too much freedom of action may come to dominate the people whom they ostensibly serve. In Congress, where members are accustomed to handling the large personal staffs allowed to them, this should be less of a problem than in other legislatures. But the danger nevertheless exists, especially in the Senate whose members have to sit on many more committees than do members of the House. Giving evidence to the Joint Committee on the Organization of Congress 1965–66 Congressman Mahon, chairman of the House Appropriations Committee, wrote as follows: 'I cannot find enough time to visit in depth with committee staff on pending matters . . . We are so preoccupied with so many district, floor and other matters that we are spread too thin . . . 100 senators have an even more acute problem than the 435 representatives'.[1]

Much of the work done by the staff for congressional committees is similar to that done for select committees in the Commons: advising the chairman and members, writing reports, handling the many administrative problems. But one main difference between the staffs of the committees of the two legislatures lies in their length of service with a particular committee. Such names as Marcellus Shield, for twenty-nine years Clerk of the House Appropriations Committee, Colin Stamm, whose service on the Joint Committee on Internal Revenue extended for over thirty years, and John Conway, for fifteen years on the Joint Committee on Atomic Energy, have carried formidable reputations in Washington. Length of service is of course far from being the only, or indeed the main, factor that makes a staff man

1. Hearings, p. 1653.

influential. His ability to speak for his chairman, his professional competence and reputation, his skill in finding weaknesses in the executive branch which would repay a study by his committee— these may all be more important than mere longevity. But the accretion of expertise that comes from long experience of a subject in Congress is in contrast to Westminster, where a clerk rarely spends more than five or six years in working for a particular committee.

Publicity

When a committee starts an investigation, it often needs as much publicity as it can get. Publicity will not only generate public interest in the inquiry, it will also alert the experts in the field to the fact that their evidence might be of value to the committee. Furthermore, by publishing the evidence as soon as possible after each hearing, later witnesses know what the committee have already been told, and can frame their evidence so as to answer or confirm the contentions made earlier. In a sense witnesses compete against each other, and the committee is better able to weigh up their assertions. Partly for these reasons committees in both legislatures have seen the value of publicizing their hearings. In Congress, though not in Parliament, proceedings in committee may be televised or broadcast.[1]

It may be that in the past American committees have been more concerned with this problem than their British counterparts because the remits of their investigating committees have been so much wider. When the subject of an inquiry is Crime, or un-American activities, it is important to make clear to the public what aspect of the matter is to come under scrutiny. But on occasion it seems that committees have sought publicity for its own sake. Douglass Cater, a distinguished journalist and former presidential adviser, has described how some committee investigations have in the past been co-ordinated in advance with the press.[2] This may sometimes be justifiable, since the purpose of an inquiry is to discover the truth and publish it in as effective a manner as possible. But it reveals that some committees conceive

1. The power to televise and broadcast proceedings, which had been enjoyed for many years by Senate Committees, was extended to House Committees by the Legislative Reorganization Act of 1970.
2. Douglass Cater, *The Fourth Branch of Government* (1959), pp. 55, 60.

it as their main function to present evidence in such a way as to make the public draw the right conclusions. The evidence in other words seems to them more important than the report to be made at the end of the inquiry. It is significant, as Cater points out, that after two of the most famous congressional inquiries of recent times—that which looked into the dismissal of General MacArthur, and that in which Senator McCarthy confronted the Army—the chairmen sought to dispense altogether with the formality of a report; for in the nature of things a committee's report, which ought to subsume all the evidence before it and add to it the committee's considered judgement, is unlikely to get more publicity than the more dramatic hearings that preceded it.

Although Lords committees always hear evidence in public, unless there are special reasons otherwise, it is only recently that select committees of the House of Commons have chosen to hear evidence chiefly in public. This was one of the changes in style that accompanied the creation of a number of new committees in the period 1966–69. It has not so far been adopted by all committees. Those looking at matters of administration, or acting judicially or domestically, have preferred to take their evidence in private and publish it, if at all, together with their report at the end of their inquiry. But those that have chosen to hold public hearings are apparently convinced that they benefit from them. One of them, the Race Relations Committee, produced a special report asking the House to authorize the televising, sound recording and photography of the committee's proceedings when hearing evidence in public away from Westminster.[1] (The House did not reply.)

Both legislatures believe in the need for privacy while committees are deliberating among themselves. The *Congressional Quarterly Almanac* noted how, in an unusual move, the House Education and Labor Committee in 1967 marked up portions of a bill in public.[2] The normal procedure is for this to be done in executive (closed) session, although sometimes an official may be present by invitation. One committee, the House Appropriations Committee, holds all its meetings in executive session, and in general the House committees hold more executive sessions than

1. House of Commons Paper 196 of 1968–69.
2. *Congressional Quarterly Almanac*, Vol. XXIII, 1967, pp. 1146–8.

do their Senate counterparts. In 1967 for instance forty-eight per cent of House committees and subcommittee meetings were in closed session compared with twenty-six per cent of Senate and twenty-five per cent of joint committee and subcommittee meetings. Overall, thirty-nine per cent of meetings were in private.[1] This compares with about fifty per cent of select committee and subcommittee meetings in the House of Commons in 1968–69 to which the public were not admitted.[2]

In the House of Representatives and the Senate[3] individual or minority views of members can be submitted and printed simultaneously with the committee report. In the House of Commons, as mentioned above, no minority report is possible. The committee's minutes are, however, printed with the report and will disclose any amendments moved to the report, and any alternative report proposed, together with the voting on them. It is thus possible to discover from the minutes the points of difference within the committee, and the views which a minority tried to persuade their colleagues to accept.

ACHIEVEMENTS OF COMMITTEES

The achievements of many of the individual committees operating in the two legislatures are mentioned at different points in this book. Since the functions of committees include legislation, the scrutiny of finance, and the oversight of the executive, those aspects of the work of committees are appropriately considered in other chapters. It will be found there that whereas Congress has entrusted its committees with the principal responsibilities in those fields, Parliament retains a large share for itself. Far more of the energy of Congress is expended in its committees than is the case in Parliament. The grievances of constituents, and even the personal ambitions of members, can be satisfied through the system of congressional committees in a manner that is quite foreign to British practice.

It is necessary to reiterate these points before going on to consider the relative effects of committee work in the two legislatures. The achievements of congressional committees are far greater than those of parliamentary committees because they

1. *Congressional Quarterly Almanac*, Vol. XXIII, 1967, pp. 1146–8.
2. Since 1968–69 there has been an increasing tendency to sit in public.
3. Legislative Reorganization Act of 1970, Section 107.

play a far greater part in the scheme of Congress. 'Congress in its committee rooms is Congress at work', said Woodrow Wilson; Parliament does essential work in its committee rooms, but that work is subsidiary to the work done on the floors of the two Houses. A description of the work done in a recent period by two committees on related subjects—the Joint Committee on Atomic Energy in Washington and the Select Committee on Science and Technology at Westminster—will help to point the difference.

The Joint Committee on Atomic Energy

The Joint Committee on Atomic Energy was created (under statute) in 1946. It contains nine members from each House, with not more than five members from either chamber belonging to the same political party. One of the strengths of the committee comes from the fact that its members also belong to other committees operating in similar fields in each House. It is a committee of formidable experience and prestige. Up to the 90th Congress (1967–68) four of its members had belonged to the committee since its inception.

Unlike most Joint Committees, it is empowered to consider legislation, which it generally reports in identical terms to each House. Besides its legislative function it oversees the work of the Atomic Energy Commission and all other government departments and agencies concerned with atomic energy. It proposes policy changes and innovations in the national atomic energy programme, and is required to keep Congress and the public informed about developments in this field. It now operates through seven subcommittees, and the internal cohesiveness of the committee is strengthened by the practice of all members sitting in on all subcommittee meetings. The subcommittees deal respectively with research, development and radiation; legislation; agreements for co-operation (with other countries, for instance); communities (in areas owned by the Atomic Energy Commission, such as Los Alamos); military applications; security; and raw materials. The committee staff, who are non-partisan and who operate closely with the staffs of related committees, comprises the staff director, six staff members (of whom two or three have scientific qualifications), and about fifteen supporting staff.[1]

1. *Current Membership of the Joint Committee on Atomic Energy, etc.;* published February 1968, for the use of the Joint Committee.

The Joint Committee has recently listed its major achievements.[1] Although these are doubtless viewed in the best light possible, they amount to a formidable catalogue. If its claims are accepted at face value, the committee can be said to have had great influence on American nuclear policy, both peaceful and military. It successfully advised President Truman to develop the hydrogen bomb, although the Atomic Energy Commission were opposed to it. As its members became apprehensive about the control of nuclear weapons outside the United States, it made a number of recommendations about how security should be improved, and these were put into effect. It played a dominant part, against the wishes of the Navy, in developing the nuclear submarine; when the Navy refused to build it, the Joint Committee persuaded Congress to authorize the Atomic Energy Commission to build the power plants which, when handed over to the Navy, became one of the mainstays of the national defence system. In the civil field, when both the Bureau of the Budget (as it then was) and the National Security Council had turned down a proposal to develop a commercial nuclear reactor in 1954, it was the Joint Committee who persuaded a House Appropriations Subcommittee to authorize expenditure for this purpose—expenditure which was to be justified by the success of the scheme. When there was a dispute between the Atomic Energy Commission and the Army about the value of preserving food by irradiating it, the hearings of the committee established that the previous tests had not been as conclusive as they seemed, and later tests proved that the system could work. It was the Joint Committee's enthusiasm that led to the first launching of a nuclear-powered satellite in 1961, and in 1965 to the operating of a nuclear reactor in space; and it has been the Joint Committee which, by substantially amending the legislation put forward by the executive branch, has refused to permit other nations to achieve independent nuclear weapons as a result of the assistance of the United States.

This catalogue, it must be stressed, reflects the committee's own interpretation of events. Even so it makes an impressive list of occasions on which the committee has affected policies and perhaps the history of the nation. But they are, obviously, high-spots in a quarter-century career; and it may be more instructive

1. Ibid.

to consider what the Joint Committee did in a normal year's work. The year chosen is 1967, the first session of the 90th Congress. In that year it held seventy-four meetings, forty-nine of them in public and the rest in executive session, often dealing with secret aspects of their remit. In their report for that year[1] the Committee lists its activities under five headings.

The first is legislation. The Joint Committee produced two bills, one authorizing the Atomic Energy Commission's appropriations for 1968, the other being an omnibus bill concerning several of the Commission's activities. The first authorized an appropriation of $2,634 million—some $4½ million less than the Administration had asked for. This was the result of extensive sittings covering the seven weeks following the President's budget message. The authorization included 15 million dollars more than requested for the weapons programme, which in the committee's opinion needed to be speeded up. It encouraged the Atomic Energy Commission to weed out several civilian reactor programmes which were not proving as successful as expected, and recommended further intensive analyses of a particular nuclear rocket engine. It approved the Commission's wish to start work on a new accelerator (though some of the Committee put in a minority report against it) while calling for a number of changes in the detailed plans that had been proposed. It also expressed concern about the failure to carry out experiments on an aspect of the Commission's plans to apply nuclear explosives for civilian use. The Joint Committee's authorization passed unamended into law, after attempts had been made in both Houses to amend it along the lines suggested in the minority report.

The omnibus bill incorporated the major provisions of five separate bills that had been submitted to the committee on behalf of the Atomic Energy Commission, as well as two others originated by members of the committee. The committee did not favour two other bills which came before it, one from the Commission and one from the Department of Defense. Three public hearings and four executive sessions were necessary before this bill emerged. It then passed through both chambers and became law.

Secondly the Joint Committee considered and agreed to four proposals to co-operate in the peaceful use of atomic energy with Australia, Norway, South Africa and Colombia.

1. Ibid. p. 53.

Thirdly the Committee held a number of 'informational' hearings on various matters within their competence. One hearing by a subcommittee was concerned with why a reactor programme was behind schedule and was costing more than expected. Another subcommittee held meetings on eleven days in order to study problems of radiation exposure; their 1,373 pages of evidence made, they claimed, 'the most comprehensive collection of information ever gathered concerning the exposure of humans to radiation incident to the mining of uranium'. A subcommittee, in conjunction with a subcommittee of the Senate Armed Services Committee, held public hearings on two occasions about the missile programme; and the committee produced a report on Chinese nuclear weapons, after hearing evidence on four occasions in closed session. The Senate members of the committee held a hearing before the Senate confirmed the nomination of a member of the Commission. For eight days the committee heard evidence before publishing a report on the licensing and regulation of nuclear reactors. Hearings were also held on five days by the committee and a subcommittee about the accelerator before making the authorization and the minority report noted above.

Fourthly the committee held a number of executive sessions in order that they could be briefed on secret aspects of defence and military intelligence. Fifthly in a number of miscellaneous activities the committee record how their members attended an international conference and how they were kept informed of the Administration's plans for future disarmament negotiations. They also detail the trips they made to foreign and domestic nuclear installations: they visited thirty-one installations from New Jersey to Hawaii, and a trip to Europe took them to six different countries.

The Select Committee on Science and Technology

It is instructive to place against this picture of a congressional committee at work a picture of the achievements of a British select committee. The Select Committee on Science and Technology suggests itself for this purpose, partly because it inquires into the same kind of matters as the Joint Committee considered above; and partly because it is a new committee, a product of the surge of enthusiasm that brought in a number of new select committees in the mid-sixties, which has lasted while some of the others have died.

The committee was first appointed in December 1966 and nominated in January 1967. Its terms of reference were 'to consider science and technology and to report thereon'. This made it a 'subject committee' rather than a 'departmental committee', a matter of some importance at the time, since the latter were planned to be of temporary duration, while the former could expect to be continued from session to session. The committee consisted of fourteen members. It chose a chairman from the government side; but its first subcommittee was chaired by an opposition member.

As the subject of their first inquiry, the committee members chose the nuclear reactor programme. Their thirteen public hearings aroused considerable interest, were widely reported in the press and led them to make a long and detailed report in October 1967.[1] In this report they proposed far-reaching changes in the structure of the nuclear industry and of the Atomic Energy Authority; suggested establishing a new fuel supply and manufacturing company, and taking new steps to control public expenditure (including a study of the U.S. Joint Committee); and offered their views on the future development of the different types of reactor. The report was debated in the House on 23 May 1968.

In the middle of this wide-ranging inquiry, in April 1967, the committee had another subject thrust upon it. In an unusual move the House (at the instigation of the government) required the committee to undertake an inquiry into the subject of coastal pollution, following public concern after a large oil tanker had been wrecked off the south-west coast of Britain. The committee (temporarily increased to seventeen persons) set up a subcommittee to go into the matter, whose inquiry thereafter ran parallel with that of the main committee into the nuclear reactor programme. The subcommittee's inquiry was continued into the next session, and the committee did not issue its report on the subject until July 1968. In the course of the inquiry the subcommittee held twenty-eight meetings (twelve of them in public). The report contained a wide review of oil pollution problems,

1. House of Commons Paper 381 of 1966–67.

and went on to criticize the government both for their lack of preparation to deal with a disaster of this kind and for the action they took when the shipwreck occurred.

Meanwhile in July 1967 the committee embarked on a new major inquiry. This was into the research and development being done in relation to defence needs. This inquiry continued into the next session, the committee's report being eventually made in March 1969. By then the committee had held 36 meetings; at 15 of these evidence was taken in public (on seven occasions at places away from London), the subcommittees had meanwhile travelled to the United States and to western Europe in search of comparative information. The committee's wide-ranging report was eventually debated by the House, but not until May 1971.

With the start of a new session in October 1968, the committee, working through subcommittees, started an inquiry into carbon fibres. Later it ran parallel inquiries into the National Environment Research Council and (following up their earlier report) again into the nuclear power industry.

Thus, from January 1967 to October 1969, the committee and subcommittees had held a total of 178 meetings, and had produced six major reports. Their reports were on the whole favourably received. There was no suggestion that the committee should not continue indefinitely into the future. It seemed to have fitted usefully and well into the system of committees that the House needed. In these circumstances it is interesting to observe the string of public complaints that the committee felt called upon to make about the conditions under which it had to carry out the tasks given to it by the House. Many of its complaints have been echoed by other committees. They offer a commentary on the difficulties faced by select committees, even when they have been created as a result of demands from the House, and even when they are believed to be doing a useful job.

The committee's first complaint was when the House referred to it the matter of coastal pollution. It issued a special report pointing out that it was already deep in a major inquiry into the nuclear reactor programme. For the House to make a habit of requiring committees to undertake a new investigation, which might divert their attention from their chosen lines of inquiry, could have serious consequences, it said, for the committee system as a whole. Although the committee did not say so, the action of the House in this regard seemed to reflect a belief that committees are its servants and must do what they are told.

When the committee produced its first major report (the report on the nuclear reactor programme), it devoted the first eight paragraphs to delineating some of the obstacles that had been put in its way. The government, it said, had delayed moving the motions in the House that were necessary to allow its sub-committees to travel abroad; and when at last the motions had been moved and carried, the Foreign Office had been dilatory in helping to make the necessary arrangements for the visits. The committee also resented the fact that it took the Ministry of Power six months to produce a paper which had been requested. When it eventually arrived, too late to be of any value to the inquiry, it was found to be so slender that the irritated committee felt justified in publishing it despite its 'confidential' classification.

There were strong complaints too at the delay of seven months that took place before the committee's report was debated in the House. It may be that this delay detracted from the interest which the report had evinced when first published. When the debate eventually took place it was poorly attended, and most of the speeches came from members of the committee.

But it was the committee's next major report (on coastal pollution, published in July 1968) that gave prominence to one of its greatest problems. An Appendix to the report dealt with the staffing of the committee. This pointed out that the committee had been assisted by a scientific assessor and a library clerk, but that its principal officer, the clerk of the committee, had had to try and service the committee and subcommittees while at all times having 'other and prior duties to perform' in other aspects of the House's service. The evidence given to the committee on this point showed that the House had agreed to an expansion in its committee system without making consequential provision for an increase in staff (and this led to subsequent changes in recruitment policy). In later sessions the committee was served by two full-time clerks.

A study of this committee therefore shows not only what select committees can and do achieve, but some of the difficulties they have to overcome in so doing. Both have to be taken into account before a true comparison with congressional committees can be made.

UNOFFICIAL COMMITTEES

This book is concerned only with the procedures and the official machinery of the two legislatures. But a passing reference must be made here to the existence of unofficial party committees, because these impinge in one way or another on the official committee systems which this chapter is considering. Here the general pattern of committees in Congress and Parliament is reversed; Congress has only a few party committees, Parliament has many.

Mention has been made (see p. 227 footnote 3) of the arrangements made by each party in each chamber of Congress for nominating their members to the various official committees. The committees on committees which operate in both Senate and House are party committees and therefore unofficial. But their right to nominate the members of the official committees gives them importance and influence.

The parties also have policy committees in both chambers. In the House the Republican Policy Committee meets fairly often, and takes informal votes on various legislative issues; the Democratic equivalent rarely meets. In the Senate one of the Policy Committees has considerable influence on events, for it is the Policy Committee of the majority party that decides which of the bills reported from committees shall be taken on the floor of the chamber. Both parties have campaign committees in each chamber, responsible for fund-raising and election strategy, and there are a handful of other general committees which the parties use to a greater or less extent.[1]

Of the various political and social groups that exist in Congress, two must be mentioned. The Democratic Study Group was founded in 1959 and in 1970 contained over 120 of the Democrat members in the House of Representatives. It provides information to its members on key liberal issues, and operates a whip system by which they are alerted to important votes. It has a professional staff and is accommodated in one of the House Office Buildings. Somewhat similar to it is the Republicans' Wednesday Club. It carries out research for its members (of whom there were twenty-six in 1970) but does not operate a whip system.

1. These and other party committees are discussed in Chapter I in the context of party organization and leadership. (See pp. 21–23.)

In Parliament the system of party committees is much more extensively organized. Each party has a sort of Committee of the Whole, a committee consisting of all their members (and, in the case of the Labour Party, of their members in the Lords); and beneath each of these there is a network of functional committees covering the whole field of government. On an unofficial level, in other words, Parliament organizes its committees in a manner not dissimilar from Congress. There is no paradox here. British ministers are not answerable to the political parties, the parties are separated from executive power; and so the parties, like the Houses of Congress, arm themselves with a series of committees to watch everything that the executive does.

THE TWO COMMITTEE SYSTEMS

In a short study of these committee systems, it has been necessary to generalize to a great extent. It would be unfortunate if an impression of uniformity is given for, in both the congressional system and the parliamentary select committee system, every committee has its own traditions and its own style. There are differences too between Senate and House committees, and between committees which are predominantly legislative and those predominantly investigatory. If an attempt is now made to suggest some conclusions, these too must be general in form.

One of the several merits of the congressional and the parliamentary select committee system is the possibility they allow of prolonged dialogue between legislators and the public. The ideas brought into a legislature, in the competitive circumstances of a series of public hearings, educate members; and the publicity given to those hearings, and to the committee's report on the subject, in its turn educates the public about the condition of their own society.

Secondly, the committees enable a legislature to scrutinize the activities of the Administration most effectively. This aspect of their work will be looked at more closely in Chapter VIII. It is particularly important in highly-developed industrial societies with the problem of ensuring that the bureaucracy remains responsive to political leadership, and where ministers are constantly faced with technical problems on which they must rely heavily on the advice given to them by their officials.

The existence of a comprehensive committee system enables a legislature to take up new problems more readily as they arise. Business on the floor of a chamber has always to be controlled by the need to get certain legislation through, while at the same time allowing a number of other routine parliamentary processes to take place. As a result there is often difficulty in finding time on the floor to examine a matter of national importance when it first arises. If a committee exists with terms of reference covering the matter in question, it can conduct the necessary examination without encroaching on the time of the House.

Fourthly it enables members to gain experience of a subject so as to exert power and influence that they would not otherwise have; and by and large it ensures that they specialize in a subject before exercising power in that field. Furthermore work done in committee is almost invariably less partisan than that done on the floor. In the exercise of the influence which committee membership allows them, the legislators are less likely to follow unthinkingly the wishes of their party whips. From the member's personal point of view the American system shows how committee work can help him to establish a national reputation, and so improve his chances of re-election.

These advantages are additional to the usefulness of committees in saving time on the floor of the House, and doing work for which the House is unsuited. But there are attendant disadvantages. Chief among them is the fact that committees gain their reputation at the expense of that of the floor of the House to which they belong; they rival the work on the floor, in other words, rather than supplement it. This was the argument put forward in the House of Commons by opponents of the proposal to create more select committees in 1967. The committees were set up; but significantly other procedural changes were made at the same time which added to the House's authority by enabling it to hold more emergency, headline-catching debates. This maintained something of the balance of effectiveness between the two.

It is said that Congress has declined in positive legislative force as a result of the strengthening of its committee system. It is certainly the case that since 1946 committees have been more effective and that Congress has lost some legislative initiative to the President. A connection between the two can be inferred, but would be difficult to prove. The same period has seen an increase in the power of governments in other countries, without any corresponding changes in the committee structure of their parliaments;[1] and if the increased power of committee chairmen has derogated from the power of the floor leadership, that in its turn ought to have made it more difficult for the President's legislative programme to get through, not less.

There is a danger in the proliferation of committees. If responsibility is splintered among too many bodies, much of their energy will be spent in competition with each other, and they may reach contradictory conclusions and issue conflicting directives. When faced with a number of simultaneous investigating bodies, any agency worth its salt will be able to play them off against each other, and this can hardly be to the benefit of a legislature. In Congress the seeds of this confusion are always present, for there is a standing committee, an appropriations committee, and a committee on government operations, in each chamber, concerned to some extent with the activities of each branch of the executive. Professor Harris has pointed out that in 1957–58 no less than twelve congressional subcommittees were simultaneously investigating the civil aeronautics agencies.[2] Yet the other side of this coin is that the more committees exist in Congress, the more accessible the legislature is to the public. Each committee is the point at which public opinion can express itself in time to have an effect on legislation.

Finally there is a danger that a strong committee system may enable small groups of members to take decisions which are contrary to the wishes of their House as a whole; may give to some members better opportunities to exert power and influence than to others; and might turn their chairmen into little Caesars. The defect of the system, in other words, is that it can give power to bodies and people who may not use it responsibly.

When these advantages and disadvantages, as they apply to the American system, are balanced, it is possible to make two general points. First, the advantages do not stem from particular facets of the American constitution; they are, or can be, features of any legislative committee system. Secondly, the defects of the system are not intrinsic in it; they arise rather from a failure by

1. *Parliaments*, published for the Inter Parliamentary Union (1966 ed.), p. 150.

2. Harris, *The Congressional Control of Administration* (1964), p. 275.

the Houses to impose the necessary limits to, or controls over, the independence of their committees. The defects would not, in other words, arise if Congress thought it worthwhile to act so as to exclude them.[1]

There are reasons for thinking that a committee system in Parliament is less likely to be subject to these defects than it would be in Congress. It will be shown in the next chapter that Parliament is not in any case the mainspring of legislation: the government, nor Parliament, mostly initiates the bills which pass into law—so Parliament's force in the legislative field is not likely to be diminished by the creation of more select committees (which do not, in any case, normally consider legislation). Furthermore, the suspicion which the House of Commons has always shown towards its committees, coupled with the fact that they are nominated by the leadership of strong political parties, make it less likely that committees or their chairmen will ever act so as to frustrate the wishes of the House, or that too many committees will be set up.

Nevertheless, it is improbable that the House of Commons will ever try to assemble a committee system comparable with that of Congress. The facilities available on the floor for the oversight of departments (see Chapter VIII) make such a system less necessary. The demands on the time of members (who do not have a congressman's personal staff) already make it difficult to man some of the existing committees, or to get members to attend them regularly. No House is ever likely to show more enthusiasm for the strengthening of the committee system than did the young House that was elected in 1966; but its demands resulted only in the creation of five or six new select committees, some of which had limited duration, and an accompanying cut in the size of the Estimates Committee.

As it happens, a test case of the House's enthusiasm for its select committees arose in February 1969. The Select Committee on Nationalized Industries, one of its most respected committees, had been anxious for some while to investigate the Bank of England, for which ministers have considerable responsibility but are not answerable to Parliament. As the purpose of the increase in select committee activity had been to make ministers more accountable, the Nationalized Industries Committee proposed

1. Lees, op. cit., p. 102.

in a report to the House that the Bank ought to be included within its terms of reference; and since the government had promised that the new committees should have 'the right to determine their own functions and activities without any interference or restriction on the part of the Government'[1], members were not satisfied when it was suggested that only some of the Bank's operations should concern them. The disagreement between committee and government came before the House in a debate on 11 February. It is hard to think when a committee had a stronger case, and when a House existed that was more sympathetic to committees as a whole. Yet in the division that followed, the government won by a comfortable majority of 101 votes to 61.

It is to be doubted then that the House of Commons will ever establish a range of investigatory committees covering the whole administration on the congressional pattern. Those who still feel that the advantages of committees are such that the House of Commons needs more, should look not to the current practice of the American committees but to their history. Congress did not organize its full range of committees out of any doctrinaire belief that that was what a legislature needed. On the contrary its committees grew up, gradually and individually, as required by the posing of new problems. That is perhaps the way Parliament will develop.

1. House of Commons Debates, 29 June 1967.

CHAPTER SIX

LEGISLATION

THE description of Congress as a legislature follows logically from the authority given to it by Article I of the Constitution, which is entitled 'the Legislative Power'. Applied to Parliament, the word 'legislature' is misleading. It is accurate in the sense that the legislative process is not complete until a bill has passed through both Houses and received the royal assent. But it misleads in not conveying that the legislative power of Parliament is in the main exercised by ministers in its midst, and that most legislation consists of what ministers decide. In the United States decisions on what bills become law and in what form are taken, by and large, by the Houses of Congress. In Britain the legislative function is primarily governmental.

It has not always been so. In Britain for centuries it was not regarded as part of the function of the Crown or the government to submit for Parliament's consideration a steady stream of measures. Under Henry VIII, it is true, Parliament passed a large number of statutes designed to give effect to the royal policy of Reformation. But in the seventeenth, eighteenth and even in the nineteenth centuries the majority of bills were private bills, *privilegia* sought from Parliament by a great variety of persons, both individual and corporate. The legislative volume was heavy and important: the face of England was changed, for example, by the enclosure Acts in one century and the railway Acts in another. But it owed little to the government in those days. Only after the widening of the franchise in 1832 and 1867 and the growing concern with the 'condition of the people', arising from rapid commercial and industrial development, did the amount of public legislation increase[1] and ministers begin to measure their achievement and importance by the number and quality of the statutes passed during their tenure of office.

In the United States the opposite tendency was at first apparent.

1. See *The Legislative Process in Great Britain* by S. A. Walkland (1968), pp. 12–15.

The early Congresses were marked by the extraordinary ascendancy of Alexander Hamilton, the first Secretary of the Treasury, who held office from 1789 to 1795. The effect of his operations on the early shape of the financial committee structure of Congress is considered later (p. 311), but it is noteworthy that his influence carried well beyond the realms of finance. The use made by Congress not only of Hamilton, but subsequently of the other two executive departments to be appointed—Foreign Affairs (State) and War—to prepare bills and plans suggested a movement towards a relationship with the executive branch in which the heads of departments took the initiative in the legislative process and the administration of policy.

This reliance on the executive was perpetuated by Hamilton's success and accounts for the delay in the development of a system of standing committees. In the course of the nineteenth century, however, that system did grow up to the point at which it spanned the whole field of government operations. The effectiveness of committees in preparing legislation has turned on a number of factors, notably the extent to which, as legislation became more complex, they have been able to recruit staffs capable of helping them to assess the testimony given by experts from the executive branch. Nevertheless, the development of a fully fledged system of committees has enabled Congress to enjoy a genuinely co-ordinate position with the executive branch, as contemplated by the Constitution.

Today the difference between Congress as a self-contained legislature and Parliament restricted to criticizing, sometimes amending, even on occasion rejecting a bill, but not fundamentally disturbing the government's legislative programme as a whole, appears to be complete. But this statement of difference needs several reservations and refinements. They can best be illuminated first by a description of the legislative process in each country and secondly by an analysis and comparison of their different features.

THE TWO LEGISLATIVE PROCESSES

The United Kingdom

Like his opposite numbers in Washington, any member of either House of Parliament has the right to introduce a bill and to have it printed and published. From that point onwards in the British legislative process the opportunities open to members cease to be equal, the scales being heavily loaded in favour of the government. In the House of Commons the time available for legislation on the floor is in practice government time, except to the extent that the House specifically provides time for private members to legislate. Over the five years from 1964 to 1969 private members had about thirteen per cent of the total time spent in the House on legislation.[1] In the House of Lords, where time is not an acute problem, there is no distinction between government time and private members' time. But since a bill must pass through both Houses to become law, it does not matter whether a private member's bill is introduced in the Lords or the Commons. It still has to negotiate the main hurdle, which is the shortage of time in the Commons.

The government, secure in the knowledge that it controls the time of the Commons, can lay a planned programme of legislation before Parliament. Herbert Morrison, Leader of the House of Commons in the Labour Government of 1945–50, has described how this programme is prepared.[2] Two committees of the cabinet are principally concerned. The future legislation committee, comprising mainly the Leaders and Chief Whips of the two Houses, draws a broad five-year plan of legislation for the entire Parliament and more specifically chooses the bills to be introduced in each session. The legislation committee, also a small body, including the Lord Chancellor and the Attorney General as chief legal advisers to the government, as well as the Leaders and Chief Whips of each House, considers the content of each bill and watches over the progress of the government's legislative programme during the session.

The projects and bills considered by the cabinet will come from several sources. First there are the annual expenditure and revenue (Consolidated Fund and Finance) bills which set the financial frame for government action and raise questions of high policy. Then there are the proposals put before the electorate by the victorious party in its election manifesto. Here the government are consciously giving effect to the choice made by the

1. This calculation does not include time spent on legislation in Standing Committees.

2. Herbert Morrison, *Government and Parliament* (1954), Chapter XI. See also P. Gordon Walker, *The Cabinet* (1970), pp. 43–44.

electorate of the programme which seemed most attractive to it in the year of election. Another source is the government machine. Each department of state is likely to have legislative projects which, it will seek to persuade its minister, are urgent and important. The picture is sometimes drawn of a long queue of such projects—desirable in the public if not the party interest—which would certainly become law, were Parliament to adopt more efficient and expeditious legislative processes. That picture has been shown to be illusory.[1] Departmental measures are nevertheless an important element in the government's legislative programme.

Another fruitful source of legislation is the repeal of obsolete and unnecessary statutes, the consolidation of enactments and the rewriting of common law in statutes. Since 1965 these have been the responsibility of law commissions reporting directly to the Lord Chancellor. The law commissions aim to cover the whole field of the law, revising it subject by subject, though there is no code of law in Britain as in the United States.

In any single session the balance between these various elements in the programme will be determined by the political actualities. The planning of the Conservative Government's programme for the session of 1962–63 was overshadowed by the possibility of Britain's joining the Common Market, with the mass of legislation that entry would have entailed. The Labour Government's decision not to introduce its controversial bill to nationalize the iron and steel industry in the Parliament of 1964–1966, notwithstanding the statement of intention in its election manifesto, was doubtless dictated by the fact that its majority in the House of Commons was only three.

The sessional programme of government bills, once decided, is announced to Parliament in the Speech made by the Queen at the formal opening of the session. It will not refer to all the measures that the government will introduce. There is always a margin for contingencies. Conversely not all the bills mentioned in the Speech will necessarily be introduced. Nevertheless the Speech is a sound guide as to the measures which are likely to occupy Parliament for much of the session.

The foundation of a bill may be the report of a Royal Commis-

1. Sixth Report of Select Committee on Procedure 1966–67, House of Commons Paper 539 of 1967, para. 9.

sion, or of an inquiry initiated by a party organization or a departmental committee or—rarely today but frequently in the nineteenth century—a parliamentary committee. On this basis the government department concerned will begin to consider in detail what the bill should contain, taking into account the views of other government departments and consulting any outside organizations and persons principally concerned. The result is converted into a bill by a parliamentary draftsman. This official is one of some twenty barristers who together comprise the Office of Parliamentary Counsel, a small and elite branch of the public service, and who work under instructions from the government. A draftsman may produce numerous prints of a complex bill before the department concerned, the legislation committee of the cabinet and the cabinet itself are satisfied that it is ready for presentation to Parliament. After that he will stay with his bill throughout its stages in each House and draft amendments to it on behalf of the government.

A bill consists of an enacting formula ('Be it enacted by the Queen's most Excellent Majesty, by and with the consent of the Lords Spiritual and Temporal, and Commons in this present Parliament assembled, and by the authority of the same as follows');[1] the provisions of the bill in the form of clauses and schedules; and a title. Preambles, setting out the reasons for legislating, are nearly obsolete except in bills of a constitutional nature (for example, altering the composition or powers of the House of Lords) or bills to ratify treaties. A bill is usually prefaced by a memorandum explaining its purport, its financial implications and its effect on the number of persons in the public service. The attention of members is specially drawn to provisions in the bill imposing any kind of financial charge or burden by printing them in italics.

Alongside the preparation of government bills, private members are making their contribution. An order passed by the Commons in each session specifies the number of days for proceedings on private members' bills. It is currently twelve days (1970–71), in addition to the time bills spend on their committee stage off the floor. The sessional order provides for twelve days to be taken on Fridays, a convenient day for members to be in their constitu-

1. The enacting formula of an expenditure or a taxation bill is more elaborate, and gives an indication of the bill's financial content and purpose.

encies and therefore a difficult day on which to persuade members to attend. As more than 550 members (that is, 630 minus 60 to 70 ministers and some others) are eligible to initiate legislation on these twelve days, a ballot is held. It cuts down the number to about twenty-five.

A private member has other legislative opportunities. First, it is always open to him to introduce and publish a bill after giving notice of his intention to do so. Secondly, under the 'ten-minute rule' on two days a week throughout the session, he can make a short speech asking leave of the House to introduce a bill. This procedure gives useful publicity to an idea for a bill even if, as the rule allows, a member's motion is opposed, and it is rejected by the House. But bills introduced by either of these two methods have a lower priority than ballot bills and are unlikely to pass into law unless they are unopposed.

A private member faces other difficulties in preparing his bill. Although a department may sympathize with his intentions, it will not be at his disposal in the often protracted business of consulting and settling with the outside interests chiefly concerned. Nor will the parliamentary draftsmen be available to draft the bill. The extent of these difficulties will depend on the source of the bill. Sometimes it may be, in origin, a departmental bill, when the preliminary work will already have been done, or the government may be willing at some stage to help with the drafting of the bill if it wants the bill to make progress. Alternatively a member may take on a project at the instance of a society or pressure group which is ready to undertake much of the necessary consultation and bear the expense of having it privately drafted. If none of these options is open, a member must do the best he can, with the help of the parliamentary offices which deal with public bills. Parliament does not put a trained draftsman at his disposal at this stage, though if the bill is given a second reading, the government may appoint a draftsman to draft amendments at the committee stage.

Whether a bill derives from the government or a private member, it has to pass through the same stages on the way to the statute book. It can start in either House,[1] and must in either case pass through all the necessary stages in each House. Here a bill's

1. But a bill with heavy financial implications may not start in the Lords (see p. 185).

progress is described from its beginning in the Commons House. First reading is a formal stage: notice of its title appears on the order paper, the minister or member in charge bows on being called by the Speaker, and the Clerk of the House reads aloud the title from a 'dummy' bill, showing the names of any supporters (up to eleven are permitted). The bill is appointed for second reading on a future day and ordered to be printed. Most bills are introduced in this way. The annual financial bills, which have to be founded on resolutions of the House (see pp. 318, 344) and private members' bills introduced under the ten-minute rule (already referred to) are the exceptions to this procedure.

Second reading is the crucial stage of a bill, when its general principles are debated and decided. The member in charge, usually the minister concerned, opens the debate and explains the objects and provisions of his bill. He will usually be followed by a spokesman for the opposition and by other interested members. Depending on the importance of the bill, the debate may last for as much as two days or as little as a few minutes. It will usually be concluded by 'winding-up' speeches from the two front benches before a vote is taken. Members have an opportunity to record objection to the bill at this stage either by voting against it or by moving an amendment to the motion 'That the Bill be now read a second time'. The amendment takes the form of either postponing the second reading for six months (the equivalent of rejection) or of declining to give the bill a second reading for certain reasons. If either amendment is carried, the bill is rejected. If a 'six months' amendment is rejected, the bill is declared read a second time; if a 'reasoned' amendment is rejected, there is an opportunity to vote on the question that the bill be read a second time.

Once the second reading has been agreed to, a money resolution covering any expenditure provided for in the bill is taken. This resolution is seldom debated because the financial as well as the other aspects of the bill come into issue in the debate on second reading. It is nevertheless important. Once the second reading and the financial resolution have been agreed to, the frame has been set within which the committee on the bill is to do its work. No amendment destructive of the principle, or beyond the scope, of the bill as agreed on second reading is in order; nor is any amendment which would have the effect of increasing the expenditure as delimited in the money resolution. These basic rules govern every committee to which a bill may be sent.

Practically all bills are sent to Standing Committees for their committee stage. Only the annual financial bills (see Chapter VII); bills of constitutional importance, such as a bill altering the balance of power between the two Houses or touching the relationship of the Sovereign with a commonwealth territory or setting up new courts of law; and bills so unimportant as not to warrant the creation of a Standing Committee to consider them are now normally considered in Committee of the whole House. A few bills are referred to select committees, with power to call expert and other witnesses before deciding the final form of the bill. These are likely to be bills without party political content— for example on obscene publications or military discipline—on which the government is content for the committee to work out the details. These bills, however, require a further committee stage, which generally takes place in a Committee of the whole House. Joint Committees of both Houses are as a rule thought to derogate from the principle of bicameral consideration and are reserved for consolidation or statute law revision bills only.

Seven or eight Standing Committees, titled alphabetically, are usually appointed in a session. Their composition and method of work have been described in Chapter V. Here it is only necessary to point out that Standing Committees have been getting smaller. Today they usually have, on average, about twenty members. The smaller the committee, the greater the difficulties of the government if the bill is at all controversial. As every committee reflects the party composition of the House, the government majority diminishes with the size of the committee. Small committees lead not only to tighter discipline but to greater governmental efforts to secure a committee with compliant rather than critical government supporters.

A Standing Committee considers the bill clause by clause. To each clause the amendments of which written notice has been given are set out on the paper of amendments before the Committee. The Chairman of the Committee has power to select from these amendments; it is the same power as the Speaker has to select amendments offered to a motion or to a bill at its report stage.[1] In a Standing Committee the Chairman exercises his

1. The Speaker's power of selection is described on pp. 140, 155-6.

power of selection less by excluding certain amendments altogether—though he is likely to exclude an amendment if not enough notice has been given of it—than by grouping a series of amendments conveniently for discussion. When the amendments to a clause have been disposed of, the whole clause, as amended or without amendment, is then debated.

The debates on the amendments and then on the clause provide the opportunity for the views of interested parties outside the House to be made known. Approaches to members, more especially by interested parties which were not satisfied by the government's own consultations before the bill was introduced, are chiefly made during the committee stage, though they continue throughout the passage of the bill. The committee has no power to hear interested parties directly: they must put their case through a member of the committee. So proceedings in a Standing Committee tend to be opposition-orientated: the dissatisfied interests, as well as the opposition's own research organizations, build up the pressure on opposition members of the committee who make the most of the running. Standing Committees sit in public and a verbatim report of their debates is published daily, so that members of the House and other persons have no difficulty in following the proceedings.

When a committee has completed its work, the bill is reported to the House. If it has been amended, it is reprinted afresh for the consideration of the House. A bill reported from a Standing Committee must always have a 'report stage' on the floor of the House to give all members of the House a chance to move amendments.[1] That opportunity is not always available if a bill is committed to a Committee of the whole House; there will then be a report stage only if the bill has been amended. At the report stage each amendment selected is considered, and an opportunity is provided for the member in charge of the bill to redeem any undertakings given in committee to think further about amendments. No question is put on a clause unless an amendment proposes to leave it out. On report the Speaker's power of selection (see pp. 140, 155-6) is aimed primarily at avoiding the duplication of debate in committee.

After the report stage, there is the third reading. Since 1967

1. Unless the House decides that the report stage should itself be taken in a Standing Committee, see below p. 273.

the question for third reading is put without debate unless at least six members have given prior notice that they wish a debate. Whether or not the bill is debated, the House has a final opportunity on third reading to vote on the bill. If, as is usually the case, it survives that vote, the bill is then sent to the House of Lords.

In the Lords the stages of a bill are broadly the same. The powers of the Lords over bills were described in Chapter IV. As in any other bicameral system a bill (other than a money bill) can be amended in the Lords. As befits a revising chamber, the opportunities for amendment are less restricted than in the Commons. Amendments may be moved as late as the third reading of the bill. Nor is any person empowered to select amendments at any stage. The government find it useful to propose in the Lords alterations which they had no time to make in the Commons or for other reasons prefer to make in the Lords. Other peers may think the bill needs further revision, more especially if for any reason discussion on parts of the bill has been cut short in the Commons.[1] If the Lords do amend a bill, it is returned to the Commons who can either accept, or amend, or reject the amendments, but they cannot reopen unamended parts of the bill. If the amendments are amended or rejected, the bill is returned to the Lords for consideration of the Commons' action. In theory this interchange may be endless; there is no procedure for reconciling differences by conference between the two Houses. In practice the Lords do not usually insist upon their amendments. If they were to do so and disagreement persisted, the bill would eventually be lost, though a government backed by its majority in the Commons has power under the Parliament Acts 1911 and 1949 to override the Lords in conditions already described (see p. 182). If the Lords do not amend a Commons bill, or if at any stage in the interchange one House agrees to the amendments made by the other House, the bill goes forward for Royal Assent.

Where a bill is introduced in the Lords, the exchanges are not essentially different. This time, after it has been through its

1. Some idea of the contribution made by the House of Lords as a revising chamber in these circumstances can be gained from the fact that it made 341 amendments to the Industrial Relations Bill 1971. For other illustrations of the Lords' function as a revising chamber, see p. 204.

stages first in the Lords and then the Commons, it is the Commons' amendments (if any) which are considered by the Lords. The exchanges continue until the bill is ready for Royal Assent or, if agreement cannot be reached, is lost. The government cannot override the House of Lords on a bill which was started in that House because the Parliament Acts do not apply to such a bill. The reason is presumably that any government bill likely to arouse the degree of controversy that makes necessary recourse to the Parliament Acts is almost certain to have been introduced first in the Commons.

The final stage of Royal Assent is a formality. Assent was last withheld in 1707. The date of Royal Assent is the date on which the bill comes into force as an Act of Parliament unless the bill itself prescribes some other date.

In both Houses steps have been taken to accelerate proceedings on bills or at least to lessen the time spent on them on the floor. In the Commons the second reading of a bill can now be taken in a 'second reading committee'—in effect a Standing Committee appointed to debate the principle of the bill. Similarly, the report stage of a bill can be remitted to a committee. In these instances, objection by a specified number of members keeps the bill on the floor for the normal procedures, so that in practice these devices are used only for non-controversial bills. Third reading can be taken without debate. So it is possible by using all these devices for a bill to pass the Commons and escape debate on the floor altogether, though up to 1971 only one bill had been so treated. Also saving time on the floor but aimed primarily at regional pacification is the reference of bills exclusively affecting Scotland to a Committee containing all the Scottish members, where the principle of the bill—in essence the stage of second reading—is debated. Similarly the committee stage of these Scottish bills is later taken in a Standing Committee composed chiefly of Scottish members. In the House of Lords pressure on the floor is more spasmodic than in the Commons. But it has been enough to oblige the Lords in 1968 for the first time for many years to take the clause by clause consideration in a public bill committee of eleven peers. One bill was so taken in 1968, another in 1969 and two in 1971. This arrangement is likely to become a regular feature during times of legislative stress in that House.

Private bills, noted above (p. 263) as seeking special powers outside the general law for corporate bodies and occasionally for individuals, are today chiefly sought by local authorities for special purposes of local government within their area. The promoters of a private bill are required by the standing orders of the two Houses to bring the provisions of their bill to the attention of anyone—for example, land or property owners—likely to be directly affected and to prove to the satisfaction of the authorities of both Houses that they have done so. Then the bill has to go through the same stages in each House as a public bill. But the treatment of the bill is different in two chief respects. First it is not normally debated on the floor, though any member has the power to secure a debate either to draw attention to a point of public policy or interest arising out of the bill's provisions, or as a means of extracting from its promoters concessions on behalf of interests affected by the bill. Secondly if petitions have been lodged by interests claiming to be adversely affected, an opportunity is given at the committee stage in each House for promoters and objectors alike to put their cases to a small committee of members, who after proceedings somewhat in the manner of a court of law, including submissions by counsel, report the bill with or without amendment to the House. In both Houses their judgement on the bill is almost invariably accepted. If no petitions are lodged, the promoters have to establish the need for their bill to a committee of the Commons and to the Lord Chairman of Committees, sitting as a committee of one, in the other House. Unlike most public bills, private bills are drafted with preambles; and whether or not petitions are lodged against the bill, the allegations set out in the preamble have to be proved to the committee's satisfaction. The promoters of an unopposed private bill can expect it to pass expeditiously through both Houses. The final stage with private as with public bills is the Royal Assent.

The United States

In the United States a proposal for legislation may take one of two forms. The most usual form is the bill, comprising a title, an enacting formula ('Be it enacted by the Senate and House of Representatives of the United States of America in Congress assembled, That' etc.), sections and paragraphs making up the text. A bill may originate in either House of Congress; it has to pass both Houses; and it must be approved by the President to become a law.

There is also the joint resolution of both Houses of Congress, beginning with the formula 'Resolved by the Senate and House of Representatives of the United States of America in Congress assembled, That' etc. Like a bill, it has a title and a text; unlike a bill, it often carries a preamble stating the reasons why it is being proposed. Joint resolutions may originate in either House. They differ little from bills, and at one time were used for purposes of general legislation. President Franklin Roosevelt, for instance, liked this form of legislation because the statement of reasons in the preamble served as 'guidance' to the Supreme Court. But normally the joint resolution is used for 'incidental, unusual or inferior purposes of legislating', such as correcting an error in an existing statute or special appropriations for minor purposes.[1] The joint resolution retains one important function: all amendments to the Constitution are proposed in Congress in this form. Joint resolutions proposing such amendments are sent to the states for ratification. All other joint resolutions are sent to the President for approval and if approved have the force of law. The legislative process in the House and the Senate is the same for a bill as for a joint resolution, and the description that follows applies to either.

The absence of ministers from both Houses of Congress means that the primary source and inspiration of bills is the individual member. His motives will vary. He is likely to be much less bound by electoral mandate to a programme of party political measures than his British counterpart. So far as he is pledged to a particular measure, it may be one chosen or accepted by himself and not necessarily by other members of the same party or region. His whole campaign may have been fought to press a particular bill on reaching Congress. Alternatively he may take action in response to pressure from individual constituents or any of the countless organizations—social, industrial, commercial, religious —who may approach him to help their case.

Other bills reach Congress in an 'executive communication' addressed by the executive branch to the Speaker of the House and the President of the Senate. The constitutional authority

1. *House Rules and Manual* (1971), para. 397.

for this initiative is clear. According to Article II, Section 3, 'the President shall from time to time give to Congress information on the State of the Union and recommend to their consideration such measures as he shall judge necessary and expedient'. The most important of these measures is the national budget. Many others come from the President himself or a member of the cabinet or the head of a governmental agency. Messages from the President or communications from departmental or agency heads frequently enclose completely drafted bills which will seek to work out in detail aspects of the Presidential message on the State of the Union delivered to Congress at the beginning of each session. It is customary for all bills emanating from executive departments or agencies to be submitted first to the President's Office of Management and Budget (see also pp. 292, 323-4). This office ensures that the bills conform to the President's legislative and budgetary policy and that the drafting is accurate and in proper form.

According to an official count,[1] of the 640 bills and joint resolutions that became public Acts in the 90th Congress (1967-68), about 170, or about twenty-seven per cent, began their congressional life in an executive communication, which leaves seventy-three per cent originating from individual congressmen. By itself, however, these figures do not give an adequate indication of the influence of the executive branch. They say nothing about the relative importance of the bills from this source, nor about the extent to which the executive branch is able to stimulate proposals actually introduced by individual congressmen. Moreover, whatever its origin, a bill that emerges from a congressional committee is likely to be the committee's bill, not the bill of its originator; and the testimony given by expert witnesses from the relevant department or agency will be an important influence in framing it. It is true that influence on legislative proposals works both ways. In any year the President's legislative programme may contain measures which have been introduced by individual congressmen in previous sessions and may even have passed one or other House of Congress. It finds its way into the President's programme because he thinks the time is ripe for it. To strike a precise balance between these various influences would need a long and elaborate inquiry. But it may be hazarded

1. Made by the Parliamentarian's office in the House of Representatives.

that at least half the legislative proposals, and most of the major proposals, emerging as Acts of Congress have had their origin in the executive branch.

As a source of legislation the consolidation of bills is not as significant in Congress as in Parliament. The reason is that the United States has a code of law, which Britain has not. The United States code, which is prepared under the direction of the House of Representatives' Committee on the Judiciary, is itself 'a consolidation—of the general and permanent laws—arranged according to subject matter under fifty title-headings in alphabetical order in large degree'.[1] Under each heading the present state of the law is set out in convenient and accessible form. Up to 1970 nineteen of the fifty titles had been recently revised and re-enacted as law, and two other titles had been amalgamated. Eventually all of them will be revised and enacted. After that they will be kept up to date. New editions of the code are published periodically—the latest (1964) being in fifteen volumes—and cumulative supplements, embodying new legislation under each heading, are published after each congressional session.

In the House of Representatives a bill is introduced when a member drops it in the 'hopper', a basket on the clerk's table. It may be a typescript of a bill, on which the name of only one member may be endorsed, although up to twenty-five members may simultaneously sponsor a public bill. A member may also introduce a petition (on behalf of an organization or group having a special legislative aim). The petition merely sets out the objects they have in mind but leaves the committee to draw the bill.

A bill or petition is recorded as having been introduced, is ordered to be printed and is referred directly by the Speaker to the committee with jurisdiction over the subject. There is no debate or comment on the floor of the House at this stage. Communications and bills sent to the Speaker by the President and executive departments are treated in much the same way, although they are not dropped in the hopper but are referred by the Speaker without formal announcement from the floor.

All references to committees are made by the Speaker on the advice of the Parliamentarian. The jurisdiction of the various standing committees of the House is specified in Rule XI. This

---

1. C. J. Zinn (lately Law Revision Counsel of the House Committee on the Judiciary), *How Our Laws are Made* (10th ed., 1967), p. 37.

Rule and the precedents set forth in a lengthy section of Cannon's *Procedure in the House of Representatives* are the basis of the advice tendered by the Parliamentarian. On occasion the House has decided to alter the reference of a bill to a committee, without regard to the rules of jurisdiction.

No legislative proposal is in order until it has been considered by the committee with jurisdiction, though the House, by suspending its rules or by unanimous consent, has exceptionally considered and passed a measure without sending it to a committee. The system of committees has been described in Chapter V. In committee a bill is subjected to its closest congressional study. Its merits are discussed and assessed, and most bills make no further progress because the committee fails to take action on them. If the committee does decide upon action, the bill may be considered either by the full committee or a subcommittee. Reference to a subcommittee may be made either by the chairman on his own initiative or pursuant to committee rules and procedures. If there are several bills on the same subject, the committee chooses one as the basis for its proceedings. A bill deriving from the executive branch will not necessarily be chosen. In the 89th Congress (1965–66), for example, the Committee on the Judiciary was confronted with three bills to set up a commission on the revision of the federal criminal law: one came from the Attorney General and had been introduced, as is customary for executive proposals, in the name of the Committee's chairman; another (identical) bill, in the name of the ranking minority member, had been tabled to indicate his support for the official bill; and a third with different provisions was in the name of another minority member. The third bill was considered by the committee most apt for their purpose and hearings were held on it,[1] rather than on the bill which was drafted and introduced to reflect the Attorney-General's proposal.

Hearings, which are as a rule public, are held on any bill of enough importance to warrant them. Advanced notice of the date is given in the Congressional Record, and invitations are sent to those whom the committee wish to testify and to interested parties who petition the committee indicating a desire to be heard. A programme of hearings is then drawn up, beginning with the sponsoring member and other interested congressmen

1. It subsequently became a statute as Public Law 89/801.

and continuing with the cabinet member, departmental officials chiefly concerned, and any other organizations or individuals whom the committee wish to hear or who wish to be heard. All interested parties are thus given the opportunity of making known their views directly to members of the committee. At the beginning of the hearings, the bill is usually read through aloud and a copy placed in the committee record. The chairman and often the ranking minority member make brief statements, and the hearings —which normally comprise prepared statements followed by a cross-examination of the witnesses by the members and staff of the committee—then begin. They may last several months. The testimony is recorded by official reporters, printed and widely circulated.

After the hearings, or if there have been no hearings, executive (closed) sessions of the committee or subcommittee are held for the purpose of 'marking up' the bill, that is, amending the basic draft to suit the members' views. The process of amendment is roughly that followed in the House (see below). Advice and help are available from the committee's staff and draftsmen from the Office of the Legislative Counsel. In this office there are eleven counsel (1970) (there is a similar establishment in the Senate, with ten counsel) who are at the service of committees and members of the House. When a subcommittee has considered a bill, it decides either to report the bill favourably to the full committee with or without amendment or to report it unfavourably or not to proceed with it. If it is reported, exactly the same procedure takes place in the full committee. As a result the committee may decide to report it favourably with or without amendments, or simply not proceed with it. An adverse report from a committee is rare, because a decision not to proceed with the bill in practice prevents further action.

In a committee and its subcommittees, a quorum—half plus one of the membership—must be present to validate a vote. For hearings this requirement is not insisted upon: as few as two members may, under the rules of the House, take testimony and receive evidence at a hearing. Each member, including the chairman, has one vote. The chairman has no casting vote: if the voices are equal, the proposition is not carried. If the committee rules permit, one member of a committee may give another member a written authority to cast a vote on his behalf, though a proxy vote does not count towards a quorum.

When the committee favours a bill, one of its members, helped by the staff, writes the report. If the bill as introduced is complicated and the amendments proposed by the committee are numerous and important, the committee is likely to report to the House a fresh version of the bill embodying its own amendments. Otherwise the amendments are set out at the beginning of the report, in which case they are not part of the bill. The report goes on to state the purposes of the bill and, where relevant, the estimated cost of giving effect to the measure. For bills deriving from the executive branch, this 'price-tag' is part of the executive communication when the bill is presented to the House. As a general rule the Legislative Reorganization Act of 1970 makes it mandatory for every committee reporting on a bill or resolution of a public character to include an estimate of its cost for the current year and for each of the next five years, or else an explanation why it is impracticable to give this information. It also requires any estimate made by a department or agency to be set beside the committee's estimate. The last part of the report indicates all changes proposed in the existing law. If part of an existing statute is to be repealed, it must be set out in full. If it is to be amended, the relevant part of the statute must be set down, with omissions and insertions shown by the type being struck through and by use of brackets and italics.[1] The bill is itself reprinted on report, showing, by use of the same typographical devices, how the committee's amendments would affect it.

When a public bill is reported by a committee to the House of Representatives, it is placed on one of the two main calendars of business, namely the Union Calendar and the House Calendar.

The *Union Calendar* comprises bills raising revenue, general appropriation bills and bills directly or indirectly appropriating money or property. In practice this definition covers any bill which imposes a charge or involves expenditure, so that most of the bills reported from committees are to be found on this calendar. The *House Calendar* comprises all bills not raising revenue or directly or indirectly appropriating money or property, that is, all public bills not on the Union Calendar. All bills reported from committees have to be considered by the entire membership of the House. As at Westminster the principle is observed

1. House Rule XIII, 3, known as the 'Ramseyer' Rule. A similar rule in the Senate is known as the 'Cordon' Rule.

that each member of the House, as well as members of the relevant committee, should have an opportunity to propose amendments to, and debate, a bill. In practice all bills on the Union Calendar are considered in the Committee of the whole House on the State of the Union (although the House by unanimous consent may waive this requirement), while bills on the House Calendar are considered in the House itself. This is more than a formal distinction. Most of the important bills, involving as they do expenditure directly or indirectly, are on the Union Calendar: and the fact that their consideration takes place in committee, with specially adapted procedures and a quorum of 100 (instead of 218), helps to expedite their progress.

A large number of bills become law without recourse to either of these consideration stages. Two other calendars, the *Private Calendar* and the *Consent Calendar*, provide avenues of swift passage for uncontroversial bills. Private bills at federal level are concerned wholly with the needs of individuals or business entities. In the main they deal either with individuals who have suffered injury through the action of a government agent but who cannot secure compensation through the ordinary processes of law, or with persons who have special problems relating to immigration or naturalization laws. In Congress private bills are usually uncontroversial and are rarely opposed after being sifted by the committee process and by the objectors appointed by the majority and minority leadership to examine the bills on the Private Calendar. Once reported, private bills are placed on the Private Calendar and are then treated in broadly the same manner as bills which reach the Consent Calendar.

Like the Private Calendar, the Consent Calendar has proved a useful and time-saving device. A member may give notice to the Clerk that he desires a bill which has been favourably reported and assigned to the House or Union Calendar to be placed on the Consent Calendar. The titles of these bills are read out on the first and third Monday in each month. If no objection is made as a bill is called, it is passed without debate. If objection is made on two Consent Mondays by one member the first time called, and by at least three members the second time, the bill is struck off the Consent Calendar. Any member may object, though six official objectors—three appointed by the majority and three by the minority for the duration of a Congress—have the express duty of studying bills on the Consent Calendar and if necessary blocking them. They work to well understood criteria, which they establish themselves and announce to the House early in each Congress.[1] If a bill involves expenditure on a substantial scale, or changes in national policy, or if for any other reason the objectors think it needs explanation or debate, it will not be passed by consent. Individual members may be more severe than the official objectors. On occasion the view has been taken that no measure involving expenditure, however small, should pass by this means.

Another manner of disposing of bills having near unanimity of committee approval and wide support in the House is a motion to suspend the operation of the ordinary rules and pass a bill. This kind of motion may be made on Consent Mondays, that is, the first and third Mondays in each month (after proceedings on the Consent Calendar), and on the last six days of the session. On the first Monday preference is given to individual members making motions on their own behalf, on the third Monday to members acting on behalf of committees. The motion has a number of obstacles to negotiate. The Speaker must agree to call the member making the motion and he will do so only if he thinks it in the interests of the House. If a demand is made, the motion must be 'seconded' by a majority of members voting, and the presence of a quorum has to be established, if requested, by a teller vote. If successful so far, the motion is debatable for forty minutes, half for those in favour and half for those against. Finally it must obtain the affirmative votes of two-thirds of the members voting, a quorum being present. If it is desired to amend the bill, the motion to suspend the rules must encompass the amendments.[2] Amendments are thus within the control of the member making the motion, and the motion once made cannot be further amended from the floor. If the motion succeeds, it is not in order to demand a separate vote on the amendments: the vote is taken on suspending the rules and passing the bill as proposed to be amended.

Some idea of the use made of these three expeditious procedures—by the Private Calendar, by the Consent Calendar and by suspension of the rules—can be gained from the fact that in

1. E.g. Congressional Record, 17 March 1969.
2. Rule XXVII, 2.

the first session of the 90th Congress (1967) eighty per cent of all the bills passed by the House of Representatives were passed by one of these means.[1] Bills so passed are normally measures of little consequence, or at least of little controversy.

How can a bill which is not passed in one of these ways be brought to the floor? Bills are added to the Union and House Calendars in the order in which they are reported. But if this order were to be followed in calling up bills for consideration, important and urgent bills could not be given priority over others not requiring immediate action. In practice the House and Union Calendars are not called. Certain bills on these Calendars are given priority for consideration on the floor by the adoption of special orders or 'rules' reported by the Committee on Rules and adopted by the House.

Before recommending a rule, the Rules Committee will usually hear the chairman of the committee reporting the bill, the sponsor of the bill and one or more members of the committee concerned in support of the claim for immediate consideration. If satisfied that the bill should go forward, the Rules Committee will propose a rule in the following terms:

> That upon the adoption of this resolution [it shall be in order for the House to resolve itself into the Committee of the Whole House on the State of the Union and proceed to consider] or[2] [the House shall proceed to consider] the bill entitled . . ., debate to be limited to . . . hours, one half to be controlled by the chairman of the Committee on . . . and one half by the ranking minority member of such Committee. . .

The Rules Committee may also propose a 'closed' rule,[3] that is, a rule disallowing amendments except by the committee reporting the bill or a rule waiving points of order (a proceeding normally followed on bills reported by the Ways and Means Committee, see p. 349).

The House of Representatives gives priority to reports from the Rules Committee, the Speaker recognizing the chairman of the Rules Committee whenever he offers a report. If the Rules

1. The *Western Political Quarterly*, Vol. XXI, no. 2, June 1968. Article by Floyd M. Riddick and Robert B. Dove.
2. Depending on whether the bill is on the Union or the House Calendar.
3. Sometimes known as a 'gag' rule.

Committee recommends an ordinary or a closed rule, and the House concurs, the bill is usually taken at once. The privileged status accorded by the House to the reports of the Rules Committee is shared by certain classes of legislation, of which the most important are general appropriation and revenue bills. No special order or rule from the Rules Committee is necessary to obtain prior consideration for such bills, though in regulating the way in which the House takes amendments and later stages, a rule can evidently speed the progress of these bills.

Another—but rarely used—method of bringing a bill to the floor is a motion to discharge a committee from its further consideration. For the motion to be admissible, the bill must have been referred to a committee not less than thirty days before; or, if it seeks to discharge the Rules Committee from the consideration of a resolution providing a 'rule', that rule must have been referred to the Rules Committee not less than seven days before. A motion of discharge requires the signature of a majority of the total membership of the House (218). It is then entered on the *Discharge Calendar*—of motions to discharge committees. These motions may be called up on the second or fourth Monday of each month. After twenty minutes' debate, half in favour and half against, the House votes on the motion. If carried, the House may then vote on the substance of the matter. In other words, where a bill is discharged from one of the standing committees, the House votes on a motion that it should proceed to the immediate consideration of the bill; where a resolution proposing a rule is discharged from the Rules Committee, the House votes on that resolution.

The exacting requirement of 218 signatures to make a discharge motion effective has meant that few motions are successful. Since 1931 when the House first adopted the Rule[1] in this form, the number of bills enacted through its operation has been negligible. It is, however, a protection for the rights of the majority in the House on a particular issue as against the rights of the relevant committees.

When a bill (from the Union Calendar) is taken up in the Committee of the Whole House on the State of the Union, there is first a general debate on the bill as reported. This debate is generally restricted to a stated number of hours by the rule

1. House Rule XXVII, 4.

proposed by the Rules Committee and agreed to by the House. Then amendments are considered one by one under the 'five-minute rule': the clerk reads the bill aloud section by section (which is the bill's second reading) and after each section a member may be recognized by the chair to offer an amendment to that section. He is allowed to speak for five minutes. One member opposing the amendment is also entitled to five minutes. In theory this is the first member to catch the eye of the chair; in practice priority is given to the chairman or a member of the relevant committee. Debate on other amendments may continue under the five-minute rule until the matter has been fully discussed or until the committee votes to terminate further debate.

When all the amendments have been disposed of, the bill is reported back to the House. In the House[1] the reported bill is subject to further debate unless the 'previous question' is either ordered or is deemed to have been ordered by the terms of the rule proposed by the Rules Committee and agreed to by the House. The previous question in the House of Representatives would be regarded at Westminster as a form of 'guillotine'. Its effect is that the House votes immediately and successively on whatever amendments have been reported from the Committee of the Whole House on the State of the Union in the order in which they were reported. Then the Speaker puts the following further questions—'Shall the bill be engrossed (reprinted on special paper) and read a third time?' and 'That the bill do pass', both debatable motions, on which the House takes its final decision before the bill is sent to the Senate. Pending the question on final passage, a member who is opposed to the bill may offer one motion to 'recommit' the bill to the appropriate standing committee, either for further study by that committee or 'with instructions to report the bill back to the House forthwith with an amendment'. The right to recognition in order to offer this motion is accorded first to a minority member who is opposed to the bill. In this way the House can be given one final opportunity to vote upon an amendment proposed by the minority.

1. Some bills are considered in the 'House as in the Committee of the Whole'. This intermediate position telescopes consideration in Committee of the whole and in the House into a single stage. It requires a special rule of the House or unanimous consent. See also p. 157.

The above description, it will be recalled, applies only to bills on the Union Calendar. If a bill is on the House Calendar, it does not have to be considered in Committee of the Whole House on the State of the Union; and there are other differences. The second reading—the bill's being read aloud in full—takes place in the House itself. Debate on the bill and on amendments is under the 'hour rule', that is, each member recognized is entitled to speak for one hour. After consideration for amendment, the House decides the questions on engrossment and third reading and on its passage, and sends the bill to the Senate.

When a bill originates in the Senate, or when it is sent there after being passed by the House, it follows broadly the same stages which can be described briefly. The bill is referred by the President of the Senate, on the advice of the Senate's Parliamentarian, to the appropriate standing committee. The committee considers it in much the same way as the corresponding committee of the House and may report it with or without amendment or simply take no action on it. If a bill is not reported within a reasonable time, a senator may move to discharge the committee from further consideration of the bill. If the motion succeeds—it requires a majority of votes cast—the bill is placed on the Calendar of Reported Bills.

The Senate observes more formality than the House in some aspects of its consideration of bills. A bill is both offered orally for introduction and reported orally by the member in charge on behalf of a committee. When a senator reports a bill orally, he may ask unanimous consent for its immediate consideration, though this rarely occurs. If uncontroversial, the bill may pass with little or no debate, with or without amendments being moved. If this summary procedure is objected to, the bill is placed on the Calendar of Reported Bills. Bills involving expenditure are not, as in the House, differentiated from other bills, by being placed on separate Calendars, nor has the need been felt for Consent, Private or Discharge Calendars. Nor does the Senate resolve itself into a committee. The Calendar of Reported Bills can be called on any legislative day.[1] When a bill on the Calendar is called, each senator may speak once and for five minutes only on any question. This restriction applies to debate

1. For the effect on a 'legislative day' of an adjournment or a recess in the Senate, see pp. 198-9.

on any proposed amendments (which are usually taken first) and
to the subsequent questions on the engrossment and third reading
and on the passage of the bill. But if objection is raised to the
bill at any stage, the restrictions of time do not apply. Similarly,
if on motion a bill is taken up out of its sequence on the Calendar,
the restrictions do not apply. Except on a general appropriation
bill, an amendment moved by a senator in committee or on the
floor does not have to be germane to the bill.[1]

When a bill is returned to the House of Representatives with
Senate amendments, the House may agree to the amendments,
disagree to them or agree to make alternative amendments of
its own. These actions are taken by the House on the initiative
of the chairman of the standing committee having jurisdiction
over the bill. He has to take account of a provision of the Legislative Reorganization Act of 1970 under which any member of
the House may demand a separate vote on each Senate amendment which, if it had originated in the House, would have
offended against the House's Rules on the question of germane-
ness. Before each vote is taken, a debate of forty minutes is in
order, one half in favour of and the other half in opposition to
the amendment. This provision is designed to give to the House's
own bills a measure of protection against the breadth and freedom
of Senate debate.

If the Senate's amendments are accepted by the House, the
bill is ready for enrolment and presentation to the President,
as it is if the Senate do not make amendments. But if the amendments are unacceptable, the member must take steps to secure
the House's approval to a formal request for a conference with
the Senate. If both Houses agree to this, the Speaker appoints
the House managers (as the conference members are there
styled) while the conferring senators are appointed by order of
the Senate on each bill. In practice they are usually drawn from
among the senior members of the standing committee concerned
in each House, with both parties represented in proportion to
their relative strength in their respective House.

A conference can decisively affect the shape and content of a
bill. It considers the subject-matter in dispute: it may not alter
any matter unless it has been the subject of amendment in the

1. An example of the importance of this rule, or lack of rule, is given on
p. 350.

second House through which the bill passed, nor insert any fresh matter. Similarly if one House amends a figure or an amount, the scope for negotiation is delimited by the two numbers; the greater may not be increased nor the lesser diminished. But if the second House has made an amendment in the nature of a substitute for the whole bill, the whole bill is thrown open for discussion. It is then possible for what is virtually a different bill to be reported. No doubt it is this aspect of its powers which has led to conferences being sometimes described as the third House of Congress.

The representatives of each House meet together in conference but vote as separate committees, each acting by majority vote and reporting to its own House. Meetings are usually held in the Senate wing and are normally closed to the public. The result is frequently a compromise of views, though either side may abandon its stated position. The agreement, when reported to the two Houses, is usually accepted by them. If the two sides fail altogether to reach agreement, they report accordingly to their respective Houses. New 'conferees' may then be appointed, and another conference held; or the first House may consider the amendments made by the second House and attempt to resolve the matter by further amendment. The House which acts first on the conference report has the additional prerogative of referring it back to the conference with instructions to its members to take a certain position with respect to the matter.

The final stage is the submission of the bill to the President in the form agreed by the two Houses. Under the Constitution[1] every bill passing the House and the Senate has to be presented to the President before it can become law. The President has ten days (Sundays excepted) from the date of receiving the bill to decide on his action. If he approves it, his signature makes it a law. If he takes no action, it becomes law when the ten days have elapsed. If he vetoes it by returning it to the House of origin with a statement of objections, that House has the opportunity to reconsider it and pass it over the President's objection. The President's veto can be overridden only if each House in turn insists on the bill by a majority of two-thirds of the votes cast. It is customary for a vote to be taken after a short debate as soon as the bill is returned to the House of origin. If the necessary

1. Article I (7).

majority is obtained, the bill is sent at once to the second House for a vote. A bill becomes law on the date of the President's approval or on the date on which the veto is overridden by the second House, unless its provisions expressly provide any other date.

A different form of veto is the 'pocket veto'. As noted above, if the President does not approve of a bill, he is required to return it within ten days (calendar days excepting Sunday, not sitting days) of the day it is presented to him. He cannot do so if Congress adjourns in that period. So if Congress passes legislation in the last ten days before an adjournment, the President can, as it were, keep it in his pocket until Congress adjourns. By this means he can effectively kill a bill without formal use of his power of veto. But if he does so, Congress has only itself to blame for allowing the President the opportunity.

The following table shows how effective presidential vetoes and pocket vetoes have been in five recent Congresses in relation to the number of vetoes overriden by Congress:

Year	Congress	Vetoed and Returned	Pocket Vetoed	Total	Overridden by Congress
1969–70	91st	7	4	11	2
1967–68	90th	2	6	8	0
1965–66	89th	10	4	14	0
1963–64	88th	5	4	9	0
1961–62	87th	11	9	20	0

CONTRASTING LEGISLATIVE FEATURES

A description of the processes of making law in the United Kingdom and the United States—such as that just completed— by itself gives an idea of their basic differences. The salient features of each system can now usefully be drawn together and contrasted.

At the outset two aspects of the constitutional framework within which Parliament and Congress make law must be noted. The first is that while one enjoys freedom in its choice of subject-matter for legislation, the other does not. Parliament can make a law on any subject it chooses. It may, and often does, devolve to a local legislature the power to make law in that locality.

But this kind of self-denying ordinance can always—in pure constitutional terms—be revoked or abridged. As Parliament's actions in regard to Northern Ireland since 1969 has shown, it retains the right to legislate over the whole of the territory of the United Kingdom. By contrast the subjects on which Congress can legislate are specifically defined in the Constitution.[1] It is empowered to levy and collect taxes, to regulate commerce within the United States and with foreign nations, to coin money, to raise armed forces and to provide for several other activities of national scope. But any one of the laws made by Congress under these heads can be challenged in the courts on the ground that its provisions go beyond the relevant authority given to it by the Constitution. Moreover, any power not delegated by the Constitution to the Union is reserved to the States.[2] Equally the congressional legislation must not traverse the Bill of Rights, as the first ten Amendments[3] to the Constitution are known. These amendments state such important freedoms as the right to the free exercise of religion, to free speech, to a free press and to peaceful assembly; the protection against deprivation of life, liberty and property without 'due process of law'; the prohibition against taking private property for public use without just compensation. Here, too, a Congress-made law may be, and frequently has been, nullified by the courts on the grounds that it infringes the Bill of Rights. In the United Kingdom a number of 'constitutional' Acts of Parliament such as the Bill of Rights 1688 resemble the American Bill of Rights in that they set down some basic constitutional rights. But Parliament could repeal them tomorrow, by the same process as it uses for passing an ordinary law. For example, in the session of 1968–69, as part of the continuing process of repealing statutes of no practical utility, several articles of the Confirmation of Magna Carta Act 1297 were repealed.[4] These articles stated a number of liberties which have been more effectively enacted in later statutes. Nevertheless the repeal technically required no more than a simple majority vote in each House at each stage.

1. Article I (8).
2. The tenth Amendment of the Constitution.
3. The first ten Amendments were proposed to the legislatures of the several states in September 1789 and became effective in 1791.
4. Statute Law Repeals Act 1969, Schedule.

The second constitutional feature vitally affecting legislation is the period of time available for a bill to be introduced and complete its passage into law. A Parliament has a maximum life of five years, and is normally dissolved by the Crown (on the advice of the Prime Minister) at some point in its last twelve months of life. Within that long-term span, the short-term working period is the session, which usually lasts one year from its opening in October to its 'prorogation' in the following October (see also p. 84). Business is effectively bound by this sessional framework. A bill introduced in one session and not passed by the end of that session dies. It cannot be carried over to the next session. If reintroduced, it must start again at the beginning of the legislative process and pass through all the stages. By contrast, although Congress has to assemble once a year and meets on 3 January, the House of Representatives is elected every second year so that a Congress runs for two years as from 3 January (in the odd numbered years). Congress thus has two regular sessions beginning 3 January (and may also for urgent discussions be called in special session by the President). But the existence of each Congress is treated as continuous, so that while uncompleted legislation dies at the end of a Congress, it does not die at the end of the first (or a special) session of a Congress. In practice a bill in Congress has two years to reach the statute book; in Parliament it has only one year. The privations imposed by the shorter period in Parliament fall not on the government—which, for as long as it commands the support of a majority, has a variety of procedural weapons at its disposal to secure its business in the time available—but on the private members whose opportunities are strictly limited. The cleaning of the slate at the end of each session, for this if for no other reason, is likely to remain a feature of the British legislative process.

In the framework so set by the constitution of each country, the legislative processes can be compared. Divergence is apparent long before the stage at which a bill is introduced. Under the British system, since a high proportion of important bills reaching the statute book are government bills, the bulk of the effective work of law-making is done before the bill reaches Parliament. The exhaustive inquiries made by the government departments (or royal commissions) concerned; the elaborate consultations with interested parties and pressure groups; the protracted study in cabinet committees as the bill begins to take shape: it is the thoroughness of these stages which leads members sometimes to complain that they are the only important and interested parties omitted from consultations when the bill is still malleable. Preparations are not invariably so thorough, as the case of the Companies Act 1967 shows, when several hundred government amendments were moved into the bill during its passage through both Houses; but such a case is rare enough to be memorable. Nor does the preparatory process in any way rule out subsequent amendments in the two Houses. This is the point at which the work done so far is tested against the political realities. Nevertheless the true legislative picture is well reflected in the enacting formula of Acts of Parliament—'Be it enacted by the Queen's most excellent Majesty, by and with the consent of the Lords Spiritual and Temporal and the Commons in Parliament assembled'. It is the Queen's government which is legislating, with the consent of the members of each House; and in the Commons House, where the government stands or falls, that legislation is backed by a majority who can be expected to support it. After a bill's presentation to Parliament, its progress is, with rare exceptions, processional and predictable.

This is the chief point of contrast to the American sequence. It is not that the bills reaching Congress from the President and other governmental sources are ill-prepared. The rising influence of the President's Office of Management and Budget has secured that all such bills are founded on conclusions drawn from extensive 'hearings' and other investigations conducted within the executive branch. It is rather that when these bills are, together with bills from other sources, fed into the congressional committees, the effective work is then done which in the United Kingdom is done within the government and the civil service. If the President or his staffs have already prepared the ground, the results may help the congressional committees concerned, but they will not abridge their customary processes of investigation to any significant degree. These committees have a duty to discharge, which in Britain would be considered governmental. As a result of their inquiries the bill may be completely redrafted. The bill which then proceeds is the committee's bill, not the executive's bill or the presenter's bill. So while in Britain the business of legislation is largely processional and predictable, in the United

States it is creative and emergent: until a bill has been moulded and shaped by a committee, its nature will not be known.

This basic divergence no doubt dictates the remarkably different approach in the two countries to the drafting of bills. In Britain this is a highly specialized and somewhat arcane activity. The small band of Parliamentary Counsel are virtually responsible for the shape and form of the statute book as it emerges, session by session from Parliament, since they draft not only the government's bills but virtually all the amendments agreed to those bills. They work to the instructions of the government, not of Parliament. Moreover because of the extent of the government's control over the time of the House and the coherence of the majority, the government's bills are usually successful; so that, though they are few in number, the productivity of parliamentary counsel (pages of statute in relation to hours worked) is high.[1] The contrast to the United States, where the knowledge and techniques of drafting are taught in universities and law schools, has lately been pointed out.[2] The need to furnish competent draftsmen for some fifty state legislatures may explain this educational provision and the much wider diffusion of drafting knowledge and practice in the United States. But the spread of drafting activity at federal level suggests a wholly different approach from that in Britain. Most of the executive departments and agencies have resident counsel who among other things draft bills destined for Congress, while each House of Congress has a special drafting section composed of about ten counsel on whose expertise committees and individual members can draw in drafting bills and amendments. But because of the nature of the legislative process in Washington —in which the committee on the bill rather than the originator, whether he is an individual congressman or a department of the executive branch, determines its content and scope—much of this extensive effort at federal level is unproductive. The drafting

1. *Cambridge Law Journal* (April 1959). Article by Reed Dickerson on Legislative Drafting in London and Washington, p. 50.

2. See *Parliamentary Affairs* (Summer 1969) Vol. XXII No. 3, p. 211. The major British study of drafting is still Thring's *Practical Legislation* (1878), supplemented by Ilbert's *Legislative Methods and Forms* (1901). In the United States, besides the classical work, Sutherland's *Statutory Interpretations* (1943), there is Coigne on *Statute Making* (2nd ed., 1965), Reed Dickerson on *Fundamental Legislative Drafting* (1965) and several manuals of drafting published for use at federal or state level.

establishment in each country reflects the needs of the system under which most of the bills are put together.

The governmental inspiration of British law-making marks all stages of its bills. Throughout there is a minister in charge. He moves the second reading which, when agreed to by the House, defines unalterably the principle of the bill. He signifies the Crown's approval to the money resolution which when agreed to defines the scope of expenditure under the bill's provisions. The committee on the bill must work within these well defined limits. But if efforts are made systematically to delay or obstruct a bill, the minister is there to move the closure on an amendment or a clause—which the chair, if it judges that there has been a reasonable time for debate, accepts and puts to the vote. Alternatively the government may use their majority to impose a guillotine, that is, an order which may either allot a specified number of days for the remaining stages of a bill, or may require the committee on the bill to report it by a certain date and entrust to a business committee the number of days to be spent in committee and on report and third reading. (See also pp. 153–54.)

The power of the government to achieve its legislative purposes within the necessary compass of time can hardly be better illustrated than by the Prices and Incomes Bills 1966 and 1967. These were among the most controversial measures proposed by the second Wilson administration. Yet though introduced as late in a session as 4 July 1966 and 5 June 1967, these measures had passed through all their stages in the Commons by 10 August 1966 and 12 July 1967, passing the Lords and obtaining the Royal Assent shortly afterwards.

This immense legislative power is exercised conditionally. The condition is that the government continues to be supported by a majority in each House. In modern times this was beginning to be taken for granted until proceedings in Parliament in 1969 underlined its continuing validity. Three bills of major importance to the government's programme for the session failed to become law. The first was the government's Parliament Bill, to reform the composition and powers of the House of Lords. Though founded on extended discussions between the leaders of the three parties and their agreed conclusions, the bill was attacked by several groups of backbench members on both sides, who for very different reasons combined to delay its progress. After eight days had been spent on the committee stage, discussing only five of the twenty clauses, the government abandoned the bill to ensure enough time for the rest of its sessional programme. The second bill, in which the government provided for a layout of parliamentary constituencies different from that recommended by the Boundary Commissions, was amended by the House of Lords in such a manner as to secure that effect was given to the Boundary Commissions' recommendations. The bill, so amended, was returned to the Commons. The government took no action to disagree with the Lords, and the bill was lost at the end of the session. The third bill was foreshadowed in the Queen's Speech at the beginning of the session: '[A bill] will be brought before you to promote improved industrial relations.' But it was never introduced, because the government were apparently unable to be sure that its majority in the Commons would be willing to carry this bill through the House.[1]

Nevertheless these were exceptional occurrences. The following table, showing the number of government and private members' bills introduced in the years 1964 to 1969 and the number that passed into law, will help to create the true perspective:

GOVERNMENT BILLS

	Introduced	Passed
1964–65	66	65
1965–66[2]	36	21
1966–67[3]	103	103
1967–68	65	63
1968–69	54	51

PRIVATE MEMBERS' BILLS

1964–65	80	17
1965–66[2]	38	0
1966–67[3]	107	24
1967–68	77	13
1968–69	94	12

1. Peter Jenkins, *The Battle for Downing Street* (1970), pp. 152–4.
2. A session cut short by an election in March 1966.
3. An unusually long session from May 1966 to October 1967.

If the 1965–66 session which was unexpectedly cut short is omitted, the table shows that about 98 per cent of the government bills introduced became law, compared with about 18 per cent of bills introduced by private members.

Given the solidity of its majority then, the British government can expect Parliament both to pass its bills and to pass them broadly in the form in which they were introduced. Perhaps because of the general acceptance of this governmental expectation, law-making in Britain appears almost too serious a business for anyone except the government to attempt. A corollary is that bills introduced by private members are not likely to pass unless they have the tolerance, if not the active support, of the government. The time available to private members is too short, and the opportunities available to opponents too large, for a bill, especially a controversial bill, to succeed without that tolerance. In the period from 1964 to 1969, it is true, an unusual number of private members' bills on important and controversial social issues—capital punishment, homosexuality, abortion, divorce—passed into law. But this was only possible because they were all given facilities by the government over and above their strict entitlement as private members' bills. The merits of these bills is not under discussion here. What is in point is that the government came under attack both inside and outside Parliament for allowing some of these important social measures to become law without all the usual exhaustive processes of inquiry and consultation having been carried out before the bills were presented to Parliament and without the drafting of the clauses having been in every case subjected to continuing oversight by the government's draftsmen during their passage through Parliament. Whatever the rights and wrongs of this criticism, it shows that the people expect the government to give a lead on important issues.

In the United States, by contrast, the predominance of one person or element in the legislative process is by no means so evident. The key or leading influence is undoubtedly the legislative committee on the bill. Here the sifting process begins. On average, in the five Congresses covering the period 1959–1968, about 17,000 bills and joint resolutions were introduced in the House. The comparable Senate figure for introductions was about 4,000. Of the total number of legislative proposals introduced in both bodies—roughly about 21,000—only about 1100 became law in any two-year period, and of these about 400 were private laws. The bill in Congress is often used rather like the 'early day' motion in Britain (see pp. 391–3), as a means of airing a point of view or pressing for action but without much expectation of its being considered or debated. Many bills are laid aside, or no action is taken on them, by congressional committees. With the bills that are chosen, the committee starts at the beginning and makes and shapes the clauses according to the results of its investigations. The method of proceeding by inquiry is appropriate to this task. It contrasts with that of the British Standing Committee, essentially an instrument for debate, designed for a test in the political arena of the details of bills on which the main consultation with interested groups have already been held by the government, and the general principles already settled by the House itself before committal.

On rare occasions, with bills which have no party political flavour, the British government has allowed the clauses of a government bill to be shaped within Parliament rather than before its introduction; the committee stage of such bills has been taken not in a standing committee proceeding by debate, but in a select committee proceeding by inquiry. The Obscene Publications Bill 1957 and the Armed Services Bill 1966 (dealing with conditions of service and discipline in the Armed Services) are two recent examples. The comparison with congressional procedure suggests that in most sessions of Parliament more bills could be sent to a committee proceeding by the method of inquiry or 'hearings', and notably those private members' bills on which the usual exhaustive processes of inquiry and consultation have not been carried out *before* the bill is presented to Parliament.

The contrast between the *debating* approach to legislation at Westminster and the *inquiring* approach in Washington is reflected in the nature of the proceedings. In Britain the debate on second reading, when the principles on which a bill is founded are canvassed and determined, is the most important stage. It sets the framework within which the detailed consideration of the clauses can take place in Standing Committee. This used to be the sequence followed in the House of Representatives. But it was effectively reversed by the progressive shortening of the processes for handling bills in the House and by the expansion of the committee system throughout the nineteenth century. The bill considered by the House came to be the committee's bill, and 'second reading' came to describe proceedings on the floor happening after, not before, the committee stage.

Again, procedure within committees is notably different in Parliament and Congress. The proceedings of a Commons Standing Committee, as befits a committee for debate, are formal. Notice has to be given of amendments, which must (with rare exceptions) be printed on the amendment paper; this is, as it were, the committee's formal agenda. Amendments and clauses are proposed, debated and put to the vote according to the classic pattern of motion, question and decision on the floor of the House. By contrast a standing committee of Congress, as befits a committee of inquiry, is concerned first with the hearing of all interested parties, and then, in informal and private 'executive' sessions, with amending the bill to reflect the committee's conclusions. While a member will often as a matter of good legislative practice make available to the other members copies of long or complex amendments in advance of their being offered, he is not required by the rules to do so, nor is any amendment paper in front of the committee.

The same bias is observable in proceedings on the floor after a bill has been reported. In Parliament there is a real opportunity for members other than members of the committee to give notice of amendments and to debate them. A paper of these amendments is before the House when the bill is being considered. In Congress greater reliance is usually placed on the committee's judgement because its processes of inquiry have been full and the resulting bill carefully prepared. In the Senate, it is true, the opportunity for other senators to offer, debate, and press amendments is virtually unlimited. But in the House of Representatives the restrictions are considerable, especially if the five-minute rule is applying. In both Houses, as in their committees, members will sometimes circulate long or complex amendments, but in neither House are they required to do so. In neither House is there an official paper of amendments of which advanced notice has been given. The Legislative Reorganization Act of 1970 provides that when an amendment is offered in Committee of the Whole (of the House of Representatives), five copies are to be sent to the majority table and five to the minority table. This may be seen as a first step by the House towards greater precision in handling of amendments. But it is a long way from an amendment paper as understood in either of the British Houses.

When reported from a legislative committee of Congress, a bill is always in charge of one of its members, usually the chairman. Once directed to report the bill, he ceases to function individually and becomes the committee's representative in charge of the bill. When the Rules Committee's resolution is agreed to, he will handle the bill on the floor, allocating the available speaking time in debate and speaking on amendments for the committee. Later he is likely to be the House's chief 'manager' in any conference between the two Houses. In the Senate if the bill finds favour with the Committee, its guardianship is assured in the same way.

All this adds up to a high degree of primacy and power for the committee and the chairman. But missing from the congressional system is the predictability of a bill's passage which is so marked a feature of a British government bill's progress. There are so many hazards along the route through Congress, so many persons and interests whose benevolence is necessary. In the House of Representatives, after the basic formative stages in subcommittee and committee, there is the Rules Committee into whose maw many bills passed by the legislative committees disappear. Efforts to bring a bill to the floor by securing its discharge from the Rules Committee have seldom been successful, so that the Rules Committee sometimes offers a formidable obstacle to legislative action. If the bill does reach the floor, the leadership of both parties, liberal and conservative groupings within each party and regional interests have each and all to be confronted. In the Senate most of these hazards have to be negotiated afresh, together with two new and major procedural hurdles: the filibuster which though nowadays exposed to a form of closure, still offers large opportunities to those wishing to hold up business; and the Senate rule that, except on a general appropriation bill, amendments do not have to be germane to a bill's subject-matter.

Finally there is the uncertainty inherent in a conference between the two Houses and the more distant threat of the presidential veto. The conference on the congressional pattern was formerly found in British Parliamentary practice. It is still recorded in Erskine May as a possible mode of communication between the two Houses, though the last occasion, in 1836 on a private bill, is crisply stated to have been 'a failure'.[1] The conference is probably more appropriate to a bicameral system in which the members of the two Houses confront each other on a basis of equality. For that reason if no other the views of the second House have to bulk large in the calculations of the would-be legislator in Congress. He has, moreover, still to cross the final fence, the President's powers of veto—not reproduced in England since 1707.

A BILL IN EACH LEGISLATIVE PROCESS

The perils of the course through Congress mean that a good deal of load has to be shed on the way. The system militates against the radical measure or the sweeping reform. In the absence of a coherent majority whipped in British style, what emerges is much more a consensus than a partisan point of view. Legislating successfully calls for much art, a sense of compromise and some luck. The complexity and sophistication of the American system has led one experienced observer to comment that 'in comparison the life of the British Member of Parliament is undemanding, simple and well ordered'.[2]

To illustrate this and some of the other points made in this chapter, it may be helpful to conclude it by considering in detail what effect the parliamentary institutions in each country have on a bill during its passage. Prime Minister Wilson's Children Bill in the session of 1968–69 and President Lyndon Johnson's Crime Control Bill in the 90th Congress (1967–68) have been chosen. They both aroused considerable public interest and, as both bills derived from the executive branch, their stories indicate what is likely to happen to a government bill on either side of the Atlantic.

The Children and Young Persons Bill 1969

The Children and Young Persons Bill 1969 was described by a Minister in charge of it as 'one of the session's major pieces of legislation'. It dealt with children in trouble. Its essence was in

1. Erskine May, 17th ed. (1964), p. 626, footnote (i). The description of procedure in a conference was however omitted from the 1971 edition.
2. Louis Heren, *The New Commonwealth* (1968), p. 62.

clause 1 which provided that when a child (under fourteen) or young person (under seventeen) is brought before a court, the court may make various kinds of order, such as requiring a parent or guardian to give an undertaking about his proper care or control, or vesting these responsibilities in some other authority. But it also laid down that a number of conditions must be satisfied before the order could be made. For example, the child or young person was found in unsuitable surroundings; was being neglected or ill-treated; was beyond the control of his parents; or had committed an offence. If one of these conditions were found, *and* he was in need of the care and control that he would be unlikely to receive without the order, the court could make the order. In other parts of the bill there were important and novel proposals for community homes for children in care and for foster children.

Much of the debate in both Houses centred on clause 1. The bill was introduced in the Commons on 12 February 1969. At the stage of the second reading on 11 March the opposition moved a 'reasoned' amendment setting out their general approach to the bill. The amendment signalled their approval of the proposals for community homes and for foster children. But it also stated that the opposition declined to give a second reading to the bill because the proposals in clause 1, among other things, were unjust as between 'different children in the like case'. In support of this proposition it was argued that the effect of the conditions would be to bring children from 'bad' homes to court, while children from 'good' homes would escape. To bring a child before a court, it was not enough that he had committed an offence. In addition he must be in need of one of the orders the court could make. This, it was said, was discriminating between one child and another and so was unjust. In reply the government argued that the bill required those concerned in the administration of the law to take account of the whole of each child's background. It was novel in that it obliged them to avoid court procedure and a court order if they could. The child's need was the basic criterion. It aimed to give more not less help to the unfortunate child, and, if anything, helped equality of treatment under the law by discriminating in their favour.

This argument was carried to a division and the opposition's 'reasoned' amendment was defeated by 200 votes to 140. In the Standing Committee which considered the bill on two mornings a week from 20 March to 13 May, the opposition moved a series of amendments aimed partly at clarifying the conditions governing the making of a court order, but chiefly at removing the basic condition that the child or young person should be in need of a care and control order. These amendments were rejected. On the major point of controversy in the clause, therefore, the government's position was not disturbed. The opposition did, however, secure a concession, by moving an amendment which was accepted in principle in committee and redrafted at the report stage, on the kind of court order which could be made, namely by adding to the various kinds of supervision order an order requiring a young person to enter into an undertaking for an amount not exceeding £25 to keep the peace or be of good behaviour. In a later clause, too, a significant change was made in regard to young persons. Its object was to deal with them outside court as far as possible and to this end it laid down that a magistrate of a juvenile court had to give his consent to the prosecution of a young person. Under pressure from the opposition, the government undertook in committee to abandon this requirement, leaving prosecutions to the police in consultation with the local authority. At the report stage, the government moved a new clause which gave effect to this undertaking.

On third reading both sides allowed that although some differences of principle remained, the bill had been improved. One measure of this recognition was that the bill passed its third reading stage without a vote being taken. The same, more cordial temper distinguished the second reading debate in the House of Lords on 18 June which was also agreed to without a division. In Committee of the whole House on 3, 7 and 9 July, several of the controversial issues on clause 1 were reopened. Again fears of a double standard carrying a danger of unfair discrimination were expressed: if a court had to be satisfied not only that a child or young person was guilty of an offence but also that he was in need of care and attention, was this not bound to separate for purposes of court orders the children of good homes from those of bad? Again the government spokesman stressed the need to deal with children outside the courts, and the purpose of the clause, to improve the possibilities of justice for those from bad homes. The amendment was pressed to a division, as the corresponding amendment in the Commons had been. But because the

Labour government did not have a majority in the House of
Lords, the amendment was carried. Later the bill was returned
to the Commons which (again on a vote) disagreed to the amendment which the Lords made, and sent it back to the Lords with
the reason stated, that care proceedings should only be brought
to ensure that the child or young person receives the care or
control which he needs. At this point the Lords acquiesced, and
the bill was given the Royal Assent on 22 October.

The Omnibus Safe Streets and Crime Control Bill 1967–68

In February 1967 the President sent a message to the House of
Representatives drawing attention to the rise in the rate of crime
and outlining a remedial bill. The draft bill, which was transmitted
by a communication from the Attorney-General on 8 February
1967, was founded on the recommendations of a presidential
commission on law enforcement and administration. The policy
behind the bill was that the federal government should not
engage directly in law enforcement, but that it could and
should give financial and technical help to local police departments. It made several proposals to this end; in particular it
provided for a grant of $50 million in 1967 to modernize local
police forces and methods of law enforcement, $100 million in
1968, $100 million in 1969 and $300 million in 1970. It also
banned the sale by mail order of rifles and shotguns.

The bill was introduced by the chairman of the Committee on
the Judiciary on 8 February and was referred to that Committee
as having jurisdiction. The Committee held hearings, and
worked on the bill for several months, finally reporting it on
17 July 1967. As amended by the Committee the bill was significantly different from the Administration's original proposal. The
proposed expenditure of $50 million in 1967 was raised to $75
million. Moreover, although the total allocation of moneys for
1968 and 1969 and 1970 were confirmed, a proviso was included
that the money should be allocated in block grants to the states
rather than be paid directly to the local communities. This proviso was carried by an alliance of Republicans and Democrats in
the teeth of the Administration's advice and pressure.

On the floor all these provisions in the Committee's bill were
approved, and two important amendments (among others) were

made. The first added an entirely new section authorizing the police to tap wires in a wide variety of circumstances. The second authorized control of firearms, but in a much weaker form than that proposed by the President. It prohibited the inter-state conveyance to individuals of pistols and revolvers and the purchase across the counter of hand-guns by persons who did not live in the dealer's state. But it exempted rifles and shotguns from any control. This, the first attempt ever made by Congress since World War II to regulate guns, was an obvious compromise, and as finally passed by the House on 8 August 1967 represented a defeat both for the President and for liberal opinion in both parties.

The bill was not taken up by the Senate until the beginning of the session of 1968, after a hortatory message from the President. It was committed to the Senate's Judiciary Committee. In this Committee the proposed expenditure in 1968, 1969 and 1970 was again confirmed, but the proposal that it should take the form of a block grant to the states was rejected by one vote. The wire-tapping provisions were approved, though restricted to police inquiries into major crimes. The Committee voted against the Administration's proposal to ban sales of shotguns and rifles by mail order. Instead they approved the provision banning the shipment of hand-guns between states or the purchase of a hand-gun by a person living out of the state.

The bill—by this time named the Omnibus Crime Control and Safe Streets Bill—was reported by the Committee on 29 April 1968 and was taken on the floor of the Senate at several sittings between 1 and 22 May. The Senate approved the total proposed expenditure for each year but it also approved the amendment to make eighty-five per cent of the totals available by block grant to the states and only fifteen per cent directly to the local communities. It also rejected amendments to delete the wire-tapping provisions from the bill. Finally it rejected a whole series of amendments to regulate the sale of rifles and shotguns, notably one proposed by Senator Edward Kennedy which would have given effect to the President's proposal to ban sales of rifles and shotguns by mail order.

When the bill was returned to the House, the consideration on 5 and 6 June of the Senate's actions was overshadowed by the assassination of Senator Robert Kennedy on 4 June. In a key vote of 318 to 60 the House decided, against the advice of the chairman of its Committee on the Judiciary, not to send the bill to conference, but to accept it as received from the Senate. The irony of this conclusion has been recorded by the *Congressional Quarterly*:[1] Senator Robert Kennedy was known to oppose the principle of block grants and any provision for wire-tapping; nor would anything in the bill have prevented the sale of the revolver by which he was shot. But the general feeling as expressed in the concluding votes was that some measure against crime ought to be placed on the statute book at once. The result was another defeat for the Administration which had hoped that a stronger bill would emerge from a conference. The President, however, acquiesced, and did not apply his veto, signing the bill on 20 June, the last available day.

1. *Congressional Quarterly Almanack* Vol. XXIV (1968), p. 237.

CHAPTER SEVEN

FINANCE

THE power over money goes to the heart of government. The nature of the financial bargain struck between legislature and executive determines whether liberty and representation are effective. In Britain the historic development of this bargain hinges on the relationship of the monarchy to Parliament and later, after much blood had been spilt, of a strong executive power operating through the Crown's prerogatives, to Parliament. Erskine May has summed up this relationship succinctly:

> The Crown demands money, the Commons grant it, and the Lords assent to the grant; but the Commons do not vote money unless it be required by the Crown; nor do they impose or augment taxes unless such taxation be necessary for the public service, as declared by the Crown through its constitutional advisers.[1]

In America the financial bargain was at a critical stage disrupted. The imposition of the tea monopoly, the dumping of the chests in Boston harbour, the ensuing coercion and eventual independence led to a Constitution with a precise delimitation of financial authority. Article I, vesting the legislative power in Congress, gives that body power 'to lay and collect taxes, duties, imposts and excises'; and in the same spirit 'no money shall be drawn from the Treasury but in consequence of appropriations made by law'.[2] The conscious exclusion of the executive branch from the grant of overall financial power basically distinguishes the American constitutional arrangements from the British. The intentions of the Founding Fathers, it will be seen, have been modified in practice. But before the present system in each country is described, it is worth looking more closely at their historical development to discover why those systems, stemming as they did from a common root, should have diverged so markedly.

1. Erskine May, 18th ed. (1971), p. 676.
2. Constitution Article I, 8 and 9.

HISTORICAL BACKGROUND

In Parliament

> That levying money for or to the use of the Crown by pretence of prerogative without grant of Parliament, for longer time or in other manner than the same is or shall be granted, is illegal.

This historic declaration in the Bill of Rights 1688 disposed finally of royal claims to impose taxation on its own authority. From the earliest days the monarch had possessed a large revenue from Crown lands and customary dues and so was independent of Parliament except for his extraordinary needs, of which the waging of wars was the chief. To cover those extra needs he had traditionally looked to the House of Commons, from whom a bill of 'aids and supplies' could be elicited. This bill provided the basis for the bargain which the Commons were able to make with the King: the Commons refused to grant supply until remedies were provided either by legislation or administrative action.

As a weapon of control the bill of aids and supplies was rudimentary. It granted the King not a definite sum of money but the power to levy specific taxes. Over the use of the money raised the House had no control. Nevertheless it came to be accepted that a bill of aids and supplies was the proper method of levying taxes, and Parliament was able to move on from that basis of acceptance to attack extra-parliamentary expedients for raising money used by Elizabeth I and the Stuarts, such as the sale of monopolies, forced loans and the sale of titles. Not until Parliament had its way—as finally enshrined in the Bill of Rights—did the next stage effectively unfold; this was the business of bringing every branch of official expenditure under regular review by the House.[1]

The foreign and defence policies of William and Mary and subsequent monarchs helped the Commons to bring into being an effective control of public finance, an essential part of which was the regular appropriation of moneys to particular purposes; in other words, to say how it should be spent. Years of warfare first in Europe and subsequently in other continents, as the great powers staked their colonial claims, impressed the need for a

1. See Kenneth Mackenzie, *The English Parliament* (7th ed., 1968), especially pp. 65–68.

standing professional army. As Redlich has shown,[1] the House of Commons was required to attend annually to a new department of public business. It had to provide each year by the Mutiny Acts for a specific number of soldiers and sailors, to grant their pay and to vote large sums for ordnance and shipbuilding. These were the old 'extraordinary' grants, now firmly appropriated to the purposes intended by Parliament in a series of annual votes. At the same time the House had been gradually extending its control over ordinary expenditure. Beginning with Charles II, the House voted the King a regular income—known as the civil list—deemed sufficient, with his non-parliamentary income, for the ordinary expenses of government. Over the years more and more of this 'ordinary' expenditure was transferred from the civil list, which the King could spend as he pleased, to the category of expenditure which was voted annually, and so was under the control of Parliament. By the end of the eighteenth century the civil list was effectively confined to the expenditure of the Royal household.

The ability to appropriate money opens up a wide range of political and procedural possibilities. In time it led Parliament to attempt a direct control of finance, to ensure, by taking a directing hand at the moment of initiation, that money voted by Parliament is spent on the policies desired by Parliament and no others. This is so large a task that Parliaments have established special machinery to undertake it. Usually a system of small committees of investigation has been built up which on behalf of Parliament ensures that a close grasp is kept on financial policy in every field of government. Committees of that kind can also oversee effectively the expert and detailed work of checking that moneys have been spent for the purposes intended. This was the course eventually chosen in the United States. In the English Parliament of the sixteenth and seventeenth centuries there were examples of small committees of investigation which could have been regarded as models or precedents for just such a development in England. The system of committees in the Parliaments of Elizabeth I and James I has already been noticed (see p. 208); in Pepys's time small committees were set up specifically to investigate the misappropriation of public funds; and under William and Mary there are examples of particular estimates of expenditure being

1. Redlich, *Procedure of the House of Commons* (1908), Vol. III, p. 165.

referred to small committees. But the committees that survived from this century were not small committees of investigation, but committees of the whole House. The Committee of Supply (starting in 1620) and the Committee of Ways and Means (starting in 1640), though committees only in name since every member of the House belonged to them, allowed the Commons to discuss the royal demands for finance informally and under a chairman of their own choosing rather than under the 'King's man', as the Speaker was then regarded.

The personal authority of the monarch was trimmed by the civil war and the revolution of 1688. But the English constitution remained monarchical in essence. The chosen way forward in England was to leave the power of initiating expenditure where it had traditionally been, that is, with the Crown, but now with the Crown acting through ministers responsible to itself. A long step was taken in this direction in 1706 when the House of Commons passed a resolution which has since become its Standing Order No. 89.

This House will receive no petition for any sum relating to public service, or proceed upon any motion for a grant or charge upon the public revenue . . . unless recommended from the Crown.

This resolution sets out one of the cardinal principles of the British constitution. Though it has been a standing order of the House since 1713, it has never been made statutory and could theoretically be overthrown by a simple majority of the House. Yet the principle has stood for more than 250 years, and the terms of the standing order have been reaffirmed and spelt out on several occasions. Its importance for members of the House can hardly be exaggerated. It prevents a private member from getting through committee any bill, or any provision in a bill, which would increase public expenditure, except by leave of the Crown (that is, the government); and it equally restrains the implementation without ministerial approval of any recommendation of a select committee which would result in greater expenditure. Finally by leaving the power of initiating expenditure to the Crown (that is, the government) the House has ultimately confined its own function in the field of supply and appropriation to criticism of what the government does. For this function the

Committee of Supply—in reality the House itself—was an apt debating forum.

Why did the Commons accept so sweeping a self-denying ordinance? As so often in British constitutional history it was a pragmatic reaction to a felt need, for one effect of statutory appropriation had been entirely unexpected. The problem was posed when money voted for a specific purpose was not entirely spent. There was a surplus in the exchequer, and as the exchequer officers were prevented under penalties from handing it over to the Crown, it was at the disposal of Parliament. Having no executive responsibility, the Commons could only use it to satisfy the claims of individuals. In these circumstances, as Hatsell recounts, petitions for pecuniary relief multiplied vastly, and members of the House were tempted to promote petitions on behalf of their friends.[1] So the standing order was aimed at removing this temptation. It was, in Redlich's words, 'a measure of protection against the easy extravagance of a large assembly'.[2] At first the order was limited to petitions. Later the House found it generally convenient and extended it to motions tabled by its own members. The House had traditionally awaited the formal demand of the Crown before granting supply. Now, it reasoned, the financial initiative of the Crown was to be safeguarded in the recommendations made by ministers; so it was right that any motion for a grant or charge on the public revenue, from whatever source, should be subject to ministerial recommendation. Equally the House accepted that the same principle should apply to the provision of revenue by taxation: only ministers were to initiate resolutions for this purpose.[3]

In Congress

Stress has been laid on this constitutional principle because it makes the essential point of divergence of the parliamentary from the congressional system of finance. Reacting from British experience—and from their own experience of British rule—the

1. Hatsell, *Precedents of Proceedings in the House of Commons* (1818 ed.), Vol. III, p. 241.
2. Redlich, op. cit., Vol. III, p. 122.
3. The sequence of events which resulted in the virtual exclusion of the House of Lords from the consideration of bills dealing with supply and taxation was described in Chapter IV.

Founding Fathers wrote into the Constitution the exclusive function of Congress to impose taxes and its duty to control public expenditure by appropriation. The supply of money was not distinguished in the Constitution from its appropriation: the two processes were then considered, and have since been treated, as inseparable.

At once Congress was confronted—as Parliament had been confronted years before—with the problem of how to supervise the business of appropriation. In the early years it was by no means clear what the answer was to be. The first Congress (1789) passed an Act setting up the Treasury department. It did so after long debate on the role and responsibility of the executive in the field of finance. Even before those debates were completed, the House of Representatives in July 1789 appointed a small Committee of Ways and Means of thirteen members (one from each state) 'to prepare an estimate of supplies requisite for the service of the United States in the current year, and report thereupon'.[1] But when the Act was finally passed in September, the order setting up the Committee of Ways and Means was discharged[2] and its function turned over to the Federalist statesman, Alexander Hamilton, who had lately been appointed the first United States Secretary to the Treasury.

One of the duties imposed by the Act on this officer was 'to prepare and report estimates of the public revenue, and the public expenditures'. It was a role and an opening which Hamilton was equipped by talent and temperament to exploit. Only thirty-two on appointment, he had made his name at the conventions at Annapolis and Philadelphia as an expert on public finance and was now to emerge as an outstanding administrator. Above all a lover of order and system, his definite policies and thrusting determination for several years dominated the political scene. From 1789 to 1795 it was to Hamilton that Congress looked for advice on estimates and appropriations; and having received that advice, proceeded to enact its substance after debate but without reference to a small committee for detailed scrutiny. Even though Hamilton as a minister could not be a member of

1. Journal of the House of Representatives, 24 July and 17 September 1789.
2. Journal of the House of Representatives, 24 July and 17 September 1789.

Congress, he had for practical purposes established the British concept that it was for the finance minister to take all the necessary initiatives in the formation of fiscal policies.

But Hamilton's fiscal policies became the keynote of controversy between Federalist and anti-Federalists.[1] His opponents attacked not merely those policies but also Hamilton's techniques of congressional arrangement. Under the leadership of Albert Gallatin, an anti-Federalist frontiersman from Pennsylvania, a move within Congress for stricter congressional control of finance found favour. In 1795 on Hamilton's resignation a Ways and Means Committee was again appointed to which the new Secretary to the Treasury was at once required to submit the estimates for 1796. From that date the Committee gradually asserted its control over matters of supply and appropriation. The Ways and Means Committee appointed annually since 1795 was in 1802 made a standing committee, and in 1811 a similar committee was appointed in the Senate. By the eve of the Civil War the House Committee had established by its tight and comprehensive control over finance the right to cut or reject policies and expenditures proposed by other committees and had won itself a privileged status which enabled it to enforce its views in the House. Despite this ascendancy, the pressure of business resulting from the Civil War forced the Committee to jettison the review of estimates and appropriation bills. In 1865 these became the responsibility of a new standing committee on Appropriations. In 1867 the Senate divided its work in the same way.

The new House Appropriations Committee was given a mandate to restrain extravagant and illegal appropriation of public funds. It took its duties so seriously that within a few years it had become very unpopular. The retrenching approach, combined with a growing tendency to graft authorizing provisions on to appropriation bills and so to poach on the preserves of the other standing committees, led directly to the dismemberment of the committee. Between 1877 and 1885 something like half of its jurisdiction was handed over to the relevant standing committees.

1. The Federalist party and the anti-Federalist or Republican party dominated national politics for the first generation of the Republic. The Republican and Democrat parties of today are their respective descendants. The word Republican today thus means the opposite of what it meant then.

But this curb on the Appropriations Committee's activities lasted only until 1920 when it was given back its entire jurisdiction.[1] This reform was linked with the important Budget and Accounting Act of 1921 which brought into being a system of national budgeting by the executive branch and set up the General Accounting Office.

The evolution of the systems of finance in Congress and Parliament has thus been very different. The House of Representatives (and subsequently the Senate) had by the beginning of the nineteenth century enforced on the executive branch a strict control of finance by using its small committees. In different constitutional circumstances, Parliament rejected this course, and left the initiative in finance, both in matters of taxation and expenditure, to the Crown, acting latterly through its ministers in Parliament. In so doing it settled for a critical, rather than a controlling, function, a choice which today marks off its procedures from those of Congress. But there has been one similarity. Parliament and Congress both found it convenient or necessary to separate the consideration of expenditure from the consideration of taxation. The division between the former Committees of Supply and Ways and Means in the House of Commons has been reproduced in the committee structure of the two Houses of Congress, so that since 1865 Congress and its committees have considered expenditure and revenue separately. The result in both countries has been a failure by the legislature to examine and debate the national budget as a whole.[2] Efforts in recent years to cure this defect are considered later in this chapter.

Against this background it is now proposed to describe the financial system in Parliament and Congress today from three angles: the control of expenditure; control through account and audit; and the control of taxation. The extent of the differences imposes its own treatment: the two systems have to be set out side by side because they are too different to be compared and contrasted at closer quarters. But the separation helps to point the differences between them.

1. A short history of the House's Appropriations Committee is to be found in the statement made in the House on 2 March 1965, the hundredth anniversary of the Committee's first appointment.

2. Professor Harris has pointed out that the term 'budget' is used in Britain to describe the Chancellor's *revenue* proposals, but in the United States to describe the President's *spending* programme: *Congressional Control of Administration* (1964), p. 288.

CONTROL OF EXPENDITURE IN PARLIAMENT

Historical Development

The function of Parliament in dealing with expenditure is to decide how much money is to be supplied to the Crown, that is, to the government in response to its demands. For this purpose the government lays annually before Parliament estimates of expenditure to cover the whole range of its civil and defence policy and administration. These estimates are today grouped into twelve classes, each of which breaks down into a number of 'votes'. Under the rules of debate in the Commons during the nineteenth century each vote was brought forward in succession. Any member could move an amendment to reduce the amount of the vote, and if not satisfied with the explanation given by the minister, could force a division. The minister would usually be sustained by the government majority, though on occasion an estimate could be reduced or defeated. Whatever the result the private member had the opportunity to enforce the closest scrutiny of an estimate in which he was interested. Joseph Hume, member of Parliament from 1818 to 1855, won a lasting reputation by his tireless search for economies through the ordinary supply procedures.

In the second half of the nineteenth century, the nature of debates on expenditure (or supply) changed. The Reform Acts of 1832 and 1867 produced a House more consistently exercised by the 'condition of the people question'. In the words of Campion 'when social reform became the dominant interest, the representatives of the people ceased to be the check, and began to apply the spur, to expenditure'.[1] The rules of debate, however, in supply remained the same. Amendments were still moved to reduce estimates. But the motive was less to seek economies than to expose and criticize the inadequacy of government policy and administration.

These two approaches to the parliamentary function of supply were classically set out in a speech made in 1896 by Arthur Balfour, then First Secretary of the Treasury, when introducing the important reforms on which procedure and practice today are based. He said:

1. House of Commons Paper 189 of 1946, p. xxiv.

Supply alone affords private members in this House that right of criticism, that constant power of demanding from the government explanations of their administrative and executive action, which without supply can never be possessed.

and again

While supply does not exist for the purpose of enforcing economy on the government, it does exist for the purpose of criticizing the policy of the government, of controlling their administration and bringing them to book for their policy at home and abroad.[1]

In the same speech he characterized the notion that the object of discussion in supply was to ensure an economic administration of public money as:

an ancient and deeply rooted superstition . . . that has absolutely no justification in the existing circumstances of parliamentary government.

The Balfour reforms, which after a period of trial became a permanent part of the House's supply procedure, were essentially two. First, a fixed number of days—computed by reference to the average number spent in previous sessions—was to be allotted to supply business in each session. By this means a more systematic distribution of supply days throughout the session became possible. Secondly, 5 August was laid down as the day in each session by which the voting of moneys was to be completed. Before this reform the session could be prolonged—as it can today in some Commonwealth legislatures—until all the money votes had been separately agreed to. Now all estimates have to be disposed of—en bloc if necessary—by 5 August. As a result of Balfour's reforms estimates were still put down for debate on a supply day, but debate increasingly concentrated on the policy that lay below the estimate, rather than on the details of the government's financial stewardship. Moreover, supply debates became increasingly a weapon for the official opposition. Before the Balfour reforms the estimates to be taken on each day had

1. Parliamentary Debates (1896), 37 cc. 724–6. Professor Gordon Reid draws attention to these key passages of Balfour's speech in *The Politics of Financial Control* (1966), pp. 69–70.

traditionally been fixed by arrangement between the parliamentary whips of the two major parties; but it was the opposition, as official critic of the government, who in practice made the selection. So, with the more systematic spread of supply days throughout the session which the Balfour reforms brought about, the opposition were given a series of regular opportunities to criticize government policy and administration on subjects of high and current political interest.

Supply Procedure Today

The cycle of supply today, as it has emerged from refinements made to Balfour's scheme in 1947 and 1966, is more elaborate but not basically different. There are now twenty-nine supply days, in practice so spaced out through the session as to allow a little less than one a week. In the latest alterations (1966) the procedural forms were brought into line with the changing nature of supply debates. The opposition now has a wide range of procedural options. It is rare for an estimate of a particular sum of money for a particular purpose to be debated on a supply day. Instead the opposition usually puts down either a motion expressing criticism of government policy or administration, or a motion for the 'adjournment', a neutral motion which conventionally serves as a peg on which to hang a discussion of government action with or without a concluding vote. The only supply days used nowadays for genuinely financial purposes are those on which the reports made by the Public Accounts Committee or the Expenditure Committee are chosen for debate (on perhaps two out of twenty-nine days) or the rare occasions when an estimate is debated (on at most two days).[1]

Debate on supply days no longer has much formal or procedural relationship to their financial basis. But the money still has to be voted, and the voting is done within the cycle of the twenty-nine supply days. For this purpose a steady stream of estimates and supporting documents are laid before the House of Commons in the course of a session. Some of the complexities surrounding the financial business of the House derive from the fact

1. The Committee of Supply, a 'committee of the whole' into which the House used to resolve itself in order to consider estimates and vote supply, was abolished in 1966. The business of supply is now taken in the House itself.

that the sessional year, beginning in October, does not coincide with the financial year, which began on the previous 1 April. So the first estimates of expenditure to reach the Commons in a new session are supplementary estimates (known as 'Winter' Supplementaries), representing demands additional to those already made for the current financial year, either to cover a revealed inadequacy in an existing vote or new expenditure resulting from government policy.

At the same time the House of Commons gets its first view of proposed expenditure in the forthcoming financial year, in the shape of a Vote on Account for civil services. This lump sum is granted by the House *before* the start of the financial year in order to keep the civil departments running until the House has voted all the estimates, which it does towards the end of the session. The civil Vote on Account comprises four-twelfths of the total civil expenditure proposed, a proportion roughly reflecting the needs of the first four months of the forthcoming financial year (April to July), the balance being voted in July when the House has completed, during the twenty-nine days of supply, its criticism of government policy and administration.

In February the main estimates, civil and defence, for the forthcoming financial year are presented to the House, comprising about 200 votes. In the same month a defence Vote on Account is laid, to provide something on account for the armed forces of the Crown, just as the civil vote on account makes temporary provision for the civil departments, the balance being voted likewise in July.

Also in February and March are laid any final supplementary estimates (the 'Spring' Supplementaries) for the current year. Once the next financial year has begun (on 1 April), the House can expect the first batch of supplementary estimates (the 'Summer' Supplementaries) for that year to be laid in June or July, in time to be voted, together with the main estimates, before 5 August, when the sessional cycle of supply comes to an end.

Three supply guillotines, as compared with one in Balfour's time, ensure that the government obtains regular supply at the proper time. On those days the Speaker has to put to the House the particular financial business that has to be secured, namely, in January (not earlier than the sixth supply day) the vote on account for the civil departments for the forthcoming year and the winter supplementaries for the current year; in March (not earlier than the tenth supply day) the Vote on Account for the Defence departments for the forthcoming year and the spring supplementaries for the current year; and in July (on the twenty-ninth and last supply day) the balance necessary to complete the sums voted on account for the civil and defence departments, together with the summer supplementaries.

The House's resolutions authorizing all these grants do not carry the force of law. This can only be given by legislation, so that after each supply guillotine has fallen a Consolidated Fund Bill is introduced and passed through the ordinary legislative process to authorize the issue of a lump sum from the Consolidated Fund.[1] The bills in January and March do this and no more. The bill in July not only authorizes the issue of more money from the Consolidated Fund, but it also appropriates the whole of the amounts voted in January, March and July: that is to say, it sets out in detail the amounts to be granted, alongside precise statements of the purposes of each grant, and it gives statutory effect to both the grants and the purposes.

This complex process of voting supply can best be summed up in a table showing how the contents of each Consolidated Fund Bill would relate to the relevant financial year during a normal session, say 1970–71.

Purpose of Supply Procedure

A deduction can be made from this survey: the House has, for all practical purposes, separated the process of voting supply from the process of debating supply. The voting of supply takes place formally on the three days when the guillotine falls, before or after the main debate on those days: on the other days when supply is debated none of the estimates is necessarily before the House. Nor is supply discussed on the various stages of the three Consolidated Fund Bills. On the day allotted to the second reading of each

1. The Consolidated Fund is the Exchequer's account kept at the Bank of England into which all revenue is paid. Issues out of the Consolidated Fund are controlled by the Comptroller and Auditor General. The National Loans Act 1968 transferred from the Consolidated Fund to a new National Loans Fund all the government's borrowing transactions and most of its lending transactions. Issues from the new Fund are also controlled by the Comptroller and Auditor General.

CONTENTS OF CONSOLIDATED FUND BILLS 1971

Date of Bill	Title of Bill	Content of Bill	Financial Year
A. January 1971	Consolidated Fund Bill	1. Civil Vote on Account	1971–72
		2. Winter Supplementary Estimates	1970–71
B. March 1971	Consolidated Fund (No. 2)	1. Defence Vote on Account	1971–72
		2. Spring Supplementary Estimates	1970–71
C. July 1971	Consolidated Fund (Appropriation)	1. Balance necessary to complete sums voted on account (A1 and B1 above)	1971–72
		2. Summer Supplementary Estimates	1971–72
		3. Appropriation of all moneys voted in January, March and July Consolidated Fund Bills	

bill in the Commons, private members can by convention raise with the responsible minister matters of their own choice, the order of subjects being determined by ballot. The committee and third reading stages of the bills are taken formally.[1] No difference is made for the Appropriation Bill (in July) when the House formally approves the purposes of the grants—as well as the grants themselves—but makes no attempt to debate the details of this appropriation.

Today it is still possible for the official opposition to put down a specific estimate for debate and to divide the house on it. The House thus retains its hold over the estimates; but the flexibility

1. The powers of the House of Lords in relation to Consolidated Fund Bills are discussed on pp. 180–1.

of the modern standing orders, enabling the opposition for example to set out in a motion a succinct statement of its objection to a particular policy or minister, allows the fullest scope for realizing the objective noted by Balfour of 'bringing [the government] to book for their policy at home and abroad'.

It should not be supposed that the movement in pursuit of this objective has been steady or single-minded. There have always been those who thought that the House should use the estimates for their natural purpose, namely, to conduct a closer financial scrutiny of the government's proposed expenditure as laid out in the estimates. In recent years pressure to re-animate this kind of proceeding has been applied, as Professor Reid has pointed out,[1] by backbenchers who have become aware that reforms of supply procedure have been at their expense. Once the number of supply days was pre-determined, and the choice of subject turned over to the official opposition, these opportunities were greatly reduced in practice. Supply debates became an instrument for the confrontation of the two front benches. Today, on a supply day the official opposition may put down a motion on its chosen subject and the government may put down an amendment stating its alternative view. It is open to a backbench member on either side to put down an amendment, either alone or with other members; but it is unlikely to be selected by the Speaker for debate.[2] The statement of grievances preceding the grant of supply has become the function of the official opposition; and the Speaker in logic selects any government amendment as embodying the official answer to this challenge. The backbencher must extract what comfort he can from the right to raise particular matters—but not to vote on them—when each of the three Consolidated Fund Bills comes up for second reading.

Scrutiny of Supply by Committees

There was a sound reason for the eclipse of the old functions of the House on supply: it is that detailed financial scrutiny cannot easily be carried out by over six hundred members or however many of them may be in the chamber on a particular day.

1. Professor Gordon Reid, *The Politics of Financial Control* (1966), pp. 72–75.
2. The Speaker's power to select amendments is described on p. 52.

The examination of estimates of expenditure in a Committee of the whole House survived for as long as it did because the total national budget coming before the Commons remained relatively small and easy to grasp. By the end of the nineteenth century these conditions were ceasing to apply; and it is significant that from 1912—some few years after the Balfour reforms were made permanent—select committees have been looking at the annual estimates of expenditure.

The Estimates Committees—appointed in 1913 and 1914—were required by the House simply to consider the estimates and make reports; no other formal limits were set to the scope of their inquiries. Since World War I, however, the Committee's scrutiny of estimates was made subject to one overriding qualification: its duty was to suggest how the policy implied in any estimates chosen for examination could be more efficiently administered, not to criticize the policy itself. It was in practice a value for money scrutiny rather than a curb on expenditure. From the end of World War II the Committee worked regularly through investigating subcommittees and within the limits set by its terms of reference covered an immense amount of ground. In these later years its inquiries afforded opportunities for the private Member which have to be set against his losses on the floor of the House.

Two examples of its work may be given. In 1958 one of its subcommittees inquired into the control exercised by the Treasury over public expenditure. This was a far-reaching inquiry which led the Committee to recommend the appointment of a small committee with access to cabinet papers to report on the theory and practice of the Treasury's control of expenditure. This recommendation was accepted by the government. A committee appointed under Lord Plowden's chairmanship reached conclusions which led to a rearrangement of the divisions of the Treasury concerned with public expenditure and to a thorough overhaul of their methods of control, especially of their 'forward look' at future programmes of expenditure.

The other example was the inquiry made in 1964–65 into recruitment to the civil service. Questions of recruitment led the subcommittee concerned to consider the functions facing the civil service and the kind of experience and skills needed to fulfil those functions. They finally recommended the appointment of a royal commission on the organization, recruiting and structure of the civil service, the last one having been in 1931. This recommendation was substantially accepted by the government. The Royal Commission, which reported in 1969, made a wide inquiry into the adequacy of the civil service today and recommended among other things, the creation of a civil service department with specific responsibilities for recruitment and organization within the government service.

These two investigations by the Estimates Committee were in a sense untypical in that they were concerned with public expenditure as a whole in one case and the operations of the civil service as a whole in the other. Specific inquiries into particular blocks of estimates were more common. Nevertheless the two broader inquries give a good idea of what the Estimates Committee was able to achieve.

Since the session of 1970–71 the House of Commons has appointed an Expenditure Committee, with wider terms of reference, to replace the Estimates Committee. The new Committee is

'to consider any papers on public expenditure presented to this House and such of the estimates as may seem fit to the Committee . . .'

Besides the estimates, the Committee can thus consider, for example, the assumptions underlying the annual white paper in which the government sets out its forecast of capital and current expenditure over the next five years. It is a larger Committee than its predecessor—49 members against 33 (in 1970); and it has decided to work through a steering subcommittee and six functional subcommittees on public expenditure in general; defence and external affairs; trade and industry; education and arts; employment and social services; and environment and Home Office. No doubt the Expenditure Committee will in due course build on the foundations laid by the Estimates Committee.

The practical limits of the power of the House and the Estimates Committee *against* the government were clear. The Estimates Committee could recommend an economy or a more efficient method of administration. The Committee's report could be debated on a supply day. The official opposition could even choose the relevant estimates for debate on a supply day, and

it could answer a minister's refusal to accept the recommendation by moving to reduce the estimate or the minister's salary. If
it were to act in this way, it would be confronted with the
minister declaring the estimate to be a matter of confidence, and
in the division that followed he would be supported by a whipped
majority. So it is rarely attempted. The official opposition
generally prefers to use its supply days for calling attention to
grievances arising from matters of major policy, which the
Estimates Committee under its terms of reference could not
abridge. It remains to be seen how far the new Expenditure
Committee, with wider terms of reference, will provide help for
the opposition in its confrontation with the executive power.

CONTROL OF EXPENDITURE IN CONGRESS

Developments in the Twentieth Century

The contrast between this picture of a House of Commons with
little power against the government of the day and the control
exercised by congressional committees, as historically evolved,
over supply and appropriation appears to be complete. In practice
however, the nature of congressional control has been markedly
affected by what has happened in the twentieth century.

The Budget and Accounting Act of 1921 strikingly altered the
balance of legislative and executive authority in budgetary
matters. Before 1921 the task of preparing the budget fell to
Congress itself. Each service or agency drew up its own estimates
and sent them to Congress through the medium of the Secretary
of the Treasury whose function was otherwise limited to adding
up the total expenditure and setting it against the expected
receipts. The total of expenditure was in no sense a superimposed
budgetary figure, but only a sum of separately formulated bids.
Within Congress these bids were considered by committees
working without close or effective coordination. Decisions were
often contradictory and overall deficits continual. Only gradually
did the ever expanding budgets force recognition of the need for
the executive branch to prepare and co-ordinate the budget before
it was submitted to Congress. The Act of 1921 gave this duty to
the President, and set up the Bureau of the Budget within the
Treasury. At first the Bureau carried out its duties in a strictly
financial sense, stressing economies in expenditure. Not until

1939, when it was transferred to the executive office of the President, did it become the instrument by which the President could consciously shape an overall budget for submission to Congress. In 1970, in order to reflect an extension of its functions, the Bureau of the Budget was restyled the Office of Management and Budget.

Today the departments and agencies send to the Office of Management and Budget by 1 October their estimates for the financial year beginning the following 1 July. The budget resulting from discussions within the executive branch is sent to Congress in January. Shorn of any taxation proposals, which are considered by the Committee on Ways and Means and its legislative proposals with accompanying 'price tags' (see p. 280), the budget is referred to the House's Committee on Appropriations and by them assigned to subcommittees for detailed scrutiny.

The House Appropriations Committee

In 1970 there were thirteen subcommittees of the Appropriations Committee—on Agriculture; Defence; District of Columbia; Foreign Operations; Independent Offices and Department of Housing and Urban Development; Interior; Labor, Health, Education and Welfare; Legislative; Military Construction; Public Works; State, Justice, Commerce and Judiciary; Transportation; and Treasury and Post Office. The full Committee has fifty-one members, the subcommittees from seven to eleven members. As a general rule a member of the Committee will belong to two subcommittees and will not be a member of any other important committee of the House. This method of assignment reflects the concentration of purpose and the independent spirit which its members bring to the work of the Appropriations Committee. Their specialized knowledge backed by their industry and stamina, which are generally recognized, account for the influence which this loose federation of subcommittees exerts over the congressional purse strings.

The Committee's duty is 'the appropriation of the revenue for the support of the government'. Directly or through subcommittees and in fulfilment of this overriding purpose, it may 'conduct studies and examinations of the organization and operation of any executive department or . . . agency',[1] and it is armed with all the necessary powers to send for persons and papers.

1. House Rule XI.

Within this general reference the subcommittees proceed by hearings at which departments have the opportunity to explain and defend their estimates. The process begins with the cabinet member or departmental head making an introductory statement of policy, and the subcommittee then works its way through the estimates of the department, division by division. Interested parties outside Congress can also make representations, and discussions may be held with interested members of the House—an important element in a subcommittee's effort to strike the balance between the desirable and the possible. A subcommittee may meet daily for four or five hours for several months to complete this part of its work.

Next a bill is drafted, and the subcommittee will meet to 'mark it up', that is, to make specific alterations up or down to the figures put in by the President. At this stage the subcommittee chairman and the senior (ranking) minority members are generally in close consultation with the chairman and ranking minority member of the full Committee. When the bill comes before the full Committee it is usually accepted after only a brief consideration and without major alteration before being reported to the House.

The process of hearings followed by the preparation of a bill differs in one important respect from that followed in other House committees. The subcommittees of the Appropriations Committee do all their work in private, though the testimony, minus any taken 'off the record', is subsequently printed and released publicly in advance of the reporting of the bill.

The Committee's function is to appropriate, not to authorize. Under the House rules funds cannot be appropriated for a purpose not already authorized by legislation. Conversely no authorizing bill can itself appropriate money.[1] This dividing line between the functions of the Appropriations Committee on the one hand and the legislative committees on the other is theoretically clear and generally applied in practice. But the subject is complex, and the case histories illuminating the borderline occupy one of the fattest sections of Cannon's *Procedure in the House of Representatives*.[2] A specific exception to the general rule is made

1. House Rule XXI.
2. Clarence Cannon, sometime Parliamentarian of the House, was Chairman of the Appropriations Committee 1949–52 and 1955–64 and ranking minority member 1947–48 and 1953–54.

in favour of a bill or provision reported by the Appropriations Committee which 'retrenches' expenditure; but whenever the Committee attaches a condition or 'rider' to a provision of an appropriation bill, it is likely to alter authorizations in existing law, and so to poach on the preserves of the relevant legislative committee.

This conflict between the legislative function and the business of appropriation does not occur in Britain. It has been shown how a bill involving expenditure, whether introduced by the government or a private member, has to be covered by a money resolution, which can be initiated only by the government. The money resolution is usually considered immediately after the House has agreed to the second reading of a bill, so that in practice the approval of new expenditure goes hand in hand with the legislation that authorizes it. The annual estimates of expenditure, main and supplementary, include all these sums, bringing together the funds already voted in support of existing programmes and the funds required for new programmes. The annual appropriation bill in Britain exactly reproduces the sums and purposes set down in the estimates. In the past it has been held that with a few recognized exceptions such as the power of the Defence departments to enter into long-term contracts in defence of the realm, new policies and programmes should be translated into specific Acts of Parliament, and that authorization should not be by the Appropriation Acts alone.

In the House of Representatives, by contrast, the conflict between authorization and appropriation is of the essence of politics. In that conflict the scales are weighted in favour of the Appropriations Committee. At first sight this may seem surprising. Individual congressmen are normally seeking programmes which will benefit their constituencies or regions; and the funding of these programmes, which may include such solid benefits as a federal building, a rocket site or a dam, brings them up against the Appropriations Committee. 'The biggest thing in electoral politics and in congressional politics is boodle, and the reputation you can get back home for being able to get boodle' said an experienced House member.[1] Yet this pressure on the Committee is somewhat balanced by a recognition of the need for economy and of the Committee's primary duty to secure it. The

1. Quoted in *The Power of the Purse* (1966) by Richard Fenno, p. 8.

Committee is expected to finance programmes and projects but also to finance them as economically as possible. The enthusiasm in the House for economy may fluctuate, but as Professor Richard Fenno, the historian and analyst of appropriation politics in Congress, has pointed out, a House member would rather be called anything else than a spender. In 1957 the *Congressional Quarterly* developed from selected roll-calls an index of 'economy voting', which rated members according to their economy-mindedness. The reaction from the lower rated members was so violent that the *Congressional Quarterly* was obliged to recast its index on a less pejorative basis.[1] 1957, it is true, was one of the years in which economies in public expenditure were seen both inside and outside Congress as specially relevant to the country's economic needs. Even so qualified, this reaction contrasts strikingly with the approach to spending of most British members in the last hundred years (see p. 314) and could reflect the House of Representatives' closer responsibilities for the realities of public finance.

The Appropriations Committee's findings also draw support from the procedure of the House. Its reports are accorded priority under the rules, general appropriation bills being taken up when the Speaker recognizes the subcommittee chairman concerned. There is no need to obtain a special rule from the Rules Committee (see p. 283), unless protection is required against points of order, for instance, where some clauses might raise doubts as to the proper scope of an appropriation bill. The printed hearings and report of the Committee must be available for at least three days before the House will consider an appropriation bill. Subject to this Rule,[2] it is the practice to bring the bill forward as quickly as possible, so that interested groups have to move with despatch to make known their reaction or opposition to the Committee's proposals. Thus the climate of opinion in, and the procedures of, the House favour the Committee's activities. Criticisms are heard of its lack of support for the legislative committees and occasionally of the secrecy of its transactions, but its bills are seldom amended in major respects.

Nevertheless the scope of the Appropriations Committee's operations has been shrinking since World War II. A feature of this period has been an increasing tendency to write into

1. Ibid., pp. 10–11.   2. House Rule XXI.

authorizing legislation a variety of 'permanent' devices by which legislative programmes are to be financed. The effect of these devices—the institution of permanent contracts and the creation of trust funds are examples—take these programmes beyond the reach of the annual appropriations process and leave Congress nothing to do except pay the bill according to prescribed arrangements. This kind of legislation is written by the relevant standing committee. But it is apt to be supported by mayors of cities, governors of states and the departments and agencies of the executive branch, who like to be able to count on a regular flow of funds without annual checks, and perhaps cuts, by Congress. Between 1945 and 1970 the percentage of total budgetary expenditure falling under these special financial arrangements—officially termed 'relatively uncontrollable'—expenditure rose from about twenty-five per cent to sixty-nine per cent. The trend has already weakened the power of the appropriation processes. There is no sign of its being halted.[1]

The Role of the Senate in Appropriations

By 'immemorial custom' general appropriation bills dealing with a number of subjects originate in the House of Representatives, though bills appropriating for single specific purposes have originated in the Senate. Once the Senate has received a bill from the House, it has equal powers. Like the House, the Senate has a Committee on Appropriations with the same task of financing programmes already authorized by legislative committees and of financing them as economically as possible. In considering the bills reported by that committee, the Senate follows broadly the same procedure.

But there are differences arising from the nature of the Senate. Larger constituencies mean stronger pressures in support of a wider variety of programmes. Because the Senate is smaller, each senator has more committee assignments. There is less specialization and less contention between the legislative committees on the one hand and the appropriations subcommittees on the other.

1. See statement of the Chairman of the House Committee on Appropriations in August 1965 to the Joint Committee on the Organization of Congress, Hearings (1965), pp. 1649–50.

In the 90th Congress (1967–68) the chairman of the Labor and Public Welfare Committee also chaired the corresponding subcommittee of the Appropriations Committee. This kind of duplication is not uncommon. The stronger pressures and the interlocking membership of Senate committees predispose senators in favour of increasing grants rather than reducing them. Professor Fenno has suggested that the Senate Appropriations Committee prescribes for itself the tasks of an 'appellate court', making decisions on appeals from departments whose estimates have been cut by the House.[1]

Who wins? This is decided by the Conference Committee, consisting of representatives of each House who are invariably members—normally the chairmen and ranking minority members—of the Appropriations Committees and their relevant subcommittees. Professor Fenno has analysed some 517 instances between 1957 and 1962 to find out whether the cash outcome was closer to the figure in the Senate bill or the figure in the House bill. In 186 cases the Senate had adopted the figure in the House bill so that there was no need for a conference. Of the remaining 331, the Senate won in 56·6 per cent of the cases, the House in 30·5 per cent and the difference was split in 13 per cent. But this does not mean that the Senate has the preponderant influence on the whole congressional appropriation process. The House, in starting the sequence, sets the form within which negotiations unfold; and nearly a third of its decisions, in Professor Fenno's analysis, were accepted by the Senate without alteration.

The table[2] that follows shows how the House and the Senate and their respective Appropriations Committees dealt with the President's requests for appropriations in the second session of the 90th Congress (1968):

($ Million)

Requested Appropriations	Agreed in House Committee	Passed by House	Agreed in Senate Committee	Passed by Senate	Finally agreed to
147,909	130,363	130,422	134,897	135,372	133,340

1. Fenno, op. cit., p. 562.
2. The rounded figures in this table are supplied by the House Appropriations Committee, to whom the authors' thanks are due.

The President and Appropriations

The President can, and occasionally does, veto an appropriation bill. Two bills—on education and on housing—were vetoed in 1970. But such a veto is a rarity for the good practical reason that the administrative need for whatever money Congress has appropriated is generally overdue.[1]

About fifteen to twenty appropriation bills and joint resolutions are usually passed each session. They should all be passed by 1 July, the beginning of the new financial year, though with lengthening congressional sessions this objective is rarely achieved. The President, however, is not without weapons against Congress. The long-drawn-out nature of the budgetary process—requiring about six or more months work in the Office of Management and Budget and at least another six in Congress (about half as much again as the corresponding period in Britain) inevitably means underestimates and deficits, and so gives the President his opening to ask for more, if the integrity of the budget is to be preserved. Delays in Congress are often attributed to the Senate. But the Senate has to wait for the House to act, and the House often takes its time. These delays and occasional deadlocks in conference between the representatives of the two Houses have made necessary provisional financing in order to keep the government solvent. To do so Congress has passed joint resolutions extending the operation of appropriations for the previous financial year until stated dates in the new year. In addition Congress is called upon in every session to consider and pass supplementary appropriation bills (relating to the year covered by the regular budgetary programme) and deficiency bills (relating to the current year) which broadly correspond to supplementary estimates submitted by the government to the House of Commons.

The figures in the table on p. 329 illustrate the power exerted by Congress over the President's proposals. The other side of the coin is that the President has on occasion 'impounded' funds appropriated by Congress; that is, he has refused to spend, or delayed spending, or apportioned to reserve, appropriated moneys. The routine use of this power has been endorsed by Congress. A law of 1950 authorizes the Director of the Office

1. For an account of what happens when the President vetoes a bill, see above p. 288–9).

of Management and Budget, in apportioning appropriated
moneys, to establish 'reserves' to provide for contingencies or to
make savings where, for example, 'changes in requirements' or
'other departments' make savings possible.[1] But there have also
been high policy differences with Congress leading the President
to impound funds. In 1949 President Truman impounded
$615 million for the purchase of aircraft. In 1959 President
Eisenhower failed to use funds appropriated to military purposes,
such as the maintenance of the Marine Corps at a certain
strength and the construction of Polaris submarines. These
actions were justified by reference to the President's constitutional
powers as Commander-in-Chief of the Armed Forces. In 1970
President Nixon vetoed an education appropriation bill on the
ground that its effect would be inflationary. The veto was overridden by both Houses; but the President could still fall back on
his authority to impound the relevant sums. These occasions
have been exceptional; but Congress has to have in mind that
Presidents have acted in these ways when the need for economy
grips them.

CONTROL BY ACCOUNT AND AUDIT

Parliament and Congress have chosen very different methods of
asserting their control over the business of supply and appropriation. But their historic decisions left outstanding the question
how the detailed, methodical examination, designed to ensure
that appropriated moneys down to the smallest sum had been
used only for the prescribed purpose, was to be undertaken. In
both countries it took what with hindsight seems an extraordinary
amount of time to find an effective solution to this problem.

United Kingdom

In England public accountancy had been fitfully attempted since
the middle ages. Audit had traditionally been conducted by
officers of the exchequer as an internal function of government;
as a rule the results were laid before Parliament. Yet even after
the revolution of 1688, when Parliament began to give serious
and continuing attention to appropriation, the House of Commons
had no means of ascertaining, through an effective system of

1. 31 United States Code 665 (c) (2).

audit, whether the money had been spent on the service for which it was voted. During the eighteenth century the House appointed various abortive committees to report on public accounts. With hindsight they can be seen as the precursors of a more systematic parliamentary scrutiny. Moreover the passing in 1785 of an Act setting up commissioners for auditing the public accounts—in response to difficulties and delays in clearing the accounts during and after the American War of Independence—much improved the internal official machinery for audit. But not until 1802, when an Act was passed requiring the production of 'Finance Accounts', was an overall statement of the national accounts first laid before Parliament. Even these did not show actual expenditure under each head but only the issues made by the Exchequer to the departments. Thirty years elapsed before this defect was pointed out in a debate on the Navy Estimates. The Navy Accounts were duly rectified, but it took another fifteen years before the same change was made in the form of the Army Accounts. Not until 1869 were the first complete accounts of actual expenditure throughout the public service, civil as well as military, laid before the House.

Before that date two important steps had been taken. In 1861 Gladstone as Chancellor of the Exchequer secured the appointment of a Commons committee of public accounts; and in 1866 the Exchequer and Audit Departments Act[1], authorizing the appointment of the Comptroller and Auditor General as an independent officer to report to Parliament, was passed. The system of financial scrutiny brought into being by these two measures stand unaltered today.

The Committee of Public Accounts is appointed every session by standing order to examine 'the accounts showing the appropriation of the sums granted by Parliament to meet the public expenditure and . . . such other accounts laid before Parliament

1. This Act is in one sense a misnomer; it nowhere mentions the Exchequer and Audit Department, which is the traditional name for the Department of the Comptroller and Auditor General. The Department was in fact set up in 1867, bringing together and superseding the offices of the Comptroller of the Exchequer (an independent officer first appointed in 1834 to prevent any issue of public money not authorized by Parliament) and the Commissioners for Auditing the Public Accounts. The two functions—control of issues and audit of public accounts—were thus amalgamated for the first time in 1867.

as the Committee think fit'. The Committee has fifteen members and its Chairman is by custom a leading member of the official opposition, usually with experience as a Treasury Minister. As a rule the Committee holds two two-hourly meetings a week from January through July and examines a wide range of accounts by questioning the permanent heads and supporting staff of the departments concerned. But it also finds time to probe more deeply into problems which may recur over a number of years. One recent example is the study it made of the form of government contracts with private industry and the accurate estimation of costs and prices. This problem was given prominence by the disclosure in 1964 of the excessive profits made by Ferranti Ltd from a production contract for an advanced guided missile system, and in the following year by Bristol Siddeley Engines Ltd, for the overhaul and maintenance of aero engines. In these instances the Committee's investigations gave much publicity to these disclosures. The excess profits were returned to the Exchequer by the companies and, after further inquiries into government contracting, a new deal was made to secure fair play between government and industry in situations of this kind.

The foundation for the Public Accounts Committee's investigations is the annual report of the Comptroller and Auditor General, a high and independent public servant, appointed by the Queen and dismissible only on an address of both Houses of Parliament. The Comptroller has invariably had a wide experience of the public service, usually at the head of one or more public departments, though after appointment he owes allegiance only to Parliament. He deploys a staff of 500 audit officials and a budget of £1,252,000 (1970–71). Some of these officials work at the Comptroller's headquarters at Audit House on the Thames Embankment at Blackfriars, but most of them are stationed in the public departments and provide the raw material for the Comptroller's annual report. This report is concerned less with the legal basis and financial regularity of public expenditure (in practice the departments themselves make sure they do not fall down on these basic requirements) than with evidence of inefficiency, extravagance and organizational weakness. The Committee is itself concerned with these aspects, as its reports reveal. The government's reply to the Committee's reports is laid before the House in the form of a Treasury minute which sets out the decisions taken as a result of the Committee's recommendations. The reports and the Treasury minute are normally debated by the House once a year when the government has another opportunity to state its case in reply to the report. The Treasury minute is considered in detail by the Committee in the new session.

The United States

Parliament can be said to have taken nearly 150 years—from the first effective instance of appropriation in 1711 to the creation of the Committee of Public Accounts and the Office of the Comptroller General in the 1860s—to develop the present comprehensive, parliamentary system of control and audit of public accounts. Congress has been scarcely less dilatory. After some early experiments in examining reports of executive officers of accounts, the House of Representatives in 1814 set up a Standing Committee for Public Expenditures. In 1816 six more committees on the expenditures of particular departments were set up, and later corresponding committees were appointed in the Senate. This elaborate network of committees seems to have proved ineffective, perhaps because expert guidance was lacking, though they remained in existence until the 1920s. During the same period audit was conducted by Treasury auditors whose operations were systematized under an Act of 1894. Their decisions and conclusions were subject to appeal to another official established by the Act, the Comptroller of the Treasury, whose interpretations of the appropriations laws were binding on departments. The reports of the auditors and the Comptroller were available to congressional committees on expenditures. But as these officers owed allegiance to the Executive, their audit could not inspire the confidence which derives from an independent audit of accounts.

This defect was rectified in 1921 with the passage of the Budget and Accounting Act, which is as much the keystone of the federal financial structure as the Exchequer and Audit Departments Act 1866 is for the British system. The 1921 Act replaced the Treasury auditors and the Comptroller with the General Accounting Office headed by the Comptroller General. The Office was declared to be 'independent of the executive departments', and the Comptroller General, though appointed by the President, was given a non-renewable term of office of fifteen years and made removable only by resolution of both Houses of Congress. In 1970 the Comptroller General had a staff of 4,500 and a budget of $74 million (about £30 million). About one-third work in the GAO Headquarters in Washington close to Capitol Hill; the remainder operate, like their British counterparts, in the departments and agencies both in Washington and in regional offices throughout the United States and in overseas offices in West Germany, India, the Philippines and South East Asia.

Soon after the Act of 1921 was passed, the various congressional committees concerned with public expenditure were merged into a single committee in each House. The jurisdiction of these two committees was confirmed by the Legislative Reorganization Act of 1946, and their name changed in 1952 to the Committees on Government Operations. Since 1946 each committee has had the specific duty (among other duties) of 'receiving and examining reports of the Comptroller General of the United States and of submitting such recommendations to the House [Senate] as it deems necessary or desirable in connection with the subject matter of such reports'.[1]

Differences between the United Kingdom and the United States

On the face of it, therefore, the present day parliamentary and congressional systems for appraising the public accounts are similar. The remit of both Comptrollers covers broadly all departments of government and agencies linked with the government, though not including nationalized industries in Britain or certain agencies in the United States, such as the Federal Reserve System. There is one curious exception: the U.S. Comptroller (unlike his British counterpart) does not audit the most important operations of the Internal Revenue Service, for lack of authority to examine records containing taxpayers' information. This Service contends that under the present arrangements the Joint Committee on Internal Revenue Taxation, and that Committee alone, has the duty of surveillance over matters of tax administration. The U.S. Comptroller is, however, seeking authority to extend his field of audit to cover this service, which handles many billion dollars of public money. Both Comptrollers

1. House Rule XI, 8; Senate Rule XXV, 1

conduct what are sometimes called 'comprehensive audits' in which attention is paid not so much to regularity of individual transactions (in the United States as in Britain the departments and agencies develop their own procedures for this purpose) but to the efficiency and economy of operations generally and the soundness of the financial system underlying them. To make these audits effective both Comptrollers are given by law access to the necessary books, accounts and records, and facilities for verifying transactions.

In carrying out this audit, both Comptrollers are concerned to ensure that the intentions of Parliament and Congress as expressed in legislation are fulfilled. The Budget and Accounting Procedures Act of 1950 requires the U.S. Comptroller General to determine how far 'financial transactions have been consummated in accordance with the laws, regulations or other legal requirements'. The official manual issued by the U.S. General Accounting Office calls for a study specifically of

> the pertinent laws and legislative history to ascertain Congressional intent as to
> 1. the purpose, scope and objectives of the activities or functions being examined;
> 2. the manner in which activities are to be conducted and financed;
> 3. the nature and extent of the agency's authority and responsibility.

'The policies established to govern agency activities' have also to be examined to see whether they conform to the 'applicable laws and intent of the Congress'.[1] Similarly, the British Comptroller under the Exchequer and Audit Departments Act 1921 is required in examining the appropriation accounts to satisfy himself that the money expended has been applied 'to the purpose or purposes for which the grants made by Parliament were intended to provide'. In carrying out this requirement, he will raise with departments cases in which, even though the letter of the law is being complied with, things seem to be happening which were not contemplated by, or explained to, Parliament. He can and often does draw attention in his report—as does the Public Accounts Committee—to the financial effect of the law with the possible result that the law is later changed.

1. s. 111 (d) of the Act of 1921, General Accounting Office Policy and Procedures. *Manual for Guidance of Federal Agencies* (*1966*), *3 GAO 13A*.

There are, however, important differences in the scope of the functions of the two Comptrollers. The first is that the U.S. Comptroller General has a general responsibility for settling claims by and against the United States; the British Comptroller has no comparable responsibility. The U.S. Comptroller was given this duty by the Budget and Accounting Act of 1921. He took over the responsibility from the Treasury Department which had been given it by an Act of 1817. In Britain the settlement of claims against the United Kingdom is, and has been, the responsibility of each government department subject to audit by the Comptroller General. Today, however, the difference between the two countries is by no means clear cut. For example Congress has placed certain categories of claim—such as those arising from legislation on internal revenue or pensions—within the jurisdiction of the department or agency concerned; while claims which do not raise questions of fact or law are paid by the department or agency concerned, subject to post-audit by the Comptroller General.

A more striking difference is that the U.S. Comptroller, unlike his counterpart in Britain, has the power to settle the accounts of the accountable offices of the departments and agencies. An auditor 'settles' an account after inspecting records in support of the financial transactions reported by the accountable officers and pronouncing on their legality and accuracy. If he thinks otherwise, he 'disallows' a part or the whole of the amount which then has to be made good by the accountable officer, either personally or by recovering the money from whoever has received it, before the account can be settled. The knowledge that they must settle with the Comptroller obliges departments to give weight to his views on all financial and legal policies and procedures. It is the usual practice to secure clearance in advance for any new kind of activity, expenditure or procedure, thus minimizing the risk of a subsequent disallowance. In this respect the American system can be said to provide a system of *pre*-control, as compared with what is basically a system of *post*-control in Britain. There the Comptroller and Auditor General has no power to settle accounts or disallow expenditures. He can only recommend disallowance, the final decision in the matter being taken by the Treasury. But in certifying the accuracy of the accounts, he will draw attention in his report to any expenditures which he thinks are not authorized by Parliament or in conformity with Treasury or departmental regulations. Departments do not need to secure advance decisions from the British Comptroller who would in any event decline to give them. A good deal of informal consultation does, however, take place, if only because particular expenditures are in many instances continuing expenditures, and the Comptroller's eyes necessarily lift beyond the confines of the year of audit to see what is happening currently.

These two differences—the general settlement of claims and debts and the right of disallowance—reflect the different approach of each country to its constitutional arrangements. In the United Kingdom these functions have been seen as appropriate for the executive rather than for the auditing authority to carry out, though the latter has an indirect control over the former through the process of audit and report to Parliament. In the United States, since the passing of the Budget and Accounting Act of 1921, they have been regarded as appropriate functions for the Comptroller General and the General Accounting Office acting in support of the independent and separate legislative power.

The same contrast is to be seen in the parliamentary arrangements for the consideration of the two Comptrollers' reports. In Congress the Committees on Government Operations in each House are primarily charged with this duty. But the Committees on Appropriations in each House interest themselves in reports dealing with matters of appropriations, financial out-turn and management performance, as well as reports on other matters of interest to them. In addition the Comptroller General frequently makes special reports on the transactions or programmes of an executive agency, either in pursuance of a specific provision in an Act of Congress or at the request of committees or individual members of either House of Congress or on his own initiative. In 1968–70 for example he made a study of the feasibility of applying cost accounting standards to negotiated defence contracts of $100,000 or more, and submitted the results to the chairman of the Armed Services and Banking and Currency Committees of each House. A related study, started in 1969, was of the profits made by defence contractors from contracts on which there was no formally advertised comparative bidding—a topic which in recent years has given rise to anxiety in Congress as well as in Parliament. Both these studies were made in pursuance of an Act of Congress. In making his own choice of initiatives the Comptroller General aims to help congressional committees in their inquiries into current and future, as well as retrospective, expenditure. In 1969, for instance, he informed the Senate's Appropriations Committee of his plans to monitor the development and production of weapons systems. He stated his intention as being

> to provide information useful to Congress where decisions still have to be made with respect to new authorization or new funding—not only to provide information with respect to costs, performances and schedules, but also to indicate problem areas and questions which we believe the Committees might wish to develop in the course of hearings with the Department of Defense.[1]

This kind of help is not confined to the Defense Committees. It has gradually been extended to all committees considering new programmes and expenditures.[2]

By contrast in Britain the direct link between the House of Commons and the Comptroller and Auditor General is the Public Accounts Committee, and that Committee alone. Efforts to make available to the Estimates Committee the expert assistance of the Comptroller and Auditor General have been resisted by (among others) successive occupants of the post on the ground that it would be inconsistent with the Comptroller and Auditor General's statutory function for him to comment, for example, on the estimates, embodying as they do proposals for future expenditure. Offers of expert help to other actual or prospective committees[3] whose work was not inconsistent with that function have, however, been made by the Comptroller, though it is

1. Statement of the U.S. Comptroller General before the Legislative Subcommittee, Senate Appropriations Committee on his Budget Estimates for fixed year 1971, pp. 12–13.

2. Statement of the U.S. Comptroller General before the Subcommittee on Executive Reorganization, Senate Committee on Government Operations on the role of the General Accounting Office in reviewing the results of general programmes, p. 13.

3. H.C. 276 of 1958–59, Q. 55 for the Select Committee on Nationalized Industries; and H.C. 410 of 1968–69, pp. 121, 130 for a possible select committee to examine the methods for collecting facts and figures on which government decisions and proposals are based.

unlikely that an individual member of Parliament would expect him to make formal inquiries or reports on his behalf.

Other differences flow from this basic contrast in the relationship of the two Comptrollers with their parent assemblies. The British Comptroller rarely makes recommendations in his reports to Parliament: they are essentially factual. But the Public Accounts Committee, the sole committee with which he is linked, does usually make recommendations to the House of Commons. By contrast the U.S. Comptroller himself makes recommendations to Congress. These are often embodied in the special reports on inquiries requested by a congressional committee or an individual congressman. Again, the U.S. Comptroller has by law to make an annual report to Congress on the activities of the General Accounting Office. The British Comptroller is under no such obligation. He reports in practice on those matters which he thinks can usefully be examined by the Public Accounts Committee. The remainder—usually a high percentage of the total —are matters which have been satisfactorily settled. The U.S. Comptroller's reports are much more voluminous and, arguably, an example of the more open style of official activity and attitude in the United States than in Britain.

The operations of the U.S. Comptroller and General Accounting Office in relation to Congress came under close examination inside and outside Congress before and during the inquiry made by the Joint Committee on the Organization of Congress 1965–1966; and comparisons were struck with the corresponding structure in Britain. The British could take encouragement from Professor Joseph Harris's authoritative study *Congressional Control of Administration* (1964), which praised the British system for providing

> one of the most notable examples of effective legislative control of administration without encroaching upon the executive function or weakening executive authority.

and reached the conclusion that the Congressional system did so encroach.[1] Whether the executive in the United States is weakened by the encroachment of the General Accounting Office must be a matter of opinion. There is certainly less sign of weakening

1. pp. 153, 159–60.

today than in 1964 when Professor Harris wrote his book. In any case 'encroachment' should not be confused with conflict. As Professor Harris himself points out, the U.S. Constitution by dividing power between the executive and legislative branches predisposes them to conflict and tension in a manner avoided in the unified British system. In that context Congress has reserved to itself the final authority to interpret its own intentions as to the expenditure of appropriated funds. The Comptroller General, as head of the General Accounting Office, is its strong right arm in carrying out this function, and he is naturally seen as a powerful ally in its efforts to control the executive power. Attempts to abridge the U.S. Comptroller's powers have foundered on this rock in the past and look like doing so in the future. The Legislative Reorganization Act of 1970 does not limit his powers: it extends them. It is to the General Accounting Office that Congress is looking for further help in reviewing and analysing the results of government programmes and activities.

CONTROL OF TAXATION

The levying of taxes is the most delicate of all acts in the relationship between government and people. In both countries, as has been shown, the powers of Parliament and Congress are rooted in major and bloody conflicts arising from the claims of government to impose taxes. It is not surprising that the processes of control and scrutiny followed in the two countries should resemble each other more closely here than in the field of expenditure.

Nevertheless there are significant differences, and the first is found at the start of the two processes. In Britain the Chancellor of the Exchequer's Budget statement is generally made to the House on the first or second Tuesday after the end of the financial year (31 March). It is an occasion of high drama, excitement and news-value. The Chancellor's measures are likely to touch the pocket of every single person in the country. They have been closely guarded secrets until the statement begins (two Chancellors who were found to have fallen short of this requirement resigned immediately). Most of them come into effect as soon as the Chancellor ends his speech; some of them may later be modified in detail, but the broad pattern of what the Chancellor proposes is likely to stand. In the United States the President usually sends major taxation proposals to the House of Representatives as part of his proposed Budget at the beginning of the biennial Congress. Further taxation proposals are sent to the House as and when the economic situation of the country makes it desirable, in the President's view, to enact them. For instance the opening of the second year (session) of a Congress, when fresh proposals for expenditure are submitted to the House, is a probable, though not an invariable occasion for the submission of new taxation proposals. So the pattern of presentation to Congress is different from that in Britain. Again, when the President sends taxation proposals to Congress, there is a lively interest but not much mystery or drama. It is true that on matters that would directly affect the market-place attempts are made, both by the Treasury Department before a proposal is sent to Congress and by the committees of both Houses when examining the proposals, to handle them sensitively. In general, however, the receipt of taxation proposals from the President is the signal for Congress to begin a long and searching examination which will effectively decide whether the President's proposals are to stand or fall. The differences of atmosphere and tempo reflects the constitutional division of power and function in each country.

In Parliament

For all its drama, the annual taxation exercise in Britain is a limited affair. As a background to his proposals the Chancellor surveys the out-turn of expenditure and revenue in the financial year just completed. The government's estimates of expenditure for the year just beginning have already been laid. The Chancellor's statement sets those estimates and any other proposed expenditure against his proposals for raising revenue, in order to strike the required balance. But only a small part of the existing taxation structure may need changing in any one year. Most taxes are permanent, having been imposed by finance or other bills of previous years. Only the income tax and corporation tax have to be reimposed annually. Otherwise the Chancellor's proposals are confined to the imposition of new taxes, the continuance of an expiring tax or the raising or lowering of a permanent tax.

The government also have the power to vary taxes on occasions other than the annual budgetary exercise. The first significant delegation of taxation power was the Import Duties Act 1932 allowing for control by the Executive of tariff rates.[1] In 1948 the Finance Act gave the Treasury power to vary the classification of goods subject to purchase tax and to apply any statutory rate of tax to goods in whatever class. The Finance Act 1961 saw the introduction of 'the regulator' allowing a variation up or down to ten per cent on any rate of purchase tax and other taxes, thus giving the Chancellor an additional weapon for dealing urgently with inflationary or deflationary tendencies. In all these instances orders have to be laid before the House allowing an opportunity of a debate expressing approval (or disapproval). Finally any government bill *may* impose a tax as part of its implementation of government policy on, for example, customs or excise duties. In that event a 'ways and means' resolution has to be passed by the Commons, just as a 'money resolution' (see p. 269) is required where a bill entails expenditure.

Nevertheless it is on budget day that the main changes in taxation are announced. The Chancellor's proposals are first laid before the House[2] in the form of resolutions—usually twenty to thirty of them—embodying those changes, together with supporting documentation. As soon as he sits down, the House passes a general resolution giving provisional statutory effect to his proposals. The consequential collection of taxes is thus immediately authorized in order to prevent untoward damage to the revenue— provided that certain conditions[3] affecting the Finance Bill are later fulfilled (see below).

Once provisional statutory authority has been given, the House proceeds to debate the budget resolutions. This it does for four or five days, founding its debate on a general motion 'that it is expedient to amend the law' with respect to 'the National Debt and the public revenue . . .' The debate extends not only to the Chancellor's resolutions but to the whole of the existing taxation structure, canvassing its adequacy to cover the estimated expenditure and to regulate the economy. At the end of the debate the general motion and all the other resolutions are successively

1. Gordon Reid, op. cit., p. 128.
2. Until 1968 the Chancellor's statement was made, and the accompanying resolutions first considered, in the Committee of Ways and Means.
3. These conditions are laid down by the Provisional Collection of Taxes Act 1968, which brought together a number of earlier Acts.

put to the vote, affording any member or section of the House the first opportunity of registering objection to specific taxation proposals in the budget. When the resolutions have been agreed to, the Finance Bill is immediately introduced formally. It is not, however, published until a fortnight later so that account can be taken—and has been taken[1]—in drafting the bill of what has been said in the debate.

The government's chief taxing proposals for the year were first brought together into a single bill by Gladstone in 1861, following the rejection by the House of Lords of the Paper Duty Repeal Bill, a taxation proposal in a separate bill (see also p. 181). Since 1894 this omnibus measure has been known as the Finance Bill. Besides imposing and altering taxes it usually includes provisions of a more permanent character designed to regulate the machinery of taxation and kindred purposes. According to Erskine May,[2] it is regarded as exceeding its proper scope if it imposes a tax for which payment is not to be demanded until after the close of the current financial year.

The Finance Bill goes through the same stages as any other bill (see Chapter VI)—first and second readings, committee, report and third reading, the only difference being that, in order to prevent the House being rushed into ill-considered proposals, each stage has by practice to be taken on a different day. First reading is, as usual, formal. The second reading is used for a wide debate, analogous to that on the resolutions themselves, lasting for one full day. To fulfil the first condition laid down by the Provisional Collection of Taxes Act the bill must be read a second time within twenty-five sitting days of the resolutions being agreed to. The committee stage is the most characteristic and important feature of the legislative process on the finance bill. The wide and increasing public interest is reflected in the number of members who take part and in the sympathetic attitude of the Treasury ministers to some amendments. Representations from interested businesses and organizations as well as constituents are channelled through members on both sides of the House, and ministers, consistent with maintaining the integrity of the budget, often make immediate concessions to pressure or promises of

1. Second Special Report of the Procedure Committee, House of Commons Paper 302 of 1969–70, pp. 119–20 and 131–3.

2. 18th ed. (1971), p. 824.

adjustment in next year's budget. The report stage provides an opportunity for ministers to redeem undertakings given in committee to reconsider amendments, and the third reading debate, though confined to the content of the bill as it has emerged so far, provides an opportunity for a backward look at the achievement it represents. In the House of Lords, which does not amend Finance Bills (see pp. 181–2), the bill passes formally through the usual stages and then is given the Royal Assent. The second condition laid down by the Provisional Collection of Taxes Act is that if the resolutions on which the bill is founded were agreed to in March or April (the usual case), the bill must receive the Royal Assent by not later than 5 August; if they are agreed to at any other time of the year, within four calendar months.

Until 1968 all stages of the Finance Bill in the Commons were taken on the floor of the House: its committee stage was taken in a Committee of the whole House. In the years following the war the amount of time needed to dispose of the committee stage has tended to rise. In the period 1946 to 1950 it was four to five days on average; from 1951 to 1967, except 1965, it was eight to nine days. 1965 was an exceptional year when the bill included provision for an increased capital gains tax and a new corporation tax. The committee stage of that bill took sixteen days. It was clear that the House would gain much time for other business if the committee stage were taken elsewhere than in a Committee of the whole House. This was the chief reason for the proposal made from time to time in the 1950s and 1960s to send the Finance Bill to a Standing Committee. It was a highly controversial proposal since it would restrict the opportunities of members at committee stage to modify the provisions of the Finance Bill. In the circumstances of 1968, when such a committal was attempted for the first time with a finance bill raising an all-time high of £923 million in new taxes, the proposal proved explosive. In 1969 a compromise solution was tried: six clauses dealing with taxes of the widest application—such as income tax, purchase tax and selective employment tax—were taken on the floor, and the rest sent to a standing committee. Four days were spent in Committee of the whole House; eight sittings of varying length were held in a standing committee. This arrangement was found more generally acceptable. In 1970 it was proposed to divide the bill on similar lines but, because a general election was called, the whole of the bill was taken on the floor and disposed of rapidly. The arrangements made in 1969 were generally followed in 1971 and are likely to be a model for the committee stages of future finance bills.

How far can members of the House cause alterations to be made in the Chancellor's proposals? From the start of the committee stage of the Finance Bill they face two important restrictions. The first is set by the nature of the budget resolutions on which the Finance Bill is founded. The general resolution ('That it is expedient to amend the law . . .') enables a member to move an amendment (or new clause) to reduce or to repeal, but not to increase, *any* tax, even if there is no reference to it in the Bill, unless specifically excluded by a proviso to the general resolution. In some years, for instance, amendments to alter the incidence of purchase tax have been excluded in this way. To the clauses in the Bill founded on the other resolutions making specific changes in taxation, a member may move an amendment to reduce or repeal the tax; but he can only move to increase it if the founding resolution is drawn so widely as to permit an increase. If his amendment offends against this rule, it will be ruled inadmissible by the presiding officer. This restriction applies to the ministers in charge of the bill as well as to members seeking to amend it, though if a minister wishes to introduce a new provision into the bill, it is open to him to bring a new budget resolution before the House. The second restriction is the power of selecting amendments (see p. 140) as exercised by the presiding officer. Selection, as has been shown, may mean total elimination of some amendments, but more often means the grouping of related amendments for purposes of discussion.

Two examples taken from the proceedings on the Finance Bill 1969 illustrate the kind of amendments that can be successfully pressed on the government. The first group were directed to a highly controversial clause which ended the allowance of interest on loans or overdrafts as a deductible expense. Only two exceptions to this general rule were to be allowed under the bill as introduced: where the loan was for the purchase and improvement of property, and where it qualified as a business expense. But as a result of debate in committee, the category of exceptions in the bill was amended to extend, with some qualifications, to loans for buying partnerships and to money borrowed to acquire part of the ordinary share capital of a close company. In addition, it was agreed that the interest on existing loans should rank as a deductible expense until 1975. The second example related to the tax imposed on gaming machines. Representations were made by members in debate that if the rates of tax laid down in the bill were maintained, the owners and operators of gaming machines would go out of business. In that event the government would lose the fruits not only of that tax but also of other taxes such as selective employment tax, purchase tax and corporation tax for which the same people were liable. This case was accepted, and the rates of tax moderated. There were other concessions in 1969, and examples can be found in the committee stage of other Finance Bills. The movers of amendments can rarely hope to throw out a tax proposed by the Chancellor neck and crop, but they can often do something to mitigate the severity of its incidence.

In Congress

In the House of Representatives the basic oversight of revenue rests with the Committee on Ways and Means. Its responsibilities for revenue extend to such related matters as customs, reciprocal trade agreements and the transport of dutiable goods. It is also concerned with the system of social security, the national debt of the United States and the security of public moneys. It is to this Committee that the Speaker of the House refers the President's budget, or rather those parts of it that relate to revenue. Sometimes the presidential message will be accompanied by the draft of a bill. This too is referred to the Committee.

The range of its jurisdiction and influence makes the Committee on Ways and Means one of the two most important committees of the House (the other being Appropriations). In 1971 its chairman had been in post since 1958, and its members were mainly of considerable seniority. The few younger members were drawn from safer seats so that their membership is likely to be prolonged. There is keen competition to belong. While all members of the Committee are in a position to bring significant influence to bear on behalf of fellow members, the Democratic members are especially influential because in another incarnation they comprise the party's committee on committees which designates members for all House standing committees. Moreover each

Democratic member of the Committee has been elected by the caucus of all the Democrats in the House.

As with the Appropriations Committee, hearings are the core of the Committee's proceedings. Ever since the Boston tea party the belief has been deeply entrenched that citizens should have the right to comment directly to their elected representatives on proposals to tax them. When the President's proposals have been received, the Committee accordingly makes a public announcement, usually giving at least two weeks' notice of its intention to begin hearings and inviting anyone to testify who wishes to do so. The first witness is almost invariably the Secretary to the Treasury, who introduces the President's proposals. He is accompanied by high officials from the Treasury and the Office of Management and Budget, and together they are examined at length by the Committee. Then it is the public's turn. The response to the Committee's invitation is usually heavy, often running into some thousands of applications from individuals and organizations. It is the duty of the Committee's staff to consolidate these applications into a manageable schedule. For example, pressure groups on the same or related subjects are usually heard together, though if there are major divisions of opinion, separate appearances are arranged. Even with this kind of grouping the schedule of hearings is heavy. The Committee sits from 10 to 12.30 in the morning and 2 to 5 in the afternoon, sometimes carrying on till 9 in the evening, on five days a week for four or five weeks. All these hearings are in public. Executive or private sessions for deliberations follow, and may continue for three or four months.

The end product is a revenue bill. Here the Committee is helped not only by the long experience of most of its members but also by a team of draftsmen from the Legislative Counsel's Office, experts from the departments and the Committee's own experienced staff. The form of the bill will owe much to the testimony given to the Committee. It is at this point, too, that the views of other congressmen are taken into account by the Committee. The responsiveness of the Committee to individual requests from congressmen will vitally affect the progress of the bill at later stages. The need to find common ground before the bill reaches the floor is one reason why the Committee on Ways and Means does not break itself down into subcommittees: if twenty-five members hear the evidence and then discuss and resolve their differences in full committee, there is a good chance that their agreement will be reproduced on the floor.

Reports of the Committee on Ways and Means on bills raising revenue (which is broadly construed to cover all bills relating to revenue) are accorded priority, in the same way as reports of the Committee on Appropriations.[1] The member in charge, in this instance the chairman of the Committee, can bring such a bill forward at any time. He is generally able to ensure that a revenue bill is considered on the floor under a rule which normally protects it from amendments; this is a fair indication of the Committee's ability to keep its proposals in line with opinion in the House as a whole. There is an opportunity for a motion to recommit the bill to the Committee on Ways and Means; otherwise the question is whether or not it shall pass.

Under the Constitution all bills raising revenue must originate in the House of Representatives. But the Constitution specifies that the Senate 'may propose or concur with amendments as on other bills'.[2] The proceedings in the Senate are thus broadly similar in both Houses, subject to the important difference, deriving from the Constitution, that the Finance Committee—the Senate's counterpart of the Committee on Ways and Means—begins work with a specific measure in the form of a bill, as received from the House, in front of it. The Committee holds hearings and executive sessions to 'mark up' the bill. A second difference is on the report of the bill to the Senate. There is no 'rule' as in the House: amendments are freely offered, and accepted or rejected. If the bill is amended, a conference of senior members of the Finance Committee and of the Ways and Means Committee is held, and when its conclusions have been approved by both Houses, it is sent to the President for signature.

How far do the two Houses of Congress alter the President's proposals for taxation? The story of President Johnson's surcharge of ten per cent on all income is instructive both as to the power of Congress as a whole and of its two component parts. The message requesting the surcharge as an emergency remedy for inflationary pressures in the economy reached Congress on 3 August 1967. It was referred to the House's Ways and Means Committee where it was strongly opposed by the chairman who

1. House Rule XI, 21.　　　2. Constitution I, 7.

questioned whether the surcharge would remedy inflation and demanded large cuts in expenditure as the price for agreeing to it. The Administration was equally strongly opposed to cuts. Accordingly the surcharge proposal stayed in the Committee on Ways and Means in 1967. In his message of January 1968 the President again called for the enactment of the surcharge, at the same time submitting a budget for 1968–69 including a rise in expenditure of $10·4 billion. Not surprisingly, no more progress was made in the Ways and Means Committee. On 2 April 1968, however, the Senate took the opportunity presented by a simple House revenue bill extending car and telephone excise duties to tack on the ten per cent surcharge on incomes, as well as a provision reducing the President's proposed expenditure for 1968–1969 by $6 billion. The chairman of the Ways and Means Committee was thus obliged to face the issue of the surcharge, though in conference with the Senate rather than in his own Committee. The conference lasted several weeks. It finally agreed to a ten per cent surcharge on income, retrospective to 1 April 1968 for individuals and 1 January 1968 for corporations; the tax was to expire on 1 July 1969. It also agreed (among other things) to a cut of $10 billion in the President's proposed expenditure for 1968–69, and a cut of nearly a quarter of a million in the number of civilian employees in the executive branch. On 20 June 1968 the House accepted the conference report, though not without much debate on whether the Senate's action in virtually initiating a tax was constitutional. On the following day the Senate accepted the report. Congress had thus taken more than ten months to enact an urgent request from the administration and had exacted a stiff price for meeting that request. The administration objected to Congress's exactions, but it was obliged to accept them.

GENERAL CONTRASTS

Expenditure

This survey of financial procedure in Parliament and Congress has thrown up several contrasts. First their approach to the control of supply and appropriation are wholly different. In the House of Commons members are powerless to propose higher expenditure (except on the initiative of ministers); and they rarely move to reduce either the total expenditure for the year or the vote for a particular department. As Ronald Butt has pointed out, this abstention reflects political realities:

> . . . for government backbenchers, who approve their leaders' policies, the consequent expenditure is no stumbling block. For the opposition, there is every incentive not to concentrate their attack on detailed spending decisions which they cannot hope to reverse but instead to use the time available to them to gain public attention for attacks on particular areas of government activity.[1]

A desire to spend on the right policies rather than to retrench, coupled with the opposition-government confrontation on the floor of the House, account for the nature of British supply procedure today.

By contrast, Congress appropriates a much larger sum of money than Parliament; in 1969 it was between six and seven times larger. Yet despite the constant pressure on congressmen for projects to advantage their state or locality, they have displayed a stronger impulse towards economy than their opposite numbers in Parliament. Instead of an opposition-government confrontation on the floor, there has been a bipartisan approach in Congress, and especially in the financial committees, to the programme of public expenditure sent over from the executive branch. The detailed scrutiny conducted by the Appropriations Committees of the two Houses and the resulting control exercised over the spending departments follows logically from the constitutional arrangements of the United States; just as the absence of detailed scrutiny (except so far as conducted by the Expenditure, and formerly the Estimates, Committee) reflects the logic of political realities in the House of Commons.

Taxation

In the field of taxation the resemblance is closer. In the House of Commons there is a genuine thrashing out of the detailed taxes proposed by the government. It is true that no proposals to raise taxes or to vary their incidence are in order. Moreover, in Britain the taxpayer, whether individual or corporate, has to make

1. Ronald Butt, *The Power of Parliament* (1967), p. 362.

representations through a member of Parliament. He has no opportunity as in Congress to represent his grievances directly to the appropriate committee, though he can make representations directly to the Treasury. Given these limitations, the British member can still make the incidence of a tax less oppressive, though he can rarely hope, as can his opposite number in Washington, to get rid altogether of an objectionable tax.

The most revealing difference lies in the amount of time and effort spent in Parliament and Congress on questions of taxation. The British Finance Bill is usually disposed of in May and June. During the 1960s in those months two days on average have been spent on second and third readings, two or three on the report stage and from ten to sixteen in committees. By contrast, the House of Representatives' Committee on Ways and Means generally spends at least a full month on hearings followed by several more months in executive session, producing a revenue bill. A similar if shorter process is followed by the Senate's Finance Committee. All this attention is devoted to the major proposals of the President. But there is in addition the non-legislative or 'study' Joint Committee on Internal Revenue Taxation consisting of ten members drawn from the Ways and Means and Finance Committees of the House and the Senate. This Joint Committee makes studies of the working and effects of the federal system of internal revenue taxation. It reports to the Ways and Means or the Finance Committees of the parent Houses. This two-pronged consideration—addressed both to the immediate and to the continuing aspects of taxation—points to a way forward for those convinced of the inadequacies of proceedings on tax matters in the House of Commons. A recent critic of those proceedings has been the Financial Secretary to the Treasury on the third reading of the Finance Bill 1969. 'We feel the need increasingly' he said 'as legislation on Finance Bills gets more and more complex, to seek a means for protracted study . . . where nothing secret is involved, in advance of more formal decision'.[1] This is one among many voices lately pressing the need for more deliberate and thorough discussion of complex taxation. If a select committee were appointed to hear expert evidence from professional witnesses inside and outside the government, and to report from year to year, it would go far

1. House of Commons Debates, 18 July 1969, c. 1165.

to remove the need for hours of debate on difficult and complex taxes, because the technical problems would have been thoroughly considered in advance.[1]

Budget as a Whole

A major defect in the financial procedure of both Parliament and Congress has been the lack of adequate consideration of the budget as a whole, that is, an assessment of the proper level and direction of expenditure in the light of available resources. In Parliament, since supply days are used for attacks on specific aspects of government policy, there have not until recently been regular debates on public expenditure as a whole; and the budget debates, though theoretically directed to the proper balance of expenditure and revenue, in practice concentrate on the Chancellor's revenue proposals. In Congress expenditure is considered by one set of committees and subcommittees, revenue by another. Once the official package of expenditure and revenue has left the President and the Office of Management and Budget, no further consideration is given to the finance of government as a whole. The package is undone deliberately, but is at no point done up again.

Here the failure of Congress's Joint Committee on the Budget must be noted. Under the Legislative Reorganization Act of 1946 this Committee—made up of all the members of the four committees of Congress dealing with expenditure and revenue, a total of over 100—was required to meet at the beginning of each session to examine the President's budget. It then had to report within six weeks, laying down one maximum figure for total federal expenditure and another for total revenue. The Joint Committee attempted this task for three years after the passing of the Act. But the two Houses were unable to reach agreement on the reports, and it was eventually thought to be impracticable to fix 'ceilings' for expenditure and revenue before the ordinary processes of hearings had been carried out. Although the statutory obligation remains, the Joint Committee no longer meets.

1. A first step in this direction was taken on 10 May 1971 when the House of Commons appointed a select committee to consider proposals put forward by the government to reform the corporation tax.

Moves have lately been made in both countries to cure this defect. In Britain a Commons committee considering the scrutiny of public expenditure in 1969 welcomed the stated intention of the government to publish annually a white paper in which estimates of capital and current expenditure over the next five years would be set out. This paper, said the committee, should provide the basis for a two-day debate, at the start of the sessional cycle of financial business, on the totality of public expenditure.[1] The government and the House of Commons followed the committee's advice. The first white paper in this series was published in December 1969,[2] and a two-day debate was held for the first time in January 1970. This sequence was repeated in October and November 1970. In Congress since 1958 the Secretary of the Treasury and the Director of the Office of Management and Budget and other officials have given evidence to the Appropriations Committee of the House of Representatives and the Senate for one day early in each session on the broad object and strategy of the President's annual budget and the assumptions on which it was based.[3] This procedure was endorsed by the Joint Committee which in 1965–66 considered the organization of Congress, and there is like provision in the Legislative Reorganization Act of 1970. In both countries, too, more attention is being given to new techniques for identifying the real, as distinct from the budgeted, cost of a project of public expenditure. In this field, in which the British Parliament has consciously sought to draw upon the experience of Congress,[4] the provision of data on real costs, if taken into account in the process of making decisions, may lead to a more rational allocation of resources.

1. Report from the Select Committee on Procedure, House of Commons Paper 410 of 1969, paras. 13 and 25.
2. Command Paper 4234.
3. Report No. 1414, dated 28 July 1966, p. 31.
4. See Report from the Select Committee on Procedure, House of Commons Paper 410 of 1969, para 2.

CHAPTER EIGHT

SCRUTINY AND CONTROL
OF THE EXECUTIVE

THE comparison between Parliament and Congress in previous chapters has shown that over large areas of their activities they do not exist to do the same job. The point needs to be made again here. The relationship between government and legislature is so different that oversight of the one by the other has different purposes in each country and takes different forms. The British constitutional system is designed to ensure that government and Parliament are working along the same lines; in the United States, the Constitution operates so that President and Congress can usefully coexist without accord between them. In the United Kingdom ministers are responsible (in broad terms) to Parliament for what happens in their departments; 'oversight' is designed to keep Parliament informed of what ministers are doing, and to allow scope for considering whether ministers should be supported or not. Ministers need to retain the confidence of Parliament, and the oversight enables Parliament to judge whether ministers are worthy of it. In the United States no issue of confidence arises at all (except in so far as Congress may impeach the President or officials). If a President loses the confidence of Congress, there is no question of his resignation from office. The oversight, while it stems from the need to carry out the duties which the Constitution imposes on Congress, has become an expression of the rivalry between two powerful bodies —each of whom is immovable until the next elections.

Furthermore in Britain the oversight is almost exclusively by one House of Parliament, the Commons. The Lords exercise little sanction over the government; a defeat there may be tiresome for ministers, and on occasion important, but no question of the government's resignation arises in consequence. In the United States, on the other hand, the committees of *both* Houses of Congress are engaged in 'constant watchfulness' of the executive. It follows that this chapter will be concerned with scrutiny exerted by the Senate, the House of Representatives and the House of Commons, but only incidentally by the House of Lords.

Within the House of Commons the extent of parliamentary control is limited in practical terms by a number of factors already described in this book. There is first the government's primacy in the field of legislation. Secondly there is the fact that only the government can take any financial initiative; members cannot propose new expenditure or taxation unless the government sanctions it, and they cannot increase expenditure or taxation beyond the limits which the government lays down. Thirdly the government controls the bulk of the time of the Commons. These factors constrain the House in its oversight of the government in a manner that has no parallel in Congress.

Another difference stems from the different character of the cabinet and of the public service in the two countries. Cabinet ministers in Britain are themselves members of Parliament and are in constant contact with other members. They have (with rare exceptions) been backbenchers and, in the normal course of events, will probably become backbenchers again. They are imbued with a sense of Parliament's importance, and are aware that their retention of office depends to some extent on the support, or at least the tolerance, of a majority of the House. In the United States the members of the cabinet have to work hard to establish their own links with Congress and exert as much influence there as they can, and the fact that they may not have had personal experience of the place puts them at a disadvantage. Congressmen know that the President's colleagues do not carry in their own right as much weight as, for example, cabinet ministers in the United Kingdom; their only sanction is the influence they can bring to bear on the President in the use of his powers. An American minister may have outstanding talents, but he is much less likely than his British counterpart to have a personal party following which could rival that of the President. The formal standing of the cabinet in the United States is less high than in Britain; the President may convene them only infrequently, and may not share his major decisions with them.

The creation of new ministries and departments of state in the United Kingdom is for practical purposes an executive act. Ministers may have statutory duties, and there is a statutory limit to the number of ministers in the Commons, but the existence and functions of departments at any given time is by the will of the Prime Minister and his cabinet. Things are different in the United States where the departments and agencies have themselves been created by legislation passed by Congress, who may at any time pass new legislation extending or confining their activities, creating or winding-up rival bodies. Such legislation may at the one time limit the control which the President can exercise over the bodies concerned, while retaining Congress's own control; in particular the Independent Regulatory Commissions, whose members are appointed for lengths of service that outlast a presidency (and in some cases, several presidencies), can act with considerable independence of the executive, but need to come regularly to Congress for funds. It is because of this financial control that all departments, agencies and the like are encouraged to establish their own individual rapport with Congress. The resulting relationship may be closer than, and it may even derogate from, the relationship between them and the President. For the President, who has not only the duties of a prime minister of the most powerful country in the world but also those of the head of state of one of the largest, is unlikely to be able to keep in close touch with the problems of an individual department. The distance between them is increased by the fact that each President surrounds himself with a large staff, appointed on a personal basis by himself. The Executive Office of the President may contain some 2,000 people, of whom 400 may work as the President's closest personal advisers in the White House office, and the others in the Office of Management and Budget and the Council of Economic Advisers. This presidential staff is not connected with departments, and tends to insulate them from the man in whom executive power is vested. This increases the natural tendency of departments to seek enhancement, or at least survival, by establishing close direct links with Congress or its committees. In so doing they may detract from, rather than sustain, the President's standing with Congress.[1]

1. Dean Griffith has postulated that the American bureaucracy has a life independent of, and possibly even opposed to, the Executive. He cites the case of the Engineer Corps of the Department of the Army, which deals direct with Congress, to the extent that its projects could not even be blocked by the disapproval of the Bureau of the Budget (as it was then called). *Congress: Its Contemporary Role* (1967), pp. 56–67.

For all these reasons the relationship between Parliament and officials in Britain is of a different kind from that which exists in the United States, where the executive and legislature are not integrated to nearly the same extent. The heads of departments do not, as in Britain, mix as colleagues with members of the legislature; nor are they, like them, dependent on the goodwill of the electorate. Although individual heads may establish close personal links with Congress (one House of which consented to their appointment), they remain part of a different—even an opposing—branch of government. Many of their senior civil servants are not neutral; they have been jobbed in by the party in power, may not expect to remain in office after the next election, and may have political ambitions of their own. Largely unknown to members of Congress, brought in specifically to pursue policies which many congressmen oppose, transient, without anyone necessarily ready to support and defend their actions in Congress, American public servants are wide open to attack. The American constitutional system leads congressmen to seek out the weaknesses in their rival body; on occasions in the past this has led some of them to be quick to raise suspicions of corruption or other shortcomings.

Against a background of these differences, both Congress and Parliament impose their will on the executive by similar means: legislative control, financial control, and control by means of a committee system. Each of these has been considered in earlier chapters. This chapter is more concerned with the machinery that exists for overseeing the executive's actions other than in those fields, though there is inevitably a certain overlapping. It will consider, first, the role of each legislature in extracting and publicizing information from the government. Then it turns to the various procedures which have been instituted by Parliament and Congress to facilitate their oversight, showing such resemblances as exist. There follows a study of the work done by each legislature in the field of foreign affairs, which serves to illustrate many of the general points made earlier.

THE FOUNT OF INFORMATION

One of the principal functions of a legislature is to inform the people about the activities of their government, and members of any parliament, if they are to carry out their duties satisfactorily, themselves need to be informed. It is thus common practice for legislation to include a requirement for government bodies and agencies to report to the legislature, at regular intervals, about their activities. Both Parliament and Congress in this way receive a constant stream of information which they duly publish.

In Congress early in each new session the President delivers to a joint session of both Houses 'information of the State of the Union', as the Constitution describes it; and within fifteen days of the start of each regular session, he submits his budget message, with its summary data and text, and the necessary supporting detail. If these are the best known of his reports, they are far from being unique; for he is by statute required to submit more than thirty reports, some annually and some at shorter intervals. In addition to these, there are the reports which Congress by statute requires from the heads of the executive departments and agencies, and the many others which its committees demand. As a result Congress receives each year several hundred reports from the executive. Each is referred to the standing committee having jurisdiction in that field, and many of them are made public. Parliament too by statute receives a steady stream of reports from many official bodies, and these can be ordered by the two Houses to be printed.[1] There is no direct equivalent of the State of the Union message, but each session begins with the Queen's Speech, which sets out the government's plans for the year ahead; and the debate which follows allows ministers to traverse the general state of the country if they so wish.

Besides the reports which Parliament has asked for are the many others which ministers make to Parliament, whether or not they have been so requested. The system of 'command' papers enables the government to publish the information they want to publish, or which they have agreed to publish as a result of requests made in Parliament. It enables them to announce new policies to Parliament and the nation. A new refinement of the system is the practice by which the government occasionally publish, as a command paper, a 'green paper' setting out the facts on which a future policy must be propounded. This is a device to stimulate public and parliamentary discussion of the

1. For a study of the use made by members of the information derived from this source, see Barker and Rush, *The Member of Parliament and his Information* (1970).

subject, in the light of which government policy will be decided. Command papers are issued at a rate of about 350 a year.

Reports made to Parliament or to Congress may not always be very informative. Bureaucrats, from whatever country, quickly learn how to say a lot without telling very much. But their skill in so doing is balanced by the capacity of legislators to look beyond the document formally before them and to inquire into matters which the reports do not mention. Whatever the content of the report, it provides a startpoint for the legislature's activities. Thus a congressional committee, charged with the duty of exercising 'continuous watchfulness' over the executive branch, can call the appropriate official before them and question him either in public or in closed session. Select committees of Parliament can do the same, and members can interrogate ministers about the reports they have laid. Thus every report, however meritorious or however anodyne, may bring congressional or parliamentary brains to bear on the workings of the executive; and the considerable number of such reports, together with the frequency and wide-ranging nature of some of them, result in a comprehensive and continuous review in both legislatures of what is going on within the administration.

While there are similarities between the arrangements made in both countries to obtain and publicize the information which the government holds, there are also major differences which stem from the different constitutional character of the two bodies. In Parliament, in contrast to Congress, with ministers and members working in the same building and sharing the same facilities, there are untold opportunities for informal contacts by which ministers may be influenced. The homogeneity of executive and legislature in Britain gives opportunities to backbenchers—more so on the government than the opposition side, but considerable on both— to make representations direct to ministers. It is impossible to quantify the effects of these largely social contacts, but they must be a considerable factor in ensuring that government policy is explained in full to members.

There are also other, more formal, opportunities open to members of Parliament to receive information from the government. For instance, after Question Hour in the House of Commons, it is possible for ministers, having given prior notice to the Speaker, to answer particular Questions at greater length than would be feasible in the Hour itself. If a minister wishes to make an important statement of government policy, he will often choose to do so by answering a Question (whether the Question had been put down for oral or written reply) at the end of Questions. The Question in other words gives him a useful peg on which to hang a statement to which he wants to attract publicity. Other statements that he needs to make can be made during the normal question-and-answer exchanges in Question Hour, or by the publication of an answer to a written Question in Hansard (perhaps with a hand-out to the press at the same time, drawing their attention to the answer and its implications).

After Question Hour it is also possible for ministers (again, having given prior notice to the Speaker, who will then alert members to the fact by means of a notice put up on a notice board) to make a statement, without the need of a Question or anything to prompt him to do so. The procedure is that after Questions (including private notice Questions—see below) have been concluded, the minister is called on by the Speaker, he makes his statement, and then answers questions from members who rise and are called on by the Speaker. A spokesman from the opposition front bench will probably ask the first question, or will in effect make a counter-statement of opposition policy. The exchanges may go on perhaps for as much as half an hour, and often offend procedural purists (as parliamentary Questions did a century or so ago) because there is no motion before the House on which members can if necessary vote.

The continued existence of this process (by which ministers make statements to the House on perhaps an average of four occasions a week) in apparent defiance of procedural propriety shows that it is useful and valuable for members. It helps to make 3.30 p.m. a peak parliamentary hour, when matters of the greatest importance are canvassed, perhaps in both Houses simultaneously, and when the people (through their representatives) can publicly react to the news. Parliament is at that moment showing itself as the heart and head of the country.

The practice has significance because it shows that Parliament has a role, different from that of Congress, as the information centre of the country. Ministers recognize that if they want to announce some new policy or news of any importance they must do so in the first instance to Parliament; and they go to great lengths to ensure that they do not offend against this principle. Even comparatively minor announcements of government action will first be made public in this way or by dint of answering a written Question which the minister himself will have 'inspired'. Sometimes the government will have needed to act without first making public profession of their intention to do so. Then the Minister concerned will make a statement in Parliament as soon as he can. Even if the facts are by then well known, he will reiterate them to members, and answer the criticism or questions which the action evokes.

There is no statute or resolution of Parliament to bind ministers on this point, but the tradition is firmly established that they should, at whatever inconvenience, unveil their proposals to Parliament in the first place. Ministers who offend in this matter find that Parliament is very jealous of its right to hear things before it reads them in the newspapers It is one of the principal expressions of Parliament's duty to oversee the workings of government.

QUESTIONS AND ADJOURNMENT DEBATES

Question Hour

The practice by which a government spokesman announces the future business of the House of Commons in answer to a question put to him by an opposition leader is of long standing; and by the end of the eighteenth century this process of question and answer was being applied to other matters of general interest. The spontaneous nature of these exchanges was curbed in 1835, when written notice was required of the Questions to be asked; and about 1850 the practice was regularized to the extent that Questions were given a definite place in the parliamentary timetable. Procedurally the process was a breach of the first principle of parliamentary debate—that there must at all times be a motion before the House on which a vote can if necessary be taken—and this often aroused the impatience of members. Nevertheless the practice prospered. Its steady expansion, up to the point at which some 24,000 Questions are now asked each session, indicates that members have found that it fills a parliamentary need.

For about an hour on Mondays to Thursdays members of the House of Commons ask Questions of ministers. Notice of each

Question must be given; so that, after its publication, a minister has time to prepare his answer. The Order Paper sets out the Questions for the day, and the Speaker calls the member in whose name the first Question stands. The minister concerned, or one of his junior ministers, rises and reads out his prepared reply. The Speaker then calls on the questioner who rises and asks a 'supplementary' Question—a Question arising out of the answer he has just been given. Although often predictable, no notice is given of the supplementary Questions to be asked and the minister has to answer these as best he can. Other members will be called on, generally from each side in turn, to ask further supplementaries which the minister answers. Generally the minister can expect to have two or three supplementary Questions arising out of each main answer; but if the matter is important, the Speaker may allow questioning to continue for some while before he calls on a member to ask the next Question on the order paper—which in turn leads on to its own inquisition.

Each Question Hour is in some measure what the Speaker makes of it. By deciding which Questions to hurry through, and which to linger over, he is in effect picking the ground on which the government is to be most heavily assailed. If the pace is too fast, and too many Questions are taken, ministers may escape the more probing supplementaries. If questions and answers can be kept short—as the Speaker constantly adjures —more Questions can be asked and more members can take part.

The ministers are questioned on a rota. Each sizeable department is allocated to a particular day of the week, together with perhaps two or three others. When at the top of the rota its minister will be questioned first and may well continue to be questioned throughout the whole of the time available; but in the following week he will be at the bottom of the rota and is unlikely to be questioned at all. In each successive week he rises one place, becoming progressively more liable to questioning until he is again fully exposed at the top of the list; after which he drops to the bottom. The result is for each minister a rhythm of mounting involvement in Question Hour.

There are two exceptions to this general picture. Some ministers in charge of smaller departments (such as the Attorney-General) are only required to answer at intervals of (perhaps) three weeks, and do so after a number of other Questions have been put. On the other hand the Prime Minister has to answer Questions every Tuesday and Thursday, from 3.15 p.m. to the end of the questioning period at about 3.35 p.m. This regular and frequent questioning of the Prime Minister is relatively novel, having been introduced in 1961. Before that time the Prime Minister's questions were set down at No. 45 (or, later, at No. 40) on the two days a week, and were frequently not reached at all; if reached, it was rare that they would take up more than five to ten minutes. This new arrangement has transformed Question Hour. Major issues can be canvassed more readily than the tight parliamentary programme would otherwise allow, and the Prime Minister has an excellent opportunity of dilating on all the political issues of the day.

At the end of Question Hour private notice Questions are asked and answered. These are Questions which are so urgent that the usual prescribed period of notice cannot apply. The judge of urgency is the Speaker, who has also to be satisfied that the Question relates to a matter of public importance.[1]

As a result only about two private notice Questions are on average asked and answered each week. The urgency and importance of such a Question, coupled with the fact that the minister will have had only a few hours' warning of it, often combine to make it something of a climax to the Question Hour.

Questions answered during Question Hour account for less than a quarter of the total number answered each year. The remainder receive a written reply (which is duly published in Hansard), either because the questioner has specifically requested such a reply, or because his Question came low in the list of those for oral answer and was not reached in the time available. A Question which gets a written answer obviously does not allow an opportunity for probing the minister's answer by means of supplementary questions. But on the other hand it evokes an answer quickly without taking up any time of the House, and members seeking information often resort to it by choice. Nearly half the Questions asked are designed for written rather than oral reply.

1. Questions to the Leader of the House about future business, including the weekly business question (see p. 28), are also allowed to be asked as private notice Questions.

A member may only ask two oral Questions a day, and must give a maximum of two weeks and a minimum of forty-eight hours' notice. He may in addition ask any number of Questions for written answer and can stipulate any day for a reply to them. A great number of rules circumscribe the content of all Questions whether oral or written. They are designed among other things to make each Question short, inquisitory, new and necessary (in the sense that its answer has not already been published). They may not offer or seek expressions of opinion, and they must be based on facts for whose accuracy the questioner has made himself responsible. They must fall directly within the formal competence of the minister, and they must not raise questions of policy too large to be satisfactorily dealt with in the compass of the Question Hour. These prohibitions were listed by Erskine May under twenty-nine general headings resembling, in the eyes of some members, Robert Browning's

> . . . *twenty nine distinct damnations,*
> *One sure, if another fails.*

The rules are applied by clerks in the Table Office. There is an appeal from their decision to the Speaker. Perhaps one Question in a thousand is subjected to appeal.

Although questions are so rigorously circumscribed there are no equivalent restrictions on the answers to them. This gives a minister a certain scope in deciding how to deal with each Question. He is likely to hold intensive briefing sessions with his civil servants in which every ramification of each Question is examined. He may then decide that a Question is actuated by a genuine desire for information or action, or by a wish to show up the shortcomings of a department, or by the hope of serving a party advantage; and he will frame his answer accordingly. He may try to evade a damaging admission, but will know that a well-phrased supplementary question may lead him to tell more than he would otherwise wish. Many a minister has been able to establish his reputation by means of his mastery of the House at Question Time. Nor is every Question potentially damaging. Many of them enable the minister to answer with good news and to publicize his successes. The minister will have friends in the House who, either 'inspired' by him or for their own motives, will ask him the Questions he wants to answer. The function of Question Hour as a scourge for a minister is well known; less well known is the other side of the coin, the fact that Question Hour can serve to create and sustain the right sort of image for him.

Enough has been said to indicate that Question Hour, and Questions in general, are far from being a simple dialogue between members and ministers. Each single Question has undertones which the public are unlikely to know of, and may be the culmination of a long campaign. The complicated rules governing each Question, and the brevity of the exchanges that result from it, require skill from the performer if he is to extract the best value from the exercise. Experienced members discover means of using Questions to their best advantage.

How effective are parliamentary Questions? Is Question Hour as valuable as its high reputation suggests? The purpose of a parliamentary Question, according to the definition in Erskine May, is to obtain information or press for action. If factual information is required, the tabling of a parliamentary Question is on the whole an effective way to proceed. Ministers may seek in their answers to put a gloss on the figures or facts asked for, but it is difficult for them to evade an answer to a specific Question. It is when the questioner asks in vague or general terms that the Minister can answer with equal imprecision. If a questioner tries to use a Question in order to give information rather than to seek it, then the result can be unproductive; and if he slants his request in a partisan way, he can expect a partisan answer. Within these limitations Question Hour can provide, quickly though briefly, an unceasing stream of up-to-date facts over the whole area of the government's competence. The value of Questions which press for action is less obvious. Frequently ministers will already have decided how they intend to act, and will not be moved from their entrenched position by a parliamentary Question; and since many Questions are asked as a last resort after a member has failed to persuade the minister by correspondence, the odds are against their succeeding. But in an area where the government has not as yet formulated a policy, it may be influenced. Indeed a steady stream of Questions in this sort of area may eventually force it to formulate a policy (in a way that may or may not be desirable to the questioner). It is by concentrating attention on problems in this area, and by keeping them constantly before the attention of ministers and the public, that members may eventually succeed in their pressure for governmental action.

Another way of evaluating the effectiveness of Questions is to consider their effect on the civil service. Here Questions can be something of a bugbear. The civil service is so large that much of the work done and decisions taken by individuals in it rarely come to the notice of Parliament. But Questions, directed at a random sample of their work, mean that every so often a functionary finds his activities being criticized in public. For example a member, irked by delay within a department in answering a letter of his, may put a question to the minister asking when a reply can be expected. By this means an answer is often quickly forthcoming, and the minister is made aware of the dilatoriness in his staff. The civil servant responsible in cases like this is unlikely to be criticized by name, but his minister—in whose name he acts—and his colleagues will know who he is and will take a view on the way he has been acting. Not every Question touches on administration, not all those that do will be critical, and not all the criticisms will be well-founded. But when these conditions are met, a civil servant's career prospects can be at risk. Many other Questions will combat aspects of departmental policy pressed on the minister by his advisers, who will be anxious to justify their advice.

Whatever the circumstances of the Question, there is not much time available for assembling the material for an answer and ensuring that the minister is briefed as fully on the matter as he wishes. Within government departments Questions are accordingly given a high priority. Other work has to be put aside in order to deal with them. They make an urgent and potentially hostile progress from desk to desk before the minister decides how strong his ground is in giving the answer that he would like to. Perhaps the simplest example of the effect which Questions have on the public service was cited by a correspondent to *The Times*. He records how in a corridor of the Ministry of Defence he once saw a General, with a parliamentary Question in his hand, *running*.

To the members who ask the Questions, things appear in a different light. They know the satisfaction they can give their constituents by raising local matters in a national context, whether or not this leads to a helpful answer. They know that Question Hour comes at a time and in a form well-suited for reporting in the newspapers, so that a brief intervention then may gain them more attention than a speech late at night. They appreciate their rights of requiring ministers to attend to matters which they designate, and they enjoy the opportunity of testing their strength against that of the minister on ground of their own choosing. This is the gladiatorial aspect of Question Hour. The fact that members continue to put down an average of about a hundred questions every day makes it clear that they find the system valuable.

To the House as a whole the system of Questions makes clear where a minister's first responsibility lies. In so many other items of parliamentary practice ministers can shield themselves from unwelcome opposition; but in Question time they have to answer as best they can a multitude of Questions from members seeking to discomfit them. This is as the House thinks it should be. It means that no minister can reach the top of the ladder without his abilities having been exposed again and again to the House. These are considerable benefits (as the House sees them), over and above the utility of the answers that are given; and there is another one. Question Hour introduces an element of the unexpected into parliamentary business. No one can be sure what a minister may not give away under pressure, or how much a member will make of the opportunity his Question allows him. Questions ensure that matters of the day are considered daily in the simplest terms; they allow early discussion of the matters which are on the nation's mind.

The benefits of Questions are not achieved without cost. There is first the literal cost: each Question for oral answer costs an average of £14 to answer, and each Question for written answer £10.[1] The total cost in a year is about £300,000. Furthermore this expenditure, and the considerable time and effort which the Commons devote to Questions, only bring benefit to a comparatively small proportion of members. For questioning is something of a minority pastime; statistics published in March 1970 show that a third of all questions were being asked by one in twenty-three back-benchers (33·5 per cent, by 4·3 per cent).[2] It is remarkable in the circumstances that the non-questioning members tolerate and sustain a system which gives so much to so few of

1. House of Commons Debates, 23 July 1970, cc. 753–4.
2. House of Commons Paper 198 of 1969–70, p. 56.

their colleagues. But they do tolerate it. They seem to appreciate the practice even when they do not want to avail themselves of it.

The Lords have a much more limited Question time than the Commons, partly because most heads of departments are in the Commons, and partly because the Lords do not have constituency problems to air. Questions may be put down for any sitting day, but a total of only four Questions a day are allowed. They are however pursued at rather greater length than each oral Question in the Commons.

Congress and Questions

The standing committees of Congress have the means of questioning members of the executive at any time about their activities. Some of them hold occasional question-and-answer sessions for the purpose, but most of their meetings are related to particular projects of inquiry and so do not constitute a regular, across-the-board interrogation of the executive. The process is not one-way, for the executive will often brief committee members about the facts of a situation or the reasons for a policy.

Proposals have on occasion been made, both inside and outside Congress, to introduce there something like the parliamentary Question Hour.[1] These are made despite the obvious difference between the two legislatures, that in Britain ministers are members of Parliament and can in some circumstances be removed as a result of action by Parliament, while in the United States members of the executive are excluded from Congress and cannot be removed by it (except through the unlikely use of the power of impeachment). But since Question Hour carries no *immediate* sanction, no *direct* consequence, it is sometimes thought to be suitable for use in countries where the executive is not accountable to Parliament; and for that reason it appears to offer 'an unusual degree of transferability to the American legislative scene'.[2]

Yet Question Hour would not be what it is if it were not backed, at however far a remove, by the sanction of a vote of censure. Congress has a sanction available in the cutting of a

1. For Senator Kefauver's proposal in 1944, see Galloway, *The Legislative Process in Congress* (1955), p. 444. For a discussion of the matter see Dean Acheson, *A Citizen Looks at Congress* (1957), pp. 77–81.

2. *Parliaments*, published for the Inter Parliamentary Union, 2nd ed. (1966), p. 294.

department's appropriation, and it would not be impossible to link a system of Questions to the financial procedure used in Congress. But it is unlikely that any change along these lines will be made—if only because so many administrative decisions are being taken, not by the executive alone, but by the executive at the behest of Congress or part of it. For a member of Congress to criticize administrative decisions would be, as likely as not, for him to be criticizing in some instances what a committee has asked for, what a congressman has contrived to arrange, what the Senate may have advised and consented to, or what a bill required. Congress is so much involved in administration that the normal purpose of Question time—to allow the legislature to query or attack decisions taken by a rival body—would not be appropriate.

It is possible that those who favour importing a Question Hour into Congress have been dazzled by the vitality it gives to a parliamentary day.[1] But viewed simply as a device for getting information from the executive, for influencing its decisions and for keeping officials on their toes, it does not carry the punch of an investigative committee on American lines.

In one respect however Question Hour is more effective than congressional procedures as an instrument for canvassing the actions of government. It allows members to cross swords regularly with the head of the executive; by contrast the President is not involved by congressional procedures in exchanges with members. Congress has to discharge its duty of overseeing the executive without being able to question its head. In Britain whatever may be the precise powers of the Prime Minister, whether they are presidential in kind or whether they derive from the cabinet as a whole, he is at the service of the House of Commons twice a week in Question Hour. On the historic occasion in February 1969 when the President in office visited the House of Commons and watched Question Hour, he said afterwards:

> It was an inspiring and compelling experience, one for which I am deeply grateful. And it was an experience in which I came away with a deep appreciation and respect for the ability of the British parliamentarian to stand up during the Question period and answer so effectively. I believe that your Question period is much more of an ordeal than our press conference.

1. *Congress: First Branch of Government*, by de Grazia and others (1966), p. 65.

The analogy with the press conference is apt,[1] because it can involve the President in the same sort of cut and thrust as take place in Questions. But the rules of the game, and the frequency with which it is played, are decided by the President; and for all its considerable utility, it is not a congressional occasion.

The Half-hour Adjournment Motion

A member of the Commons who is dissatisfied with the answer he has received to a parliamentary Question, or who wishes to discuss a matter for which the brisk exchanges of Question Hour are inappropriate, can seek to raise it 'on the adjournment'. In this context (there are other types of adjournment motion, one of which, the 'urgency' adjournment motion, is considered below), the adjournment motion is the half-hour debate which is initiated by a back-bencher and takes place at the end of every day's sitting. The motion before the House—'That this House do now adjourn'—is formal and allows any matters to be debated that fall within the responsibility of ministers. The right to raise a matter of one's own choice 'on the adjournment' is highly-prized, and is decided on four out of the five sitting days each week by a ballot held fortnightly; on the fifth day the adjournment is allotted by the Speaker to a member whose subject ought, in the Speaker's opinion, to have priority. Members successful in the ballot can raise any matter that falls within the current administrative grip of ministers; this would automatically exclude any request for new legislation (which would indicate a change in *policy*), but the rule on this point was relaxed by a standing order made in 1960, and the member may now make 'incidental reference' to the need for new laws.

The debate must conclude within half-an-hour (although if the business of the day should finish early, extra time is added to the fortunate member's entitlement of half-an-hour). Time taken up by interruptions such as points of order is time lost to the member concerned. As a result the debate is generally quiet and orderly; a typical adjournment motion sees a member debating with a minister, with perhaps only two or three other members present in the chamber. But the press will be in their gallery

1. The comparison is usefully made by Douglass Cater in *The Fourth Branch of Government* (1959), Chapter 8.

above, reporting a case which by its nature often hinges on the ill-treatment of a constituent at the hands of authority—in this case the government machine—and which may be of interest to newspaper readers.

Under these conditions the member sets out his case and the minister replies to it. Most adjournment motions comprise a direct and simple confrontation between the two, although there is occasionally opportunity for another member or two to interpose a few words before the minister replies. A clear-cut case can receive a clear-cut answer, and it is accordingly an ideal vehicle by which a member can raise an administrative grievance, can publicize it and can receive at least an explanation of the government's attitude and at best some concession. It provides an admirable examination, fuller than a Question and less easy to dodge, of a minister's handling of the matters in his charge.

Much the same sort of debate can develop in the House of Lords on an 'unstarred question' (see p. 196), though there is no fixed time-limit for these.

The 'Urgency' Adjournment Motion

Under Standing Order No. 9 members of the Commons have an opportunity of seeking to raise debates at very short notice on matters of urgent public importance. If the Speaker, who has an unlimited discretion in this matter, feels that the subject raised is of sufficient urgency and importance, he can allow it to be debated on the following day (or, if the urgency is very great, at a later hour on the same evening).

It is rare that the government welcomes a debate of this kind, taken as it must be while the government is still reacting to a situation and formulating plans to deal with it. Thus these debates are generally anti-government occasions. They do not take place very often, perhaps on four occasions in a session, but they can be damaging and are invariably inconvenient to a government.

The standing order was re-drafted in 1967. The old standing order had been so hedged around by rulings made by successive Speakers in their interpretation of it that it was hardly possible to invoke at all. The new standing order forbids the Speaker to give reasons for his decisions and removes the danger that its provisions may become ossified by precedent. But as the Speaker's decisions are no longer based on known precedents they cannot be as easily predicted. The change has lent more vitality to the House of Commons' business, which otherwise might become unduly rigid. The possible impact of the standing order is the unknown factor in every day's business, enabling the House to react swiftly to an emergency.

Special Orders and Analogous Procedures in Congress

In contrast to debates in Parliament the day's business in Congress is much more frequently interrupted by speeches in which members raise points which concern them individually. Under the one-minute procedure members of the House of Representatives can be given permission to speak for a minute. They draw attention to a matter and, when authorized, they can revise and extend their remarks for the written record. As a result the day's record contains a considerable number of observations on a variety of matters, which can range from a member's views on forthcoming legislation to an *apologia pro vita sua*. Such a speech can be geared to a campaign which a member is fighting with other weapons in the House. Add the judicious use of a press release, and the result might be to bring pressure to bear on the executive at the right time.

The House also grants, by unanimous consent, a 'special order' to members to speak for a certain time towards the end of a sitting. The period of time, which might typically be an hour or half-an-hour, enables him to raise any matter he wishes. He can yield to other members, enabling them to interrupt and argue with him, so that a debate can take place.

There are obvious similarities here to the half-hour adjournment debates in the Commons, and the obvious difference that there is no minister in Congress to reply to the debate. Another important practical difference is that in the House of Representatives, a failure to keep a quorum of 100 members can bring the debate to a precipitate end. In practice most members granted a special order do not use it to make speeches publicly in the House, but instead take advantage of their right to have their speeches written into the Congressional Record.

THE OMBUDSMAN
Influenced by experience gained from the work of the Ombudsman in Sweden and later in New Zealand, Parliament decided in a statute passed in 1967 to create a Parliamentary Commissioner for Administration to investigate the complaints of citizens of injustice resulting from maladministration by government departments. It is important to note that he was to be a *parliamentary* commissioner. It was a deliberate decision that he should not be part of the judiciary, or an independent tribunal. He was to act on cases passed to him by members of Parliament and he was to report to those members on the results of his investigations. In addition he was to report annually to Parliament on the performance of his functions, with the option of making other reports in respect of those functions as he thought fit.

The Commissioner is appointed by the Sovereign, acting on the advice of the Prime Minister, and continues in office until he is sixty-five or resigns at his own request, or is removed on a motion passed by each House of Parliament. His prime task is to investigate complaints of 'maladministration'. But his remit does not cover the whole of the public service. He cannot for instance concern himself with matters affecting the armed forces, police, hospitals, the local authorities and the nationalized industries; nor with matters for which a tribunal already exists or for which there is a remedy at law, unless he is satisfied that it was unreasonable to have resorted to the tribunal or the courts. These limitations have been criticized as being unduly restrictive of his office.

In the first thirty-three months of the existence of his office, the Commissioner received 2,950 complaints from 569 of the 630 members of Parliament. Of the 2,820 cases completed in that period he found that 1,733 were outside his jurisdiction, and 223 cases were discontinued after he had made a preliminary investigation of them. Of the 864 cases he completed he found that 105 involved some elements of maladministration leading to some measure of injustice—one in eight, a high enough proportion to suggest that the office has a useful job to do.

Apart from the reports he makes to members on individual cases, his annual report to Parliament gives details of the cases (without names) where he has found the departments at fault, and a representative selection of other cases. It also explains the decisions taken on the extent of jurisdiction.

As soon as Parliament had created this new office, the House of Commons set up the Select Committee on the Parliamentary Commissioner for Administration, to examine his reports to Parliament and related matters. The Committee has eleven members who have chosen a chairman from the opposition side. It has power to take evidence. With the Commissioner and the Committee the House of Commons now has a useful weapon for attacking bureaucratic injustice.

An example of how the weapon can be used is given by the Sachsenhausen case. Twelve persons who had been prisoners of war at Sachsenhausen during the war claimed that they should have shared in the compensation paid by the Foreign Office under the Anglo-German Agreement of 1964 for victims of Nazi persecution. This claim was rejected by the Foreign Office on the ground that they had not been imprisoned under concentration camp conditions. Four of the persons complained to the Commissioner, through a member of Parliament, about the decision itself and the damage to their reputation by the dismissal of the evidence they adduced. He investigated their case and found that they had been victims of maladministration. He criticized the Foreign Office for basing their decision on 'partial and largely irrelevant information', and for the way they had treated the complainants' evidence. He also recorded that the general compensation rules, the merits of which he could not question, meant that some claimants had to pass a more severe test than others. So far as the men's reputation had suffered, he thought that his report would remedy the injustice. So far as they had complained of their failure to receive compensation, he suggested that the Foreign Office should review the evidence and take a fresh decision in each case. He was careful to say that whether a financial award was appropriate for any of the claimants would depend upon the result of that review.

This report was made on 20 December 1967. A debate 'taking note' of the Commissioner's report took place, in government time, on the following 5 February. It was opened by the Foreign Secretary who rejected the findings about maladministration, but said that he would nevertheless make financial awards to all the claimants 'out of respect for the Commissioner's judgement and to support the authority of his office'. In the three hour debate which took place, members generally showed themselves satisfied with this outcome.

But the Select Committee was not satisfied. It regretted that the Foreign Secretary should have precipitated the debate before it had been able to consider the matter and report (which it did in May). However, the minister's impatience meant that the Select Committee was able to compare his remarks with the Commissioner's findings. This led the Committee to endorse the Commissioner's belief that the Foreign Office had based their original decision on partial and largely irrelevant information and had maintained it despite the additional evidence available. The Committee also agreed that there had been maladministration, though it considered it arguable that the Commissioner had gone too far at one point in describing as 'minor' some of the discrepancies in the evidence. The Committee then turned to the remedy, and criticized the department for the way it had made the award only out of respect for the Commissioner: it should have done as he suggested and gone back over the evidence, making an assessment of what the complainants were entitled to under the regulations. The Committee was also dissatisfied with the remedial measures that had been taken in the department to prevent a recurrence of the failure.

Several points combine to make this an interesting example of how this new parliamentary weapon can be used. In the first place it shows how the Commissioner and the Committee interact, the latter sustaining the former (without necessarily accepting all he says), advising the House on the general issues involved, and following up the case to find out what the department is doing to prevent a recurrence.

The way in which the Parliamentary Commissioner acted can be taken as typical. He did not question whether the rules of the Foreign Office on this matter were at fault, but devoted himself instead to the question whether they had been incorrectly applied in this case. The Committee thought incidentally that he took 'too narrow a view' of his authority here: but it thought he was right in not suggesting what financial remedy would be appropriate, and leaving it to the department to assess this in the light of their own rules.

The case also brings out how readily Parliament can now become involved in matters of departmental administration. Bad cases like this must occur occasionally in all departments. When they do, it only takes one person to complain to his member for the train of inquiry to start, ending in a major parliamentary occasion at which the minister faces his critics. The case also makes clear that neither ministers nor officials are exempt from the strictures of the Commissioner or the Committee. In this instance the Foreign Secretary robustly took the traditional view that he was responsible for the defects of his department because it is 'a minister's job to see that he had all the necessary information'. But the Committee, while not absolving him, implicitly rejected that view by holding that there were shortcomings on the part both of officials and ministers. It did not name the officials concerned, because the advice given to ministers had been their collective, and not individual, responsibility.[1]

It must be noticed that this new machinery undermines to some extent the traditional doctrine of ministerial responsibility. When Sir Thomas Dugdale (as he then was) resigned office in 1954 because of the shortcomings of his officials discovered in the Crichel Down case, he was acting as Parliament expected a minister to act. He was responsible for what went on in his department, and had to suffer for its faults, even when he had not been personally implicated (and may not have known of the matter until it was too late to apply a remedy). Contrast this attitude with what happened in the Sachsenhausen case. In that later case the minister accepted the traditional view, the Dugdale view, that if his civil servants had made a mistake he was responsible for it; he told the House so when the case was debated. But the Select Committee thought otherwise. It said the blame lay on both the ministers and the civil servants concerned. So a group of members, representative of the House as a whole and under the chairmanship of a senior opposition ex-minister, can be seen to be throwing doubt on this principle that responsibility lies solely with the minister.

The case may however prove untypical in the order in which its principal events took place. The Committee's view is that in future the best order of proceeding would be for the Commissioner to make his report, for the department to announce the

1. The effect of the Ombudsman system on the doctrine of ministerial responsibility is considered in the Committee's Second Report of 1967–68, House of Commons Paper 350, paras. 24–30. The Committee makes clear that it has the right to examine the civil servants directly concerned in the matter.

remedy, for the Committee to report, and then for the debate to follow. In the case described they found themselves acting, as they specifically did not wish to act, as a court of appeal from a dispute between the Commissioner and the department.[1]

The United States and an Ombudsman

In the American governmental system the Comptroller General of the United States performs a function in this field. If a contracting officer in a department of the executive branch awards a contract erroneously, anyone whose economic interest is involved in the award may make a 'bid protest' to the Comptroller General or his office, the General Accounting Office. The Comptroller General's decision is final and conclusive. Some of the bid protests are channelled by the aggrieved party through a congressman, but they may be sent direct to the General Accounting Office. A decision is reached, on average, in ninety days. In the three years 1967–69 something like 1,500 bid protests were made in this way, of which about 100 were sustained by the Comptroller General. To these must be added the many cases where protests were withdrawn before judgement was reached, frequently because the contracting officer was prudent enough to offer some satisfactory relief to the protester.[2]

Apart from this machinery, nothing like the Ombudsman exists in the American central governmental system,[3] although the standing committees can investigate administrative failings which come to light, and many complaints made to congressmen are taken up with the executive departments or agencies concerned or with the General Accounting Office. It is interesting though to observe that there has been some pressure for an Ombudsman to be set up in the United States. The Joint Committee on the Organization of Congress in 1965–66 considered a memorandum on the subject that was put to them,[4] but they did not recommend any action on it in their final Report.

1. House of Commons Debates, 5 February 1968; House of Commons Papers 258 and 134 of 1967–68, and 134 of 1966–69.
2. *The Government Contractor*: briefing paper, June 1970 (Federal Publications Inc.).
3. One state (Hawaii) has had an Ombudsman since mid-1969.
4. See the Report of the Hearing before the Joint Committee on 12 May 1965.

NATIONALIZED INDUSTRIES AND
PUBLIC CORPORATIONS

Although there had been a number of industrial concerns in Britain operated or part-operated by the government for a long while before World War II, it was only in the Parliament of 1945–50 that the problem of parliamentary control of the nationalized industries[1] became a major issue. That Parliament brought about the nationalization of the railways, road transport, gas and electricity industries, coal-mining, and the Bank of England, and the extension of the state's participation in air transport. With ministers operating in so many new fields, it was not surprising that members of Parliament should seek to oversee the work they were doing.

The statutes nationalizing these industries have many similar features. A typical Act requires the minister to appoint a chairman and board of management, with a duty to balance its accounts over the years. The board can borrow money up to a stated limit, and has to make an annual report to Parliament and to publish its accounts. The minister is given certain specific powers, such as that of making the regulations necessary for public safety, can call for such information as he wants and can give the board directions of a general character about the way it is required to operate. These powers, especially those of appointing the board, controlling its expenditure, and giving it general directions, are enough to ensure that the industry is run along lines laid down by the minister. But the responsibility for the day to day management of the industry is placed on the board.

Faced with important industries under novel forms of ministerial control, members found that the parliamentary opportunities for questioning and debating what ministers did were limited. Several days a year were given over to debates on the annual reports and accounts of the boards or to general debates on supply days, or on government policy proposals for the industry, and in

---

1. A 'nationalized industry' is something of a term of art. It refers to a whole industry, or a major part of an industry, which has been nationalized by statute and whose income is largely derived from its own operations. It does not cover several other semi-governmental organizations which depend on government funds, provision for which appears in the Estimates.

addition the need for new legislation (affecting a board's borrowing powers, for instance) gave periodic opportunities for reviewing an industry's performance. But when members sought to question a minister in Question Hour, not about his own handling of his statutory powers, but about a board's use of theirs, the Questions met with a refusal by ministers to answer. The ministers were not responsible for managing the industry. That was for the board to do. Though there was no doubt that ministers had a statutory power to get hold of the information for which they were asked, they declined to use it. Persistent attempts to ask about the day-to-day operations of the industries met persistent refusals to answer, and so invoked the rule which forbids the reiteration of the same or similar Questions. In other words members found that they could not ask parliamentary Questions about the day-to-day affairs of the industries.

Members in due course found some ways round this particular difficulty. They could, for instance, ask the minister to use his powers to give a general direction to a board about some aspect of its day-to-day affairs; the minister would probably say no, but he might be pressed in supplementary questions to ensure that action was taken in the way desired. Various easements of the practice with regard to Questions on nationalized industries were made over the years, and it is now possible to ask for national—but not local—statistics of a board's operations.

Nevertheless members remain unable to ask parliamentary questions about day-to-day matters because the government's responsibility does not extend to matters of detail. Yet it is these matters which greatly affect constituents everywhere, and it is on these matters that they are constantly enjoining their members to take action.

No such bar exists on the debating of these day-to-day matters in the half-hour adjournment motions. On these occasions ministers answer freely and at length on administrative details. Although they are not responsible for these details they have power to require information from the boards, and this they freely pass on to the House during adjournment debates. There is no procedural rule, as there is in the matter of Questions, by which ministers can refuse to answer these debates. In these circumstances ministers are answerable to the House on matters for which they are not themselves responsible.

The story of the Select Committee on Nationalized Industries, and its liberation from the policy bar, has been described earlier.[1] The successful functioning of this committee has done much to satisfy the earlier misgivings of members in regard to the industries. Since 1966 it has had power to set up subcommittees, and this has enabled it to keep more industries under surveillance at the same time.

In the United States

The United States does not have any nationalized industries in the sense that Britain has. There is a certain amount of public subsidization of industry—of the transport and farming industries, for example—but operations are left to the private owners concerned. Where the government pursues some form of public enterprise on a national scale—in afforestation, for example, or atomic energy—it is generally undertaken in special political circumstances. Where the corporations are administered by the departments, the normal forms of congressional oversight apply to them as to all other kinds of departmental activity. But Congress has created some special government-owned corporations, with terms of reference laid down by legislation, to undertake specific tasks for the public good with an organization akin to that used by comparable private organizations. Of these the Panama Canal Company and the Tennessee Valley Authority are well-known examples. During World War II the number of public corporations of this kind rose to over a hundred, but they have declined considerably in number since then.

Compared with other government agencies their chief characteristic is the extent of their independence. In establishing them Congress as a general rule requires them to submit periodic reports, and these provide material for the oversight of their functioning by the appropriate standing committee. But the other main congressional control, through annual appropriations, may not operate because the corporation may be able to make ends meet as a result of its own operations.

Congress has shown itself suspicious of this form of semi-governmental body. The high point of distrust was in the era of President Franklin Roosevelt. It was mitigated to some extent

1. See pp. 234–5. See also Coombes, *The Member of Parliament and the Administration* (1967) for the history of this Committee.

in 1940 by bringing the employees of the national agencies—which included the corporations now being considered—under the system of merit appointment operating within the central civil service.[1] Since 1945 the corporations have been made to submit themselves to annual scrutiny by the President's Office of Management and Budget and the General Accounting Office.

Since these changes were made, Congress has appeared content with the existence and functioning of the corporations and of its control over them. New corporations are occasionally set up; legislation on five new ones was pending in 1970. In the attitude of Congress to them there is some resemblance to Parliament's scrutiny of the nationalized industries. But it would be unwise to press this analogy too closely—first because the American constitutional system tends to involve Congress in all aspects of administration; and secondly because the corporations, although comparatively numerous, do not operate on so wide a scale, and do not affect the national economy to anything like the same extent as the industries nationalized in Britain.

DELEGATED LEGISLATION

In the United Kingdom

From its early days Parliament has seen the advantage of sometimes leaving it to the government of the day to work out the consequences of the laws that Parliament passes. By this means a government department can escape from the rigidity which a statute might otherwise impose. The impact of the statute can be varied as circumstances require, or it can be brought into operation whenever the preparatory work had been done. The necessary subsidiary details of an enactment are often technical matters which Parliament is unfitted to pursue; and these can appropriately be worked out by the department concerned. Parliament may not be sitting at a time when it is necessary to alter the incidence of its Acts, and during its sittings it does not have time to consider the details of the law it makes.

For these reasons Parliament delegates to government the duty of making the lesser laws necessary to give a full effect to Acts of Parliament and, from time to time as necessary, to vary those

1. The T.V.A. was exempted, apparently because it had already developed a well-publicized merit system of its own.

proposals. All types of delegated legislation, whether in the form of rules, orders or regulations, have since 1946 been known as Statutory Instruments. In 1968 seventy-seven public Acts were passed and 2,079 general and local Instruments made. The volume of public statutes for the year comprises 2,426 pages; the volumes of general Instruments take up 5,660 pages of roughly the same print. (The comparison is misleading in that delegated legislation is by its nature of lesser importance, but it gives some measure of the scale of government action in pursuance of parliamentary powers.)

Parliament's primary control is exerted when it passes a bill which formally delegates authority to the government. So far as general (as opposed to local and personal) Instruments are concerned, it decides at that point whether or not it wishes to place any restraint on the government in their use of the delegated power. It also decides whether an Instrument should or should not be laid in draft before it is made. There are various grades of restraint. In general, the bill may require (i) that a general Instrument should receive the formal consent of one or both Houses before it comes into force or is continued in force ('the affirmative method'); or that (ii) either House should, if it wishes, be able to annul the Instrument within a certain time ('the negative method'); or that (iii) the Instrument should be laid before Parliament, so that Parliament is at least aware of what it contains. Finally (iv), Parliament may decide that it does not need to place any restraint on the government departments who will make the Instrument. Parliament chooses the category appropriate to the Instrument, in the light both of the importance of its subject matter, and Parliament's possible desire to retain some later control on it. In the session of 1968–69 general Instruments were placed into these four categories by the following percentages:

Affirmative %	Negative %	Laid, without other proceedings %	Total before Parliament %	Not laid before Parliament %
9	56	6	71	29

All the Instruments made under the affirmative method duly come before Parliament in a debate which is, in some circum-

stances in the Commons, limited to one-and-a-half hours.[1]
As the government's majority ensures that Parliament assents
to them, it may be argued that the affirmative control is little
more than a paper threat. But the arguments advanced in
debate, irrespective of the result of any vote, may lead to changes
in government policy, and can affect public opinion on the rights
or wrongs of policy. This, coupled with the fact that the government are forced by the affirmative method to provide time for
debating matters they might otherwise have wished to avoid,
makes the affirmative method very attractive to the opposition
of the day. It results in close oversight by Parliament of these
Instruments.

The negative method is less effective. Each House has a period
of time[2] in which it can annul an Instrument by passing a motion[3]
to that effect. In the Commons, debate on such a motion must
conclude (or be adjourned) at 11.30 p.m. (5.30 p.m. on Fridays).
The government has little difficulty in keeping a majority until
that hour, so again it is rare for a hostile motion to succeed. Since
debate on these motions generally does not start until the main
business of the day has been completed—which is rarely before
10 p.m. and often much later—it has become increasingly difficult
to arrange these debates in the Commons within the time-limit
allowed by statute.[4]

In its handling of Statutory Instruments Parliament can
accept or reject the propositions of ministers. There is no middle
ground, no chance of amending each Instrument. It is sometimes
suggested that this is a weakness in the system of parliamentary
control. But to give Parliament a say in the wording of Instruments would be to depart from the principle of delegated legislation—which is to allow ministers to resolve how best to solve
their problems. Although Parliament retains a power to veto

1. Standing Order No. 3 (1). Alternatively, it concludes at 11.30 p.m.
2. Generally forty days, excluding time in which either House is in
recess.
3. The formal wording of the motion 'prays' the Sovereign to annul the
Instrument; so that the motion is colloquially known as 'a prayer'.
4. In recent sessions the government have on occasions arranged a
debate on an Instrument *after* the forty day period has elapsed. If such
a motion were carried, there would be no statutory onus on the government to withdraw the Instrument in question although they might well
feel obliged to comply with the sense of the House.

some Instruments, it is not fitted to do the detailed work of drafting the Instrument. If Parliament had the power of amendment, it would imply the duty of trying to improve every Instrument, and the ensuing delays would paralyse a process that had been introduced in order to give swift results. Furthermore the period in which both Houses can now concurrently act on an Instrument would have to be almost doubled, since the second House's consideration of an Instrument could not satisfactorily begin until the first House had agreed to the wording of the text, and a new procedure would be necessary for settling differences between the Houses.[1] It is in any case so comparatively simple at the present time for a minister to withdraw an order and present it anew in amended form, in order to meet the objections of members, that it would be retrograde to introduce a clumsier system.

Parliament's primary controls over delegated legislation are supplemented by the appointment of committees in each House to examine Statutory Instruments. In the House of Lords the Special Orders Committee reports on rules or orders requiring an affirmative resolution. The Committee has in the past advised the House on whether the Instrument raised an important issue of policy or principle, on whether it was precedented or not, and on whether it deserved special attention or required special inquiry before the House agreed to it. If the Committee found that an order was 'hybrid'—that some private interests were affected—then it allowed the persons affected to petition against the order, and would not report until the petition had been considered. If the Committee was doubtful about whether a minister acted within his powers in making the order, it was required to say so. Proposals for broadening these terms of reference were agreed to in 1970. As a result the Committee may now draw to the attention of the Lords any aspect of an order they think necessary.

The Special Orders Committee can thus go deeply into the comparatively few Instruments which attract the affirmative process. In the Commons the Select Committee on Statutory Instruments goes less deeply into a far greater number. It con-

1. An experiment to allow the amendment of certain India and Burma Orders under the Government of India Act 1935 was not repeated because of the difficulties inherent in a situation where the two Houses could come to conflicting decisions.

siders all general Instruments—that is, all Instruments other than those which are local or personal—and special procedure orders,[1] but it looks at them in a different way from the Special Orders Committee. It does not question the policy which led to the making of the Instrument, nor its merits—it is in other words one of the select committees subject to the policy bar[2]; and it can do nothing about the hybrid aspect of an Instrument. It can however draw the attention of the House to various unusual or undesirable aspects of an Instrument—for instance, that it creates a charge; or that, without express provision in the parent Act, it purports to act retrospectively. If an Instrument makes unusual or unexpected use of a statutory power, the Committee will alert the House to it; and bad drafting, or a failure to carry out correct procedures, will also attract its displeasure. It is fair to say that by its reports over the years the Committee has had a strong and beneficial influence on the drafting and presentation of Statutory Instruments.

The success of the Statutory Instruments Committee owes much to the advice its members receive from an officer of the House of Commons, the Counsel to Mr Speaker, who examines every instrument within its remit and advises accordingly. Similarly in the Lords the advice of the Counsel to the Lord Chairman is available to the Special Orders Committee. With the help of these two officials, the scrutinizing committees of both Houses are able to apply consistent standards of judgement to the many Instruments which emanate from all government departments.

In the United States

In the United States as in the United Kingdom much legislative power has been delegated by the legislature to the executive in the twentieth century. As in the United Kingdom (see page 382), the basic reason is the need in a large and complex industrial civilization to restrict legislation to the fixing of objectives, while departments or specially created agencies devise the means of attaining them. No direct parallel can be drawn with

1. These are orders, generally on local matters, made by ministers, which attract a special parliamentary procedure. Members of the public can petition against them, in which case a joint committee may consider the petition. Either House can then, if it wishes, annul them on a motion. Recently there have been about thirty of these orders each year.

2. See p. 233.

the statistics of delegated legislation in Britain, since much that is there administered by the central government falls within the responsibility of State government in the United States.

It is fair to note that there does not seem to have been in the United States the same criticism of the principle of granting these powers to the administration as was heard in Britain (*The New Despotism*, and *The Passing of Parliament*)[1] especially from the 'thirties to the 'fifties. American public opinion seems to have accepted the growth of regulations as an inevitable development in the nature of present-day government. The substance of regulations issued is often criticized but not the process itself. This is especially interesting because a theoretical case can be made out that the process is unconstitutional. On a strict interpretation of the Constitution and of the principle of the separation of powers, the delegation of legislative powers to the President ought to be impossible: *all* legislative power, the Constitution says—not just some—shall be vested in Congress. Nevertheless, in the last few decades the executive has been invited to roam in fields previously reserved for Congress. The Supreme Court has objected to delegation that amounted to giving the President a blank cheque; but within its fairly liberal bounds, there has been so great a move of delegated legislative power to the executive as to constitute almost a transfer of function.

In a nation which time and again shows itself sensitive to constitutional nuances, it is significant that this delegation arouses little controversy. One reason must be the care taken to ensure that the regulations made are as acceptable and as well-publicized as possible. The steps taken by the executive in the United States before making rules and regulations have proved more successful in allaying public anxiety than similar efforts in Britain. The opportunities afforded to interested parties to participate in the rule-making process, to petition for new rules or for the repeal of others, seem to satisfy the interests most closely involved. These preparatory steps are prescribed by statute (the Administrative Procedure Act of 1946), so that a failure in their observance can be questioned in the courts.

Congress does not have the power of directly annulling delegated legislation (apart from its legislative veto—see below), but

1. By Lord Hewart (1928) and Professor G. W. Keeton (1954) respectively.

it exercises a number of other controls. Administrative agencies are required to submit periodic and special reports on their activities, which may have included the making of regulations; and Congress may pass resolutions formally requiring information on particular matters. On the floor of the Senate and the House of Representatives members may call attention to particular regulations, the Congress may go on to pass new legislation withdrawing and altering the powers it has delegated. The law which delegates the power may limit the executive's discretion in the use of it, and may specifically allow appeals by persons affected to independent tribunals. Above all there is the power of committees to investigate the scope and effect of rules and regulations in their field, and to summon the administrators to give evidence before them.

These safeguards, coupled with the considerable influence which congressional committees are able to bring to bear on agencies and departments while the regulations are in preparation, have hitherto proved satisfactory. But it is sometimes argued that legislatures in the twentieth century might benefit from a reduction in the time spent on legislative details.[1] The British system, under which delegated legislation can be made subject to Parliament's approval, is one way in which the legislative load can be lightened. Congress itself has sometimes used a different device—the legislative veto.

Congress and the Legislative Veto

Congress has on many occasions dictated the means by which the executive branch operates. Under the Constitution the executive's function is to carry out the laws made by Congress; but it does so through the departments and agencies which Congress itself creates by statute. In some cases Congress has even determined the internal structure of departments and agencies, though on other occasions this has been left to the executive branch to decide.[2]

1. See for instance Wheare, *Legislatures*, 2nd ed. (1968), p. 157.
2. All fifteen departments of the executive branch have been set up by statute, as have the forty-five independent agencies. Of the approximately eighty boards, commissions, authorities etc., most were set up by statute, the rest by executive action pursuant to statutory authority.

Generally speaking it is only in wartime that Congress has abdicated its right to shape the framework of government. It has however, become increasingly clear that the reorganizing and improving of departments of the executive branch is a more sensitive process than a normal statute can effect. There are obvious advantages in letting the executive branch reorganize itself, but Congress has been unwilling to give up its rights in this field. To do so would be to pass some power from the legislature to the executive; and it is in the abrasive attempts of each branch of government to gain power, rather than to lose it, that so much of the vitality of the American system resides.

Accordingly Congress devised a new method of control which gave to the executive branch the initiative in revising its methods of working, while leaving it to Congress to permit the change or not. The Legislative Appropriation Act of 1932 authorized the President to reorganize departments and agencies; but his proposals in this regard have to be submitted to Congress sixty days before coming into effect, and they can be set aside by a simple resolution of either House.

Thus was born the 'legislative veto', a system which has obvious affinities with the British system of control of delegated legislation. It is an aspect of congressional control which has been the cause of controversy ever since it was introduced. It invites the executive to take part in legislation, and requires the legislature to sit in judgement on an executive decision; so it deliberately confuses the separate roles which the Constitution devised for each. Its validity was questioned by the Attorney-General at the time and has been criticized by many constitutional authorities since.

Because of such constitutional objections the Executive Reorganization Act of 1939 contained a legislative veto of a slightly different kind. It provided that the *plan* for an order reorganizing governmental agencies, rather than the order itself, should be subject to congressional veto. This veto was to be imposed by a concurrent resolution—passed by a majority of the members of each House—within sixty days. President Roosevelt assented to the Act after a long legislative struggle, and it became the pattern for later applications of the legislative veto. During the war Congress allowed the executive sweeping powers to make the necessary changes in its organization. But when these powers expired, Congress insisted in the Executive Reorganization Act of 1949

that the plans of the President should again be subject to annul-
ment on a majority vote of all members. In 1957 the veto power
was amended so as to be operated by either House on a simple
majority of those voting. Many reorganization plans have since
been made. One was rejected by veto of the House in the 86th
Congress (1959–60), and three in the 87th. The veto was not used
again in the 1960s, but was used to reject a reorganization plan
in 1970.

The successful use of this device led Congress to apply it in
other fields of administration, in addition to that of reorganization.
Examples of the powers which Congress has assumed in this
manner, so enhancing its oversight of executive decisions, are
those to review and set aside the suspension of the deportation
of aliens by the Attorney-General (1940): to disallow the disposal
of federally-owned property, such as obsolete vessels (1946); to
terminate assistance to a foreign country (1957); to approve the
allocation of highway aid to the states (1956); and to disallow the
exchange of atomic energy materials with other countries (1958).

If the original use by Congress of the legislative veto had been
controversial, a development that took place in 1944 must have
seemed far more alarming. A bill passed then required the Secretary of the Navy to 'come into agreement' with the Naval Affairs
Committee of each House before undertaking certain real estate
transactions. The department in other words could only carry
out certain functions after the committees had agreed to its
proposals; the committees thus had the power of vetoing the
department's administrative decisions. This was the first instance
of a legislative veto by a committee. In this case the will of the
executive branch could be thwarted not by Congress, not by either
House of Congress, but by a small group of members in one
House. The President signed the bill, although he announced
his disagreement with the principle of veto by committee when
the same device was incorporated in a later Navy bill. Nevertheless this kind of veto has been used on many subsequent occasions.
Its application by committees—the 'committee veto'—rather
than by Houses became a normal feature of the legislative veto.
An extraordinary extension of this power came with an Act of
1952 which gave the effect of law to certain regulations of the
Bureau of the Budget (as it then was) relating to housing allowances, but provided that any amendment of the regulations

should require the prior approval of the chairman of the House Appropriations Committee. Here, in other words, the veto could be operated by a single individual.

In more recent times, Congress has chosen to link a veto of this kind to its function of appropriation. Certain actions had to be approved by congressional committees before funds would be appropriated for them. This device has been effectively applied by Congress to such measures as those relating to grants for flood protection or land reclamation—projects which, because of their local importance, are of particular interest to congressmen. The linking of the veto to the committee's undoubted rights in the matter of appropriation has apparently been accepted by Presidents as being within the proper powers of Congress, and has accordingly become the usual way in which the veto is authorized.[1]

In a system based on a written Constitution, any departure from the normal forms can expect (and deserve) close scrutiny. So it is hardly surprising that the invention and operation of the legislative veto has attracted a great deal of interest in the United States and elsewhere. But, to British eyes at least, accustomed to the constant flow of governmental orders and regulations in the shape of Statutory Instruments coming before Parliament for its yea or nay, it is important not to get the veto out of perspective. By British standards it is rarely employed. In a twenty-year period, from the 1940s to the 1960s, it appeared on average in about two Acts per year;[2] of these Acts, several lapsed before long, and it was never necessary to invoke the veto power in others. So despite the theoretical similarity to Parliament's use of the affirmative procedure, in practice it has not so far amounted to a major weapon of oversight or control.

EARLY DAY MOTIONS

There is a device available in the House of Commons by which members can give public notice of their attitude towards public events. This is the 'early day motion'—a motion put down on the order paper by a member, theoretically for debate on an

1. For a fuller description of this subject, see Joseph Harris, *The Congressional Control of Administration* (1964); and Norman Smale, *The Committee Veto—its Current Use and Appraisals of its Validity* (1967) (for the Library of Congress Legislative Reference Service).

2. Joseph Harris, op. cit., p. 206.

unspecified date ('an early day'), but actually to test the response of fellow-members to a particular proposition. The motion can be supported by members ad lib, and the names of supporters are published; perhaps hundreds of members will make a public protestation of their views on a particular issue (frequently an issue of up-to-the-minute interest). Since it is rare for an early day motion to be debated members feel free, almost to the point of abandon, to table their own motions and to subscribe their names to others. The proliferation of these motions is largely a feature of the post-1945 era; in recent years, well over 500 motions have been tabled during a session. It is true that the rules of the Labour Party require their members to show each motion to their Chief Whip before tabling it, and he can hold it up for a day if it displeases him. But that is the extent of the power of party discipline in this matter. Many early day motions are tabled by members in criticism of the attitude taken up by the leaders of the parties. The leaders know that the tabling and supporting of these motions is a paper exercise and not a practical threat to their policies, but they cannot ignore them. The precise number of signatories to a motion is not itself significant, in view of the haphazard way in which members are persuaded or persuade themselves to sign, but the volume of protest and the type of member joining it may well affect a policy.

The strength and the weakness of the early day motion can be illustrated by considering one tabled in 1967. The government planned to build a new London Airport in Stansted, Essex. The proposal raised great controversy both locally and elsewhere, and an early day motion calling for an independent inquiry into national airport policy, and thereby obliquely criticizing the decision, was tabled by members of all parties and was strongly supported. Eventually about half the members of the House signed the motion, including nearly one hundred government supporters. Now although it is unusual for an early day motion to be debated, it is possible. A private member who is lucky in the occasional ballots for motions can nominate whatever motion he likes for debate; or the opposition can table the motion for debate on a supply day. On this occasion the opposition nominated the motion for debate on a supply day, and it came up for discussion in June 1967. On a motion critical of their handling of events, the government insisted on the support of their members.

As a result almost all the hundred government supporters who had signed the motion went into the lobby to vote against it. This at first glance makes brutally clear how little a party leadership has to fear from an early day motion. But it is a fact of parliamentary life under strict party discipline that the voting can have a different significance from the debate itself. In a debate members argue the merits of a case; in a division they vote on whether the present government is better than its alternative. So perhaps a fairer assessment of the value of the early day motion as a weapon against policy is to note that it played its part in forcing the government to think again. Eight months after the debate the government cancelled their plan to use Stansted and agreed to set up an independent inquiry on the siting of the new airport.

In the Lords there is nothing strictly comparable to the early day motion because, generally speaking, motions in that House are not put down for propaganda purposes; and, in any case, only one name may be put down to any one motion. There is however a running list of motions and unstarred Questions, each one of which may eventually be put down for a specific date and then debated. This list gives the government an idea of some of the subjects upon which it may be called to account in debate during the session.

As pointed out earlier (see p. 297), many of the bills introduced into Congress fulfil something of the same function—of publicizing a point of view—as do early day motions in the House of Commons.

CONGRESSIONAL PROCEDURES FOR CONTROL OF THE EXECUTIVE

This chapter has so far considered procedures of scrutiny and oversight which are either peculiar to Parliament or common to both Parliament and Congress. There are other procedures peculiar to Congress which flow from the relationship between legislature and executive in the United States and can usefully be considered in isolation. Principal among them is the control exercised by the standing committees of Congress.

Oversight by Committees

The power of committees to oversee departments and to conduct investigations is not granted by the Constitution. Congress has inferred, from its duty to legislate, that it has an inherent right to inform itself on a subject in order to be able to pass intelligent legislation about it, and the system of inquiry by congressional committee has sprung from this. The system was formalized with the passing of the Legislative Reorganization Act of 1946, in which Congress specifically assigned to the standing committees of both houses the job of supervising the administration. Section 136 of the Act says that

> . . . each standing committee of the Senate and the House of Representatives shall exercise continuous watchfulness of the executive by the administrative agencies concerned of any laws, the subject matter of which is within the jurisdiction of such committee.

This Act, with the changes in committee structure and the strengthening of staff that accompanied it, have made Congress far better equipped to control the executive. Its effectiveness is such that scholars now ponder on whether Congress does not exercise more influence over administrative agencies on a day-to-day basis than does the President.[1]

The work done by the standing committees has been considered in Chapter V of this book. In addition to oversight by the standing committees which each House has set up to scrutinize a particular field of government, departments and agencies are also subject to the interest of the Appropriations Committees and Committees on Government Operations in both Houses. Many of these committees receive assistance in their investigations from the General Accounting Office.

The activities of the Appropriations Committees have been described in Chapter VII. Their consequences in terms of administrative scrutiny should be noticed here. The powers of investigation by the subcommittees of the Appropriations Committees leads them to range over the whole area of the department's activities, its organization and its competence. Some idea of the scale of their activities can be gained from the two years of the 88th Congress (1963-64) when there were well over a thousand subcommittee meetings of the Committees on Appropriations (590 in the House, 444 in the Senate), together with ninety meetings of the full committees (twenty-four in the

1. Hyneman, in *Congress: First Branch of Government* (1966), p. 38.

House, sixty-six in the Senate). As a result of these multifarious examinations, Congress is able to impose its own views on the amount and balance of government expenditure, favouring some policies and restricting others. At the hearings, or in their reports, the members of the subcommittees can give oral or written instructions to the agencies which cannot be ignored. The agencies may for example be required to submit periodic reports of their activities, or notify the appropriate congressional committees before or after taking specified administrative decisions. The fact that every part of the executive may not be granted the money estimated for its needs, and that the money it gets may be granted with or without conditions, brings an element of uncertainty into the administration of the country which is foreign to the British practice and which, even without the other differences already observed, makes the relationship of the American public service to Congress completely dissimilar to that between government and Parliament in the United Kingdom.

Each House also has a Committee on Government Operations[1] charged with the duty, among others, of 'studying the operation of government activities at all levels with a view to determining its economy and efficiency'. Each committee acts through subcommittees which may sit anywhere and at any time (whether or not its House is sitting). It can subpoena witnesses and require the production of such documents as are necessary for its inquiries. It is to these committees that the Comptroller General, and through him the General Accounting Office (see p. 338), primarily report.

The work done by the Government Operations Committee in the House of Representatives during the 89th Congress (1965–1966) may be cited as typical of the way in which the two committees go about their business.[2] This Committee, then consisting of thirty-four members, appointed eight regular subcommittees; in addition two other subcommittees were set up during the period to conduct special inquiries. In the two-year period, they:

1. Until 1952 each Committee was called the Committee on Expenditures in Government Departments.
2. *Activities of the House Committee on Government Operations, 89th Congress, First and Second Sessions* (December 1966).

Conducted, and reported on, 46 investigations;

Issued 14 'committee prints'—documents of a background nature for committee and congressional use;

Considered 367 bills and resolutions, coalescing 103 of them into the 24 bills which they reported (of which 19 were enacted into law);

Approved 10 plans which the President had submitted for the reorganization of public bodies, all of which were duly permitted by the House and Senate to be implemented; and

Considered 431 audit reports from the General Accounting Office, calling for more information on most of them, and using the information so gained in order to further the special investigations and reviews they were making.

A work-load of this size, carried by thirty-four congressmen supported by a committee staff of sixty-three, is some indication of the role being undertaken by the Government Operations Committee. A list of the subjects considered by the Committee ranges from the government weather programme to the unshackling of local government; from the fraudulent obtaining of grain storage contracts to satellite communications; from a shortage of coins to medical research on the ageing; from the conflict between research programmes and higher education, to the use of lie detectors; from sewage disposal to the auditing of defence contracts; and from the military programme in Vietnam to the coastguard examination of foreign passenger ships.

A specific example of the Committee's work is the investigation by a subcommittee of the sale of grain storage contracts. It held twenty-one days of hearings and numerous other meetings, conducted an exhaustive search of government and private files, interviewed 125 people, examined 200 reports of investigation by the FBI and other agencies, and obtained other information from 300 firms and individuals. As a result it found no evidence of bribery of government employees, but disclosed that the contracts had been gained by false statements, and that inadequate procedures, lack of alertness and poor judgement contributed to the mistakes that had been made. It found that previous irregularities in the behaviour of a particular man involved in the contracts, over a period of twelve years, had been investigated on many occasions by various government agencies; as a result, the subcommittee concluded that there had been an almost total lack of effective co-ordination between the departments and agencies involved. The Committee recommended that action should be taken to recover the profits involved; and the Justice Department later filed claims of nearly $10 million against the firm concerned. The Committee recommended that a comprehensive review of federal audit and investigation activities should be undertaken to secure better co-ordination in future; and noted the action taken by the Department of Agriculture to improve its procedures in future, which included the placing of all its audit and related activities under an inspector general. The Committee's investigation later led the Department to reduce storage rates by nineteen per cent, resulting in an estimated saving in the following year (1967) of over $25 million.[1]

Here then is an organization, almost an executive in itself, scrutinizing and sitting in judgement on all government operations. As the House of Commons Estimates Committee used to do, it can pounce on any matter where it suspects that the executive branch have been showing negligence. It can expose mistakes, and it can call for remedial action. It differs from the Estimates Committee in style, in scope, in its far greater workload (including legislation) and in its greater power to insist on remedies for the shortcomings it discovers.

The extent of these committee investigations into the detailed functioning of departments and agencies must raise the question whether they are conducive to efficiency in the public service. It is clear that the proper concern of any legislature with the functioning of the executive is always likely to lead to some derogation from the initiative and the managerial ability of the public service; and the depth to which Congress has immersed itself in this matter will obviously have a considerable effect on the quality of the work done by the executive. This may be regrettable; but it is the result of the search by Congress for a greater goal—the search for an open society, in which the public service works publicly for the public. The balance between the two needs—of efficiency on one side and openness on the other—is difficult to strike, and there will always be doubts as to whether it has been struck correctly. Someone has to decide where the balance lies, the buck must stop somewhere; and there are reasons for thinking that Congress will decide this better than most. For Congress is

1. House of Representatives Report No. 196.

not only the body seeking the open society; it is also the body charged with seeking for efficiency and economy in government; and the reconciliation of these two themes is proper for it to make.

Advice and Consent

The Constitution says that the President shall nominate all 'officers of the United States' (apart from those specifically provided for in the Constitution itself) 'by and with the Advice and Consent of the Senate'; but allows Congress, by law, to divest itself of any interest in the appointment of 'inferior officers'. As a result the civil service today consists of a small number of senior functionaries who have been appointed by the President by and with the advice and consent of the Senate, and a great number of career officials in a competitive system created by Congress where positions are gained by merit alone, without regard to political fortunes.[1]

A recent assessment[2] is that eighty-four per cent of the federal civil service comes within the classified or merit system. The remaining sixteen per cent, comprising 375,000 posts, constitutes the patronage sector. Of this, a relatively small proportion are in the most influential positions. These include some 1,200 'excepted' posts—secretaries to the heads of department, and other confidential positions—and some 300 presidential appointments. Most of these latter are subject to confirmation by the Senate. In addition there may be some 500 posts filled by persons from outside the civil service.[3] But outside this core of influential appointments, there are many patronage posts at all levels, such as postmasters, customs officials and marshals.

The advice-and-consent procedure, in which the House of Representatives plays no part, is that the President's nomination is referred to the standing committee of the Senate which has jurisdiction over the department concerned. The committee may hold public hearings as well as closed private meetings where the suitability of the nominee is considered, and then it reports its view to the Senate. The Senate usually considers the

1. See Joseph Harris, *The Advice and Consent of the Senate* (1953), for a full examination of the Senate's role in this field.

2. By M. Shaw, in *Anglo-American Democracy* (1968), pp. 110–11.

3. Figures supplied by C. J. Zinn, lately Law Revision Counsel, House of Representatives Committee on the Judiciary.

matter in public, but can by a majority vote decide to consider the matter in a closed session—in which case all subsequent proceedings on the nomination take place in secret. The final question to be decided is 'Will the Senate advise and consent to the nomination?'; but if no decision has been taken by the end of the session, the President has to renew the nomination (if he wishes to press it) in the following session. The President may withdraw a nomination, if he so wishes, even after the committee has reported on it, but the Senate cannot revoke its consent once given (except on impeachment by the House, which is a different story). If a vacancy occurs during an adjournment, the President can fill it without Senate approval, though such an emergency appointment will automatically expire at the end of the following session (unless the Senate has meanwhile been asked to consent to it and has done so).

The Senate's powers to advise and consent may not affect the great bulk of the public service, but they are an important feature in the choice of its top ranks. The need to appear before the appropriate committee provides an ordeal for newly-appointed members of the cabinet, or senior executives, ambassadors and the like. Although statistically the number of direct refusals is minuscule, there is significance in the number of nominations that have been withdrawn, or have remained unconfirmed for various reasons. In 1960 a Senate dominated by the party which opposed the President held up a large number of appointments so that the incoming President would have a free hand in making his own nominations. In a different field, that of the judiciary, several presidential nominees for the Supreme Court were rejected by the Senate in the last years of President Lyndon Johnson and in the early years of President Nixon. These incidents showed how considerably the President can be embarrassed by the use of this power by the Senate. But perhaps of more overall importance is the effect that the system of advice and consent has on the quality of the public service. The constant threat of senators stumbling on disagreeable (and perhaps irrelevant) aspects of a nominee's character may mean that, especially in the higher ranks, the safe man is more likely to get the President's nomination than a more talented, but less predictable, competitor; and a head of department can be deprived by this means of the free choice of his own assistants.

SCRUTINY AND CONTROL OF FOREIGN AFFAIRS

As an example of the relationship between the legislatures and the executives of the two countries, a useful comparison can be made of the control which the elected bodies are able to exert over the foreign policies of their governments, and over foreign affairs in general. There are one or two considerations which need to be stated before a comparison can usefully be struck. Especially in Britain, where the government has wide powers of action without needing parliamentary approval, foreign policy is largely conducted without the need for legislation; so the control which Parliament exerts by dint of its legislative powers is not so pronounced as in many other fields. This is an area in which the British government can operate largely under the royal prerogative—that is, it has an inherent right of action which does not require it to seek prior parliamentary approval. Secondly there is the fact that in Congress one chamber, the Senate, has the constitutional responsibility of sitting in judgement on the treaties which the executive wish to make and on the choice of the ambassadors they wish to use. This distinguishes the Senate's role from that of the House of Representatives and means that the two chambers have different attitudes towards the subject.

If these considerations make foreign affairs something of a special case in any study of the procedure of Congress and Parliament, it is nevertheless true that no subject is of more importance to the electorate.

Parliament and Foreign Affairs

In Parliament treaties can be debated before they take effect. Under the Ponsonby rule, instituted in the 1920s by Arthur Ponsonby, then Under-Secretary of State for Foreign Affairs, the government has agreed not to ratify any treaty it has entered into for a period of twenty-one sitting days after the treaty has been laid before Parliament. During that period Parliament has the opportunity of debating it and if necessary dissenting from it. This so-called rule is no more than a self-denying ordinance on the part of government; on occasion it has been waived or modified if expediency requires a treaty to be ratified more hurriedly.[1] Since Parliament never has needed to use the provisions

1. See, e.g., House of Commons Debates (1961–62), 651, cc. 940–5.

of the rule in order to dissent from a treaty, it is not clear whether the government would have to refrain from ratifying in those circumstances. But the inference is that it would not ratify.

Only treaties are affected by the Ponsonby rule. Other forms of international action are not. Foreign policy is however now rarely regulated by treaty, and Parliament has to employ other means of exercising oversight. These means do not include anything like the Senate's advice-and-consent power. There is thus no parliamentary control over diplomatic appointments, although they can be criticized. The fact that all but a few top posts are filled by career diplomats means that they are protected by the normal regard for the political neutrality of the public service. But the extent of the controls that are available to Parliament can be indicated by an examination of parliamentary activity in a recent session, 1968–69.

The House of Commons does not have a committee on foreign affairs;[1] the principal method by which it keeps itself informed of government policy and activity in foreign affairs is by the regular questioning of the Foreign Secretary and his junior ministers. The pattern of Question time has been described earlier. It brings the Foreign Office to account every three or four weeks: in 1968–69 some four hundred oral questions (together with two or three supplementary questions on each) were answered in the House by the Foreign Secretary or his colleagues. These amounted to about ten hours of exchanges in the House, spread evenly over the thirty-three weeks for which the House sat during the year. In addition close to a thousand questions received written answers from the same ministers in that period. There must be added to these the number of urgent questions which the ministers answered by private notice at the end of Question Hour, and the number of occasions on which ministers made statements to the House about aspects of foreign policy and answered questions arising out of them. These amounted, in the same year 1968–69, to an approximate total of seven-and-a-half hours. Members also took advantage of the half-hour adjournment

1. Though in the past the Estimates Committee has investigated the administration of the Foreign Office and similar subjects; and the new Expenditure Committee has appointed a subcommittee on defence and external affairs. The idea of a substantive foreign affairs committee is considered by P. G. Richards in *Parliament and Foreign Affairs* (1967).

debates at the end of each day's sitting to raise matters for which the Foreign Secretary was responsible. Some of these occasions enabled criticisms to be made of the Foreign Office's administration overseas—points being raised about the treatment accorded to British individuals by British embassies abroad, for instance. But some also enabled a member to raise broader issues, and amounted to a reasoned attack on a particular part of the government's foreign policy. There were four adjournment debates on foreign affairs in the session 1968–69, taking two hours. Debates on Consolidated Fund Bills during the session allowed another four-and-a-half hours to be spent on foreign affairs; and a private member's motion accounted for a further one-and-a-half hours.

In addition to the opportunities afforded by these procedures to individual members, there are the number of times each session when the House of Commons debates foreign policy. These debates are generally of two different kinds. There are debates on a single specific issue of international concern—issues which have aroused concern throughout the country, which it is the function of the House to express. In such debates there is a sense of urgency, often underlined by the fact that an emergency session of Parliament has had to be convened (during the summer recess, perhaps) in order that these matters can be debated, or that they take place under the urgency provisions of Standing Order No. 9. In the summer of 1968, for instance, Parliament was recalled in late August in order to consider the incursion of Russian troops into Czechoslovakia, and the civil war in Nigeria. The first debate allowed an impressive sense of national unity to express itself. The second debate showed, as effectively, the deep national divisions of opinion that existed. Each debate showed the value of these occasional foreign affairs debates on specific issues of importance. Additionally, in 1968–69 there were two debates on foreign affairs under Standing Order No. 9, taking three hours each.

But besides urgent debates the House also holds occasional debates, sometimes lasting two days, in order to survey foreign affairs in general. On these occasions, the speeches of members traverse all the problems of the world:

> Let observation with extensive view,
> Survey mankind from China to Peru.

These debates are less satisfactory; too many issues may arise for an agreed view to emerge on any of them. Nevertheless, even on these occasions, a group of members can let it be known in advance, perhaps by tabling an amendment to the motion for debate, that they intend to press for a change in a particular aspect of government policy. They can express their view in the debate, and by forcing a division at the end of it (as is always possible) can provide an opportunity for their numbers to be counted. So even in these general debates it is possible for a positive alternative to government policy to be put forward and pressed. Some five days in 1968–69 were taken up by general foreign affairs debates. In addition to the above opportunities, Parliament occasionally needs to spend time legislating with regard to some aspects of foreign affairs; it spent one-and-a-half days doing so in 1968–69.

If all these opportunities are added together, they amount to the equivalent of about eleven full sitting days in that session— that is, the equivalent of about one day's debate in every fifteen.[1] On most of these occasions the House put the Foreign Secretary on trial and enabled alternatives to his policy to be put forward and their supporters to be counted. It also enabled a sense of national resolve to be expressed when this was appropriate. These are useful and important functions, which frequently cause governments to trim their policies in order to meet the criticisms expressed. By and large though, here as in so many other fields, it is not for the House to take the initiative in formulating new policies. Its main task is to sit in judgement on the initiatives undertaken by the government.

The House of Lords has a great deal more freedom in arranging its affairs, so that it can turn more readily to foreign affairs than the Commons. Its debates in this field generally take place on a motion asking for 'Papers'—a lordly procedure of unknown origin and uncertain effect, which does not usually lead to a division where the government's supporters and opponents can be counted. But though these debates do not pose any threat to the government, they must pay regard to the views expressed, since they are often expressed by men of great expertise (ex-

1. These figures do not include the time spent debating the immigration and aliens laws, which in Britain fall to be considered by the Home Office.

ambassadors and former ministers among them) who sit in that House. In the session of 1968–69 the House of Lords devoted the equivalent of approximately six days to debates on foreign affairs.

Congress and Foreign Affairs

The normal sanctions employed by Congress against the executive all operate in the field of foreign affairs, and by themselves have considerable effect. The manner in which Congress constantly cuts appropriations in order to impose its view on what should be the size and shape of the foreign aid programme; the countless laws it passes about such matters as aliens, foreign commerce, and customs; the resolutions passed by either House on matters of foreign policy; the visits made by members of congressional committees to other countries to see things for themselves; the public examination of the credentials of people designated as ambassadors, leading to a vote where a simple majority of the Senate can refuse a nomination; the activities of committees in both Houses—all these are examples of the normal congressional processes being applied to matters of foreign policy, where they clearly add up to an influencing factor. By themselves they ensure that Congress has an important role to play in the conduct of foreign affairs. But to them need to be added the effects of certain other specific constitutional duties.

The Constitution says that Congress shall have power to regulate commerce with foreign nations, to provide for naturalization, to deal with offences on the high seas and offences against the law of nations, to exercise various controls over the forces, and to declare war. It then goes on to declare, in the 'necessary and proper clause', that Congress shall make all laws necessary and proper for executing the pre-mentioned duties; and it adds the requirement that two-thirds of the Senate shall advise and consent to treaties before they can be ratified. In foreign affairs, then, Congress has been given responsibilities which are additional to those it exercises in domestic matters. These additional responsibilities are now to be considered. Principal among them are the power to make treaties and the power to make war.

Making Treaties

There is nothing to prevent the President's negotiating a treaty without any reference to Congress, though in view of what occurs later the President or the Secretary of State may well consult senators while the negotiations take place. Once the treaty has been signed, a certified copy is transmitted to the Senate with a message asking for that body's concurrence. The Senate sends it to its Committee on Foreign Relations, where the practice is to allow the treaty to pend for a considerable time, so that the public can study it and let the committee have their views on it. Consideration of the treaty by the Committee usually takes place in closed session. At least half of the Committee must be present when votes are taken, and a simple majority of them can decide all questions that arise at this stage. The Committee deal with the treaty like a bill. They report it back to the Senate with or without amendment, or they may decide not to report it at all, which is likely to prove fatal to the treaty. In the Senate the treaty is proceeded with, article by article, with the Committee's amendments being considered first and then other amendments which senators may propose; decisions at this stage are made by a simple majority of votes. A resolution is then framed to approve the treaty, with or without certain amendments or reservations. To carry the final question on whether to advise and consent to the ratification in amended form or otherwise, the concurrence of two-thirds of senators present is necessary. Current practice in the Senate is to hold a roll-call vote on each treaty or each group of similar treaties.

There are four ways in which the Senate might qualify its consent to ratification of a treaty. In the first place it might advise and consent to ratification, while making its views known in the committee report; such views have no legal effect. Secondly it might include in its resolution words expressing its understanding or interpretation of the treaty; such words are not likely to have any legal effect, but would be communicated to the other parties. Thirdly the Senate may include a reservation in its resolution. (In their handling of the Nuclear Test Ban Treaty (1963) for instance the Senate included in the resolution of ratification a preamble requiring that any subsequent amendments to the treaty should themselves be submitted to the Senate for ratification.) A reservation affects the contractual relationship imposed by the treaty, and has to be communicated to the other parties, who may thereupon make reservations of their own or even refuse to proceed with the treaty. Fourthly the Senate can actually amend the treaty, in which case it would have to be negotiated again.

Provided that the reservations or amendments are acceptable to the President, he will then reopen negotiations on the wording of the treaty. When agreed to by the parties concerned, it may again need to be submitted to the Senate unless the only changes made are those that the Senate asked for. If the Senate's proposals are unacceptable, the President may not proceed any further with the matter. But if final agreement can be reached between Senate, President and the other parties to the treaty, the President attaches a statement of ratification to it, duly signed and sealed, and issues a proclamation that the treaty has taken effect. At that point it comes into force.

It is clear that this procedure gives to senators, if they so wish, an effective control over every treaty. No President is able to bind the United States by treaty without the agreement of a large majority of the Senate, and for this reason he needs to keep senators informed of his policies and to carry them with him. Since the support of two-thirds of them may be necessary at some stage, a bipartisan foreign policy can be expected.

In practice, however, the Senate now seldom deals unfavourably with a treaty. In 1960 an optional protocol to the conventions on the law of the sea, concerning the compulsory settlement of disputes, failed to get the necessary two-thirds majority vote. 1935 provides the last occasion before that. What usually happens is illustrated by the Senate approval of fifteen treaties in the 89th Congress (1965-66). They dealt with such matters as the amendment of the United Nations Charter, the extension of the international wheat agreement, double taxation agreements with various countries and a treaty of friendship with the Togoland Republic. Each went through a roll-call vote, and on none was there a single dissentient vote.

To some extent this picture of an acquiescent Senate is misleading. As noted above, treaties only come for the Senate's approval after they have been examined by the Foreign Relations Committee. It is there that perhaps their highest hurdle has to

be jumped. If any of the treaties in question had seemed objectionable to the Committee, there is a chance that it would never have
been reported. In that way the treaty would have effectively been
killed. Of the thirty-seven treaties and conventions pending with
the Committee at the end of 1970, ten had been there for at least
ten years.[1]

Today treaties are probably less important than the numerous
executive agreements which the administration enters into with
other countries. These include decisions to take part in various
international organs, joint projects of military or technical
assistance, and the cultural initiatives by which a government
furthers its foreign policy. Executive agreements of this kind are
made by the President after Congress has by law given him a
general authorization in the particular field. Of the agreements
which the United States made with foreign governments in 1968,
226 were executive agreements, and only fifty-seven were treaties.[2]
These executive agreements, not being formal treaties, do not
require the consent of the Senate. Their widespread use has
consequently increased the influence of the House, *vis-a-vis* the
Senate, in this field.

Here then, with the increasing use of executive agreements,
the role of Congress has been changing. Congress has apparently
been content to leave it to the President to make agreements of
this kind, for some of which speed is essential, without the need
for the agreement of the Senate. If the President has been able to
enter into agreements of which the Senate has later disapproved,
senators have only themselves to blame. For in the past Congress
has seemed unperturbed by the possibility that the President
might circumvent the Senate's constitutional power by the use of
these agreements. They have rarely been challenged in Congress,
and when in 1955 a proposal was put forward (the 'Bricker
amendment') which among other things sought to regulate the
President's use of executive agreements, the Senate did not agree
to it and the House of Representatives did not consider it.

An example of how important some executive agreements may
be is that under which American bases were set up in Spain.

1. Committee on Foreign Relations, Legislative Calendar, 91st Congress.

2. Figures given by Senator Javits in an article in *Foreign Affairs*,
January 1970.

This was a logical step in pursuance of American foreign policy, and as such the Senate were content to leave it to the President to negotiate. It was later however learned that, as a part of the agreement, the administration had entered into a commitment to keep American troops in that country.[1] If that had been known at the time the agreement was signed, the Senate would undoubtedly have wished to express its opinion.

Because of cases like this, Congress has been having misgivings about the use by the President of the power to make executive agreements. There is a much stronger feeling that Congress should be able to reassert itself in the way the Constitution had envisaged. In 1969 the Senate passed a resolution[2] stating that no national commitment should be entered into and no American troops should be used abroad until Congress had formally approved.

Declaring War

If the Senate's duty with regard to treaties has been increasingly taken over by the President, so too has the sole authority to declare war which the Constitution gives to Congress.[3] The intentions of the Founding Fathers in this respect have had to be adapted to the circumstances of a later age. Congress recognizes that world events often require rapid, unqualified reactions from the government of the day, and this the process of congressional ratification may not permit. The President alone commands the intelligence network and the machinery of diplomacy and negotiation, and in times of emergency Congress accepts that it is his duty to give a lead to the nation.

Presidents do not themselves think that any action by Congress is constitutionally necessary before steps are taken to deal with an emergency situation. They think that the inherent powers of their office, coupled with their authority as Commander-in-Chief and their duty to execute the law (which includes treaties), is a strong enough basis for them to act on. Although the Constitution says

1. Senator Javits, loc. cit.
2. S. Res. 85, 91st Congress, first session. See *Documents Relating to the War Power of Congress, etc.*, printed for the use of the Senate Committee on Foreign Relations, July 1970.
3. Article 1, Section 8.

that Congress alone can declare war, this has not stopped Presidents sending American troops into action on a number of occasions since Congress last made a formal declaration of this kind in 1941. For instance President Truman committed his troops to a war in Korea in 1950 on his own initiative, following a United Nations decision, on the grounds that the United Nations Treaty was part of the law of the land which it was his duty to execute faithfully. Congress subsequently endorsed his decision, but not until three months later. His action was repeated by other Presidents who, on their own initiative, sent American troops to the Lebanon (1958), the Dominican Republic (1965), and Cambodia (1970). It would seem that Presidents try to carry Congress with them at these times of crisis, if circumstances and timing so allow. Thus in 1955 President Eisenhower asked Congress for a mandate to employ forces in the Far East in the event of attack by Communist forces, and within three days both Houses had passed a joint resolution giving him the authority he sought.

Events following a similar crisis in 1964 have recently had a profound effect on the attitude of many congressmen towards their duties in this regard. In that year an incident in the Gulf of Tonkin was thought to place some American troops in danger. This led both Houses of Congress to adopt by large majorities a resolution giving the President wide powers of action. These powers were subsequently used to involve the United States in the Vietnam war to an entirely new extent. Dissatisfaction in Congress about the outcome of this resolution merged in time with a suspicion that Congress may not have been fully informed in 1964,[1] and have led to suggestions that Congress needs to reinforce its authority here. However the action taken in the Senate—the adoption of the 'National Commitments Resolution' of 1969, mentioned above—has not been repeated in the House.

But the changed mood of Congress has been revealed, not so much in any reassertion of its special constitutional powers, but in a more vigorous use of its other weapons, its weapons as a legislature. It has been revealed pre-eminently by the use of its power of the purse. In the 91st Congress (1969–70) amendments were offered (albeit, not carried) to bills which, if accepted, would have terminated the supply of funds necessary for carrying out government policy, whether it was for continuing the war in

1. See *The Pentagon Papers* (1971), Chapter 5.

south-east Asia or developing new defence systems. In the latter instance in particular there were signs that Congress was no longer so willing to accept without question the expert testimony given to it by the administration, but had gone out to hear different testimony from advisers of its own choice.

The conclusion to be drawn is that the role of Congress is now different to some extent from that envisaged in the Constitution. The special duties given to it there have to some extent been eroded. But it is as a legislature, using its committee system and its power of the purse, that it continues to play so important a role in foreign affairs.

Committees on Foreign Affairs

To complete the evaluation of the present role of Congress and to bring out the contrast with Parliament's oversight of foreign policy, a look has to be taken at what its two Committees on foreign affairs habitually achieve. An example is the work of the Senate's Committee on Foreign Relations in the 89th Congress (1965–66). In their report (published in February 1968) they mention that in recent years there has developed a recognition for the need of even greater emphasis on the oversight function; in pursuance of this they held a number of hearings, 'sometimes called "educational"', designed to examine and illuminate a broad spectrum of foreign policy problems. These hearings—which were in addition to the many other meetings on legislation, the approval of treaties, nominations and other topics—numbered fifty-six in 1965-66; of them,

> 8 were on the world situation,
> 11 on Vietnam and south-east Asia,
> 10 on the Dominican Republic,
> 11 concerned Latin America,
> 4 were on the activities of the Central Intelligence Agency,
> 3 were on the North Atlantic Treaty Organization, and
> 2 were on the United Nations Organization.

The others covered such matters as disarmament, Greece, eastern Europe, and international air travel. On nine occasions the Secretary of State, Mr Dean Rusk, gave evidence to the committee. Nineteen meetings were addressed by an Assistant Secretary of State or an Under Secretary of State, eleven by various ambassadors, seven by heads of agencies and the others by various people who included the Vice-President, the President's Special Adviser on south-east Asian affairs, and the like.

Of particular interest here are the meetings which considered the situation in the Dominican Republic. Civil war broke out there in April 1965, and the President despatched 23,000 American troops to the island on 30 April. On the same day Mr Dean Rusk appeared before the Committee and told it something of the situation. Three days later the Under Secretary of State was examined about it. On 21 May Mr Dean Rusk was again before the Committee. On 14 July the Committee began a series of hearings with evidence from the State Department, the Ambassador concerned, the Central Intelligence Agency and others. By now the Committee, and through it the Senate, was fully briefed on the extent of American commitment on the island. On 3 September a provisional President was installed in the Republic, and the civil war ended. The Committee held a meeting in June of the following year in which it considered the state of affairs in the country after elections had brought a new President into power.

The calibre of the witnesses appearing before the Committee and the frequency of the meetings,[1] seen against a background of the numerous other meetings which the Committee holds on legislative matters and the many other direct contacts they have with officials, combine to make the members of the Committee extremely well-informed. But the giving of information at Committee hearings is not only in one direction. The witnesses, who are in the key positions in the public service, are also made aware of the views of the senators. It is possible for senators themselves to suggest initiatives and to pursue them at later meetings; and in view of the sanctions available to Congress—the control over appropriations, the setting in train of special investigations, the ability to refuse legislation which the administration wants—the witnesses have to pay regard to what is said. If they cannot refute the suggestions made to them, they may have to agree to them or to something like them.

1. In his four years as Secretary of State (1949–53), Dean Acheson calculates that he spent about one-sixth of his working days in Washington in meeting congressional committees or preparing for such meetings—*A Citizen Looks at Congress* (1957), p. 65.

This description of the Senate Committee's work-load illustrates the extent to which Congress immerses itself in the details of foreign policy. In addition the House Committee on Foreign Affairs is covering much of the same ground. It does not have the duties with regard to treaties and appointments which the Constitution has placed on the Senate. But it does have a special concern for appropriations and the last decades have shown the growing importance of the economic aspects of foreign policy in such matters as Marshall aid and overseas development. In addition there are the Committees on Appropriations in each House—already studied in Chapter VI—which review all legislation touching foreign policy and in part determine the role of Congress by deciding how much money should be spent for each purpose. Between them these four Committees constitute a formidable restraint upon the executive's policies. All of them receive help, when appropriate, from the Comptroller General.

In addition to the work of the Committees, there are the occasions on which major matters are brought up for debate on the floor of each chamber, particularly the Senate, and, if necessary, in secret session. Such occasions are comparatively rare but—as when the Senate in the 82nd Congress (1951–52) debated the constitutional responsibilities of the President and Congress in the involvements in Korea and Europe—can be of the highest importance.

The total effect of these activities is to make Congress a power in the actual formulation of foreign policy. According to Dean Griffith,[1] it was Congress that first analysed the nature of Chinese communism and first insisted on the controls to be placed on the use of the atomic bomb. The role of Congress in forcing the purge of Communists from American public life is also well known. It was a Senate resolution, proposing that the United States should associate itself in peacetime with countries outside the Western hemisphere, that paved the way to the North Atlantic Treaty. The immense publicity that attended the hearings of the Senate Foreign Relations Committee on Vietnam in 1967, and so gave a voice to the many general misgivings on the subjects, undoubtedly influenced the administration to the point of modifying its policy there. It can be said of Congress, to an extent that it could never be said of Parliament, that there are times when it initiates foreign policy.

1. *Congress: Its Contemporary Role* (1967), 4th ed., p. 175.

INDEX

Note: In this Index, the following abbreviations are used: (HC) for House of Commons, (HL) for House of Lords, (HR) for House of Representatives, (S) for Senate, (C) for Congress, (P) for Parliament, (UK) for United Kingdom, (US) for United States